LOURDES COLLEGE

3 0379 1000 1235 2

DUNS SCOTUS LIBRARY
LOURDES COLLEGE
SYLVANIA OHIO

230
U71a
mR
RL

ANSWERING FOR FAITH

D1227365

also by Richard Viladesau
published by Paulist Press

THE REASON FOR OUR HOPE

ANSWERING FOR FAITH

Christ and the Human
Search for Salvation

RICHARD VILADESAU

PAULIST PRESS
New York/Mahwah

067674

Paulist Press gratefully acknowledges use of excerpts from *Systematic Theology* by Tillich, vol. 2, 1957, used by permission of The University of Chicago Press.

Copyright ©1987 by
Richard Viladesau

All rights reserved. No part of this book may be reproduced or transmitted in any form or by any means, electronic or mechanical, including photocopying, recording or by any information storage and retrieval system without permission in writing from the Publisher.

Library of Congress Cataloging-in-Publication Data

Viladesau, Richard.
    Answering for faith.

    Bibliography: p.
    1. Theology, Doctrinal.   2. Apologetics—20th century.
3. Christianity and other religions.   4. Salvation.
I. Title.
BT75.2.V52   1987   230   87-7018
ISBN 0-8091-2882-9 (pbk.)

Published by Paulist Press
997 Macarthur Boulevard
Mahwah, New Jersey 07430

Printed and bound in the
United States of America

TOPICAL OUTLINE OF CONTENTS

(Subsection headings which do not appear in the text are placed in parentheses)

V: GOD'S WORD IN HUMAN WORDS—THE WESTERN RELIGIONS

VI: A FINAL WORD OF GOD? THE DIALECTIC AND CONVERGENCE OF RELIGIONS

VII: JESUS THE CHRIST AS GOD'S WORD   196

TO MY TEACHERS, COLLEAGUES,
AND STUDENTS AT THE
SEMINARY OF THE IMMACULATE CONCEPTION

PREFACE

After having spoken many times and in many ways to our ancestors through the prophets, in these last days God has spoken to us through his Son. . . .

Heb 1:1–2

Reverence Christ in your hearts as Lord, and always be ready to give answer to anyone who asks the reason for the hope which is in you. . . .

1 Pet 3:15

This book represents the second part of a foundational theology conceived as an introduction to a Christian theological anthropology. The first part, entitled *The Reason for Our Hope*, began with an examination of the human subject and attempted to establish, on the basis of the experience of transcendence, that there are reasons for affirming the existence of God and the possibility of a revelation from him. This volume, after a brief resume of its presuppositions, examines the notion of revelation and, beginning with the fact of religious experience, attempts to uncover the grounds for affirming a divine revelation in the history of religions reaching its culmination in Christ.

As in its antecedent, the anthropological perspective in this study consists in the adoption of the transcendental "turn to the subject" as the starting point and methodological principle behind the entire project. The entire content of both volumes may be conceived as a progressive series of answers to Kant's question "What is humanity?" posed in its most ultimate perspectives: What can we know? What dare we hope? What ought we to do?

The purpose of this work, as its title indicates, is "apologetic" in the sense of an effort to uncover the rational grounds for belief in Jesus Christ as God's salvific "word" to humanity. The basic structure of the argument roughly parallels that of "classical" Christian apologetics; the major differences I believe will be found in two areas: (1) in the use of a transcendental and dialectical method to uncover the bases of faith, and (2) in the treat-

1

ment of non-Christian religions not as rivals to faith in Christ, but as its presupposition and extension.

Karl Rahner remarks in his *Foundations of Christian Faith* that because the offer of God's grace is universally operative, it should be possible to find in the world's religions a "searching Christology": that is, an implicit anticipation and hope for what is revealed historically in Jesus the Christ as God's definitive Word. Rahner himself establishes only the dogmatic principle; he leaves to theologians working with the history of religions the task of establishing *a posteriori* its actual existence and forms. This book is in part an attempt to confront this task, at least in an initial way.

At the same time the phenomenology or typology of religions undertaken here has relevance to belief in Christ itself; for this study suggests that what the "searching Christology" in world faiths is seeking is revealed as not *simply* identical with the Jesus Christ of history. Rather, it proposes an identity in a dialectical way, mediated by the proleptic character of Jesus' resurrection. In this way, the great world religions are not simply subordinated to Christianity, but retain a validity of their own, even within the affirmation of Christ as God's final and saving Word.

The overall progression of the book's argument can be succinctly stated. The expectation of salvation, with which *The Reason for Our Hope* ends, leads to an examination of religious experience in general to establish the fact of God's action in history and to a phenomenology of religions to examine the concrete claims of having encountered a saving word or illumination. In the context of the dialectic and convergences of world religions thus uncovered, the Christian claim is discussed, and an attempt is made to justify Christian conversion by means of transcendental and dialectical method.

Although this book is intended as a logical sequel to the anthropology constructed in *The Reason for Our Hope*, I have also attempted to present the material in such a way that it can stand alone. For this reason the first two chapters are essentially a resume of the contents and method established in the earlier book. I have however substantially expanded the treatment of the need for salvation by the addition of a section on theodicy, and have appended to the affirmation of God's saving activity an examination of how an "act" of God can be understood theologically.

The central chapters discuss the locus of revelation: first in general, in the phenomenon of religion, and then specifically in the higher world religions. The final three chapters pose the question of a "special" divine revelation and attempt to show the reasonability of faith in Christ as God's "eschatological" word and saving act. Finally, the implications of the acceptance of Christ are explored, particularly with regard to the plurality of world religions.

Both in method and in content this work is largely indebted to the works of Karl Rahner and Bernard Lonergan. I have attempted to synthesize their complementary approaches to foundational theology through the "turn to the subject." If explicit references to Lonergan's work are fewer in number, it will nevertheless be seen that his reflections on theological method, as well as his foundational categories—in particular that of "religious conversion"—form the very basis of my treatment. At the same time, I have attempted to go beyond the explicit concerns of either Lonergan or Rahner by applying their methods and insights to new areas, especially in the dialogue with world religions.

A word must also be said about the limitations of this study. This book is written by a Roman Catholic and, to that extent, from a point of view which stems from a particular formulation of the Christian conversion experience. Its theological context—as the references to Lonergan and Rahner show—is above all Roman Catholic theology. At the same time, the intent is to pursue a *foundational* theology, based in philosophical grounds which are potentially common not only to other Christians, but also to non-Christians and even non-believers. The major distinctiveness of this treatment will probably be found more in the kind of "philosophical faith" that grounds it than in any specifically confessional or dogmatic issues.

At the same time, the philosophical underpinnings, if not specifically Christian, clearly come out of a Christian and Western context, and thus represent a bias toward a particular epistemological-metaphysical-anthropological position. Rather than try to escape from this bias, I have tried to bring it honestly into the discussion with other philosophical and theological traditions, in the hope that the ensuing dialectic may lead to mutual clarification.

The treatment of the non-Christian world religions in a work of this length can only be introductory and typological; it is intended to open the way for further study. Furthermore, I can make no claim to a specialist's expertise in this field. Nevertheless, I am convinced that theology today can no longer responsibly be done within only one tradition; my modest efforts at presenting several of the classic religious movements will, I hope, be taken as an initial contribution to a dialogue that must expand both in breadth and depth.

Within the text there are sections which are printed within brackets. These represent elaborations or explanations which I considered too important to be relegated to the footnotes, but which are not absolutely crucial to the main line of thought of a section, and which can be skipped over without losing the continuity of ideas. The footnotes for each chapter are independent, so that citations of references are not carried over from one chapter to the next.

The sub-title of *The Reason for Our Hope* described it as an *introduction* to Christian anthropology. The same description also applies here. The proper sequel to these two books should be an exposition of Christian anthropology proper: that is, the Christian view on human being as created, sinful, and engraced in Christ. The anthropological perspective in these books is a progressively narrowing one, centered on the notion of "revelation": from the human subject in general as seeker for God's word, to the subject of religious conversion as receiver of that word, to the Christ as the final word or revelation of authentic human possibilities. The foundational theological anthropology which will stem from this will follow a correspondingly widening course, centered on the mystery of God's self communication as "grace": from Christ as the exemplar of self-realization in God (Christological dimension of grace), to the Church as the expression and continuation of Christ's life (ecclesial dimension), to all of humanity as called to share in the divine life (universal dimension of grace).

Thanks are due to the many people who made this book possible: to the late Rev. Francis M. Tyrrell, who first as a teacher and later as a colleague served as an inspiration for my studies; to the students I have taught, who were my principal motivation in writing; to my colleagues at the Immaculate Conception Seminary for affording me the opportunity of the Sabbatical semester during which the book was written, and especially to Sr. Mary Maher, SSND, who generously assumed my duties during my absence; to Bp. John R. McGann for his approval of my Sabbatical plans and to Msgr. Peter Pflomm for his assistance in implementing them; to Prof. Robert Sommerville and the Department of Religion at Columbia University for granting me the status of visiting scholar during that period; to Msgr. Harry Byrne and the staff at Epiphany Parish in New York for the gracious hospitality which provided an ideal ambience for writing; and to Doug Fisher of Paulist Press for his continual encouragement and help.

I. HAS GOD SPOKEN?

PRELIMINARY SUMMARY: STATE OF THE QUESTION

The White Rabbit put on his spectacles. "Where shall I begin, please your Majesty?" he asked.

"Begin at the beginning," the King said, very gravely, "and go on till you come to the end: then stop."

Lewis Carroll, *Alice in Wonderland*

"In my first book, O Theophilus. . . ."

Acts 1:1

The first thing that must be noted about this book is that it is a sequel. This in itself is a problem. A reviewer in *The New York Times* once wrote that there have only been two sequels in the entire history of literature which have managed to surpass the works they followed; these were *Huckleberry Finn* and the New Testament. In this case, there is no question of living up to anything of the quality of the Old Testament, or even of *The Adventures of Tom Sawyer*. The problem is rather that the entire argument of this book is based upon premises whose validity is examined elsewhere. It is impossible, under the circumstances, to take the King of Hearts's advice and "begin at the beginning"; the essential epistemological and metaphysical positions upon which these reflections are based must be presupposed. On the other hand, since they are so vital to the development of the present subject, it seems wise to begin with a brief summary of the purposes, the method and the conclusions arrived at in my earlier work, *The Reason for Our Hope*.

Continuity in scope and method

Like its predecessor, this work is intended as a contribution to the field of fundamental or foundational theology. It aims at exploring the reasonability of the act of religious faith. The first volume dealt with the most basic issues that faith must encounter in an attempt to justify itself: the

5

existence of an Absolute or God, the possibility of knowing and speaking of such a being, the conditions of such knowledge in the human subject, and the need for salvation which leads people to expect and seek dialogue with God. This volume will set out from this expectation to explore the reasons for explicitly Christian conversion.

There are four points of continuity which should be noted with regard to scope and method.

1. First, the scope of this work as a "theological anthropology" is "apologetic," in Paul Tillich's sense of that word. That is, it is not "positive" kerygmatic or dogmatic theology: it does not aim at exploring the interconnections or the implications of the content or message of faith; it rather aims at correlating faith with general human experience. Specifically, it is an attempt to give reasons for faith to people in our society; first of all, ourselves, who for the most part share the predispositions and thought context of our contemporaries.

In line with current trends in theology, one could look at this enterprise as a "hermeneutical" venture: if one looks at theology from a semiotic viewpoint, the whole of theology is a hermeneutic, or systematic interpretation, where the "text" to be interpreted is life (or the converted life) itself. In that schema of thinking, fundamental theology comprises the principles of hermeneutics; that is, it asks the question, "On what bases do we make our religious interpretation of the conversion experience, and how are they related to the other principles of interpretation, the symbols with which we face the rest of life?"

It must be noted first of all that there are limits to this kind of approach. Theology today has been made more aware than ever, by the critique of "ideology," that theory cannot be separated from praxis; likewise, that any hermeneutic or interpretation of existence cannot be separated from the concrete stance of the persons doing the interpreting, including their socio-economic conditions and the society in which they live. Our particular project is very much influenced by the culture of unbelief in which (or at least with which) Western people have lived since the Enlightenment. The dialogue between that unbelief and the believer has taken different shapes in the several centuries since the beginning of the "Age of Reason," or the "scientific revolution"; but the basis of the conversation is the same: it is an intellectual conversation between believers and unbelievers.

This is of course not the only form that foundational theology can take. Dialogue with a "secular" world which was formed basically in the era of the Enlightenment and the European revolutions depends upon peculiar cultural condition which does not exist in most of the rest of the world. This naturally limits the relevance of our theology. We are not addressing every situation, but a particular "modern" situation in which we happen to find ourselves at this moment. We may not find ourselves in that same "modern" situation in another ten or twenty years. (This is always true of philosophy and theology, although they have not always been aware of it.) Harvey Cox in his book *Religion in the Secular City* talks about the emergence of a "post-modern" theology which will no longer be in dialogue with the Enlightenment scientific mentality and the secular world. We can already see in this country the beginnings of such a post-modern attitude in the powerful emergence of fundamentalism, which is certainly (in Cox's sense) a post-modern attitude; it does not regard scientific knowledge as being critical; it rejects the Enlightenment. One can see another form of post-modern theology emerging in "Liberation Theology," which likewise rejects the whole of the culture of the Enlightenment as being "bourgeois"—the mental counterpart of the structures of colonialism and exploitation—and constructs its basis on a peasant culture, as Mao did in China with Marxism. These movements are responding to different conditions from the "modern," and demand a different theology to speak to them. We also may shortly find ourselves in a post-modern era—where the "post" does not necessarily indicate progress, but merely succession; such an era may have many characteristics of the pre-modern era, as fundamentalism and liberation theology both have.

Nevertheless, it seems to me that even if this study is necessarily dated, even as it goes on, there is something permanently valid in the questions it faces—the questions that were raised by the Enlightenment and by secularization—and something therefore permanently valid in the effort to reply to them. Harvey Cox himself insists that a responsible post-modern theology will have to integrate the insights of "modernity," particularly with regard to critical thought. This is, it seems to me, especially important, because the great temptation of the kinds of post-modern theology that we can already observe is to be uncritical in their thinking, to neglect what was the great contribution of the Enlightenment: scientific method and the critique of "self-evidence." Indeed, if Cox is right in thinking that post-modern theology must be performed in the light of the plurality of world religions, the kind of fundamental theology envisaged here will make a very definite contribution.

2. From this project of "correlation," in which we attempt to correlate faith with the attitude of critical reason, arises the basic principle behind our method, namely the "turn to the subject" or "anthropological turn." A primary characteristic of the post-Enlightenment age in thought has been the critique of "taking for granted"—*Selbstverständlichkeit*—the presumption that there are areas of existence which do not need to be examined. The Enlightenment in contrast poses the challenge that *every-*

thing can and should be examined, that there is nothing that can simply be taken for granted.

The "turn to the subject" is based upon the need for a radical posing of the question about human experience—including the experience of religious faith. Can we *verify* what we say in faith? This turn to the subject in our field of fundamental theology also arises from the effort of philosophy to meet the particular problems that characterize the modern age—the problems for example which I have called relevance, integration, radicality, and praxis (including the critique of "ideology" which we find in Marxism and in liberation theologies).

The turn to the subject means that this form of foundational theology can be conceived of as an "anthropology." This is a departure from the usual use of the term "theological anthropology," at least in Roman Catholic circles, where the name generally designates a part of systematic theology. In the perspective adopted here, fundamental theology is an "anthropology" because it turns to the subject as the starting point of theology. It indicates not so much the theological doctrine of humanity as found in the Scriptures or the Church's tradition, but rather a stance which sees reflection on existential human existence as the basis of theology.

This implies that our perspective is significantly different from that of a "dogmatic" approach. Although it concerns conversion, and is taking place (presumably) in people already committed to Christian conversion, this study does not take a single point of view on conversion; it does not presume the truth or the authenticity of every aspect of conversion, or, indeed, its basic integrity. It takes many points of view, and new questions are raised by every integration that we arrive at.

[This point may perhaps be illustrated by a reference to the history of art, which frequently reflects the difference in consciousness found in various eras.

Probably the two greatest and most famous statues of David are those of Michelangelo, in the Accademia in Florence, and of Bernini, in the Villa Borghese in Rome.

Michelangelo's "David" is of gigantic proportions. The instinctive reaction of the viewer is to walk around it, looking at it from every side. This is the way it was meant to be seen: it does not presume any single point of view, but is sculpted "in the round," so that the viewer himself must move, creating many different angles, each of which makes sense and none of which is complete.

Bernini's "David," on the other hand, is a life-sized and highly realistic figure. It was intended to stand against a wall (although it does not now do so). One is meant to look at it from one particular point of view: only from the front—like a photograph. (In this sense, Bernini's is the much more "modern" work of art.) When looked at from this viewpoint, the statue creates an aesthetic space in which the viewer is involved.

Michelangelo's statue has no particular time or space; this David is not "portrayed" at any specific moment; it represents rather the "ideal" David, the "Platonic" David, indeed the ideal "man" (hence his very un-Biblical nudity) for whom the Biblical figure and his story provide the inspiration and context. Bernini's David, on the other hand (although like any great work of art it possesses a wider significance), is definitely the character of the story. He is dressed appropriately, and he is shown at a particular moment in the narrative: right at the moment when he is about to fling the stone at the giant Goliath. This statue creates its own space. Indeed, standing in the position intended by the sculptor, one is confronted with a life-sized figure about to hurl a stone directly over one's head; one is involved in the action. This represents a different artistic ideal and a different way of thinking from Michelangelo's; the viewer must *decide* how to see the David in the Accademia; Bernini has decided the question for us.

The two statues are to some extent symbolic of the ages that produced them: Michelangelo's of the questioning spirit of the early Renaissance, Bernini's of the certitudes and commitment of the era of the Council of Trent, when things were becoming increasingly systematized under a definite point of view, excluding others.

Since the time of the Council of Trent, until very recently, most Roman Catholic theology has been more in the spirit of Bernini than of Michelangelo. Like Baroque art, it presupposes a point of view and a definite "space" or context of engagement: that is, exactly where and how one's commitment takes place. Most Catholic theology has tended to be "dogmatic": presupposing a commitment and the stance which that commitment implies.

What we are doing, on the other hand, is much more like what Michelangelo did: not presupposing a particular point of view, but taking a circular approach, looking at the same commitment under many different aspects. Such an approach will necessarily be less neat, certain, and complete; it will leave more unanswered questions and more possibilities for looking at things differently, with equal legitimacy.]

It seems to me that this foundational approach is particularly fruitful for dealing with our situation. Karl Rahner, in his article "Faith Today," states that a central task of modern theology is precisely to face the loss of the context in which the "dogmatic" point of view was acceptable. (In fact, this task seems to have taken root in the Western theological world; almost all contemporary theology tends to integrate the "foundational" questions, even in the midst of highly systematic or dogmatic concerns.) Concerning the teaching authority of the Church, Rahner writes: "First of all, as a matter of fact the teaching authority of the Church has been given a very secondary existential place in the 'system of belief' of a contemporary person."[1] (In America, this has been shown by studies such as Andrew Greeley's to be statistically true; no matter what the bishops may say, people who define themselves as Catholics do not necessarily follow "authentic Church teaching" in such matters as birth control, abortion, remarriage, or a number of other moral issues. The Church's teaching authority is not for them the sole or supreme criterion of Catholic faith or practice.)

In this sense, says Rahner, the attitude of the contemporary Catholic with regard to faith coincides more with the methodical concerns of fundamental theology than with a type of dogmatic theology which takes such matters as settled and can appeal to an established and accepted authority:

> The teaching authority of the Church is certainly one of the contents of the Catholic faith but, again from the viewpoint of fundamental theology, it is not the beginning of faith nor its ultimate foundation.
>
> In theory this was always true of Catholic fundamental theology, since the latter justified its teaching on the existence of God and on the possibility and reality of a revelation, as well as its teaching on Jesus Christ as legate of God, *before* presenting an ecclesiology doctrine on the teaching office of the Church and on scripture as inspired source of revelation. But at the practical and kerygmatic level a different mentality was present, at least under the surface. People argued along the lines of St. Augustine's famous statement that he would not believe the gospel if he were not moved to do so by the authority of the Church. They experienced the Church, her authority, and the inflexible absoluteness of her teaching as the sole real bulwark behind which they knew themselves to be protected against their own skepticism and the disintegration of all certitude. . . .
>
> Even today, of course, there are many people whose psychological bent and social conditioning make them feel the same way. Moreover, there is no way of forecasting whether this experience of the Church may not once again become generally the almost self-evident way of approaching the Christian faith as a whole. . . . But, even granting all this and taking it into account, it is a fact that belief in the Church and especially in her authoritative teaching office is today, on the whole, a conviction which plays only a belated and secondary role in the genesis and overall structure of the Catholic faith.[2]

This means, according to Rahner, that proclamation of the Christian message inside the Church cannot differ from proclamation "outside"; the fundamental or foundational aspect of theology must permeate not only systematics, but also the Church's preaching.

If we look at theology as "hermeneutic," as the interpretation of experience, then in foundational theology we are seeking the bases of the interpretation, its principles. It is impossible, of course, to attain to an absolutely certain Cartesian starting point, with no presuppositions. We theologize and philosophize from within experience, which includes a social setting. As Schillebeeckx points out, experience is always already interpreted experience.[3] In this sense, theology is always the interpretation of a particular tradition. Nevertheless, we theologize not merely within a tradition, but also *from* within a tradition; that is, we can purposely and consciously distance ourselves from our starting point in order to examine it critically. In doing so, we look for the radical basis in ourselves—in the existing subject—for our own actual faith commitment.

3. The "turn to the subject" in our method implies the adoption of what Lonergan calls a "moving viewpoint." The "subject" here is not a Cartesian "cogito," but a ratio-vital human being; the starting point is not an absolute zero, with no presuppositions, but the living subject examining his presuppositions, including that of faith.

The method of subjectivity as we practice it, therefore, includes both a *transcendental* and a *dialectical* movement. Purely transcendental method has been criticized by theologians like Metz and by the liberation theologians, for beginning with an unreal transcendental subject without concrete historical conditions. This is exactly what is not presupposed here. We begin not merely with the thinking subject and the *a priori* conditions in consciousness for being in the world, but also the existential living subject in dialogue with the historical world.

For this reason, our method includes a dialectic between method and content, in which the questions asked are continually posed in the light of the situation in which we find ourselves; and within the content, we find that every transcendental movement implies a dialectical/categorical movement, so that we not only transcendentally ask about the conditions of possibility of being a believer in the world, but we also dialectically expose and respond to the possibility of a non-believing foundation for human existence; we not only affirm the existence of God as the ground to meaning, but we also examine the problem of evil as the challenge to that meaning.

In this second part, there is even more a dialectical as well as a transcendental movement, as the "moving viewpoint" expands to cover more inclusive and more concretely existential conditions.

4. In terms of Lonergan's "functional specialties," this study can be regarded as falling under the two categories of "dialectics" and "foundations."[4] Both of these center on the reality of conversion, that is on the

level of decision in human existence. Dialectics examines the alternatives; foundations examines the consequences of the conversion decision once made. This volume represents the movement from the former to the latter.

Because of the anthropological centering of this study, this volume also touches upon areas which are traditionally considered within the sphere of systematic theology—namely grace and the "theological virtues." But our treatment remains within a "foundational" and dialectical perspective insofar as those questions are posed here not from the standpoint of the Church and its dogmatic authority, nor even of the Scriptures, but from the standpoint of the dialectic of world religions on the question of human salvation.

Continuity in content

> If humankind evolved by Darwinian natural selection, genetic chance and environmental necessity, not God, made the species. Deity can still be sought in the origin of the ultimate units of matter, in quarks and electron shells (Hans Küng was right to ask atheists why there is something instead of nothing) but not in the origin of the species. However much we embellish that stark conclusion with metaphor and imagery, it remains the philosophical legacy of the last century of scientific research.
>
> Edward O. Wilson: On Human Nature

The first part of the introduction or foundation to "theological anthropology" set forth in *The Reason for Our Hope* dealt with establishing the possibility of revelation and the criteria for identifying a revelation from God. The quotation given above from Pulitzer-prize winning scientist Edward Wilson summarizes the context in which the questions are asked: in the light of modern science and of alternative philosophical systems of meaning, there is doubt whether and where the notion of God is meaningful for modern man.

First, *whether:* Wilson admits that it is legitimate to ask why there is something rather than nothing, and that this is how the question of God arises. But the question does not necessarily receive a positive answer (not from Wilson himself, for example).

Second, *where:* if there is a positive answer to the question of an ultimate, an Absolute "behind" the existence of the world, how does such a being relate—if at all—to existence *in* the world? It is certainly not sufficient for the common religious mentality to affirm a God who is the final explanation of quarks or electron shells, but who has nothing to do with the origin—and the present existence—of the species; a "Deist" God, in other words, who may be the source of the world, but who does not intervene in it, and with whom, therefore, there can be no relationship. Most forms of religion and religious philosophy—with important exceptions—are interested in God actually acting in the world, not simply being its foundation.

The part of my earlier study which we are now summarizing dealt explicitly with the first question, in the hope of providing a basis for exploring the second. The first task was to show the necessity of even asking the question about God. The question of God occurs when we ask about *meaning;* that is, it arises not directly as an explanation of the physical world, but rather when one enters the world of consciousness, of human *Existenz* with its search for authenticity and value. Such a question must be arrived at genuinely by each person; and therefore such a "study" cannot be a merely academic pursuit, but depends upon the student's willingness to enter into an experiment in the appropriation of his or her own consciousness.

Within human consciousness the problem of ultimate meaning arises because of the phenomenon of "transcendence." Analogously, there is some kind of transcendence in the objective world process that is examined by the scientist; but we advert to transcendence especially when we turn our attention to the process by which we understand the world, including ourselves. We note transcendence in the principle behind every scientific explanation (and as well—although we have not explored this—every aesthetic explanation, every "feeling" response): the principle of intelligibility. On a first level, then, Wilson is right; the question about God arises metaphysically when we ask, "Why is there something rather than nothing?"

This same question can also be posed in other, more existential terms:

Why is there intelligibility, rather than nonsense?

Why is there value or purpose rather than absurdity?

Why is there becoming rather than stasis?

Why is there order rather than chaos?

—and so on; the question can be posed from many points of view.

Even in asking such questions, we are already taking a stance: namely, in favor of intelligibility. By our practice, we are already affirming a value: at least the value of asking the question, which presupposes that there may be an answer. This indicates a predisposition in favor of intelligibility—at least the intelligibility of asking metaphysical questions. Asking such questions also evinces a certain "ultimate concern," under which there is already a kind of basic "faith," a trust in existence and its meaningfulness.

There is, therefore, an existential presupposition in favor of meaning in our very practice. This presupposition, however, does not invalidate

what we are doing as critical thought, for two reasons. First, such a presupposition is unavoidable. It is impossible to live as a human being without some kind of implicit faith in the meaningfulness of existence; the
alternative is madness. Second, the presupposition is not invalid precisely
because it is conscious of itself as a presupposition. It is not a "dishonest"
presupposition. But this implies also that it is radically revisable. (This is
the reason for the dialectical movement of our study; we must be ready to
question the possible "ideological" elements in our presupposition.)

The first task, then, was to examine whether this basic human trust
in meaning and value, in a purpose to existence, is grounded in reality;
whether it can in some way be justified. This question was asked dialectically, that is, in dialogue with various other positions which attempt to
ground human transcendence: existentialism, dialectical materialism,
non-theistic religion. The dialectic consists of contrast: not merely between one position and another, but also and more significantly between
each position's concepts and the performance of the living subject holding
them. We find that despite what non-theistic systems may say, there is in
actual performance an assent to an ultimate value which the conceptual
systems are incapable of grounding or explaining. From this arises the
question of God.

[Strictly speaking, of course, we do not *discover* the God question in
the dialectic; it is with us all along in our religious commitment. But we
come rationally through the dialectic to the need of taking with ultimate
concern in the realm of reflection what religious symbols are pointing to:
that is, we find the need to ask the God question personally.]

The question of the existence of an Absolute Ground was again posed
from the standpoint of subjectivity: is there an ultimate reason or foundation for my basic trust in reality, in meaning and value? Of the various
approaches to the existence of God, transcendental method appears the
most radical, in that it places metaphysics within the more basic epistemological framework, exposing the principle of intelligibility which seems
to underlie all approaches to God.

The establishment of the existence of God by transcendental method
as the condition of possibility of the actual performance of the subject as
knower and lover allows us at the same time to state our most fundamental
relationship to God: namely, that to be human is to be a creature and to
be "open" to the Absolute as the only adequate horizon and goal of our
existence. At the same time, it tells us something fundamental about God:
namely that he transcends as well as grounds (the "analogy of being") what
is graspable by the human mind, and is known not conceptually, but sim-

ply—at least at this level of reflection—as the term or end of human transcendence.

The establishment of the existence of God allows us—indeed, forces us—to ask a further question: What is the meaning of human existence in the light of the existence of God or of ultimate intelligibility? Existentially, this is the question of *salvation;* for we find that the existence of God indicates a goal and meaning to human life which we are in danger of missing. At the same time, the existence of God—and our existential experience of him—leads us to look for a solution to the dilemma of existence in some sort of dialogue with God and with our fellow beings. This leads us to the possibility and the need of revelation.

This last section may be summarized as a series of progressive answers to the question, "What is a human being?"

1. To be human is to be "spirit": that is, a being in whom the transcending processes of the world come to self-knowledge, so that matter is subsumed into the realm of consciousness.

2. To be human is to be a finite freedom: that is, a material consciousness which constitutes its own transcendence toward being and goodness through the exercise of intelligent and responsible decision—i.e., through love—and which does so in the context of history and community.

3. To be human is to be a creature orientated to the infinite; the human is thus a finite spiritual being who listens for a possible further dialogue with God, in fulfillment of a basic and unrestricted desire for knowledge and love.

4. To be human is to be alienated spirit, who therefore seeks salvation and authentic human existence in God's "answer" to the problem of evil.

5. To be human is to be a religious being, who seeks to find and express salvation in history as a collaboration of love with God and with others; this collaboration is in the world, but points beyond it.[5]

SEEKING GOD'S WORD

Faust: "The essence of the like of you is usually inherent in the name; it appears in all too great transparency in names like 'Lord of Flies,' 'Destroyer,' 'Liar'; all right, who are you, then?"
Mephistopheles: "I am a portion of that power which always works for evil, and always accomplishes good."

Goethe, *Faust*, Act I

It was not the fault of creation that it was frustrated; it was by the will of him who condemned it to frustration, in the hope that creation itself would be set free from its bondage to decay, and have the glorious freedom of the children of God.

Rom 8:20–21

Our study presupposes two major affirmations of anthropology: first, the ontological possibility of revelation: the fact that we look for meaning in existence, and cannot find it within the ambit of merely worldly life, and therefore are ontologically oriented toward the transcendent, or God. Second, that we find ourselves in a dilemma; we find ourselves in the midst of a problem of evil; and thus we look toward the transcendent not simply as some sort of theoretical goal beyond life, corresponding to the infinite capacity of spirit, but as a means of salvation from the problem in which we find ourselves in worldly life itself. The human is therefore a religious being who seeks to find and express salvation in history as some kind of collaboration with God and with fellow human beings.

We enter next into a dialectical moment, in which I will attempt to clarify by contrast the position outlined. The metaphysical position presupposed here is that expounded by Bernard Lonergan in *Insight:* namely, that evil is a *problem.* This means, in Lonergan's terminology, that evil is, *in itself,* unintelligible; it is the "surd." Nevertheless, it has some intelligibility in the light of the existence of God. It is thus a "problem" in the sense that we can ask about and attempt to discern that higher intelligibility which God gives to the fact of evil.

The Need of Salvation: The Problem of Evil and God

The position I have outlined is by no means self-evident, nor is it universally held; therefore it will be useful to differentiate our presupposition from other possible positions on man facing the fact of evil. For some, evil is a *mere fact,* with no intelligibility either in itself or in any higher synthesis. On the other hand, some would consider evil a *mystery;* it is not unintelligible, but it cannot be questioned because it is an ultimate, an intrinsic part of the mystery of being, which has its intelligibility only in itself.[6] If evil is either a mere brute fact or an aspect of the mystery of being, then there can be no question of salvation or of a saving revelation; our attitude could only be one of fatalism.

In contradistinction, evil for us is a *problem,* in a double sense. (1) The *fact* of the *existence* of evil is a problem to our intelligence: How can evil exist in a world made by a good God? How can there be a lack of intelligibility in being, if being and the good are one? (This is the classical problem of "theodicy," and was addressed in outline form in our first volume.) (2) Evil itself is a problem for *our* existence: How can we be saved from evil? What is God doing about evil? What further intelligibility does this unintelligible serve?

Evil can be a "problem" in both of these senses only if: (1) God exists; (2) evil is truly evil, i.e. unintelligible and diametrically opposed to good; (3) God is absolute Good; (4) God is omnipotent; (5) God is relevant to the existence of evil.

Each of these conditions can be used to define positions which are distinct from ours. Let us take each in turn:

(1) *Evil is a "problem" only if God exists.*

If there is no God, then evil is simply a brute fact, an absurdity in a fundamentally absurd world. Indeed, on this hypothesis "good" also becomes ultimately absurd; that is, value words would have no final ontological referent; they would merely express human convention, based on our preferences. Evil would have neither intrinsic intelligibility, nor the possibility of a solution, because there would be no ultimate meaning to "intelligibility" itself. Evil might be considered a "problem" in the practical sense: "What shall I do to avoid pain?" etc.; but a metaphysical or religious problem of evil could not arise.

Our position is therefore distinguished from any atheistic philosophy of pessimism, like that of Schopenhauer (the world is the product of blind, meaningless drives; all that is, is evil; we exist in the worst of all possible worlds) and from atheistic existentialism like that of Sartre or Camus (man is a "useless passion"; "good" and "evil," like all terms expressing meaning, are inventions of our minds, and have no intelligibility apart from what we give them). As Dostoievski already remarked in *The Brothers Karamazov,* "If there is no God, all is lawful"—that is, evil ceases to be a meaningful term.

(2) *Evil is a "problem" only if evil truly exists as diametrically opposed to good.*

There is no problem of evil if evil really does not exist, or if we cannot distinguish it from good. There is likewise no problem of evil if it is not really evil, if it is an intrinsic part of the mystery of being. Such a position is found in systems of monism or pantheism. Various Oriental philosophies take such or similar positions. Thus for example the Taoist scriptures advance the notion that our existence is a dream, and therefore we cannot know how to value things properly; perhaps when we awake, we will find that what we loved as good was delusion, and what we feared as evil was desirable.[7] At the same time they teach that all opposites, including good and evil, are really identical in the Tao; the wise man therefore does not even make such distinctions.[8]

In Indian philosophy there is also a strong current of thought which holds that this life is—at least in some sense—illusory.[9] For the philosophy of absolute non-dualism, God is finally All; therefore the world, plurality, and evil are all simply "appearance." The Vedantists commonly speak of God's attitude in producing the world as "*lîla*"—"playfulness"; the world is a thing of play, a dream or illusion. As we shall see, even the strict non-dualist system does not hold that the world is *completely* unreal, but that its reality is not ultimate. Nevertheless, the significance of worldly good and evil is certainly de-emphasized, and at the limit denied.[10] Thus in the *Bhagavad Gîtâ* the Supreme God, Vishnu, counsels the wavering hero, Arjuna, not to hesitate to wage war and kill his kinsmen, for

> He who imagines this embodied one a slayer
> And he who imagines this embodied one to be slain,
> Neither of them understands;
> This, the embodied one, does not slay, nor is it slain.
> Neither is it born nor does it die at any time,
> Nor, having been, will it again come not to be.
> Birthless, eternal, perpetual, primeval,
> It is not slain when the body is slain.[11]

Certain forms of Mahâyâna Buddhism likewise play down either the reality or the distinctness of evil. Evil arises from attachment to the illusion of a personal "self": once that illusion is surpassed, all distinctions disappear. Certain forms of Tantric Buddhism (the "Left-Handed Tantra") emphasize the unity—and hence the goodness—of all being to such a degree that various forms of "immoral conduct" are used as sacramentals in their rites, and the defiance of ordinary morality is considered a means of spiritual growth.[12]

In the West we find examples in philosophies of "optimism" of a rationalist or pantheist type. Spinoza, for example, holds that all finite being is a self-modification of God's own substance. Everything that exists, therefore, is absolutely necessary, as God is necessary. There is thus no room for evil; all that is, is good.

For Hegel, the finite has a necessary place in the dialectical development of the Absolute. The achievement of Spirit is always the product of a synthesis of a positive and negative moment. The negative moment in the dialectic is therefore necessary to the progression; without it, the higher synthesis could not take place. This means that evil loses its absolute character, since it is in the last analysis an intrinsic moment in the production of a higher good. Evil is thus something that must and ought to be, even though it must also be surpassed and "sublated" ("*aufgehoben*") in a higher level of reality. Because reality is seen as dialectical in nature, evil *as evil* is eliminated; it is only relatively opposed to good, and is finally necessary to it and integrated in it.

We may also remark here on the temptation for the theistic (especially Christian or Muslim) believer to take a kind of "short-cut" with evil: that is, immediately to integrate evil into a kind of theological fatalism which eliminates its problematic quality and considers it intelligible as a part of God's "providence." The religious person is tempted to say: "God gives the world as it is, including evil; therefore, is not evil simply a part of God's will, and thus a necessary element in God's ruling of the world?"

Clearly, for the believer there is a truth here; that is, if God in fact creates or gives the world, then everything that exists, including evil, must be seen as in some way God's "gift" *to me*. That is, it is a factor in the "givenness" of existence, to which I am invited to respond. To this extent, one might regard evil as an element in God's "word" to humanity.

On the other hand, such a view seems problematic, at least in some respects. What happens to human freedom in such a view of providence? Is humanity in no way responsible for evil—even including that evil which is performed by us? Does not such a view presuppose a completely categorical and anthropomorphic idea of God's "will," seeing it in terms of control and power rather than transcendental causality? Does this view finally make God immoral—or at least amoral?

Nevertheless, we have all had experiences of good coming out of evil, and even, presumably, of good coming to be which would not have existed except in response to evil. In this sense, could evil be providentially "necessary" for the good? The Catholic Easter liturgy proclaims even with regard to the "original" sin: "O happy fault! O truly necessary sin of Adam!"—because it makes possible so great a work of redemptive love on God's part. If it is misleading, from a metaphysical point of view, to think of God as "responding" to the human situation—as though humanity sins and God subsequently finds a remedy—is it perhaps better to think the other way around? Does God "plan" humanity's intimate union with him, and permit/create sin and evil as the necessary means for such intimacy? Must we have sin, in order to have redemption?

In short, is Hegel right in seeing the relation between good and evil as a necessarily dialectical one? Does evil exist in order to make possible a greater good?

There seems to be at least some support for this idea in the Christian tradition. Do not the Synoptic Gospels tell us that the repentant sinner is more loved than the one who had no need of repentance? And, conversely, is not the one who is forgiven more, all the more capable of loving?

Yet if we generalize this idea and push it to its logical conclusion, it seems to lead to strange consequences in the field of morality. St. Paul faces this dilemma in his Letter to the Romans:

> If our wrongdoing brings out the uprightness of God, what are we to say? Is it wrong in God (I am putting it in ordinary human terms) to inflict punishment? By no means, for then how could he judge the world? But, you say, if a falsehood of mine has brought great honor to God by bringing out his truthfulness, why am I tried for being a sinner? And why not say, as people abuse us for saying and charge us with saying, 'Let us do evil that good may come out of it'? Such people will be condemned as they deserve! (Rom 3:5–8).

> Greatly as sin multiplied, God's mercy has far surpassed it, so that just as sin had reigned through death, mercy might reign through uprightness and bring eternal life through Jesus Christ our Lord. Then what shall we conclude? Are we to continue to sin, in order to increase the spread of mercy? Certainly not! (Rom 5:20—6:1).

The fundamental difficulty with the view that evil exists as the providentially willed means to a greater good seems to be that it finally threatens the very distinction between good and evil. It can lead at the extreme to a sort of mystique of evil as the necessary means to God—a position which, despite St. Paul's vehement denouncement, has appeared occasionally in Western heresies,[13] as well as in the "left-handed" Tantra of Buddhism.

[Perhaps the most eloquent Western expression of this necessary or "providential" view of evil is found in Goethe's treatment of the "Faust" legend. While in earlier moralistic versions of the story the magician Faust is damned, for Goethe Faust is saved—if not precisely *by* his straying, at least through it, as the expression of his striving. Indeed, the agent of temptation and evil, Mephistopheles, is presented as God's collaborator and agent. The notion of "the Satan" as a member of God's court whom God uses to test us and prove our virtue is of course already present in the book of Job. But Goethe takes the idea a step farther: the improvement of humanity not only justifies the evils that befall us as a test (as in Job), but even justifies our giving in to temptation. Thus, God affirms that "Man will stray so long as he strives"; evil is inevitable in our pursuit of the good. As long as the striving continues, however, the "detours" of evil are of no account, for "the good man in his dark and secret longings is well aware which path to go." But because "man's diligence is easily exhausted," we need the devil to spur us on.

This idea is made clear in Faust's first interview with Mephistopheles, in which Faust demands to know his guest's identity. The devil responds: "I am a part of that power which always wills evil, but always achieves good."

In the end, Goethe's Faust is not damned, but saved, despite his bargain with the devil, as a mystical chorus proclaims: "the Eternal-Feminine draws us onward." All of Faust's straying is merely the expression of his groping journey toward God, who draws him onward by the attraction of his infinite love (the Eternal-Feminine).

The same view is put forth by the representative of Satan in C. S. Lewis's theological/science-fiction novel *Perelandra;* not only is man's fall necessary to human progress, it was the necessary condition for the supreme moment of humanity, the Incarnation itself. Can the believer deny that good came of the archetypical sin, the fall of man? Lewis's hero replies:

> "Of course good came of it. Is [God] a beast that we can stop His path, or a leaf that we can twist His shape? Whatever you do, He will make good of it. But not the good He had prepared for you if you had obeyed Him. That is lost forever. The King and first Mother of our world did the forbidden thing; and He brought good of it in the end. But what they did was not good; and what they lost we have not seen. And there were some to whom no good came nor will ever come. . . . "]

We shall have occasion to return to some of the positive elements in this line of thought later. For the moment, we may point out the insight which lies at the center of Kierkegaard's critique of Hegel's system: sin is not, of itself, a dialectical move toward the good, but is on the contrary a move away from the good. If left to itself, it does not imply a higher synthesis, but a loss. If good does in fact come from evil, it comes *despite* the dynamism of sin, not because of it; and there is no assurance that the good which comes from the correction of evil will be a "higher" good than otherwise possible.

On the metaphysical view we have proposed, God indeed "gives" the universe as it is; he gives the being of all. It does not follow, however, that we may say that God wills the *lack* of being which is sin. If evil is seen as a lack of due order or being, then it is by nature what does *not* have being, i.e., it is what is *lacking* to existence, and therefore in itself cannot be "willed" or given by God.

Again, to acknowledge that evil can dialectically serve a good purpose is not to say that this is its natural or normal course. Sin does contain the germ of its own reversal, precisely because it is self-contradictory; it affirms a good "for me" which is in opposition to *the* good; it goes against a fundamental human drive. In this sense, it is what Lonergan calls a "surd," an unintelligible. For this reason, there is a dialectic on the moral level as well as the intellectual: every "position" (apprehension of the true or the good) calls for its own development; every counter-position (whether intellectual or moral) calls for its own reversal. On this view, however, it is *good* which is dynamic; the development, even in the reversal of evil, comes from the fundamental drive toward being and the good, not from the surd of sin itself. Thus even in the affirmation of a salvific Providence, evil remains a "problem" in both senses we have defined.

(3) *Evil is a "problem" only if God is totally good, that is, if Being and Goodness coincide.*

There is obviously no problem of evil if the Absolute reality itself can be thought of as evil—as in Descartes' hypothesis of the *"malin Génie."*

There is also no problem of evil if God somehow *includes* evil; this would be the equivalent of the position outlined above, in which evil is an intrinsic part of the mystery of being. We have seen that monist or pantheist systems tend to such an idea; but it may also be coupled with the notion of God's absolute transcendence. In the Old Testament, for example, it is presumed that God is responsible for both the good and evil in the world: "Out of the mouth of the Most High proceedeth not evil and good?" (Lam. 3:38). It is God who hardens the hearts of the wicked; he saves whom he wills, and not others, by the arbitrary choice of his favor, apart from goodness or merit.

These notions stem from the recognition of the complete *otherness* of God. "My thoughts are not your thoughts, nor are my ways your ways." What *we* think is good or evil is not necessarily what God considers good or evil. God may be totally "good," but his goodness is quite other than what we find good. At the extreme, this would constitute a denial of the analogy of being and the analogy of goodness. Human moral standards would not be a reflection of God's being, but rather humanity's own sinful norm, or an illusion, or else an arbitrary *command* of God, based upon his absolute will, but not on his essential nature (voluntarism). It is of course true that any human idea of the good falls short of the reality of God; but if the word "good" is used in a simply equivocal way of God and the world, if there is no real analogy between God and the human good (and the lack of it, evil), then the problem of evil disappears, for it no longer makes sense to say that God is "good."

(4) *Evil is a "problem" only if God is omnipotent, that is, the creator of all, not opposed by anything.*[14]

Once again we are affirming the absolute ultimacy of God alone; no other reality exists of itself. Apart from God's goodness and creativity, there is nothing; everything that is exists in dependence upon God.

There is no "problem" of evil in the first sense, then, if God is not the sole ultimate power of the universe: if evil is an equally primal, equally ultimate force, standing against God. Such is the position found in dualist and polytheist systems.

In true polytheism there is strictly speaking no "God" in our sense of the term: that is, the metaphysical Absolute. There may be a *supreme* god, but not an *omnipotent* god. Goodness and evil are, so to speak, divided up among the gods; likewise power. Such religious ideas—as found in ancient Greek popular religion or in Hinduism on the village level—really do not reach the metaphysical level of the problem of evil.

In dualist metaphysical systems, on the other hand, God is the ultimate Good, but he is not omnipotent; he is opposed by some other primal force. In classical Zoroastrianism, there are *two* primal spirits, one all Good (Ahura Mazdâ or Ohrmazd) and the other completely evil (Ahriman). These two are from the beginning locked in a cosmic struggle, which God will win at the end of time. God finally *will* be omnipotent when evil is conquered; but he is not so from the beginning.

[Zoroastrianism thus avoids any responsibility of God for the existence of evil; the "problem" of evil is avoided, since evil is itself an ultimate reality. However, another problem inevitably arises for such a dualism: if both spirits are equally primal in reality, what does it mean to call one "good" and the other "evil"? Do these terms not become arbitrary designations for one's choice of sides in the struggle? Once again, there is a lack of ontological identity of "the Good" with Being, since Being in this system is dual. The movement of Zurvanism within the Zoroastrian religion tried to solve this problem by positing a more primal being from whom both great Spirits proceed. But this only raises the classical problem which dualism attempts to avoid: why does evil proceed from the primal Being?]

For other systems of thought, God's power is limited not by an opposing spirit, but by pre-existent *matter* (or by the intrinsic *nature* of matter). One finds this idea in certain philosophical schools of Hinduism, as well as in the emanationism of Plotinus and the Gnostics. God in such systems would not be the Creator; some lesser and imperfect principle would be responsible for the existence of the world, and there would be a natural and necessary degradation from spirit toward matter, which is intrinsically un-Godlike and to that extent evil.

(5) *Evil is a "problem" only if God is relevant to evil.*

There can be no "problem" of evil if God has nothing to do with the world—as is the case for example with the God of Aristotle, a Prime Mover who is perfect in himself and has no consciousness of any being outside himself.

Likewise the theological "problem" of evil is eliminated if evil is totally explained without reference to God, as in the Hindu doctrine of *karma.* Here the explanation of evil in the world is found in guilt accumulated in previous existences, extending infinitely but not remembered in present life. Evil is the automatic consequence of this guilt. The system of *karma* is self-contained within the world of *saṁsāra* or finite (and "illusory") existence; God or the Absolute simply does not enter into it.

Finally, there is no "problem" of evil if the question of God's relationship to it cannot even be asked. For the Buddha, such questions are profitless; the only problem of evil is the practical one of getting out of it. [15] The existence or non-existence of God is irrelevant to this. In Islam, on the other hand, God is recognized as the omnipotent source of the world and all that exists in it; but the act of posing a "problem" of evil would be a questioning of his creative will. For Islam, the only proper attitude toward God is submission. If there is a problem of evil, it is not with God, but with us, for not accepting his will. Islam, as Van der Leeuw notes, never produced a Job.

TYPES OF RELIGIOUS-PHILOSOPHICAL THEODICIES

Having clarified the notion of the "problem" of evil with regard to God, we may now proceed to ask about its possible solution. We shall first examine some of the general patterns of religious theodicies; then we will look more closely at the major Western attempts at finding a higher intelligibility to our existential encounter with evil in the light of the existence of God.

We can discern in world religions five major categories of solution to the problem of theodicy. [16] It will be noted that there is a certain overlapping and intermixing of themes among them. Furthermore, they do not all address precisely the same aspect of the problem; therefore any particular theodicy might employ several of these categories at once.

(1) The *aesthetic* solution holds that the *whole* of existence is good, either despite or even because of the evil of some parts. A very simple form of this solution would point out an imbalance between good and evil; the whole remains good simply because there is more good. On a more sophisticated level, it might be claimed that the evil aspects of creation are somehow needed in order to give relief to the good—just as in a work of

art the light must be set off by darkness, or as in music the major key sounds stronger when contrasted with the minor. Or, finally, the evil of the world might be recompensed by greater good, either in this life (as in the present non-original ending to the Book of Job) or in an after-life ("I consider the sufferings of this life to be as nothing compared to the glory that will be . . ."—Rom 8:18).

(2) A second type of solution sees evil as the result of *free will*. This category may also be subdivided. One type would see evil as the product of God's justice: God punishes humanity for sin. The sin may be personal, or communal, or "original" (see Rom 5:16). We find instances in the New Testament of the common assumption that even physical illness is a punishment: "Master, for whose sin was this man born blind? For his own, or for that of his parents?" (Jn 9:2). Another interpretation sees evil in the world not as a "punishment" from God, but as a privation which stems directly from bad will (individual and communal) itself: by the misuse of freedom, we deprive ourselves and each other of the good which God wills. Finally, there is an aspect of prevention: God may permit or use lesser evils (physical evil) in order to prevent greater (moral) evils. Suffering may serve as a warning (as C. S. Lewis puts it, pain is "God's megaphone").[17]

(3) A third category of solution centers on *teleology:* the evils that we suffer are a means to a good end; suffering is a kind of "discipline" or "education:" in some way it builds or perfects character. (Clearly this applies basically to evil suffered, rather than evil performed; if it were extended to the latter, we would have a position similar to Hegel's on the necessity of evil.)

This type of solution finds expression in many scriptural passages. God in allowing us to suffer is like a loving father who disciplines his children (Heb 12:6ff., quoting Sir 30:1); suffering is a test, or a trial, which purifies us as precious metals are purified in fire (1 Pet 1:6–7; 4:12); the frustration suffered by creation is by God's will, for the sake of the glory of his children (Rom 8:20). In some Hindu theology the point is stated even more baldly: God introduces evil into the world because humanity needs it.

(4) Another category, often linked to the above, sees evil as being, at least in part, *illusion*. If suffering is really a test or a trial, or is a means to a better end, then it is not in the last analysis evil at all; we only think it so because of our limited perspective. As we have seen, if this idea is presented in its most radical form (the entirety of human existence is illusion; we cannot know good from evil at all) it would eliminate the problem altogether; but in a more limited sense it may be taken as a partial explanation for evil. As St. John of the Cross puts it: "no sabe el hombre ni

dolerse bien, ni gozarse bien; porque no sabe la distancia del bien y del mal"[18] (we do not know either how to grieve or to rejoice rightly, for we do not know the true proportions of good and evil). Since we have only a partial perception of what is good—even for us—and since we are ourselves sinful, we frequently imagine evil to exist because of our distorted sense of values (see for example Jas 4:2ff).

(5) Finally, there is the category of *limitation:* the existence of the good willed for the world by God is limited, not by a lack in his power, but by resistance: either of a personal adversary to the good (Satan, the devil), or of an impersonal evil substance (matter), or of the unavoidable imperfection of creation.

THE MAJOR TYPES OF CHRISTIAN RELIGIOUS THEODICY

Each of the categories outlined above features to some extent in all the major religious theodicies, Western and Eastern. They are present, however, in different degrees, and are used in different ways; some are more theoretical explanations, others more imaginative analogies. In attempts to formulate a systematic response to the problem of evil, there is generally a dominance of one theme, to which the others are subordinate.

There are three such major systematic approaches which have been influential in the West:[19] a dualistic theodicy, the free will theodicy associated with the fall of man, especially as presented by St. Augustine, and, in more modern times, an evolutionary theodicy.

(1) A strictly dualistic approach on a systematic level—the positing of some evil principle, whether spiritual or material, equally primal with God—would of course come into conflict with the Christian doctrines of creation and omnipotence. Not surprisingly, therefore, the explicit adoption of such a system is primarily found among heretical groups like the Manichaeans or the Cathari. Nevertheless, a dualistic mentality has often existed on the level of imagination and piety even among theologically orthodox Christians. Not infrequently it is the image of a *struggle* between good and evil, a "war" mentality, which has dominated spirituality in the West. The evil principle has often been portrayed as a personal adversary, the devil, who from the beginning to the end of salvation history must be combatted, and from whom humanity must be "redeemed"—literally, bought back.

At the same time, there has often been an explicit or hidden "Platonic" current in Western thought, frequently bringing with it a matter-spirit dualism. The "world" of John's Gospel and the "flesh" of St. Paul are interpreted in Greek categories as referring to material being. Matter, although in theory recognized as God's (good) creation, is implicitly and practically treated as the realm of the devil.

(2) The major theoretical attempt to explain evil, however, was in terms of free will. Its classic expression is in the theology of St. Augustine.[20] For Augustine, all evil, moral and physical, in humanity and in the world, is due to the *fall* of mankind at the beginning of history. This fall is due not only to human freedom, but also to temptation, which stems from the enmity of the devil (here we find the introduction of the sub-theme of the spiritual Adversary). His existence is in turn explained by another fall: that of the angels, before human history. Augustine's theodicy therefore takes on the aspect of a great cosmic drama of creation, salvation, and judgment.[21]

The first part of the drama takes place before the creation of the material world. God creates first the spiritual beings, the angels. Put to the test by God, a certain number of the angels fall—Augustine specifies that their sin was that of pride (later theologians were to speculate that they refused to accept God's plan of self-Incarnation, which he revealed to them). The fallen angels are expelled from God's presence, but retain the powers of their nature.

[The fall of the angels already figures in the writings of St. Athanasius and other earlier Fathers, who got the idea from the intertestamental literature. It is interesting to note, however, that in the books of Enoch and Jubilees, the sin of the angels occurs *after* the fall of man, and is indeed identified as intercourse with human women.

The fall of the angels allows Augustine to explain more easily the fall of Adam; but it poses another problem: Why did the angels fall? Augustine states that God did not give to those who sinned the same knowledge of eternal bliss that he shared with those who would not fall.[22] Is this the equivalent of saying that God predestined certain ones to fall by not giving them the grace that would be needed to avoid sin?]

Only after sin has already come into existence does the creation of humanity take place, as described in the Book of Genesis (according to some, mankind is created to make up the number of the fallen angels). Adam and Eve exist in Paradise with extraordinary ("praeternatural") gifts. They are tempted by the devil (note that this is not the view of the author of Genesis; it was only later speculation which identified the talking serpent with a fallen spiritual being). They fall, and are expelled from God's presence and grace into a situation of hardship and death. Because of their sin, *the world* becomes a "fallen" place; it no longer serves humanity, but becomes disordered, hostile and pain-filled. The descendants of Adam and

Eve not only come into a fallen world, but are born in a *fallen state:* they are not only without the praeternatural gifts, but are weakened and ignorant in their nature, alienated from God by the transmitted "original sin," and with a tendency to personal sin.

God, however, does not leave humanity in this state; he sends his Son, the Christ, who "atones" for sin by his death and once more frees human freedom, by his grace, from the slavery of sin. It becomes possible for humanity, in grace, to choose the good; but the effects of the original sin remain operative in the world, so that salvation must come about through a participation in the cross.

The last part of the cosmic drama will be played out at the end of history, when God will judge the world. All who have lived will enter into their everlasting destiny: glory or damnation. (In Augustine's view, the majority would be lost.)

Clearly, the Augustinian theodicy as presented in the Adamic myth is a magnificent theological creation. It presents in imaginative form many of the crucial elements of a metaphysical and Christian perspective on the problem of evil:[23] that God is totally good, and is not the cause of evil; that human free will is responsible for our alienation from God and the world; that humans form a community, and are intimately linked to each other, so that there is truly a communal dimension to both sin and salvation; that evil is of its nature a privation of good, not a positive force, since the final metaphysical reality is a totally good God; that there is a distinction between humanity's alienated state and personal sin; and, finally, that we stand in need of salvation from God.

Nevertheless, there are also clearly problems with this form of theodicy. If it is accepted as a "myth," there is much existential meaning within it; but it is presented in the form of salvation *history,* and has generally been taken as such. As an historical account of the origins of suffering and evil, it is simply unacceptable to a modern world view. We know from studies of pre-history, for example, that physical evil, at least, pre-dates the origins of humanity on earth; the sin of the first humans can hardly be held as the source of the struggles, suffering and pain or of the natural conditions that caused them in the millions of years before the appearance of the species.

Moreover, this schema is inadequate as an explanation on several counts. The wholesale condemnation of humanity because of the sin of the first parents seems totally unjust—especially if one holds, as Augustine did, that "original sin" suffices for a person's damnation in the absence of the grace of baptism. The omnipotence and/or the goodness of God seem compromised by the power of evil as represented by the devil. The "transmission" of the original sin is not adequately explained. And, finally, the original evil—that of the fall of the angels—is unexplained, unless we accept the hint of predestination. As subsequent Christian history has shown, the Augustinian schema easily leads to a dualist mentality, to a theory of predestination, and to a masochistic attitude: the acceptance of guilt for unjust suffering.

(3) The failures of the Augustinian myth to provide an adequate explanation for evil, at least on the level of theory, have led modern theologians—among them John Tennant and Teilhard de Chardin—to attempt to disengage its existential and ontological meaning from the mythic framework, and to present that meaning in the light of a modern anthropology, taking into account an evolutionary view of the world and of humanity. John Hick has linked this attempt to the name of St. Irenaeus of Lyons, calling the evolutionary explanation of evil the "Irenaean theodicy."[24]

St. Irenaeus in his interpretation of Genesis held that humanity (symbolized by Adam) was not created in a finished state, but as a being in process; man was made in the "image" of God, but has not yet attained to God's "likeness."[25]

Transposing this theological notion into a modern scientific evolutionary context, Hick and others see humanity as having been "created" through a long process of evolution which would already include physical (or "pre-moral") evil as one of the conditions for evolution itself. Once humanity appears, moreover, it is not in a state of perfection, but in a state of incipient growth, in which humans are responsible for progress *toward* God. This responsibility necessarily includes the possibility of mistakes and also of genuine moral evil or sin.

Hick's theodicy therefore centers on a *teleological* solution, in the line of many scriptural texts.[26] He writes:

> One who has attained to goodness by meeting and eventually mastering temptations, and thus by rightly making responsible choices in concrete situations, is good in a richer and more valuable sense than would be one created *ab initio* in a state either of innocence or of virtue.[27]

A world in which there would be no trials, a world of pure pleasure, according to Hick, would *not* be the product of a loving God. It is better for humanity to be free and responsible for itself, to have the task of *becoming* the best possible self, than to live in a perfect or paradisical world. For Hick, it would be un-loving of God to create a world without the possibility of pain.

One may take this line of thinking one step farther, in accord with the insights of Teilhard de Chardin. For Teilhard, a progressive and evolutionary world is not merely *better* than a world of static perfection; it is in fact the only *possible* kind of world for finite, embodied spirit. Spirit which is "in the world" (in Rahner's phrase) must have a material and temporal kind of existence; it cannot have its being all at once, but must come to itself through what is not itself (the world, matter, the other). It must therefore realize its being through a freedom which is not simply transcendental self-possession, but is categorical choice.[28] Such spirit as humanity is, is necessarily progressive in its being; it must create and choose values. It must therefore also have the possibility of making morally evil choices.

The kind of world in which finite spirit can exist and realize itself must be a world which contains both order and randomness. It must, in short, be an evolutionary world. But in such a world, "physical" or pre-moral evil is inevitable; it is the very condition of the randomness which allows progression. It is also inevitable that spiritual, intelligent and free beings will come into conflict, to some degree, with both the order and the randomness of the world; for the freedom of the subject does not automatically coincide with the "laws" of nature. The evolutionary view holds, therefore, that a world in which finite spirit can come about and can engage in encounter is necessarily a world which contains pre-moral evil; and the very existence of finite freedom in the world includes the possibility of moral evil and the kinds of suffering that derive from it.

This view does not eliminate the notion of a "fall" of humanity as the existential cause of evil in the world. Indeed, it is necessary to posit the entry of sin into history as the explanation of our actual situation; for we are confronted not with the mere *possibility* of moral evil and its consequences, but with the *fact* of its existence. That fact could only come about through human choice.[29] Furthermore, once that choice of moral evil has occurred in history, it affects the whole human situation. Because we create the environment or context for each other's lives, the existence of moral evil in the human community leads to the permanent conditioning of our situation by a certain pre-personal alienation from the good—or the situation which the Christian tradition calls "original sin."[30]

THE ANTICIPATION OF GOD'S "SOLUTION" TO EVIL

In our consideration of the problem of evil, thus far we have attempted to show that evil is a complex phenomenon, and that we should therefore not be bewitched by our own language into thinking that evil is one thing, or even that it is "something"; this would lead to a wrong posing of the problem.

The complexity of the problem of evil is compounded by our own restricted knowledge and goodness; a being which is itself not totally good cannot with total adequacy pose the question about goodness; part of the problem of evil is ourselves, and we must recognize this in posing the problem.

Furthermore, evil in its many forms is a *problem,* or a series of problems. In our vocabulary, to say that evil is a problem means that it is not something to be accepted, to be wondered at, as we wonder at the mystery of being. To call evil a "problem" is to say that the only correct attitude toward it is rejection: the "solving" of the problem. It is to say that practically speaking one must take a stance against evil. This practical stance corresponds to evil's being also an intellectual problem; it is because evil is absurd, unintelligible in itself, that we must practically face it as something to be "solved."

Nevertheless, evil is a problem only because it is not *simply* absurd but has, existentially, a further intelligibility in the light of the fact of God. We distinguished above a double sense in which evil is a problem: intellectually, there is the question of how evil can exist in a world made by a good God; and existentially, there is the question of how we can be saved from evil—what God is doing about it. If the evolutionary theodicy gives us some insight into the first question, it leaves us still with the existential problem. How we finally react to evil will depend upon what—if anything—we think God is doing about it, and upon what we are doing about it, if anything. How we regard evil will largely depend upon ourselves either collaborating with it or resisting it.

If God in some way "responds" to the problem of evil (which is a different question from whether God "reveals" himself; for we could conceive of a divine "response" to evil in which God remained "silent" for man), then evil is not merely evil, but is also an element in a higher synthesis. It never becomes good in itself; but some evil, at least, may become a relative good, under some aspect, because of its circumstances.

Obviously if this approach to evil as a "problem" is correct, then the distinction between different kinds of evil becomes absolutely crucial: particularly the difference between what I have called "physical" evil and "moral" evil. There is a critical distinction between evil which is a part of an evolution toward the transcendent, and evil which is so because it *opposes* the movement of transcendence. The one kind of evil is to be "advanced": one "solves" it by advancing the situation to a new horizon, by furthering the process; the other kind is rather to be "reversed": it is opposed by the opposite motion of repentance, restitution, the return of good for evil. If our analysis is correct, then whether a particular evil ought to *be* is a relative matter; what is absolute is that evil ought not to *remain.*

On the basis of this analysis we can distinguish some different kinds of evil. (This is not intended to be an exhaustive analysis, but only an example of the kinds of distinctions we would have to make in order to meet the complexity of the problem.)

1. Simple physical evil: the conflicts and clashes of an incomplete and evolving world, in which both order and the element of chance or indeterminacy mean that there will be events and contacts between things that will not be completely ordered. This is compounded by the fact that the conflicts caused by the indeterminacy of material things are also experienced by conscious beings who can feel the conflicts as pain.

2. Moral evil: sin, the conscious and purposeful evil. In its root, this is an evil that one performs against oneself, because sin is by definition a movement against the drive to transcendence (and therefore St. Thomas Aquinas held that "God is only offended by that which we do against our own good").

3. Physical evil that people inflict on each other: directly, by sin; or indirectly, as a consequence of sin; or accidentally, as physical agents in an evolving world (and perhaps with no conscious volition at all); or as moral agents in dialogue with each other, in a dialogue which is not necessarily sinful, but is still conditioned materially by an imperfect world, and which therefore includes misunderstanding and mental conflict, pain, and physical evil.

4. Suffering: mental evil, or the conscious reaction to a real physical or moral evil.

5. Unnecessary suffering: the conscious reaction to a falsely perceived physical or moral evil. Such a false consciousness could be the result of many other evils: illusion, fear, ignorance, misperception, or sin. The basis of much of the problem of evil is precisely the fact that we tend to absolutize what is actually relative, thus creating or enlarging evil.

6. Suffering from being loved by God: God's call to spirit (whether it is conceived as "revelation" or not) can itself be a cause of suffering precisely because God is love, and we are not completely loving; that is, there is a movement of transcendence toward God, and transcendence always implies breaking out of a present horizon. There is thus a tension to overcome, a demand for work, a necessary loss of the present good for the sake of a greater; and in this there is the possibility of suffering. When sin enters the picture, the tension between lower and higher integrations is increased; there may actually be resistance to being loved, insofar as this calls for growth.

7. Suffering caused by loving and being loved by others: St. Paul speaks of returning good for evil, and how it "heaps burning coals" on the head of the sinner. Goodness does not always cause pleasure, but can cause pain as well. The psychological effect of love on a resentful consciousness, for example, may be suffering. Even in the human world, love

by or for another may cause physical evil or the suffering that comes from a call to growth.

8. Suffering that people take upon themselves: sacrifice. Clearly, some of this suffering is perverse: masochism. But it would also seem that there may be legitimate forms of sacrificial suffering, at least in a sinful world. Such suffering may take place in order to perform a service of love for others which otherwise could not be accomplished; or in order to return good for evil, and break out of the cycle of self-perpetuating evil; or possibly in order to worship God in a way not otherwise possible (for example, in fasting or celibacy. It is doubtful, however, whether such acts of sacrifice can ever be separated completely from the first form, i.e. in service of others; the act of sacrifice seems always to have at least a witness value to others regarding the need to attend to a higher context).

As there is no single source of evil or meaning of evil, so there is no single mode of response to evil (even if we do speak, for the sake of convenience, of "the solution" to the problem of evil). There are different attitudes which may be correct, both in the receiving of suffering and in the causing of it.

[So, for example, we find in the Gospels the idea that the poor are blessed; on the other hand, there is condemnation for those who do not meet the needs of the poor: that is, for those who accept the poverty of others without doing something about it. Obviously, then, the "blessing" of poverty is relative; being poor is not good in itself, but the poor are blessed because they are open to a higher good.

Similarly, one reads in John's Gospel of a Jesus who accepts death, who thinks of it as the grain of wheat going into the ground, who will not pray that this hour be taken from him; while in the Synoptics, Jesus does pray that the cup be taken away; he weeps at his impending death, and feels abandoned by God on the cross. These two pictures are reflected in two theologies of redemption: a contrast theology, in which *man* sinfully puts Jesus to death, and God, by contrast, raises him up; and, on the other hand, a sacrifice theology, in which God himself delivers Jesus to death as a part of his saving plan.

On the one hand, we read that peacemakers are blessed; on the other hand, "I have come not to bring peace, but a sword."

In short, one cannot simply take a synthesis from the religious view toward suffering without neglecting part of the message.]

We must therefore reject every simplistic approach to the problem of evil: either a simple acceptance of evil, in every form, or a simple rejection of every evil. How we are to face evil concretely, as we have noted, will depend upon what we believe God is doing about it. We have not yet reached a point in our considerations where we can identify God's "word" to humanity; thus far, we have merely established that humanity necessarily seeks for such a "word," both as the fulfillment of our essential orientation to being and as the "solution" to the problem of evil. Even before we make any identification, however, we can anticipate God's saving word; indeed, it is only in the light of this anticipation that we can regard evil as a "problem." Furthermore, we can at this point formulate that anticipation as a "heuristic structure": that is, by naming the problem and its context we can determine the minimal elements which any solution which meets that problem must have. We shall turn to Bernard Lonergan's *Insight* for the essentials of this formulation.[31]

First of all, we recognize that the "solution" is in fact the actual order of the world—even though within our "moving viewpoint" we have first considered the "problem" in abstraction from it. In order to meet the problem, God's solution must be like the problem an "existential" of human existence: the "solution," that is, must be (at least implicitly) an intrinsic factor in the condition of every human being.

Any solution to the human dilemma must be in continuity with our basic human "nature" as "spirit in the world": i.e., a dynamic openness in freedom to being and the good, realized within the material and intersubjective world. The answer to the problem of evil, then, cannot *simply* consist in an "afterlife" in which the alienation of this life is overcome. Our spiritual reality does indeed presuppose a hope for eternal validity which goes beyond the present world; it also presupposes, however, that the attainment of that validity can only come about *in and through* our historical existence.

A divine solution to the problem of evil, therefore, must provide a higher integration of human life in the world, including the irrationality of sin and evil. Since it cannot consist simply in the abolition of these realities (because they are inextricable conditions of the world in which free finite spirit exists), it must provide a means by which evil, in its many forms, can be transcended, transformed and integrated into a higher good.

The higher integration of existence which we anticipate must be dynamic, because it occurs within the actual evolutionary world order and the actual dynamic of human spirit. God's "answer" to the human dilemma, therefore, must come to us through our own apprehension and consent, and within our history. History, however, is not a homogeneous flow; the possibilities of realization of human spirit are conditioned by material, cultural, and intersubjective factors which vary with times and places. Our concrete capacity for apprehending and responding to God's solution will therefore be variable. Hence we may expect that salvation will include not only a full realization, in the "fullness of time" (Eph 1:10), but also an entire series of "emergent trends" through which the appearance and acceptance of salvation become effectively possible.

As the fulfillment of our spiritual being, the solution to evil must mean a higher integration of freedom, that is, a new or transcendent dimension of love. Physical evil exists as a condition of the progressive realization of finite freedom, while moral evil contains the implicit self-contradiction of an absence of good within a dynamism which necessarily seeks the good. The overcoming of evil, therefore, will consist in the reinforcement and restoration of the dynamism toward the ultimate good. That dynamism is love, which transcends evil by providing a motivation for responding to evil with good, thus transforming even the irrationality of evil—including sin—into a potential for transcendence. Such love is of necessity "self-sacrificial" in some degree, for it not only seeks a final good outside the self, but does so in the face of the concrete lack of a proportionate present satisfaction.

Because free love is the highest act of rational self-consciousness, it is of necessity connected with meaning and truth, and must involve the mind. A solution to the problem of evil must therefore involve a higher pursuit of the true meaning of existence. Because our existence is intrinsically intersubjective, historical and social, this pursuit must be a collaboration in the apprehension and formulation of meaning. It must hence include a dimension of "faith," at least in the philosophic sense of trust in meaning and in a human collaboration which goes beyond one's self-generated knowledge. The collaboration of humans in the pursuit of meaning will be in some (undetermined) sense institutionally or socially embodied, as a condition of its continuance and progression.

Since God's solution must come to us as free, intelligent, rational beings who construct our lives in dialogue with others, it will include a need for collaboration on our part, despite the fact that it remains God's work. We will be called to realize and further the solution by becoming part of it: by participating in the collaboration of love, by formulating and making it known, by adapting it to changing human circumstances, by explaining it and its conditions to ourselves and others.

As we have seen, the problem itself is complex and multidimensional. The solution, then, although it must have its own unity as a dynamism to a single goal, will also be manifest in many dimensions. "Love" is an analogous term, like "the good," and its concrete meaning must be worked out in response to the varying circumstances which it is called to meet. Furthermore, the solution must integrate not only the higher levels of freedom and intellect, but also the bodily and sensitive levels of existence; it must exist not only as a transcendental dynamism but also as a categorical realization, not only as act but also as idea, not only as insight but also as image and symbol, so that every aspect of the human person is involved.

We may also expect, in a solution which respects our freedom, that sin and error, as well as physical evil, will remain within our collaboration with God; nevertheless, as God's work, it must finally be victorious, and show itself as such.

Lonergan concludes his heuristic anticipation of God's saving action by recalling that such a heuristic structure is of its nature limited in its scope. God's actual action may go beyond what is indicated merely by a grasp of the problem; it may open up for humanity an unanticipated dimension, totally transcending a mere "answer" to our need. We cannot determine the extent of God's "word" to us prior to our actual identification of it. But from the perspective of our "moving viewpoint," before we can make any identification we must first clarify an essential question, the answer to which will serve a hermeneutical function in our further progress: In what sense can God "speak" to us, or "act" in the world? What is the meaning of a "word" or "action" of the Absolute within the context of the relative and finite sphere of history?

II. GOD HAS SPOKEN

DOES GOD SPEAK/ACT IN HISTORY?

In many and various ways God spoke of old to our fathers, by the prophets; but in these last days he has spoken to us by a Son, whom he appointed the heir of all things; through whom, also, he created the world.

Heb 1:1–2

"Do you believe in a personal God? I know, of course, how difficult it is to attach a clear meaning to this question, but you can probably appreciate its general purport."

"May I rephrase your question?" I asked. "I myself should prefer the following formulation: Can you, or anyone else, reach the central order of things or events, whose existence seems beyond doubt, as directly as you can reach the soul of another human being? I am using the term 'soul' quite deliberately so as not to be misunderstood. If you put your question like that, I would say yes. . ."

Werner Heisenberg: *Physics and Beyond*

We have been considering the problem of evil as a presupposition for posing the question about a possible revelation from God. We began with the need of man for meaning, or for a higher integration of his life; we expanded this with the idea of the need for salvation from evil.

There exists, in fact, a quest for higher meaning and a collaboration to overcome evil; there is as well a perceived relevance of God to both questions. The question still remains: Is this all "from" God, as his creation, but in such a way that the activity is entirely on our side, or does God actually "enter into" the collaboration? Is God merely the horizon in which the dialogue takes place, or is he a participant in the dialogue? Is God reached by us in some sense analogous to the way in which we reach each other as spiritual beings?

Before we can adequately respond to this question, we must examine certain presuppositions regarding the nature of God and his relationship to the world.[1]

37

Can God "Speak" to Us?—The Meaning of "God"

First, regarding the meaning of the word "God" itself: as used here, this word refers to an ontological reality: God is the absolute horizon which is revealed as the condition of possibility for human transcendence. (In the method used in *The Reason for Our Hope*, this horizon was especially revealed in the treatment of intellect; but it is also revealed in human morality, or in aesthetics.) There can be no question of "defining" God, or of having a concept of God in the proper sense of the term; our speech about God can only refer to the fundamental experience in which we anticipate the non-objectifiable ground of all existence, the source and goal of our own dynamism to transcendence.

Of primary importance, then, is the fact that God is mystery: that is, that we do not know what God is. It is easy, when speaking in a religious context, to forget the transcendental basis of speech about God, and therefore its merely analogous character. Since we have no intuition of the "essence" of God, on the one hand, and since on the other hand God is not an "object" which can be known within the sphere of proportionate being, all our rational knowledge of God is simply an explicitation of what we are knowing when we judge *that* God exists. In this sense, our basic theology can be seen as anthropology: we do not say what God is in himself; rather, everything that we can say about God is as the goal of our existence. We can name God in different ways by his relationship to our transcendent dynamism.

(It must also be recalled that we are speaking from within a "moving viewpoint"; we are abstracting from some of the affirmations that faith makes about God, precisely in order to examine their basis and validity. What we can say at this point may have to be expanded as our point of view includes higher syntheses. Nevertheless, those higher viewpoints will not contradict, but will depend upon the lower, so that whatever faith has to say about God on the basis of "revelation" must be received and interpreted on the basis of the principles expounded in our basic ontology/anthropology. To put it another way: our anthropology is the hermeneutic principle by which we will interpret any "revelation.")

THE DIVINE "ATTRIBUTES"

With this caveat, we may proceed to speak of certain "attributes" of God. To provide a brief summary of these, as seen in a transcendentally-based philosophy, we shall encapsulate and comment upon Bernard Lonergan's treatment in *Insight*;[2] then we will return to certain critical points, particularly regarding God's relationship to the world, where further development is needed.

From the very notion of God can be derived certain "attributes": the transcendentals: being, unity, truth, goodness; and certain implications of the very fact of God's being.

First, God is the completely intelligible: what Lonergan calls the "Idea of Being," an unrestricted act of understanding.[3] The "primary component" of the Idea of Being is God's understanding of himself as the "primary intelligible," the absolutely unconditioned. This is to say that God is self-explanatory, the only reason for himself. Were this not so, God would not be complete intelligibility. Thus, there is no "why?" beyond God's existence; God is the ultimate answer to the question about meaning, and it is meaningless to ask "why?" about God. In understanding himself, God also understands everything else that exists by his act of creation: the "secondary intelligibles," that is, everything whatever that is. This Lonergan calls the "secondary component" of the Idea of Being.

What is known by true understanding is "being"; and therefore the primary intelligible is also primary being. We should note that a transcendental affirmation of the existence of God does not permit us to say that God is *a* being: he is rather Absolute Being, *esse subsistens*. God does not fall within a more general category of "being" as one of the instances of its reference; God is not alongside beings. God is both "above" beings (and Heidegger's "being of beings") and "within" beings, since there is no limitation to his being. But it would be misleading to speak of God as though he were *one of the beings* of the universe. (The apparent inevitability of mythic religious language speaking in just this way is one of the main reasons for the need of the critical theological enterprise.)

The primary being must also be perfect being, because outside God and his goodness there is nothing. In this sense, God must transcend the finite world and contingency. This must be understood carefully: to say that God transcends the world must not be understood as an *exclusion*, as though we were saying that God is unlimited in being, opposed to nothing, *except* the finite world. Infinite being must include the finite as participating in its being; otherwise, it would not be infinite, but finite. God is thus being in all its fullness, with no limits.

God must also be unconditional being; as the Absolute, he can be in no way contingent, for then he would need some explanation outside himself. God is revealed in transcendental method as the absolutely unconditioned on which every virtually unconditioned depends. (This is exactly the content of the so-called "proof" of the existence of God.)

It follows also from the unconditioned character of God that his being must be completely simple. The absolute or unconditioned being cannot contain parts or divisions because such parts would have to be finite, and a being composed of such parts would itself be finite. The Absolute must be the One, immutable and unchangeable; otherwise there would be duality in God.

[Here we meet with a difficulty, however. We have described God in Lonergan's formulation as the Idea of Being, and have said, with Lonergan, that this Absolute Intelligibility has two "components": knowledge of self and of the contingent world freely posited by him. But now we say that God is completely simple. How can a completely simple being have two "components"? On the other hand, the distinction between the two components cannot be done away with: for God's knowledge of himself is necessary, while his knowledge of the world is freely posited; to identify the two would result in pantheism.

The response is first of all that God is not literally "composed," as Lonergan himself recognizes.[4] Both aspects of his knowledge are identical with his very being in its absolute simplicity:

> Though the secondary intelligibles are distinct from the primary, they need not be distinct realities. For knowing does not consist in taking a look at something else and so, though the secondary intelligibles are known, they need not be something else to be looked at. Moreover, the primary being is without any lack or defect or imperfection; but it would be imperfect if further realities were needed for the unrestricted act of understanding to be unrestricted.[5]

This implies that the reality of the creation (the "secondary intelligibles") is identical with God's own being. At the same time, that being is free, and capable of expressing itself by positing what is "distinct" from itself. If God actually is Creator of the world, then that fact is *of* the divine being itself (cf. Lonergan's "principle of contingent predication"), without its thereby being "necessary" to the divine being.[6] (Does this not imply, however, that God's being—in its intrinsic immutability—*includes* change? We shall return to this point when considering the relation of God to the world.)]

It follows from God's simplicity that his knowledge must be non-receptive; otherwise it would be contingent and incomplete. Therefore, also, God is beyond the world of relativity defined by the epistemological *a priori* of space-time. God as eternal does not exist "within" space-time; he is rather an entire present. God is therefore absolute Spirit—absolute and complete consciousness of himself and of all that is.

God is also the goal and the source of our being. To be the source of a non-necessary being is to be an act of love; for God freely posits beings whose existence and value depend upon his knowing and willing them.

God As "Person"

Because we may speak of God as the Idea of Being and the Act of Love, we may also speak of him as "personal." However, we must not think that God is *a* person, in the sense of a finite individual. God's being is the foundation of what we mean by personality; thus we may call him "person" by analogy. But if by person we mean an intrinsically incomplete being, relational because necessarily opposed to and dependent upon another, then in this sense God is not personal; he would have to be qualified as "supra-personal."

[One of the characteristics of Western biblical religion is that it tends to imagine God as a person with anthropomorphic qualities. For Eastern religions like Hinduism and Buddhism, on the other hand, the Absolute is clearly above personality in the human sense; the Western conception frequently seems a naive and even idolatrous idea. There is here, I think, a real divergence of views, particularly on the nature of "analogy" and the value of "personality" (to this we shall return in a later section); but much of the conflict is also a matter of misunderstanding of context. At least upon a metaphysical view, the God of Western religion cannot simply be called "person" in every sense of the term.]

The Relation of God to the World

From what we have said regarding the Absolute, there arises the question of the relationship between God and the world.[7] The basic principles of explanation are already contained in what has been said; what follows is merely a matter of further clarification.

First of all, within the very experience which allows us to affirm the existence of an Absolute ground is contained at the same time the intuition of our own dependence or non-necessity. Thus the *distinction* of God from the world is a primary transcendental datum of consciousness. Indeed, as Karl Rahner remarks, this distinction is not only necessary; it is *the* distinction which makes possible all others.[8] The differentiation between the ineffable term or "horizon" of human transcendence and all finite being is precisely what allows us to perceive objects *as finite,* and thus to differentiate them from the absolute horizon itself and from each other.[9] For this very reason, the absolute horizon, as the condition of possibility for all categorical distinctions, cannot itself be differentiated by the same categorical norms that apply *within* the horizon. The distinction between God and the world is completely *sui generis,* and can be grasped only in the originating transcendental experience. It cannot be understood as simple duality, as though God "and" the world were two entities which form part of a larger whole. The distinction is rather included "within" the being of God:

> the difference between God and the world is of such a nature that God establishes and *is* the difference of the world from himself, and for this reason he establishes the closest unity precisely in the differentiation. [10]

> . . . this nameless and indefinable term of transcendence . . . is distinguished from everything else only from its own side, and hence differentiates everything else from itself. [11]

Rahner remarks that there is thus a certain truth in pantheism: namely, that God is the only absolute reality, the originating Ground and ultimate Term of all transcendence. [12] The preaching and theologies of the theistic religions, particularly in the West, have not always avoided the danger of presenting God's transcendence on the model of finite "otherness," thus actually destroying his infinity. [13] (Within the Thomist tradition, the persistence of the Platonic notion of the "analogy of being" and its correlative doctrine of "participation" have served as a corrective to the finitizing of God; but this aspect of Thomism has also frequently been forgotten. [14])

On the basis of a transcendental understanding, there is the most intimate unity between God and his creation. Indeed, there is a sense in which one can say that there is "nothing else" but God: in himself or in his creatures. The divine creative act is essentially identical with God (because of the divine simplicity); at the same time, this very act in its effect (*"terminative"*) constitutes the being of creatures. [15] Thus St. Thomas can say that the being (*esse*) of God is the being of all things, [16] and Rahner states that the difference of beings from God is itself "identical with God." [17]

This reality may be expressed in a number of ways. The classic notion of "participation" must of course not be taken in its most obvious literal sense, as though the divine being had divisions or parts; [18] but combined with the notion of God as subsistent Understanding (the "Idea of Being") it gives some intelligibility to the subsistence of the many in the One: for understanding is one, but is understanding "of" a plurality. [19] Donceel suggests that God might be spoken of as the "quasi-formal" cause of all things (the "formal cause" being the essence, what makes a thing itself; the "soul" is formal cause of the body); but this term has been appropriated by theologians to speak of the relation of "grace." [20]

Others have developed the notion of creation as the "image" of God; this theme, common in the Platonic theology of the early Church, is taken up in modern times by Fichte. For him, there always and only exists the Absolute ("Light"): either *in se,* or in his "appearance" or exteriorization ("image"). Finite beings are never totally "real," but are in perpetual self-making toward the infinite horizon. (Gómez Caffarena suggests that this is a more dynamic way of stating what St. Thomas Aquinas holds as the relationship between Being and beings, expressed by him in terms of "exemplary" causality.[21])

The same theme (with perhaps more explicitly Hegelian inspiration) is present in Rahner's notion of creation as the *"figura,"* "symbol" or "self-expression" of God, outside himself. God, who is in himself immutable, can nevertheless *himself* become, *in* his finite "other," creation:[22] "he himself *becomes* what has come from him, without having to become in his own and original self."[23] Creation is thus God's self-expression or symbolic manifestation outside himself. As Joseph Wong has shown,[24] Rahner's epistemological basis for metaphysics may be stated in terms of his theory of symbol. God is present "sacramentally" in the finite; in "reading" the symbols of finite being, we not only penetrate to their "essence," but implicitly perceive a reference to the ultimate symbolizer, God.[25] From this point of view, metaphysics does not so much arrive at the positive knowledge of God as at a knowledge of the world as the "revelation" or symbol of God, in which he is intimately present.[26]

If transcendental theology rejects a dualistic interpretation of theism, it must likewise reject the extreme of pantheism or monism. As Pseudo-Dionysius taught, and St. Thomas repeated, "participation" in the divine being is also "imitation." Creation is not merely God's self-expression; it is so God-like, participates so much of the being of God, that it is, like him, a "self," and thus "other" than God in himself. For St. Thomas the "taleity" or "suchness" of beings, what makes them distinct, is precisely the imitation and participation of the being of the Absolute.[27] The creature is so much "of" God that it is like him in the very thing that makes God himself: "aseity," selfhood, freedom—in the different degrees in which creatures "have" being. At its highest point, the creature is thus not *only* the self-expression of God, but also his "other," to whom he can be related in dialogue, in free interpersonal communion.

Our position also differs from pantheism (and from some forms of "panentheism") in insisting that the "emanation" of the world from God, or creation, is by no means a necessity to God. God remains always what our original transcendental experience preapprehends: the absolutely Unconditioned. If a Hegelian "principle of universal correlativity"[28]—

everything is itself by being related to something else—can be applied to God, it is only because he freely posits an "other" in love, and not because of necessity.[29] God is related to his creatures not out of need, but out of superabundance: "God does not move Himself because He is in potency; He does not change because He is in need; He does not become because He is incomplete. To believe such things would be to make God a copy of human misery."[30] God as the Absolute cannot become "more" than himself, cannot "gain" by creating; but his perfection would be less "if in addition to being infinite, he could not become *less* than he (always) is."[31]

The fact that God *can* be himself as the Unconditioned and at the same time share his being with others, without detraction from himself, is the mystery of the divine nature itself; it is the source of our "wonder" at our own contingent existence, as a participation in being which is, yet need not be. What we can finally say (from our present perspective) about the relation between God and the world is precisely what is contained in our knowledge of the fact that there *is* such a relation. As with the existence of God itself, ultimately all we can say is *that* there is a relationship, not clearly *what* it is; for in order to say what it is, we would have to be able to say what God is (since God not only posits but finally *is* his own free act).

The God-world relationship, therefore, is a mystery—ultimately identical with the mystery of God himself; it cannot be reduced to a case of some more universal or more ultimate principle. (To say "mystery," in this context, is to indicate what cannot be "resolved." In contrast to a "problem," mystery can only be lived into; it is intelligible with a meaning that invites us onward, but does not admit of being contained by our thought.[32])

What we can finally say about this relation comes down to the absoluteness of God and the relativity of the world. Concretely, this means that we cannot speak metaphysically of God as a being within the horizon of the world, but only as the condition for the being of the world. Therefore, when we ask whether God enters the collaboration of humanity against evil, or whether God acts in the world or "speaks" a word to us, we clearly cannot mean to ask whether God acts *in the way a finite being acts*, as *one of* the actors in the world, one of the elements in the situation.

On the other hand, the perspective of the absoluteness of God and the relativity of creation means that in some sense *everything* whatsoever is a "word" or an "act" of God. Everything that is participates in God's being, and thus "manifests" or reveals God, in some way and on some level. Indeed, one finally has to say that everything that is, insofar as it is, is God expressing himself outside himself.

The Question of Revelation/Salvation

What, then, is the question? We might phrase it this way: Is there a dimension to our experience of God, in which God is not merely the "asymptotic horizon" of our being, but is also experienced as the fulfillment of the dynamism toward that horizon? Is there an experience of the absolute overcoming of evil, even while we are in the midst of it?

To pose the question in more religious and imaginative language, we might ask whether God has "spoken" to the world a revelatory and saving word—not merely spoken "in" or "through" the world, insofar as everything can be taken as a word of God, but spoken *to* the world, so that within the "all" of revelation we can and must distinguish elements which lead beyond the mediation of creatures. God might reveal himself, and answer the human dilemma of evil, by remaining "silent"; for this also would be significant for us; has he done so—or has he spoken a word in history?

When we ask whether God has "spoken," we are using a metaphor or analogy. Clearly we do not mean to ask whether God has produced vibrations which are accessible to the human ear. What exactly, then, does the metaphor mean?

Speech in its widest sense (including the language of action, or gesture) means several things. First, speech implies freely positing a sign of oneself outside of oneself. Second, such a sign addresses someone, calls for a reaction, invites a dialogue. Third, speech gives some content: it may give information; it may communicate emotion; it may give aid; it may somehow give the person himself. Finally, speech mediates and leads toward encounter: it tends toward unity, on some level (although in ordinary speech the level of union or love might be no more than politeness or the human collaboration in knowledge; even where it mediates conflict, however, speech presumes some contact and communal relation of the persons involved).

To go back to our opening quote from Heisenberg, then, what we are asking is: Can God be reached, encountered as a "Thou," and not merely as the horizon of every "I-Thou" relationship—in, and not merely "through," his creation?

[Because we will be posing this question in the light of world religions, we should note that it is not necessary to conceive of God's revelation or speech in "inter-personal" categories—which to some religious traditions seem inescapably mythic, and derogate from God's absoluteness. One could also conceive of what we are calling God's "word" in a visual metaphor—for example, as "enlightenment." In such a case, revelation might not be conceived so much as a relation between an "I" and a

"Thou" as between the conscious "I" and deeper "I" which grounds it—
in other words, an awakening to the "true self."]

Do we, then, experience ourselves as "addressed," "spoken to" by
God? Do we find within the world of experience signs which point beyond
it, to the Absolute? Do we experience a "content" of lived knowledge
which transcends the horizon of the finite? Do we experience ourselves as
united with, or at least tending toward, a goal beyond the possibilities of
any creaturely existence? Do we have an intimacy, an immediacy, with
God?

GOD HAS SPOKEN

The Affirmation of God's Word/Act

At the end of our last section we asked the question: Has God
"spoken" or revealed himself to humanity in a way which goes beyond
the revelation implicit in the very fact of the world's existence? Can
God be known in a way which it would not be totally false to compare
with the knowledge that one human being gives to another in dialogue?
Existentially speaking: Do we have an experience of the Absolute, not
merely as the ground of creation, but as engaging us in a transformation
of our personal horizon? Do we have a kind of experience which cannot
find sufficient explanation within the horizon of proportionate being, or
is God's communication with us so entirely mediated by creatures that
it is really experienced as a "silence" of God? Do we experience the
tension of a calling to God "beyond" the human horizon, or is the highest
point of our encounter with God one of complete "devotion to the
world"?[33]

The answer to such questions, of course, must be given by each
person individually, through the examination and appropriation of consciousness. Furthermore, it is in any case clear that the affirmation of
such experiences on any level is not without conditions on the part of
the subject; if there is a "dialogue" with God, our ability to discern it
depends upon our personal engagement in it, and hence the depth of
our "converted" existence. There exists, however, a large body of testimony to give direction to our inquiry, and we may point to instances
in life in which the subject may recognize and interpret a depth of experience which has hitherto gone unreflected. Such instances are treated
more fully in *The Reason for Our Hope;* for our purposes here, it will
suffice to give a brief summary.

The religious history of humanity witnesses clearly to belief in a revelation from God; the phenomenon of mysticism, in all cultures, gives evidence of experiences which are interpreted as direct contact with the Absolute. However, there are perhaps also more commonplace experiences which point to the presence in life of a dimension of "mystery" which can only have as its source an encounter, even if highly unreflective, with the Absolute Mystery of being, in an intimacy beyond the mediation of the world.

> If someone perseveres in final faithfulness to his conscience, even when there is no reward; when someone manages to love selflessly, so that it is no longer merely a question of getting along with someone, or a union of egoisms; when someone allows himself to be drawn into the night of death calmly and without a last protest; when the whole of a person's life—despite all contrary experiences and disappointments—quietly opts for the light and the good; when someone—perhaps in apparent total hopelessness and doubt—nevertheless hopes that he hopes . . . there human freedom has become identified with that hope which is the fundamental structure of man's existence: the hope which constantly underpins human freedom through all the individual events of life. In such hope there is already unthematically experienced and known that which is really meant by "God." . . . God himself is the most profound dynamism of this unlimited movement of hope toward himself. And insofar as God in grace makes himself the dynamism and goal of our hope, revelation is already taking place.[34]

> Have we ever kept silent, despite the urge to defend ourselves, when we were being unfairly treated? Have we ever forgiven another although we gained nothing by it and our forgiveness was accepted as quite natural? Have we ever made a sacrifice without receiving any thanks or acknowledgement, without even feeling any inward satisfaction? Have we ever decided to do a thing simply for the sake of conscience, knowing that we must bear sole responsibility for our decision without being able to explain it to anyone? Have we ever tried to act purely for love of God when no warmth sustained us, when our act seemed a leap in the dark, simply nonsensical? Were we ever good to someone without expecting a trace of gratitude and without the comfortable feeling of having been "unselfish"?
> If we can find such experiences in our life, then we have had that very experience of the Spirit which we are after here—the experience of the Eternal, the experience that the Spirit is something more than and different from a part of this world, the experience that happiness in this world is not the whole point of existence, the experience of trust as we sink into darkness, the experience of a faith for which this world provides no reason. . . .

Now if we have *this* experience of the Spirit—by accepting it—then we who live in faith have in fact experienced the supernatural, perhaps without quite realizing it.[35]

If we experience ourselves, at least at our deepest moments, living by something from beyond ourselves, grounded in mystery and received as a gift, which makes possible commitments, hopes, and convictions which we implicitly know to be right and responsible, although the reasons for them cannot be founded in worldly life itself, then by our very lives we are affirming an experience of God revealing himself.

Particularly in the experience of self-giving love is the presence of God, revealing himself, implicitly affirmed as the condition of possibility of the act. If we love another finite being unconditionally, we can only do so by virtue of the fact that the only unconditional Object of love is somehow present in and united to our concrete neighbor. If we can recognize within ourselves an impulse and imperative toward such agapic love, then we have reason to affirm that our spiritual nature is directed implicitly toward God, not merely as transcendent and "asymptotic" horizon, but as an immediate presence in life; that is, we have reason to affirm that God reveals himself in our history.

A second question now imposes itself: If God reveals himself, "acts" in our lives, or "speaks" a word of dialogue to us, of which we can recognize the traces in the inmost dynamism of our concrete being, does that "word" remain merely internal and transcendental, or does this "word" or "act" also become an external word and deed, a revelation of God in and through the world? Does the immediacy of the Absolute preclude every mediation by the world, including human thoughts and words, so that the finite becomes a locus of revelation only by its own negation, or does the world have a positive role even in God's revelation of himself?

An answer to this question is already implicit in our reflections up to this point. First of all, on the basis of our anthropology, a "supernatural" immediacy of the Absolute to a finite being can only be understood as a "mediated immediacy"; for at least the subject's own subjectivity must serve as the "medium" through which the Absolute is experienced. As Rahner writes:

It is easy to perceive that immediacy to God in himself (however this is to be understood more exactly) either is completely impossible, or is not prevented by the fact that there is also some kind of mediation. If there is immediacy to God at all—that is, if we really can have to do with God, in himself—then this immediacy cannot depend on the fact that the non-divine simply disappears. . . . Mediation and immediacy are not simply

contradictories; there is, with regard to God, a real mediation of the immediacy.[36]

Furthermore, the context in which we experience the mysterious "more"
which points to immediacy with God seems always to include a commitment to and love of the world, especially our fellow human beings. It is
indeed in such commitment that we find our primary evidence of God's
presence. But this already implies that the finite is not merely the "locus,"
but also the means of God's self-revelation; for the concrete object of our
love somehow stands for and makes present the transcendent Goal of love,
which is not experienced otherwise.

The analysis of our existential experience, then, leads us to expect and
hope for a genuine "word" or "act" from God which communicates himself
to us, but which does so in and (in some sense) through the finite world.
We may therefore affirm that God "speaks" to us in dialogue, "acts" in our
history, reveals himself. We must now however examine these notions
more closely. In the light of our anthropology and theology, just what does
it mean to say that God speaks or acts? How are such notions reconcilable
with the absolute transcendence and immanence of God? What is the relationship between God's own being and the historical events/actions
which "manifest" or "reveal" him?

Understanding the "Acts" of God: Possible Interpretations

*And the anger came on Peleus' son, and within his shaggy breast the
heart was divided two ways, pondering whether to draw from beside his
thigh the sharp sword, driving away all those who stood between and
kill the son of Atreus, or else to check the spleen within and keep down
his anger. Now as he weighed in mind and spirit these two courses and
was drawing from its scabbard the great sword, Athene descended from
the sky. . . .*

*The goddess standing behind Peleus' son caught him by the fair hair,
appearing to him only, for no man of the others saw her.
Achilleus in amazement turned about, and straightway
knew Pallas Athene and the terrible eyes shining.
He uttered winged words and addressed her: "Why have you come now,
o child of Zeus of the aegis, once more? Is it that you may see
the outrageousness of the son of Atreus, Agamemnon?*

Yet will I tell you this thing, and I think it shall be accomplished.
By such acts of arrogance he may even lose his own life."

Then in answer the goddess grey-eyed Athene spoke to him:

"I have come down to stay your anger—but will you obey me?—
from the sky; and the goddess of the white arms Hera sent me,
who loves both of you equally in her heart and cares for you.
Come then, do not take your sword in your hand, keep clear of fighting,
though indeed with words you may abuse him, and it will be that way.
And this also will I tell you and it will be a thing accomplished.
Some day three times over such shining gifts shall be given you by
 reason of this outrage. Hold your hand then, and obey us."

Iliad bk. 1, vv. 190–210

When they arrived at the place God had pointed out to him, Abraham built
an altar there, and arranged the wood. Then he bound his son Isaac and
put him on the altar on top of the wood. Abraham stretched out his hand
and seized the knife to kill his son. But the angel of Yahweh called to him
from heaven. "Abraham, Abraham," he said. "I am here," he replied. "Do
not raise your hand against the boy," the angel said. "Do not harm him,
for now I know you fear God. . . ."

Gen 22:9–12

We have adverted to the fact that religion in general is characterized by a conviction that God *acts* in history and thus reveals himself, to save humanity; God can be "reached," and reaches us, in some way analogous to the intercommunion between persons. We have likewise contended on the basis of existential experience that there are elements in life which are inexplicable except on the basis of God's self-revelation. We now must ask: How can we understand, in the light of our ontological position on the transcendence of God, the notion of a divine act in history? What does it mean to say that God "acts"? How is such action reconcilable with the absolute transcendence and immanence of God?

Many modern Christians, Jews, and Muslims (and to some extent other believers) seem to fall into an ambiguity with regard to the notion of God's action in the world, vacillating between two mutually exclusive positions. On the one hand, they affirm the reality of the scriptural God, who personally interacts with us in our history; they pray for specific goods, and expect that God in some way "answers"; they "listen" for God's personal word of inspiration for their lives; they expect his salvation to appear as a transforming power. On the other hand, most modern people also take for granted the world-view of modern empirical science, which posits a world independent of God, a world whose explanations are to be sought entirely within the interplay of natural causes.

The modern believer has, for example, no difficulty in "demythologizing" the gods of Homer. When Achilles listens to "Reason," we quite easily understand this as *his own* reason, personified in mythic fashion. But would the same believer be equally comfortable in making the same kind of analysis of God's revelation to Abraham? Is the voice which tells Abraham to spare his son simply the voice of (his own) reason? Nor can the problem be dismissed by qualifying this particular story as belonging to a non-historical literary genre; for the same problem arises with regard to Moses, the prophets, Jesus, and the "inspiration" of the biblical authors themselves.

Although the problem of understanding how God can "act" in the world and still be transcendent occurs in all higher religions, it is particularly acute in the West, where we are accustomed to being told that the particular contribution of Hebrew religion was its conception of God as engaged in history, acting for his people.[37] Certainly this idea is prominent in the practice of Judaism and Christianity. (So, for example, the Second Vatican Council's document *Dei Verbum* characterizes revelation as an interconnected series of "words and deeds" of God, and the fourth Eucharistic Prayer of the Roman Catholic liturgy proclaims, "All your actions show your wisdom and love.") At the same time, the West is the home of the secular and empirical world-view, which is taken for granted in daily life, and even enters into biblical studies themselves. As Langdon Gilkey put it:

> Whatever the Hebrews believed, *we* believe that the biblical people lived in the same causal continuum of space and time in which we live, and so one in which no divine wonders transpired and no divine voices were heard. Nor do we believe, incidentally, that God could have done or commanded certain "unethical" deeds like destroying Sodom and Gomorrah or commanding the murder of the Amalekites. The modern assumption of the world order has stripped bare our view of the biblical history of all the divine deeds observable on the surface of history, as our modern humanitarian view has stripped the biblical God of most of his mystery and offensiveness. . . . In sum, therefore, we may say that for modern biblical theology the Bible is no longer so much a book containing a description of God's actual acts and words as it is a book containing Hebrew interpretations. . . .
>
> Perhaps the most important theological affirmation that modern

> biblical theology draws from the Scripture is that God is he who acts, meaning by this that God does unique and special actions in history. And yet when we ask: "All right, what has he done?" no answer can apparently be given. Most of the acts recorded in Scripture turn out to be "interpretations by Hebrew faith," and we are sure that they, like the miracles of the Buddha, did not really happen at all. . . . [38]

Gilkey rightly points out that only on the basis of ontology can the notion of an action or revelation of God in history have "intelligible and credible meanings."[39] We must therefore return to our ontological presuppositions in order to find on what basis, if at all, we may affirm the activity of God which seems to be central to the religious conviction of salvation. Before doing so, however, it will be helpful to review, in summary fashion, the principal positions which have been proposed on the issue of how God's activity is to be understood. We shall examine five possible solutions.[40] (Needless to say, there is no question here of presenting a complete or adequate understanding of any of these positions, but merely an overview of their main lines. The frame of reference of the discussion will primarily be Christian theology; but the same possibilities of understanding will generally apply as well within Judaism and Islam, and *mutatis mutandis*, within other theistic systems of belief, e.g. in Hinduism.)

(1) Literalist Scriptural understanding

According to neo-orthodox and fundamentalist theologies, the act and word of God are to be understood exactly as they are presented in the Scriptures: God reveals himself in special, objective acts in history. These acts and words of God give rise to faith (and so are not to be seen as the mere subjective interpretation of existence by faith). God acts, therefore, in a way analogous to the way a human person acts. He acts only in some events, and of these he is the sole cause. Owen Thomas refers to this position as "an analogy without a theory,"[41] since it proposes an understanding of God's special activity as analogous to human performance, but does not provide an ontology of God's action and relation to the world in general. In the words of Prof. Frank Dilley:

> What is being discussed here is the God that Tillich decries as the God of personalistic theism, the God that William James suggested is a finite God working alongside man. Such a God is a superior being who has created nature outside himself, and who works in and with the world that he has created, guiding its working, taking steps to correct man's evil, punishing and rewarding with storms and gentle rains where appropriate, and quite capable of aiding a band of fugitive slaves with an

east wind [the Exodus]. Such a God is the sort which the man on the street worships, although it is not the God of the theologians and philosophers. . . .

A finite God of this sort is not the Biblical God as presented by theologians, although a good case can be made that it is the Biblical God presented by the Biblical writers themselves.[42]

There are a number of problems with this position. While it may be, as Dilley states, that it represents the notion of God held by "the man in the street," even at this imaginative level most modern Christians or Jews would have difficulty in ascribing to God *all* the acts attributed to him in the Scriptures—for example, the rule of *charem,* or the extermination of Israel's enemies in the invasion of Canaan; the affliction of Job; the attack upon Moses; the "hardening of hearts" of sinners; etc. One can avoid these embarrassments by holding God responsible only for acts affecting inanimate nature (the parting of the seas, etc.). But basic difficulties still remain, among them the following:

(a) From the point of view of modern science, such a position must be methodically excluded (although it cannot be strictly disproved) because it presupposes breaks in the causal nexus of the world. It violates, therefore, the basic assumptions of the empirical world-view.

(b) From the point of view of metaphysics, a God who acts on the same level as finite beings is not (as Dilley notes) the metaphysical Absolute, but is himself a finite being, "alongside" the others. There can be no metaphysical justification of the affirmation of such a God's existence; indeed, metaphysics would have to posit an Absolute Reality beyond such a "God."

(c) From the psychological point of view, an anthropomorphic God is open to the suspicion of being a projection of the human mind. Only the notion of a totally transcendent God can meet this objection to religious belief. Furthermore, a conception of God which is divorced from an ontological basis is "supreme" not in a metaphysical sense, but only in the sense of being the most powerful of the beings in existence. He becomes in some sense a competitor with the world, as the humanist/atheist critique points out. Finally, such a God seems directly responsible for evil, or at least for particular evils in the world; there is, in any case, no basis for identifying this sort of deity with the ontological absolute good.

(d) From a religious point of view, this position has difficulty in explaining why some of the acts of God seem to contradict others. Which is the "real" God—the God of compassion, or of vengeance? Furthermore, modern scriptural studies are well aware of the different literary genres present in the Bible; this position (at least in its radical fundamentalist form) takes no account of them.

(2) "Classical" Western theology

In classical Western metaphysical theology, as represented for example by Thomism and mainstream Protestant orthodoxy, God is conceived as the transcendent cause of the world. As such, he creates the whole of the finite universe, in every aspect, as its *primary* cause. At the same time, *within* the finite world *secondary* causes—those discernible by empirical science and by reason—are at work and, on this level, are a sufficient explanation of all (ordinary) phenomena. God works *in* and *through* these secondary causes insofar as his "providence" guides and governs the entire world, without interfering with the natural and/or free processes within it.

This theory also leaves room for God to "act" in a special way in new instances of creation (for example, of each spiritual soul or of new levels of being) and in miracles, in which created causes surpass their normal effects. On this position, God acts in *all* events (as primary cause), and is also the sole and direct cause of some special events.

The difficulties with the classical view come from two directions. On the one hand, what happens to the God of the Bible, the God involved in history and in human life? Does the transcendence of the classical metaphysical God eliminate the "living" God, the "God of Abraham, Isaac, and Jacob"? On the other hand, how is one to explain the "special" acts of God, in particular miracles? Is a metaphysically conceived Absolute who intervenes in *some* cases any more acceptable to the modern empirical worldview than the God of fundamentalism?

(3) Existential theology

A negative answer to the last question leads to the position of the "existential" interpretation of the accounts of God's action, as formulated especially by Rudolph Bultmann and subsequently espoused by much of Protestant liberalism. In its essentials, this position agrees with classical theology in affirming God's primary causality and his absence from the world of secondary causes; but it goes yet farther by eliminating also the possibility of miracles or extraordinary interventions of God. The finite causal nexus is completely closed and events in the world can have only inner-worldly causes. The other side of the coin of the existential interpretation, therefore, is the demythologization of any religious statements which portray God as inner-worldly and thus finite. God acts as primary cause and providential guide of all events, but as the sole cause of none.

The fact that we may existentially interpret particular historical events as bearing a word of God for us is an aspect of the paradox of faith, the great "nevertheless": "Faith 'nevertheless' understands as God's action here and now an event which is completely intelligible in the natural or historical connection of events."[43] That is, in faith one is able to see in the naturally caused events of history the hand of God.

The existential interpretation must face several significant questions. How, on this basis, can there be any "special" revelation of God, as Christianity claims to be? How indeed can there be any genuine revelation *by God* at all, if every so-called "act" of God is in fact a human interpretation? If the answer given to this is "faith," then what is the connection between the affirmations of faith and human reason? If there is no "objectively" knowable reality of God's action or revelation, does not faith in these become completely detached from reason every bit as much as for the fundamentalist?

(4) Process theology

The philosophies of Alfred North Whitehead and of the American Charles Hartshorne propose a concept of God which differs significantly from the classical metaphysical view, and has significantly influenced such theologians as Ogden, Cobb, and Griffin. Whitehead rejects the notion of an "eminently real, transcendent creator, at whose fiat the world came into being";[44] for him, we can know nothing beyond the temporal world in which we live—which according to Whitehead is made up of a multitude of "epochal occasions," or concretions of diverse elements into real unities—and the formative elements that constitute it.[45] God can be nothing other than one of these elements, subject to the same metaphysical laws as the rest of reality. The three formative elements are:

> 1) The creativity whereby the actual world has its character of temporal passage to novelty.
> 2) The realm of ideal entities, or forms, which are in themselves not actual, but are such that they are exemplified in everything that is actual, according to some proportion of relevance.
> 3) The actual but non-temporal entity whereby the indetermination of mere creativity is transmuted into a determinate freedom.[46]

The last of these elements is what Whitehead means by "God." God and world stand in mutual requirement and relationship, brought together by the principle of "creativity." Through God, the multiplicity of the world attains perfected unity; through the world, God attains conscious, fully actual being.[47] It follows that, like all actual entities, God has a "dipolar" nature: a primordial nature which is infinite, conceptual, complete, but deficient in actuality, and a consequent nature which derives from the temporal world and which is incomplete and consequent upon the creative advance of the world, is conscious, and is fully actual.[48]

While it is not possible here to examine all the aspects and ramifications of this concept of God, we must note its import for the conception of God's activity in and on the world. "Creativity" per se is indeterminate, and has boundless possibilities. God's action upon the world is precisely what allows creativity to become determinate and orderly.[49] God is "the lure for feeling, the eternal urge of desire";[50] he acts in all events by his "influence" or "persuasion." God is "prehended" or experienced by every emerging event; God grasps the emerging possibilities for good of such events, and gives to each a "vision" of its initial aim, that is, the value it can attain. This aim is realized to a greater or lesser degree, dependent upon the creature's "free" (i.e., undetermined) response.[51] (This indeterminacy has various levels, from the merely physical to conscious choice.) God is thus active in all events, is the partial cause of all, and the sole cause of none.[52]

This position has some obvious advantages in conceiving an "act" of God. Since God works by "influence," his causal activity can be greater on the higher levels of freedom. Furthermore, it is possible to conceive God as loving all and "acting" for all equally, while at the same time holding that the concrete realization of that loving action can differ (according to the degree of collaboration of the creature), and hence that there can be "special" loci of God's action/revelation.[53]

On the other hand, there are serious difficulties with the conception of God which seems to be implied here. (It is to be remembered, of course, that "process" thinkers differ considerably in the way in which they interpret, adapt and expand Whitehead's basic ideas.) Whitehead's basic assumption, that temporality is the only mode of being we can know, is challenged not only on the epistemological and metaphysical levels, but even on the level of contemporary science, which in both sub-atomic and astro-physics seems to deal with events of existence which cannot be simply included within the concept of time as experienced in the macro-cosmic world.[54] The "God" of Whitehead, conceived on the basis of a universal application of temporality, does not transcend the universe, but is a part of it. Furthermore, beyond God there is a more ultimate power, that of "creativity." Does process theology, like biblical literalism, finally save God's activity only by sacrificing his divinity?

(5) Advaita Vedânta

Finally, we look briefly at a Hindu approach to the problem. The Advaita (non-dualist) school of Vedânta philosophy explicitly attempts to come to grips with the problem of reconciling the metaphysical affirmation of the transcendence of the Absolute, Brahman, with the faith of the common person in an active and self-revealing personal God.

Unlike the theologies of the biblical religions, Vedânta begins with the absoluteness and illimitation of the Ultimate Reality. One might indeed say that *the* philosophical problem is: If the Absolute (Brahman) is real, how can anything *other* than the Absolute be?

The answer to this question is: by reason of *"mâyâ."* This term is generally translated "illusion," but while it can have this meaning, it actually refers more generally, in the theological context, to Brahman's creative energy. It does not imply illusion in the sense of "unreality," but in the sense of phenomenal existence, appearance. There are different theories of how *mâyâ* relates to Brahman, expressed in three major schools. Of these we shall consider only that of the Advaita, or non-dualist school, as the predominant school and as the major expression of what is uniquely Indian in relation to our question.[55]

The principal and classic formulator of Advaita thought (although not its founder) was Śaṅkara (788–820 A.D.), a mystic, poet, philosopher, religious reformer and founder. Stated summarily, the doctrine of Advaita is that Being is one; there is no duality, no coming-to-be or change in it. Duality is a distinction imposed on the essential non-duality of Being by *"mâyâ."* The *real* (cf. Plato's "really real")— τὸ 'ὄντος ὢν does not change. All change is unreal; causality thus does not exist. Thinking that causality and change are real leads to rebirth, a failure to attain the ultimate goal of existence. The "production" of all things is only apparent; for dependent existence, the existence of the world, is not "real" existence.[56]

Thus Brahman, the Supreme Reality, is, *in se* changeless, absolute, and complete. Brahman is *"nir-guṇa,"* without attributes; that is to say, Brahman *is* all that he is. Although Brahman is without qualities, Śaṅkara is nevertheless at pains to refute the Buddhist view that the ultimate is *"śûnya,"* or void: Brahman is *"sat-cit-ananda,"* Being, Consciousness, and Joy—a plenitude, not an emptiness.

The world, by contrast, is not "real" in the ultimate sense; it is illusory, compared with the truth of knowing Brahman. But the world still has *empirical* reality; on the level of experience, its existence is not contradicted. When viewed from the ultimate perspective, all is Brahman. Apart from Brahman, objects do not exist; they are to that extent unreal. Their appearance is due to *mâyâ*. *Mâyâ* is not Being (*sat*), but neither is it non-being (*asat*); it is the undefinable, mysterious cause— ultimately identical with Brahman himself—owing to which the world of distinct individuals exists. *Mâyâ* is not a real entity; it is simply "wrong" (or non-ultimate) knowledge; it has no existence independent of the fact of being perceived. Yet *as* finite perception/appearance, it does exist.

Śaṅkara's metaphysical vision might be presented as a series of "higher viewpoints," each of which sublates—i.e., both contains and corrects—the lower, as in the following diagram (based on K. Puligandla[57]):

Level:	kind of being:	known by:
The REAL (Brahman/Atman)	ultimate; cannot be sublated or corrected in judgment	pure intuition
	sublates	
	sublated by	
Appearance	real entities	correct knowledge of world
	sublates	
	sublated by	
	entities (existents)	common knowledge (opinion)
	sublates	
	sublated by	
	illusory existents	mistaken knowledge (may still be datum of experience)
Unreality	neither sublatable nor unsublatable	unknowable (cannot be datum of experience)

When associated with *mâyâ*, the creative power, Brahman is *Îśvara* or the personal God of religion, who has attributes, acts in the world, hears prayers, enters into relation with his devotees, etc. One cannot ask *how* Brahman is associated with *mâyâ;* this relation does not begin in time, and is thus outside the realm of worldly knowledge; it is the mystery of Brahman himself. For Śankara, as for Aristotle, causality produces no change in the cause, but only effects the being of the caused. Thus there is a one-sided relation (of dependence) of the world of appearance to Brahman. Since the world is simply appearance, due to ignorance of the ultimate, that Ultimate itself is not affected. *Îśvara*, the personal God, belongs to the realm of *mâyâ*, and has the same status in reality: that is, is merely the *appearance* of Brahman; his creative acts are likewise part of the general appearance of the world. Compared with the Ultimate, they are illusory; yet empirically they are real. (It is noteworthy that Śankara himself worshiped God in personal form, and was indeed a major force in the spreading of *bhakti* [devotional] Hinduism.[58])

The problems raised by Śankara's theology (and Advaita in general) are indicated by the strong criticism it received within religious Hinduism. Madhva, a one-time disciple of the Advaita, broke away to found a school of metaphysical dualism (*Dvaita*), which teaches the reality of a personal God, the plurality of things in the world, and the ultimate difference between Brahman and the self. Madhva's disciples claimed that Śankara's system was no better than materialism or crypto-Buddhism. Less extreme but more philosophically and religiously important was the reaction of Râmânuja, the principal exponent of the *Viśishṭâdvaita* (non-dualism of the differentiated, or "qualified non-dualism") school. Râmânuja criticizes Śankara on epistemological grounds: if Brahman were totally without qualities, we could not know it at all. More significantly, Râmânuja objects that Śankara's system contradicts the Scriptures, which do not reveal a characterless Absolute, but a personal God; *Îśvara* and the ultimate Brahman are the same, and his relation to the world is that of soul to body. While the world and human spirits have no reality *apart* from Brahman, neither are they identical with him. God has filial affection for his creatures, and he intervenes to save them and remove their sufferings.

The Hindu reaction against Advaita points to its principal weaknesses from the point of view of an explanation of God's activity in the world. In the extreme monist interpretation, it eliminates the reality of the world altogether, so that every personal relation with God becomes illusory— even if these illusions are encouraged for those who have not attained final knowledge. On a less extreme interpretation, Advaita has at least the same problems, from a religious point of view, as classical theism or existential theology.

Understanding the "Acts" of God: Transcendental Interpretation

Forgive me, O Śiva, my three great sins: I came on a pilgrimage to Kâsi, forgetting that you are omnipresent; in thinking about you, I forget that you are beyond thought; in praying to you, I forget that you are beyond words.

Śankara

The God who made the world and everything in it, being Lord of heaven and earth, does not live in shrines made by man, nor is he served by human hands, as though he needed anything, since he himself gives to all life and breath and everything. And he made from one every nation to live on all the face of the earth, having determined allotted periods and the boundaries of their habitation, that they should seek God, in the hope that they might grope after him and find him. Yet he is not far from each one of us, for "In him we live and move and have our being."

Acts 17:23–28

Having considered some of the ways in which God's action in the world may be understood, we proceed to ask how God may be said to "speak to" and "act in" the world in a transcendental theology.

The basis of our understanding must be a return to the foundational source of all our knowledge of God, that which allows us to affirm that there exists a God: namely, the experience of self as spirit in the world, a finite transcendental dynamism toward being and the good. This experience of our own spirituality is also the condition of possibility for the reception and recognition of any "revelation" from God; and therefore it is also the fundamental hermeneutical principle for interpreting any such revelation. This experience leads to the affirmation of God as the necessary and absolute condition of possibility of the self, in its knowledge and love, and of the world which is its situation.

On this basis, we have made two fundamental affirmations. First, God is the cause of the world: that is, God is affirmed as the goal of the mind's anticipatory grasp of being and goodness, the dynamism which constitutes the condition of possibility of all intelligible judgments and responsible decisions. As such, God is the ultimate intelligibility which accounts for the existence of the universe, its "cause." Second, existential experience leads us to affirm that God is self-revealing; he is known not only as the Mystery which draws us forward to an infinite and infinitely receding goal, but as the Source of an experience of intimacy, of fulfillment of our being which is not adequately explained by the category of causality. This dimension is referred to by the categories of revelation and grace. It implies already in the world an "immediacy" of the human subject to God, an immediacy beyond the natural proportions of a finite spirit-in-world—that is, in some way beyond the mediation of God by the self and by other finite beings in the world. This immediacy is the source of the religious conviction of "intimacy" with God, on various levels and to varying degrees.[59] Let us examine each of these in turn.

God is the ultimate or "primary" cause of all being. As such, he is the condition for the existence of every secondary or finite cause, and acts "in" every secondary cause, in that his creative act is the source of all finite causality, both in its existence and in its ability to effect change. God as primary cause does not act either "alongside" or "instead of" secondary causes. Neither is he the first member of a causal series.[60] Rather, God is the immediate condition of possibility of *each* being. (Therefore, as Rahner points out, there is no difference between the demonstration of God's existence and the affirmation of his *continual* causality, sometimes referred to as the divine "concursus.") God is the ground of the totality of the real. His causal activity is thus not an item of experience, but is the *ground* of every experience.[61] The primary causality of God, therefore, is always known through the mediation of finite things, the "secondary" causes of the world.

At the same time, it is possible on this basis to affirm that some events are more revelatory of God's activity than others, because they represent a higher degree of participation in God's being and goodness. God is the first actor "in" every agent, but analogously, and to different degrees, because there are different degrees to which creatures participate (and not, therefore, because of a different level of activity on God's part). The more the action of a creature reflects its groundedness in the absolute source and goal of existence—that is, the more acts are free, intelligible, loving, good—the more God can truly be said to act in the given event. Thus God's transcendent causality and finite responsibility are *directly*, not inversely related. The more free and creative are human acts, the more they participate in and manifest the act of God in the world.

[An understanding of this view of the relation of God to finite causality depends upon a grasp of the transcendental source of the metaphysical concept of "cause." As Rahner points out,[62] for transcendental method the meaning of such terms as being, operation, causality, etc., is encountered first of all in the being of the spiritual subject himself. The physical world, to which we apply these terms analogously, is, on this view, a "deficient mode" of spirit. A genuine notion of causality, therefore, is to be obtained from the analysis of the operation of our own spirit in its acts of knowing and loving.

A transcendental analysis reveals that every human spiritual act is grounded in a dynamic orientation of spirit beyond itself to being, and thence toward Absolute Being. This dynamism is the condition of possibility of reflective self-awareness and of objective knowledge and decision.[63] There exists, therefore, a non-conceptual and implicit term of the transcendence of spirit in its acts of knowing and loving. Mind and its activity cannot be understood apart from it. This term is immanent in the dynamism of our spirit, and at the same time is beyond it. It is thus at once the goal and (precisely as such) the cause of every spiritual act.

There is in our spirit a goal which is present to us, orients us, and transcends us; it is this goal which allows us to be *self*-moving; and it is in precisely this experience of being self-determining within the enabling transcendent goal that we have our primordial experience of the meaning of causality. Our own spiritual activity, precisely as our own, is dependent upon the pre-apprehended Absolute for every aspect of its being and activity. Every other notion of "cause," according to Rahner, derives from this immanent and implicit experience (which is transcendentally validated in our acts, even should we explicitly ignore or deny it). All other causes are analogous to and deficient modes of this primary cause.]

On the basis of his transcendental grounding of the notion of cause, Rahner can understand all finite becoming as entirely dependent upon (= caused by) God and at the same time as completely the result of inner-worldly causes. Every finite act of becoming or of causing is always a going-beyond, an advance in *being* beyond what the agent is already. Thus change is always a matter of self-transcendence. This can take place, according to Rahner, because Absolute Being (or Act) is the ever-present cause and ground of the self-movement of the creature. A finite being can become and can cause more than it is because its being and act are grounded in (= created by) the immanent total Act which is God. Therefore the "essence" of any being does not determine in advance the limits of what such a being can become or can produce beyond itself.

This does not mean, of course, that anything can become or can produce simply anything else; the "what it is" or "essence" of a thing indicates the direction and limits of its act and its becoming; this is especially true, Rahner notes, of non-spiritual being.

Nevertheless, for Rahner, in line with the metaphysics of St. Thomas, the "essence" of any finite being is not an absolute and closed limit; every creature is not only "what it is," but is also a potency to become, a dynamism (corresponding to the attractive or final causality of God) to transcend itself. This potency, moreover, is not confined to the "natural" limitations of the powers of any being; for there is also a potency which is "obediential," that is, open to a becoming, by God's causality, that which is beyond the possibility or horizon of the creature in itself.

Applying this line of thought to an evolutionary view of the world, we may say that every introduction of qualitatively new being (including the appearance of humanity on earth from animal ancestors, or of any single new spiritual "soul" from the act of human reproduction) implies a "creation" by God and at the same time a total production by the finite antecedents. That is: the created causality is of such a kind that the agent, by virtue of the immanent divine causality, exceeds its own "essence" and transcends itself in the production of new being. (This is not to be thought of as a kind of "partnership" between God and the finite cause, as though each produced part of the new reality; each is totally the cause of the whole, but on different levels.) In the process of evolution, there will necessarily be particular moments in which significant and sometimes dramatic change occurs (Teilhard's "thresholds"); this does not imply, however, that God's action should be conceived as an arbitrary intervention occurring at a definite point in time and space, even though we may correctly speak of such moments as *manifesting* God's (continuous and transcendent) causality in a special way, and hence as being revelatory "acts" of God (as Creator) for us.[64]

Our second basic affirmation was that God is self-revealing not only as Creator, but on a level which draws us into intimacy with himself and gives already an experience of immediacy to him as the absolute goal of existence. Here again the notion of the "potentia obedientialis," the essential openness of finite being to God, is crucial to Rahner's understanding. Humanity is constituted by a dynamism toward God as our ultimate horizon. If God reveals himself, not merely as asymptotic goal, but in his very Being, this indicates an "elevation" of human intentionality to a level of participation in the absoluteness of God. God's act of self-communication consists in his becoming the transcendental ground of our being, knowing, and caring in such a way that their goal, already experienced as anticipation (parallel to the *Vorgriff* of being, and not adequately distinguishable from it in experience), is *God himself*, and not merely the finite world within God, its horizon.[65] (This situation is what Rahner calls "the supernatural existential.")

Such a revelation of God is, on the part of the creature, a transcendental experience; that is, it goes beyond all objective experiences and is the condition of possibility for our actual mode of relating to them.[66] It is an experience of what Rahner calls (borrowing Hegel's celebrated phrase) a "mediated immediacy" (*vermittelte Unmittelbarkeit*) to God. Because God is present *as* himself, that is, as transcending every object, there can be no objective mediation of his being; in this sense, there is an immediate experience of God. At the same time, a purely transcendental experience for a human—i.e., a spirit which attains its spirituality by being *in the world*—is impossible; every human consciousness, including the most basic awareness of the self, is in some way mediated by the "other," its "real symbol." The immediate experience of God, then, is also in some sense "mediated"—not by any object, but by the very self which experiences the attraction to God in himself, and which comes to itself through the non-self. This experience of the self (and, with it, its dependence on memory, habits of thought, bodiliness in general) is at least implicit even in the experience of the transcendent.[67]

Furthermore, this experience of God's self-gift must have a history; that is, the immediacy is mediated not only by the self, but also by the world. Because we exist in the world, God's self-gift or self-revelation cannot remain for us merely transcendental; in order to engage us in our full human being, this transcendental gift must become graspable through experience, understanding, judgment, and responsible decision; for otherwise it could never be "ours." The transcendental experience, therefore, becomes categorical in and through the subject's *apprehension* of it and *response* to it. This apprehension and response are necessarily conditioned and limited by the subject's interaction with the categorical world. Thus God's revelation is not only a trans-historical *gift*, but also an historical *achievement* on the part of humanity. The achievement is a mediation of the immediacy of God in and through categorical history.[68] The structure of revelation or grace, therefore, is like the structure of human consciousness itself: a "mediated immediacy" which comes to full self-possession by the encounter, in intelligence and freedom, with the non-self, the world. That is to say, the encounter with God necessarily has a "sacramental" structure, in which the transcendent reality of God is mediated by categorical symbols, and thus becomes objective for our minds and freedom. Furthermore, the historical human apprehension of God's self-gift itself becomes a factor in subsequent history, so that God's revelation is not only a transcendental cause, prior to the order of "secondary" causality, but is *also*—in its human mediation—a causal factor *within* the world, an "influence" on the human situation.

The Rahnerian understanding of God's activity toward the world thus implies a divine self-giving which has a transcendental and categorical aspect, the latter being determined concretely by the receptive potency of subjects in history. This explanation has a number of advantages.

First, it preserves both the transcendent-immanent absoluteness of God, and the reality of his activity in and for the world. On this understanding, God *is* his act: to say that God acts is to say what and how he *is*, but *in relation to us*. The action of God is thus "uniform," in the sense that we need posit no change (and thus finitude) in the divine being *in se*. At the same time, there are really different levels and degrees of God's activity in the world, according to the various potencies and dispositions of the finite receptors of that activity. Thus the relationship between God and the world really changes; God "acts" differently, is revealed differently, in diverse historical circumstances. The divine simplicity and absoluteness are not compromised; at the same time, what God effects, he effects as participating in his being; and since God's "participated being" changes, God himself changes, acts and reveals himself variously, *in* his "other."

Second, this understanding flows from the epistemology and metaphysics of the self-appropriation of the subject. Its conclusion is in line with Rahner's insight that every theological statement is (also) anthropological; when we speak of God, we reveal the conditions in ourselves for the apprehension of God. God, "in himself," remains the Absolute, and is absolutely Mystery for the human mind (*reductio in mysterium*). It is also in concordance with Lonergan's "principle of contingent predication," which states that anything truly and contingently predicated of God must be constituted by the very divine essence, but in such a way as to demand a suitable "ad extra" term (i.e., an existing creature).[69] This explanation, then, finds an epistemological and metaphysical basis for its positions in the transcendental metaphysics which arises from asking the conditions of possibility of the subject's actual performance. It proposes a theory, therefore, which is in principle "verifiable" through the examination of one's own subjectivity. Furthermore, the explanation proposed is in accord with the basic structure revealed by finite spirit in-the-world: that of a "mediated immediacy" to being.

Third, this explanation is capable of "retrieving" or subsuming the capital points of the other major explanations.

It is of course clear from the outset that the transcendental explanation, especially as represented by Rahner, is a development of classical Thomism. It preserves both the transcendent absoluteness and the immanence of God: his "distinction" from the world, and the fact that this distinction itself is posited by God as a participation in his being. At the same time, the modern transcendental version of Thomism is able to integrate within itself the evolutionary view of the world presented by modern science. By emphasizing the transcendental character of our statements about God, it is also able to avoid the objectifying tendency which too frequently characterized classical Thomism.

By the same token, Rahner's position is in essential agreement with the "existential" interpretation. Nevertheless, because it conceives the finite changing world not as a "closed" system but as a process of self-transcendence, essentially "open" to God's continuous causality, it allows for

the possibility of "extraordinary" acts of God in history, or "miracles";
these, however, need not be conceived as interventions which "break" the
chain of natural causes (see below). Because the "degree" of transcendence
depends upon the creature's response and creativity as well as upon God's
transcendent causality, it is necessary to affirm higher and lower stages of
the revelation of God through the world, and even the possibility of a "special" revelation in which God would be manifest more completely than
elsewhere. Furthermore, the concept of the "obediential potency" in nature allows us to see a continuity between the orders of nature and grace
or revelation; thus the affirmation of historical events as God's acts and as
God's "word" to us does not depend upon a paradoxical "nevertheless" of
faith, but is grounded in the rational recognition of the openness of the
world to God.

Our position agrees with the fundamental intuition of Advaita Vedânta, that God is Absolute and that the world's reality is deficient compared to his. But because transcendental method begins with the subject's
experience of knowledge in true judgments and freedom in responsible
decisions, and arrives at the Absolute as the Condition for these, it conceives the reality and value of the world positively. The world is "mâyâ"
in the sense of being totally derived from the mystery of God's creative
energy; but the notion of "creation" emphasizes the positive aspect of this
relation: the world is seen as the "real symbol" of God, rather than as mere
"appearance." Brahman is ultimately *Nir-guṇa:* nothing that we say of God
captures or contains his reality. Nevertheless, the ideas of participation
and of the analogy of predication allow us to speak of God's "attributes"
(Brahman as *Sa-guṇa*): those qualities in us which are most real and valid
are derived from and reflect the reality of God, whose being is their em-
inent reality. The God who acts in the world and relates to us is (as for
Râmânuja) the *real* God, communicating himself outside himself.

While explaining God's activity in terms of transcendent creativity
("primary" causality), the transcendental position is able to agree with
process theology in asserting that God *also* acts as an "influence" on the
indeterminate ("free") behavior of creatures (secondary causes). He does
so first insofar as he is the "final cause" of all things, *prehended* as the ultimate value and goal of every creaturely dynamism. Here Whitehead's
description of God's activity seems to be quite consonant with transcendental theology. Second, God acts as an "influence" on freedom insofar as
he is *apprehended,* with varying degrees of adequacy, by finite subjects,
who can make "God's will" an explicit factor in their decisions. Thus God
is both the complete cause *of* the world of secondary causes, and becomes
a factor *in* that world through the creatures themselves.

Although the transcendental explanation rejects a literal or finitizing interpretation of God's activity, its purpose nevertheless is not to deny but to give meaning to the affirmation that God really acts in the world. It therefore preserves the basic intent of symbolic-mythic speech about God in his relation to us, while avoiding the pitfalls of fundamentalism. God's activity may even be spoken of as his "intervention" in the world, insofar as the events which concretely realize his continuous creativity and grace are unexpected on our part, and at least in their human meaning go beyond the "natural" course of events.

[Rahner gives the example of a "good idea" which comes to me unexpectedly and proves subsequently to be valid. Such an idea can be explained on the level of the finite causes of my personal history: psychological associations, insights, etc., even if at the moment I am not aware of them all. Nevertheless, if I experience myself as a subject "before God," this good idea is the concrete expression of a conscious positive decision for him, and is thus something which goes beyond my "natural" powers, and is willed by God and freely "given" by God to me.

" . . . a good decision along with everything which it presupposes as its mediation correctly has the character of an intervention of God, even though this takes place in and through human freedom, and hence can be explained functionally to the degree that the history of freedom can be explained, namely, insofar as it is based on elements objectified in time and space."[70]]

The purpose of the transcendental explanation is precisely to validate the existential religious meaning of statements about God's activity for us; it does not destroy (as some fundamentalists claim) but gives intelligibility to the "naive" assertions of symbolic speech about God.[71]

A final advantage of the transcendental explanation of God's activity in the world is that it gives us a horizon for understanding extraordinary "interventions" of God—miracles—in a way which is both closer to the biblical notion and more comprehensible to a modern scientific consciousness. A miracle may be seen as a *sign*—an event apprehended as meaningful—which brings to consciousness in an extraordinary circumstance the total and continual dependence of the world and the subject upon God's creative and transformative activity, and thus invites the subject to an act of religious faith, an existential affirmation of the subject's own relation to God.

From the time of the Enlightenment, Christian apologetics has generally started from the definition of miracle given by David Hume: "A miracle is a violation of the laws of nature." Such a description not only presupposes an imaginative schema in which God acts as a factor in the world "alongside" or in place of empirical causes, but is also based upon an antiquated classicist and determinist notion of science.

In an evolutionary context, the world process may be seen as a series of what Lonergan calls "emergent probabilities."[72] The "laws" of nature are not inflexible statements of an invariable and absolutely determined world-structure, but are descriptions of the probabilities at work on the various levels of intelligibility: physical, chemical, biological, etc. These levels form a series of "higher viewpoints," culminating in the level of *meaning*, and in which the higher levels cannot simply be reduced to the lower levels which they subsume and upon which they depend. (This idea has its philosophical antecedent in the Thomist notion of the "obediential potency": the "essences" of things are not closed-off and static realities, but are fundamentally "open"; every level of being is (1) a potency for self-realization, by its natural dynamism, enacted by God's continuous final causality, which gives every dynamism its goal, and (2) a potency for transformation to a higher level, by means of God's transcendent causality.)

In this context, a "miracle" may be conceived as a transformative action of spirit on the empirical world in such a way that a lower level of being is brought beyond its ordinary possibilities into the sphere of human meaning as a sign of transcendent reality, so that the observer is invited to make an existential self-disposition toward that reality.[73] A new material situation is produced by a spiritual act (e.g., a healer produces a movement from sickness to health). This material transformation signifies a new spiritual reality or relationship (v.g., the movement from the alienation of sickness to the peace and unity of healing is a sign of the transformative power of God's creative love). The action points to the Absolute as the source of the spiritual power, at least insofar as this act anticipates and signifies an ultimate good (v.g., in the New Testament miracles are explicitly meant as signs of God's kingdom); for God is the "final cause" of the entire dynamism of transcendence. A miracle must be an act whose intelligibility (not only on a physical level, but on the level of its meaning) demands reference to the transcendent: to the grounding source of spirit itself. It is, then, an act which causes "wonder"; it makes manifest to human consciousness the fundamental metaphysical question, the need for explanation, which underlies *all* finite existence and all transformation. A miraculous act shows the irreducible presence of the reality of spirit as the cause of this event, and thus invites the beholder to stand before the mystery of one's own spiritual being and its Ground.

In this conception of "miracle," it is neither necessary nor sufficient that the act involved be beyond the limits of the "natural" powers of a human being.[74] Indeed, from a scientific point of view, these limits are as yet unknown. While it is clear that there is a certain power of mind over matter, at least in the instance of one's own body (psychosomatic illnesses and cures, interference with normal reactions under hypnotic suggestion, etc.), the exact extent of the relation of spirit to matter remains an open question. Thus in this area we cannot determine *a priori* what is "beyond" the spiritual possibilities of humanity, or "supernatural." Nor is it necessary to do so; for, as we have said above, the fact that an event is explainable in finite terms does not preclude its truly being an "act" of God. A miracle is not an event which is unexplainable. The miraculous is at most only unexplained on a certain (physical) level; on the level of spiritual reality, it is intelligible precisely through the openness of human spirit to God and the dynamism of self-transcendence toward him and within his creativity. The simultaneous presence of lower levels of explanation does not affect the validity of the act as a "miraculous" sign; indeed, it is exactly the phenomenon of transcendence on these lower levels which calls for an ultimate explanation and cause. Therefore an event which is within the ordinary (or extra-ordinary) physical-psychic-spiritual powers of a human being (for example, if one were to consider healings by prayer or exorcism as due to some psychosomatic influence) may still be "miraculous" if it fulfills the criteria of manifesting the irreducible presence of spirit, creating a sense of awe, and constituting for the beholder a sign of the presence of the transcendent creative power.[75]

It is true that this understanding introduces a strongly subjective element into the notion of the miraculous.[76] As Rahner writes, miracles

> are miracles in the first instance for a *definite addressee*, and this is very
> important. They are not *facta bruta* but an address to a knowing subject
> in a quite definite historical situation. Miracles which just happened,
> but which did not intend to say anything to anyone, and in which God
> would, as it were, merely correct the objective course of the world, are
> an absurd notion to begin with.[77]

The transcendental method itself is based upon the principle that the irreducible presence of spirit and the unthematic consciousness of the Absolute are implied in *every* truly human act; "miracles" are the limit cases, in which our knowledge of causality breaks down and the transcendent ground becomes more apparent. Thus in principle the simplest and most ordinary of human actions might, for a particular individual, provoke the sensation of wonder or awe which confronts one with the subject's own spiritual being standing within its Absolute Ground (as indeed is intended to happen in Zen exercises leading to *satori*). For an "enlightened" person, all of life might then be "miraculous." Such an idea is not foreign to the Judeo-Christian tradition. The rabbis state that a single drop of rain is as miraculous as the Flood; St. Augustine speaks in a similar vein.

[A further consequence of this understanding of miracle is that an event of spiritual power does not in itself guarantee either divine origin or the presence of grace, for, as we have stated above, the limits of the powers of mind are not yet known. On the other hand, even if one were to presume that such an event takes place in the context of divine grace, this would not of itself assure that the interpretation or message accompanying the event is adequate. Spiritual power, even along with sanctity, does not of itself legitimate its bearer as a divine messenger.]

In conclusion to this section, we may summarize the ways in which a transcendental theology can understand the notion of an "act" of God. God acts first of all as the primary and transcendent cause of all that exists, in its being and in its dynamism. In this way God acts as cause *of* the world, and of everything within it. Insofar as the Absolute is unthematically "prehended" or thematically "apprehended" by any creature (or any epochal occasion, in Whitehead's system), as the supreme value for which it may strive, God may also be said to act as an "influence" *in* the world. On a second level, God acts by giving or revealing himself to human consciousness. Here again we may distinguish two modalities. There is first a *transcendental revelation,* which consists in God's unthematic and ineffable presence to the human spirit. Secondly, there is a *categorical revelation,* in which that presence is interpreted and made concrete through human expression. In the process of interpretation of the transcendental experience, the unthematic presence of the Absolute exercises the causality of love, drawing the human spirit beyond itself to the accomplishment of transcendence. (Here again we may use Whitehead's category of "influence."[78]) On yet a third level, the human interpretation itself becomes a "word" of God for others, so that God acts also "outside" himself, in and through his "other."

Within the general history of categorical revelation, we may distinguish certain "special" acts of God: whenever the transcendental revelation of God becomes categorical in such a way that it actuates the creature's openness for self-transcendence (*potentia obedientialis*) and transforms the creature to an entirely new level of being. This takes place (1) when "thresholds" are reached in the evolutionary process, bringing about a higher and more spiritual form of being, (2) in "miracles," when events manifest the irreducible presence and power of spirit in an extraordinary way, and (3) when human beings achieve a free decision for absolute love: that is, for a supernatural mode of existence.

III. THE LOCUS OF GOD'S WORD

RELIGION

Religion that is pure and stainless in the sight of God the father is this: to look after orphans and widows in their trouble, and to keep one's self unstained by the world.

Jas 1:27

Religio est [virtus] per quam redditur debitum Deo. . . . Religio non est fides, sed fidei protestatio per aliqua exteriora signa.

Thomas Aquinas, 1a2ae, q. 60 art. 3, c;
2a2ae, q. 94 art. 1 ad 1

Religion is the self-consciousness and self-feeling of man, who has either not yet found himself or has already lost himself again. . . .

Karl Marx: *Toward the Critique of Hegel's
Philosophy of Right*

Our religion is the poetry in which we believe. Mere poetry is an ineffectual shadow of life; religion is, if you will, a phantom also, but a phantom guide.

George Santayana: *Poetry and Religion*

Religion is unbelief; *religion is a concern—but one must immediately add: the concern of the* Godless person. *. . . Religion is a contradiction to revelation, the concentrated expression of human unbelief, that is the attitude and behavior that is precisely contrary to Faith.*

Karl Barth: *Church Dogmatics*, I

If we can affirm the positive answer to the question posed in the last chapter in that our experience leads us to affirm that God is not merely the asymptotic horizon of human existence, but is somehow encountered "within" history—that is, that God "speaks" to man and reveals himself in a way similar to dialogue between persons—then we have entered the realm of religious conversion.

Although all of human existence may contain elements of the divine revelation, it is above all in "religion" that we find the claim of an experience of salvific encounter with God embodied and formulated. Our next step will therefore be a turn to the phenomenon of religion in an effort to discern God's "word" and salvation.

It is obvious that we cannot here perform an adequate phenomenology of religions; at best, we can give certain indications and overviews which may suffice for our purposes of dialectical comparison of the manifestations of categorical revelation.

It is also clear that the category of religion is a complex one. Religions are not only the expression of "religious conversion," in the sense of a dialogue of love with God, but are also social and historical phenomena which incorporate other meanings and influences. Any religion is both a mixed reality and an evolving one. If we are concentrating our attention on a particular—if crucial and primary—aspect of religion, we are not thereby denying that other aspects exist. Religions may therefore legitimately be studied from various viewpoints: social, political, aesthetic, ethnological, biological, economic, etc.—as well as theological. In our concern for the last we must also recognize the presence of all the further dimensions of religious reality.[1]

The Meaning of "Religion"

Our first task will be a delimitation of the subject. In general, we know by our common sense experience what the word "religion" refers to. But if we are to examine a wide range of phenomena, we will need a more exact and theoretical description which will allow us to set limits to our study. Are we to consider Marxism, for example, a religion? Can a religion be atheistic? Are phenomena like magic and superstition to be considered religious? Can a philosophical system like those of Socrates, Plato, or Śankara be considered a religion?

[It would be theoretically possible to formulate a theological definition of religion, identifying it with conversion, the love of God, or the reception of revelation. Such an a priori definition, however, would be completely abstract at this point; it would leave us completely uninformed about the actual historical phenomenon of religion in its plurality, which is exactly what we wish to examine. We cannot therefore begin by defining religion in relation to a theological criterion, but in relation to historically verifiable objective criteria: events, contents, purposes, etc. Only at the end may we possibly be able to relate these actual religions to the theological notion of salvation to arrive at a theologically normative idea of religion.]

A phenomenological definition of religion, however, is notoriously difficult, because "religious" phenomena are so diverse, so complex, and so changing. Concrete religions, when seen over a long period, seem always to be in a state of becoming, and scarcely to have a definite "essence." We cannot define religion (as might seem an obvious course) as man's thought and action regarding God; for there are many religions (on the primitive level) which have not reached a concept of "God," while among the higher religions there are some (Buddhism, monistic Hinduism) that are trans-theistic. On the other hand, it will not suffice to define religion by "its one universal objective trait,"[2] relationship to transcendental reality, because such relationships are not exclusively religious; a relation to the transcendent, as our anthropology has shown, can and does take place also within the secular sphere, and indeed in the whole of the human situation, even if it may not be thematically reflected upon. Similarly, William James rejects his own suggestion that religion could be defined as "any total reaction upon life," for some attitudes toward the whole of existence may be trivial or escapist; they may not face the question of ultimacy.[3]

Emile Durkheim, in his pioneering work on the sociology of religion, *The Elementary Forms of the Religious Life*, bases his definition of religion on the distinction between the sacred and the profane, which he claims is "the distinctive trait of religious thought."[4] Religion is thus the totality of beliefs and rites which form a system of sacred things and their relation to each other:[5]

> A religion is a unified system of beliefs and practices relative to sacred things, that is to say, things set apart and forbidden—beliefs and practices which unite into one single moral community called a Church, all those who adhere to them.[6]

Durkheim's definition separates religion from magic by insisting that religion is "eminently *collective*";[7] it is a social reality. The socio-biologist Edward Wilson agrees: " . . . religion is above all the process by which individuals are persuaded to subordinate their immediate self-interest to the interests of the group."[8]

On the other hand, the psychologist William James defines religion as "the feelings, acts, and experiences of individual men in their solitude, so far as they apprehend themselves to stand in relation to whatever they may consider the divine."[9] Similarly, Whitehead holds that "religion is what the individual does with his own solitariness";[10] religion is above all interiority, the transformation of the individual.

In the face of such differing perspectives, we would perhaps do best to abandon any effort to give an essential definition to "religion," and to admit, with James, that we are dealing with a collective name which includes varied phenomena. We may nevertheless attempt a *descriptive* definition that will gather together the characteristics which seem to typify actually existing religions. In doing so, we shall follow the insights both of James and of the great phenomenologist of religion, Gerhardus van der Leeuw. We may distinguish seven major features:

(1) Religion always aims at *salvation* of some kind. As van der Leeuw says: "Religion is always directed towards salvation, never towards life itself as it is given; and in this respect all religion, with no exception, is the religion of deliverance."[11] Religion combines a dissatisfaction with present empirical reality with a hope for ultimate liberation.[12] William James points out that under all creeds, there is a common nucleus which consists of two points: an uneasiness, and its solution:

> The uneasiness, reduced to its simplest terms, is a sense that there is *something wrong about us* as we naturally stand. The solution is a sense that *we are saved from the wrongness* by making proper connection with the higher powers.[13]

(2) Religion seeks salvation, as James says, by contact or relationship with a higher—finally, an ultimate—Power. The religious attitude means that humanity does not simply accept life as given, but seeks to "elevate" life, to gain deeper value and meaning. Furthermore, we do not find the means to do so simply within ourselves; we are not altogether the masters of life. Therefore, we seek connection with a Power which transcends us.

There are, however, various levels of association with the transcendent power, ranging from an attempt to control and use it to submission to it in worship and love.[14] (In our sense of the word, therefore, "religion" includes magic, the attempt of man to retain his autonomy and to use the superior power for his own ends. As religion deepens, however, so does man's sense of dependence on the transcendent.[15])

(3) The religious quest for an increase of life, or salvation, by contact with the transcendent power confronts us with the limit situation of life: we encounter the dimension of "ultimacy." The search for salvation *for* human life leads to the question of the meaning *of* human life, its final significance and purpose: "The religious significance of things, therefore, is that on which no wider or deeper meaning whatever can follow."[16] Re-

ligion is the "last word" about our existence. The dimension of ultimacy reaches beyond the mere use of the world, or the understanding of it in order to subjugate it. It includes a sense of "wonder" at existence, and an openness to a "beyond." We find, however, that we cannot attain or possess this "beyond"; it stands always above us.

(4) Therefore we are confronted in religion with the *sacred*, the mystery of being: Otto's "numinous," the *mysterium tremendum et fascinans*. Humanity recognizes the Power as wholly "Other" than the empirical self and world, and qualifies it as "holy." The religious attitude toward the Holy may vary from awe and astonishment to faith and love; but it always includes some kind of harmony. This again may vary from a mere attempt at appeasement (as in primitive religious sacrifice) to a sense of intimate unity (as in the Hindu intuition of the ultimate identity of the human spirit with the Absolute).

(5) The discovery of union with the sacred also gives unity to the rest of human existence, giving it purpose and an ultimate meaning. It therefore affects man's present life by producing assurance, healing power, courage, etc. As Louis Dupré notes:

> The religious act is not a simple experience, but a complex movement by which the mind discovers a new reality which, although lying beyond the phenomenal and contrasting with it, ultimately integrates all reality in a higher synthesis.[17]

(6) Since human existence is not only individual but also social, this integration of life tends to take social form. This form, however, can vary from a minimum—a learned religious language, for example, which is used in an almost purely individual and private way—to the opposite extreme of an almost purely social and ritual religion, with little personal involvement or transformation of life.

(7) Religious life tends to include a dimension of belief. Concrete religious beliefs of course are extremely diverse, but they generally include the three elements discerned by William James: a conviction that the visible world is part of a more spiritual universe from which it draws its deepest meaning, a sense that union or harmony with that higher sphere is our true purpose in existence, and a belief that prayer or inner communion with the Transcendent spirit can produce effects in the present world. Furthermore, these beliefs tend to produce the psychological characteristics of new zest in life and a temperament of peace, assurance, and love toward (at least some) others.[18]

From these general traits, we may now attempt to formulate a synthetic description. "Religion," as we shall use the term, signifies a unified system of beliefs and practices, individual and communal, in which man seeks salvation (at some level) through relation to a transcendent power (of some kind), and in which life is experienced as increased, unified, and given meaning through union with this sacred reality.

Excursus: Origins and Socio-biological Basis of Religion

[As we have already noted, religion in the concrete will always be more than what we have discerned as its typical characteristics. Because it is intimately involved in the whole of human life, it can serve other purposes than the strictly "religious." It will also be related to the whole complex of human activity on its many levels: not only spiritual, but also psychological and even biological. Man as spirit is the culmination of an evolutionary process; our spiritual activity is related to and depends upon pre-spiritual manifolds. The same will also be true of religion. We may therefore assume that the origins of religion will have a basis in man's psychic and social evolution.

If religion is defined in the sense given above, we find that it is a virtually universal human phenomenon. Within history and ethnology, there has been no people found without religion—although of course there has been a very wide variety of types. Even pre-historical remnants (in art, burial sites, etc.) give indications of its presence.[19] Exactly how far back religious practice goes is unknown; but it is only modern man, as far as we know, who has attempted to live on any wide scale without religion.[20]

Edward Wilson, who describes himself as an agnostic and a scientific materialist, comments:

> The predisposition to religious belief is the most complex and powerful force in the human mind and in all probability an ineradicable part of human nature. Emile Durkheim, an agnostic, characterized religious practice as the consecration of the group and the core of society. It is one of the universals of social behavior, taking recognizable form in every society from hunter-gatherer bands to socialist republics. Its rudiments go back at least to the bone altars and funerary rites of Neanderthal man. At Shanidar, Iraq, sixty thousand years ago, Neanderthal people decorated a grave with seven species of flowers having medicinal and economic value, perhaps to honor a shaman. Since that time, according to the anthropologist Anthony F. C. Wallace, mankind has produced on the order of 100 thousand religions.
>
> Skeptics continue to nourish the belief that science and learning will banish religion, which they consider to be no more than a tissue of illusions. The noblest among them are sure that humanity migrates toward knowledge by logotaxis, an automatic orientation toward infor-

mation, so that organized religion must continue its retreat as darkness before enlightenment's brightening dawn. But this conception of human nature, with roots going back to Aristotle and Zeno, has never seemed so futile as today. If anything, knowledge is being enthusiastically harnessed to the service of religion. The United States, technologically and scientifically the most sophisticated nation in history, is also the second most religious—after India. According to a Gallup poll taken in 1977, 94% of Americans believe in God or some form of higher being, while 31% have undergone a moment of sudden religious insight or awakening, their brush with the epiphany. The most successful book in 1975 was Billy Graham's *Angels: God's Secret Messengers*, which sold 810 thousand hard-cover copies.

In the Soviet Union, organized religion still flourishes and may even be undergoing a small renaissance after sixty years of official discouragement. In a total population of 250 million, at least 30 million are members of the Orthodox Church—twice the number in the Communist Party—five million are Roman Catholics and Lutherans, and another two million belong to evangelical sects. . . . Still another twenty to thirty million are Moslems, while 2.5 million belong to that most resilient of all groups, Orthodox Jews. Thus, institutionalized Soviet Marxism, which is itself a form of religion embellished with handsome trappings, has failed to displace what many Russians for centuries have considered the soul of their national existence.

Scientific humanism has done no better. . . . [21]

Not only is religion virtually universal, in human societies, if not in individuals, but it is also apparently a *uniquely* human trait. According to Wilson (who as a socio-biologist is not slow to draw parallels between human activity and animal behavior, and to find the origins of the former in the latter):

Religion is one of the major categories of behavior undeniably unique to the human species. The principles of behavioral evolution drawn from existing population biology and experimental studies on lower animals are unlikely to apply in any direct fashion to religion. [22]

Nevertheless, religion does, of course, have a relationship to the underlying strata of human evolution—to man's survival as a living species. Wilson is not the first to suggest that a predisposition to religion has become part of the human species' biological inheritance, through the interaction of genes and culture, in the evolutionary process of the survival of the fittest. Religion survives and becomes part of man because it confers biological advantage:

I am suggesting . . . that the mental processes of religious belief—con-
secration of personal and group identity, attention to charismatic lead-
ers, mythopoeism, and others—represent programmed dispositions
whose self-sufficient components were incorporated into the neural ap-
paratus of the brain by thousands of generations of genetic evolution. As
such, they are powerful, ineradicable, and at the center of human social
existence.[23]

How does religion confer evolutionary benefit? By counteracting
tendencies to selfishness and the individualism fostered by high intelligence. Not all religions do so equally, of course; but "within broad limits
any set of conventions works better than none at all."[24]

Religions survive and evolve, Wilson suggests, according to rules of
"a kind of cultural Darwinism"; that is, they evolve in directions which
enhance the welfare of their practitioners either as individuals or, more
importantly, as a group. Since in the long run altruistic behavior is favor-
able to the species as a whole, those religions which inculcate a morality
of self-sacrifice for others will be more in accord with humanity's needs
and will be more successful over long periods.

Before we pass on to an examination of the kinds and stages of
religion that have in fact appeared in human history, a word is perhaps
in order on the relevance of the socio-biological perspective we have
just presented.

A "heuristic anticipation" of God's word addressed to the human dilemma leads us to expect that any divine "solution" must be in accord with
the structures of human existence. It should therefore not seem strange
that religion, which claims to embody a revelation from God, should conform to the social and biological needs of humanity as well. At the same
time we should point out that the fitting of religion in its origins and development into the general evolution of the species has no direct bearing
on its *truth* value. The fact that religion confers evolutionary value does
not imply that religion's truth or meaning can be *reduced* to that value; the
fact that religion has its origin in psychic needs likewise does not imply
that its claims to knowledge are false. As William James pointed out already at the turn of the century:

> To plead the organic causation of a religious state of mind, then, in re-
> futation of its claim to possess superior spiritual value, is quite illogical
> and arbitrary, unless one has already worked out in advance some psy-
> cho-physical theory connecting spiritual values in general with deter-
> minate sorts of physiological change. Otherwise none of our thoughts
> and feelings, not even our scientific doctrines, not even our *dis*-beliefs,
> could retain any value as revelations of the truth, for every one of them
> without exception flows from the state of its possessor's body at the
> time.[25]

Just as opinions in science are not judged by their author's neurotic constitution, but by logic and experiments, neither should religion's claims be judged on extrinsic grounds, but on their intrinsic merit. The *origin* of an idea—religious or otherwise—is not a useful criterion for its truth. The same remarks can also be applied to other species of reductionism—Marxist, for example, or Freudian—which take one aspect of religion's function and reduce the truth value of the whole to that aspect. While any element in human consciousness—including science, philosophy, the whole search for meaning—has a biological and psychic ground, the higher synthesis that such consciousness represents may not legitimately be reduced to its supporting sub-levels (what Lonergan calls the "lower manifolds").

On the other hand, religion is not simply immune to the reductionist critique; for any higher synthesis can sink to a lower level, while preserving the outward forms of the higher. The fact that religion *per se* has a justifiable role on the spiritual level does not mean that it is always operating on that level; like any other higher content of consciousness, religious thought (like philosophical or political or scientific thought) can be used as an "ideology" supporting a vested interest on a political or economic or social or psychological level. This danger, as history shows, is particularly acute for religions. It is for this reason that the rational examination of religion ("giving answer" for faith) is so crucial.]

RELIGION AS REVELATION

Yes, vain are all those who have not known God, and who, through the goods things that are visible, have not been able to discover He-who-Is, and have not recognized the Artist in considering His works; but rather they have regarded fire, or wind, or ether, the starry vault, the impetuous wave, or the lights of heaven, as gods, the masters of the world! But if, charmed by the beauty of these things, they have seen them as gods, let them learn how much superior their Master is to them; for it is the Source of beauty Himself who created them. And if their power and their activity have struck them with admiration, let them deduce how much more powerful is the One who formed them; for the grandeur and the beauty of creatures lead us, by analogy, to contemplate their Source.

Yet these are only slightly to blame; for perhaps they only strayed in searching for God, and wishing to find him; living among His works, they attempted to understand them, and were trapped by appearances, for what they saw was beautiful.

Nevertheless, they are not blameless; for if they were capable of ac-

quiring enough knowledge to examine the universe, why did they not sooner discover its Master?

Wisdom of Solomon 13:1–7

[The Blessed Lord said:]
"Even those who lovingly devote themselves to other gods and sacrifice to them, full-filled with faith, do really worship Me, though the rite may differ from the norm. For it is I who of all sacrifices am recipient and Lord, but they do not know Me as I really am. . . . "

Bhagavad-Gîtâ 9:23–24

The ire of God is revealed from the heavens against all the impiety and sinfulness of those who keep truth captive in unholiness; for what can be known of God is manifest to them: God indeed has shown it to them. He who is invisible from the creation of the world can be perceived by the intellect through his works, his eternal power and divinity; so they are without excuse, for having known God, they did not render him the glory or thanksgiving due to God, but rather they lost their senses in their thoughts. . . .

Rom 1:18ff

Father, we acknowledge your greatness; all your actions show your wisdom and love. You formed man in your own likeness and set him over the whole world to serve you, his Creator, and to rule over all creatures. Even when he disobeyed you and lost your friendship you did not abandon him to the power of death, but helped all men to seek and to find you. . . .

Eucharistic Prayer IV of the Roman Catholic Liturgy

Our explanation of God's activity in the world has already involved a preliminary discussion of the nature of a divine revelation. It is now necessary to pursue the notion of revelation at greater length and to relate it to the phenomenon of religion.

As we have seen, the ontological structure of human existence forms the condition of possibility for the receiving of a "word" or "deed" of God in the world. The nature of finite being and experience led us to the affirmation that a revelation from God necessarily has a "symbolic" character, and is experienced as a "mediated immediacy": God's giving of himself as transcendent is mediated by what is outside himself, the finite beings which are the "real symbols" of God on various levels. When God's universal "deed" of self-giving is apprehended by human consciousness, we may speak of it as "revelation." "Word," "speech," and "dialogue" are appropriate metaphors for this action of God, for in these activities a subject expresses and gives self by means of a sign outside the self.

"Religious Conversion" as Gift and Achievement

The human apprehension of God's unique and transcendental act of self-giving has a history. The structure of revelation, therefore, can be expressed in Rahner's terms as "transcendental" and "categorical" revelation. These terms correspond to God's action *as* primary cause, and through and *in* secondary causes. We may also speak of revelation as being both God's absolute *gift* and a human *achievement*[26] of transcendence—bearing in mind, however, that these two are not on the same level; rather, the "achievement" is grounded in and created by the gift, so that the human collaboration is itself God's gift.

The achievement of transcendence in the acceptance of God's absolute gift may be termed "conversion." It implies a transformation of the subject and the subject's (personal) world. This achievement has two interrelated aspects: the actual interior *performance* of conversion, and the interpretation or *formulation* of that conversion in the available language. The former will again take place on various levels, all interconnected: there is intellectual conversion by which true judgments become a person's standard of reality, moral conversion by which "the good" is defined through rational decision rather than self-interest, and religious conversion by which God or the Absolute is chosen as the supreme goal of life and norm of living. The formulation of the achievement of transcendence consists in the attempt to reflect upon and express conversion in language or symbols.[27]

The performance of conversion is never totally contained or expressed in reflection and language; on the other hand, the conversion of heart needs to be concretized and expressed symbolically in order to be examined and lived on a reflective level; in this way it can be more complete and spiritual, can grow and be integrated with the whole of the subject's life and personality, and can be shared with others. The interpretation or formulation of conversion is not primary, but it will in its turn affect not only the way in which conversion is understood, but also how it is lived. Thus intellectual conversion strives to come to formulation primarily in philosophy, moral conversion in ethics, religious conversion in religion; and the philosophy, ethical norms, and religious practices of a community will affect how a person comes to and reacts to the experience of the transcendent. Thus the history of categorical revelation will include the whole human effort to express God's self-revelation in human terms, including the history of philosophy and ethics and above all the history of religion.

The level of performance intends total conversion of life in accord with the transcendental openness of human spirit. Nevertheless, only that is *actually* and fully converted which is within the "language" (in the widest sense) of the subject or his community. (As Wittgenstein remarks, "The limits of my language are the limits of my world.") For this reason there is a need for continual progress in conversion. For this reason also there is a certain ambiguity in the categorical revelation of God; the history of religions shows not only the human expression of God's grace, but also the limitations of that expression. For, as Whitehead remarks, "A language is not a universal mode of expressing all ideas whatsoever. It is a limited mode of expressing such ideas as have been frequently entertained, and urgently needed, by the group of beings who developed that mode of speech."[28] The same principle may be extended to human symbols in general, so that the history of the formulations of conversion will necessarily have higher and lower points, according to the adequacy (or lack of same) of the symbols found or invented to express and realize the ineffable experience of the transcendent.[29]

This brings us to an important expansion of our treatment of religion. We have thus far presumed a positive relationship of religion to God, and have even identified religion as the central categorical point of expression and formulation of revelation. But when we look at the actual history of religions, it is far from clear that it represents an unalloyed achievement of transcendence or conversion.

THE AMBIGUITY OF RELIGIONS AS REVELATION

In fact, religions themselves do not generally agree with Rahner's identification of world religion with a "general categorical revelation." Even the comparatively tolerant Hindus and Buddhists differentiate between different levels of revelation, faith, religious knowledge, and response to God (or realization of the Absolute), and hold that some views, at least, are erroneous or misleading. But especially in the religions inspired by the biblical tradition, there has long been a tendency to exclusivism.

[The fourth Eucharistic Prayer of the Roman Catholic liturgy, echoing the teaching of the Second Vatican Council,[30] praises God for helping *all* people not only to seek him, but also to find him. But the Book of Wisdom, for example, despite its comparatively understanding attitude, ends up saying the opposite: the pagans have indeed *sought* the true God, but they have *not* found him; rather, they turned to the worship of creatures and man-made idols (Wis 13:1–7). On the whole, in fact, the Old Testament tends to look at other religions not as a general form of revelation, but rather as the *rejection* of revelation. In this it is followed by St. Paul (Rom 1:18–25). Leaving aside the exegetical question of whether Paul means to say that non-Jews ever actually *had* a "natural" knowledge of God, or whether this was only an unrealized possibility, it is clear that existentially, for Paul, pagan religion is not faith in the true God. St. Augustine takes the implications of the biblical view to their logical conclusion in his judgment that "omnes dii paganorum daemonia"—"all the gods of the pagans are actually demons"; and his attitude is widely imitated in the Christian tradition.]

Indeed, the biblical critique goes even deeper; for the prophets teach that even Israel's *own* religion can be a rejection of God.[31] Jesus' critique of the Judaism of his day and Paul's critique of the religion of the law follow much the same line of thought. Outside Israel, we find that the prophets' indictment of the folly and idolatry of pagan religion is echoed by the pagan philosophers: Heraclitus, Xenophanes, and Socrates against the mythological piety of the Greeks; the Buddha against the unenlightenment of the polytheistic Hinduism of his day; Lao Tse against ancient Chinese ritualism.

Furthermore, an unbiased study of history reveals that religion has frequently been the source, directly or indirectly, of many evils: intolerance, superstition, warfare, witchhunts, persecutions. The poet Lucretius' famous *tantum religio potuit suadere malorum* (*De Rerum Natura*, 101) has echoed frequently and all too justly through the ages.

Is it possible to reconcile Rahner's view of religious history as "general categorical revelation"—and the optimism of the Second Vatican Council, as of universalist forms of Hinduism and Buddhism—with the undeniable facts of history and the mutual and self-critiques of the religions themselves?

A measure of understanding may be gained if we return to our original anthropological presuppositions. We take it as established that the world is an evolving process, a series of "emergent probabilities,"[32] and that humanity and its history are likewise (although on a new level) involved in the same evolutionary scheme. In this process, higher integrations or syntheses arise out of and subsume lower ones. The lower manifolds, however, are not simply abolished or replaced; they remain intact within the transcending higher system. (So, for example, a human being remains biologically an animal, a living thing, and a physical object, subject to all the laws of these realms, even while transcending them as "spirit.") The same is true of religion as a higher integration of human life and contact with the transcendent: it does not remove or replace human nature, or the other existentials which affect human existence in the world.

All human achievement, therefore, is conditioned by many factors. The achievement of transcendence, or what we have called "conversion"—intellectual, moral, and religious—insofar as it is not simply the result of God's creative power, but also of human freedom, represents, in varying proportions, the interplay of "grace" and freedom. The freedom involved, moreover, is not purely free, but is restricted and conditioned by the concrete human situation of the individual or group. (Here Whitehead's analysis of the "epochal occasion" is helpful: the ideal value seen by God and given as a possibility is itself not the "pure" ideal, but is the best that can be attained concretely by this occasion; furthermore, its full attainment is not assured, for the prehension of the value given by God is only one of the influences on the freedom of the occasion.)

For this reason the history of conversion—and hence the history of revelation—is partially conditioned by and partially produced by aspects of human existence which are prior to the level of conversion (the available "language": cultural forms, symbols, etc.) or even opposed to it (unconversion on the intellectual, moral, or religious plane: the intrinsic pluralism in human existence, with the consequent inability to integrate life completely; lack of insight; the working of the "biases";[33] individual or group refusal of transcendence, or sin). These opposing influences may be to some extent "objectified" in the situation in which human freedom operates, thus limiting the available possibilities for the attainment or expression of transcendence,[34] and/or they may affect the individual's free choice itself.

If we combine Rahner's notion of transcendental and general categorical revelation with Lonergan's categories of transcendence as "gift" and as "achievement," we might represent the resulting schema in this way:

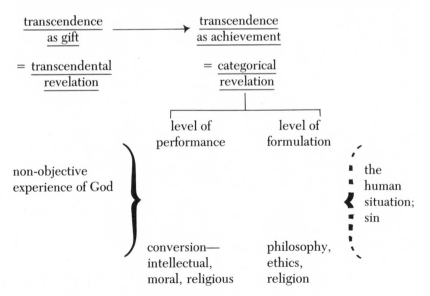

[the entirety of the level of achievement is the result of and expression of the gift; but both the act of conversion itself (performance) and its symbolic expression (formulation) are limited and to some extent conditioned by the existentials of the human situation, including the lack of conversion and sin.]

Religion, therefore, as the expression of "general categorical revelation," is not perfect, but ambiguous; it has degrees of correspondence to its transcendent source and goal; it admits (as we have seen earlier) of other, "lower" motives and functions, besides its properly religious or transcendent one. Authentic religion will always have to be defined in relationship to the move away from in-authenticity, which always remains a possibility and a temptation. In religion as well as in philosophy, the "positions" of conversion invite development, the "counter-positions" invite reversal.[35]

In this perspective and for this reason Rahner writes:

> The history of religion is at the same time the most explicit part of the history of revelation and the intellectual region in which historical misinterpretations of the transcendental experience of God occur most plainly and with the most serious consequences, and where superstition most clearly flourishes. But it is always a case of both, and always in an ambiguity which is for us inextricable.[36]

THE QUESTION OF A "SPECIAL" CATEGORICAL REVELATION IN RELIGION

These considerations bring us to face the *de facto* plurality of religions. The question that must be posed is: What is the relationship of the various categorical expressions of revelation to each other and to God's transcendental self-revelation? Is the history of categorical revelation uniformly "general"—or may there be some point in which God's revelation and his "solution" to the human dilemma are manifested finally and triumphantly, not merely as humanity's halting and imperfect collaboration, but as the victory of grace? Is there any religious achievement which is in some way a normative or final expression of our relationship to God?[37]

A priori, there seem to be only three possibilities:

(1) There is no normative or final form of religion, nor any critical advantage of any religion over any other. The only ultimate norm is the faithfulness of the individual to the transcendental precepts in the performance of conversion. While a public formulation of religion is inevitable and necessary, such formulations serve only as the starting point and aesthetic expression of personal existential faith, which always goes beyond any societal expression. The relationship of the individual to God is determined

solely interiorly, by the intention of conversion rather than by its always inadequate thematization. All religions, although they have unequal possibilities as "languages" of transcendence, are essentially equally viable means for catalyzing existential faith. Another version of this position would hold that all religions, of whatever level of culture, say or *mean* substantially "the same thing," despite the differences in symbols.

(2) There are substantial differences between the thematic formulations of revelation, and some of these are more adequate than others. Furthermore, the level of formulation is not a mere extrinsic addition to the performance of conversion, but "sacramentalizes" the performance: gives it concrete human reality and so *affects* the possibilities of conversion itself. The subject's existential faith, although primary, is not complete in itself, as an interior act, but can never be totally removed from its "language."

On this position, the relation of religions (and other formulations of conversion) to each other may be conceived in a variety of ways:

(a) Complementarity: there is an irreducible pluralism in religions, each particular one making a unique contribution to the expression of the finally ineffable revelation of God. No individual can hope to reach a final form or synthesis, but can only recognize and adopt the religious expression which is best (most fitting, easiest, most meaningful, etc.—whatever the criteria may be) for this particular subject. (This kind of religious relativism is sometimes found among Hindu and Buddhist theoreticians—although less frequently among common believers—and also among a good many post-Enlightenment Westerners.)

(b) Dialectic: the pluralism of religious expressions is resolved in a dynamic evolution to ever higher, more adequate and more synthetic forms; but there is no final point of arrival to this evolution.

(c) Dialectic/complementarity: some combination of the two positions, with different degrees of emphasis.

(3) There exists, or can exist, some final, normative, or even absolute form of categorical revelation.

On this position, one would have to ask the further question concerning the relation of this final form to the rest of the history of religious expressions. Such a relation might be dialectical (à la Hegel), or synthetic (a syncretism of religions), or a combination of these, or perhaps yet some other possibility. It should be noted, however, that if our conclusions thus far are correct, the relation can *not* be that there is one religion (or formulation of conversion) which is true, while all the others are simply false. We have already accepted Rahner's assertion that *all* religions (and also philosophies, ethical systems, etc.) form part of the general (and ambiguous) history of revelation. The question here is whether one set of conversion performances and/or symbols can be in some way the culminating point of that general history. To use Rahner's terminology again: Is there a *special* categorical revelation?

(It is clear from the outset that at least one religion, Christianity—if not invariably, then certainly in its traditional and orthodox form—makes the claim to be such a "special" case of revelation; it will be part of our task to discern the credibility of that claim.)

Clearly we cannot decide among these possibilities by an *a priori* judgment; we must turn to the actual history of religions to ask whether there is reason to affirm that some forms are (in some way) "superior" to others, and whether any form can claim a privileged status. At the same time, our turn to history can only be profitable if we have established criteria of judgment, or norms against which we can compare the historical phenomena; for otherwise, we could not even know where to look in the history of religions, nor what to look for. Such criteria are provided by two sources: (1) our basic anthropology, which has uncovered the human conditions of possibility of any revelation, and has provided a heuristic anticipation of the "solution" to the human dilemma, and (2) our own existential experience of conversion on the level of "performance" (even though the latter is already influenced and informed by a particular religious and philosophical formulation, for to the extent that our inquiry is honest, our commitment to these formulations is subject to the possibility of expansion or even revision, should it be warranted).[38] The measure by which we shall judge religious history, therefore, is the extent to which each formulation corresponds to our view of human existence, as known through our own existential and transcendental experience; for, as Pascal writes, a religion can only be true to the extent that it knows humanity.[39]

The Question of Progress in Religions as Expressions of Conversion

The historical phenomenon of religion, as we have already had occasion to note, is vast and complex. Our first task in asking about differentiations within categorical revelation will therefore be to attempt to narrow our field of inquiry.

We may do so by first dealing with the possibility that all religions are *equally* valid forms of relating to God or the Absolute. Clearly, on the level of thematic expression some religious forms are more primitive than others; the idea of the Supreme Being itself shows a significant progression, as do forms of cult, the kind of spiritual power aimed at, the relationship of religion to magic, etc. The question, however, is whether these ideas and other symbolic forms are crucial to the relation of the subject to God, or whether all such forms are relative and only the interior disposition of "faith" behind them is ultimately significant.

As long as the subject's relationship to the Absolute is thought of as a purely interior, spiritual and personal act, this position seems possible. Our transcendental anthropology, however, holds that every human transcendental relation in order to be real must also be genuinely in the world.[40] The transcendental relation itself is affected and limited by its "language," even though it is not fully contained in it; likewise, every level of categorical "performance" is already, at least implicitly, limited by the symbolic forms and level of human development on which it takes place (so that there is, for example, a real difference between the faith of a child and that of an adult; it is not merely a matter of the latter's having a more developed means of expression).

Furthermore, religious conversion requires integration with the whole human being; that is, it calls out for intellectual and moral conversion as well. But these must all attain intellectual formulation in order to be self-critical and to progress, in order to be communicated with others, and in order to establish a measure of objective control over one's actions. The inevitable thematization of one's basic attitudes will in turn affect how one subsequently acts (it will make a difference, for example, whether one *thinks* of the Absolute as Love or as arbitrary Power; for one will to some extent [although not completely, for we are concupiscent and inconsistent] model one's own behavior and ethical norms on this conception).

Moreover, our analysis has led to an anticipation of a divine "solution" or revelation in which we collaborate both with God and among one another.[41] Such a collaboration requires that that there be a thematic and social dimension to conversion; and the level of collaboration possible will depend largely upon the adequacy of the formulation. (Comparative religion points out, for example, the difference between tribal religions and "world" religions—that is, those which have a universal horizon. While the former tend to exclude others from relation with God and/or with his "people," the latter include others within the relation, thus allowing a wider and more perfect collaboration.)

On these bases we may from the outset reject the position holding that all religious formulations are necessarily of the same value. This of course does not mean the rejection of any religious formulation as the means of revelation for a particular individual or group; nor does it mean that objectively less adequate formulations cannot be transcended in the personal faith of a particular subject—even to the extent that this faith may, in specific cases, be more integral and authentic than that of a person who enjoys the availability of a "higher" formulation. It does mean, however, that the words "lower" and "higher" have meaning when applied to the adequacy of religious formulations of the conversion experience.

[Even the "relativism" sometimes ascribed to Hinduism, in particular, generally admits of at least this much differentiation among religions. In the *Bhagavad-Gîtâ* Krishna (who is here the one supreme Absolute) states:[42]

> Even those who lovingly devote themselves to other gods and sacrifice to them, full-filled with faith, do really worship Me, though the rite may differ from the norm. For it is I who of all sacrifices am recipient and Lord . . . (9:23–24).

This is certainly a great deal more tolerant and universalist than the utter condemnations of pagan religion found in the Old Testament. But Krishna continues:

> . . . but they do not know Me as I really am, so they fall (back into the world of men). To the gods go the gods' devotees, to the ancestors their votaries, to disembodied spirits go the worshippers of these, but those who worship Me shall come to Me (9:24–25).

Again, Krishna says that he not only accepts, but confirms the faith of those who worship other gods:

> Whatever form (i.e., whatever god) a devotee with faith desires to honor, that very faith do I confirm in him, making it unswerving and secure. Firm-established in that faith he seeks to reverence that god, and thence he gains his desires, though it is I who am the true dispenser (7:21–22).

Yet there is a value to seeking and finding the "true" God, for there is differentiation in the final state:

> But finite is the reward of such men of little wit: whoso worships the gods, to the gods will surely go, but whoso loves and worships Me, to Me will come indeed (7:23)]

Just as we recognize in physical evolution the occurrence of turning points or "thresholds" in which a new and higher level is reached, so also in the history of human spiritual development we must admit the possibility of the appearance of qualitatively different forms. An a priori egalitarianism would in fact deny the possibility of progress in the spiritual realm.

If we must reject the possibility of complete equality among religions, may we then see in the history of religions a *progression*, a spiritual evolution? Is there a progressively true revelation of God in the course of the dialectic of history?

This notion is congenial to modern Western thought because of our belief in evolution and in progress.[43] Our normal model for collaboration in knowledge and belief is science, which is eminently progressive. We must be cautious, however, in applying this parallel to the formulation of revelation. First of all, we must recall that history—even the history of science—does not show uninterrupted linear progress; there are rather periods of progression interspersed with periods of decline. We can see progress only by looking to the large historical picture; we cannot in any case assume that later forms of culture are necessarily higher (even in science; many discoveries of the Greeks were lost and replaced with less advanced ideas during the Middle Ages).[44]

More profoundly, we may ask whether religion is the *kind* of knowledge or collaboration that is progressive, like science. If we take science as our model, an evolutionary schema, at least over the long run, seems most likely. But can the same be said of other realms of human culture and spiritual achievement? For example: Is there an evolution or progression to higher forms in art or in music? Clearly there have been many technical advances over the centuries in these fields, but it is not immediately clear that later periods in art are necessarily better than earlier ones. (A modern person may still marvel at the *beauty*—not only the historical interest—of the pre-historic cave paintings at Altamira.)

The question is complicated by the fact that in fields such as music, art, and literature, we generally recognize "classic" forms. These are in some way seen to be "normative" for excellence;[45] yet they may be neither primitive ideals (from which everything else declines, as in the Chinese vision) nor yet modern achievements (to which everything has led, as in the evolutionary-progressive vision). The "classic" periods in the various arts, indeed, do not coincide with each other. Their normativeness is not the automatic result of their chronological placement. These fields do not favor the model of invariable higher development. While many might disagree, a person would at least not be thought absurd to claim that the music of Bach or Mozart is superior to anything produced before or since.

A similar situation obtains in a field closely related to the religious, namely in philosophy. A. J. Ayer notes at the beginning of his *Philosophy in the Twentieth Century* that an objection frequently brought against philosophy is precisely that it fails to exhibit any clear progress. While no one today would hold that the astrophysics of Kepler or Galileo, for example, is superior to Einstein's, "it is otherwise with philosophy":

> The historian of philosophy can, indeed, trace the influence of one philosopher upon another. . . . There is, however, no question of one of these philosophers superseding another. . . . One can still maintain, without forfeiting one's claim to competence in philosophy, that Hume was right and Kant wrong on the point at issue between them, that Locke came nearer to the truth than either Berkeley or Hume, that as against Kant it was Hegel who took the wrong turning. One can still be a Platonist while fully understanding Aristotle's criticism of Plato, and without being ignorant of all the positions that different philosophers have taken in the centuries that have passed since Plato lived. [46]

Progress in philosophy, according to Ayer, consists not in the contributions of individual philosophers, but in the "evolution of a set of perennial problems,"[47] in a "change in the fashion in which the problems are posed, and in an increasing measure of agreement concerning the character of their solution."[48]

We may suspect that something similar may hold true in the sphere of religion. Revelation and its embodiment in religion and its allied forms comprise a highly complex phenomenon. It is not a matter of pure interiority, but of the mutual interdependence of interiority and external interpretative elements, of individual and social realities. While there can be no assurance of linear progression in the human capacity for or achievement of "conversion" itself, we may nevertheless expect a development over the long run, as in philosophy, in the cultural and socio-political conditions that foster the capacity to formulate certain interpretative elements: the intellectual, moral, and religious insights that permit (but do not guarantee) an expansion of the religious achievement to new levels.

Concretely, there appear to be what Karl Jaspers calls "axial periods" in the development of the human mind, occurring in conjunction with enabling social conditions. These periods represent developments in the way the mind itself works; that is, they are stages in humanity's coming to consciousness, and are therefore relevant to our possibilities of spiritual activity. Such developments advance the human ability to objectify our spiritual life, and thus to subjectivize the self and the world. The increasing differentiation of consciousness (from a stage in which everything is within the single realm of "common sense," to a differentiated realm of theory, of interiority, and of transcendence)[49] permits the spirit to come to itself on new levels of self-awareness. In this sense, there are within the history of spirit moments comparable to the "thresholds" of physical evolution, turning points which raise the process to a new level of possibility.

While it is true, as Ayer says, that a twentieth-century philosopher can still be a Platonist, it is doubtful whether one could equally well be a follower of Thales or Anaximander; for precisely with Socrates and Plato there occurred the final turning point of that discovery of mind which permitted philosophy to disengage itself from mytho-poetic consciousness and enter into a critically differentiated way of thinking.

In religion as well there appear to be "axial" periods of development, in which revolutionary new horizons are attained in human thinking and in the capacity to objectivize spirit in the world. One such period seems to have occurred early in history, when religious consciousness moved away from a centering on ritual and emotion, and into the sphere of rationality and belief. Another is marked by the ethical and metaphysical revolution represented by the Hebrew prophets in Israel, Zoroaster in Persia, Socrates and Xenophon in Greece, the Buddha in India, Lao-Tse and Chuang-Tse in China, in which a new consciousness of interiority was introduced. Another—or a continuation of the same—saw the rise of universality in religion, with the worship of a God or Absolute beyond both humanity and nature.

The development of new human horizons, therefore, is relevant to our question not only on cultural grounds, but precisely to the achievement of the expression of God's self-communication. As our heuristic anticipation already indicated, revelation must come to us in accord with the relevant emerging probabilities, not only in nature, but in human history;[50] among the probabilities that must arise are the capacities for deeper levels of self-awareness and freedom through the thematic discovery of mind itself. At the same time, the kind of evolution or progress involved here is not inevitable, nor is it necessarily cumulative and open-ended in the manner of scientific progress. There is no assurance that further, higher forms of consciousness will or can arise; nor are later developments necessarily higher. But it is possible to conceive the development at least of certain "classic" forms of religious consciousness which represent a high point of the achievement and formulation of categorical revelation.

In the next section we will attempt to explore more concretely and on the basis of historical data in what sense religions "evolve" and to sketch in its general lines the development of the higher forms of religious consciousness.

The Emergence of the Higher Religions

About the historical origins of religion there is very little that can be said. Surviving data from pre-history are minimal and ambiguous, and attempts to extrapolate from living religions to some kind of common ancestral form have all been doomed to failure from the outset.[51]

Although we cannot therefore speak of any originating form of religion, we may observe (in line with Lonergan's observation concerning the gradually increasing differentiation of consciousness into various "realms") that the emergence of religion as a *distinct* phenomenon, separate from other areas of life, is comparatively late in history (occurring probably in the last six thousand years, in comparison to some sixty thousand years of the known existence of religious behavior). Our concern here is only with differentiated religious consciousness, and especially the later part of its development, in which religion attained to explicitly personal and universal consciousness.

The increasing rationalization and personalization of religion had to await the development in human consciousness of the relevant language, ideas, and values. This transformation appears to have taken place in a number of separate cultural contexts during Jaspers' "axial period" beginning perhaps some one thousand years before the Christian era. Alfred North Whitehead theorizes that during this time—in part because of relatively improved social conditions—it became possible for the individual to travel in comparative safety. This permitted an expansion of thought beyond the tribal community consciousness and led to the development of "world" consciousness. Dissociation of thought from its immediate surroundings also permitted a more "objective" way of thinking, so that the bias of the group or tribe could give way to a search for objective, essential ethical rightness, and the notion of the power of God, conceived as arbitrary will, could give way to an idea of absolute goodness. All of this fostered the creation of universal and personal religion.[52]

At the point where religions become rational, universal and personal, we may speak of the appearance of "higher" religions. (We note again that there is no single path of development to this point; nor is it necessarily later in time than other forms.) The historian Arnold Toynbee notes that the higher religions of the world have all in fact arisen out of generally similar historical circumstances which permitted the formulation of a notion of a transcendent object of worship and of personal responsibility toward that absolutely transcendent.

Toynbee points out that human worship (using the word in its widest sense of a personal relation to the ultimate) has only three possible objects: nature, humanity itself, or some absolute Reality which is beyond both humanity and nature. (This Absolute may be conceived as "personal" or as "impersonal," in the sense of beyond personality. Both conceptions are generally found in all higher religions, although with differences of emphasis and formulation.[53])

The oldest and most deeply rooted form of religion—as far as we know—consists in the worship of nature.

[Toynbee remarks that the thesis of Fr. W. Schmidt, which posits a primitive monotheism (based on observation of surviving primitive societies—a method whose shortcomings we have noted above) may have validity; it is possible that people did not begin to worship nature until they had begun to manipulate their surroundings; "for it would perhaps be difficult to worship a power which one had no hope of being able to influence," and the idea of exerting power to change nature could only arise when people had already begun to do so. If this is the case, then nature worship would have flourished during and after the period of humanity's transformation into hunters and fishers, after the period of passive food gathering. This would place nature religion in the upper Paleolithic Age.[54]]

The power which man encounters and relates to in nature is manifested and symbolized by the gods—necessarily in the plural, for nature appears as disconnected and sometimes conflicting forces.

We have noted that a characteristic of all religion is a search for salvation, in the sense of some integration or elevation of life. We may now distinguish between a totally immanent kind of salvation, which is entirely centered *within* the world as it actually exists, and a salvation which transcends the present world, and is a salvation either *of* the world or *from* the world as it actually is. The latter form is characteristic of the "higher" religions (in Indian thought, the present world is "mâyâ," not totally real, and salvation consists in escape from false existence; for Zoroastrians, the actual world is a mixture of good and evil, which comes about by the agency of the evil spirit, and salvation consists in its purification and transformation to pure good; for Israelite religion, the present state of the world is the result of a moral "fall," and salvation is reconciliation; etc.). In nature religion, by contrast, the world is accepted *as it is*. Salvation is not from the present world, but only from particular evils, and toward particular goods, within the world. Edward Wilson notes that contemporary anthropology and history "support Max Weber's conclusion that more elementary religions seek the supernatural for purely mundane rewards: long life, abundant land and food, averting physical catastrophes, and the conquest of enemies."[55]

The reason for this is clear from the nature of these religions: polytheism is (in general) without any "high" or transcendent soteriology because the gods are *immanent* in the reality of this-worldly experience, i.e., they are personifications of nature itself. Their function is to guarantee the stability of the present world, not to transcend it.

[This means that reality, as it is, is divine, and therefore not only that it is stable, but also that its stability is *desirable*. In polytheistic religions we find that reality, including the normal human condition—even where its harshness is recognized—is accepted . . . as the permanent manifestation of the will and the nature of the gods: for this reason it does not need salvation.[56]]

The stability of the world, however, is not a changeless stasis; it is rather a recurring rhythm. Hence nature religion typically embodies what Eliade calls the "myth of the eternal return." The gods of polytheism "save" the whole of reality (nature) periodically, by re-establishing the origins of the world. They do not save humanity *from* the world and its present conditions, since a God who transcends the empirical world is not conceived.

It follows that for nature religion, since there is no transcendent and omnipotent Absolute, the problem of evil, as we have conceived it, does not exist. What men call "evil" is simply a fact of existence, one of its intrinsic aspects. The worship of nature gods, in fact, normally has a dual aspect, corresponding to the harsh and the beneficent aspects of nature itself. In Toynbee's image, nature is worshiped both as "Mother" and as "Monster": as creative and self-sacrificing and as threatening, demanding and destructive.

[It is to be noted, as Toynbee points out, that the worship of nature frequently remains embedded secretly within forms which are ostensibly those of higher religion—especially on the popular and more mythological levels. Thus one finds alongside its sophisticated and metaphysical theology the Hindu worship of Kali (Durga), or of Śiva in the form of the *linga*. In Christianity likewise one finds the popular worship of the Mother and Child sometimes taking forms far from acceptable to the official theology. In particular humanity is tempted to worship that part of nature which has never yet been conquered: that is, our own psyche.[57]]

In Toynbee's view, the polarization of the worship of nature into its positive and negative aspects sets the stage for the appearance of the other possible objects of human religion. The worship of nature as "monster" gives way to humanity's "suicidal" worship of humanity itself, that is, of human power, while the worship of nature as beneficent and self-giving leads into the worship of a transcendent God who sets the example of self-sacrifice.

In its second major form, human worship passes from the adoration of nature's power to center instead on power in humanity itself. Toynbee distinguishes three forms: the idolization of parochial communities, of the ecumenical community, and of the self-sufficient individual.

As civilization advances, the power of nature becomes less mysterious and numinous; humanity emerges as the center of its own world, and the power of the human community becomes the most potent immediate force in life. Alongside and in association with nature worship, then, there develops the worship of the community's own collective power, embodied in the state. This form of religion is commonly found in what Toynbee calls "civilizations of the first two generations," before the axial period in which higher civilizations and religions emerge. Typical forms are the worship of the personified city-state (e.g., Athena as the goddess of Athens, etc.) or the association of the king with a nature god. The old nature gods are not rejected, but are co-opted to become gods of the community. (So for example Yahweh, who appears to have been originally some kind of mountain god or storm god, is adopted as the war-god of the Hebrew confederacy.[58])

Salvation in this kind of religion is still fundamentally mundane and communal. Because of the natural rivalry between states, however, the adoption of nature gods as local patrons turns polytheism into a destructive force. While the worship of nature is unifying of different communities, since nature is common to all and provides a focus outside the self, the worship of the parochial community is an expression of communal self-centeredness and thus sets people at odds with others. The identification of the group with deity adds force to the already potent allure of the group bias. Furthermore, the collective ego and collective power are more destructive than any individual manifestation of egotism, not only because the community is larger, but because it is more at the mercy of subconscious passions, being beyond the control which intellect and will impose on the individual ego. Thus, although such civilizations may make great cultural advances, it is at the price of war and destruction.[59]

The eventual longing for peace which results from the period of warring states leads to the rejection of the deification of the parochial community and a search for a higher form of divinity. At this point humanity can either turn to the Absolute (as we shall see, the higher religions have the possibility of arising precisely in the circumstances of the dissolution of parochial states and the disillusionment with the local gods), or can engage in other forms of worship of itself.

Of the latter, Toynbee distinguishes two major forms: the idolization of the ecumenical community and, at the opposite pole, of the self-sufficient individual.

Ecumenical or "world" communities of imperial form provide a solution to the problem of warring states (as exemplified in the "Pax Romana" and its parallels in the Persian and Chinese empires). They also provide a more universal and less self-centered focus for devotion. But the imperial state as a god (generally still with some admixture of nature-worship) is impersonal and remote. A tendency arises, therefore, to personify the state in the imperial ruler ("Divus Caesar," the Pharaoh as son of the sun-god). Such a form of religion, however, is highly artificial; it exists for reasons of state, but has difficulty in capturing the hearts of the people. These circumstances again provide an opportunity for the rise of transcendent religion.[60]

On the other hand, they also provide a context for the development of the idolization of the individual. In primitive societies, humanity is preeminently social; its self-centeredness is plural in form. The development first of strong parochial communities and later of ecumenical states allows the development of the independent individual.[61] In the spiritual vacuum left by the failures of the worship of the parochial or ecumenical community, there arise philosophical religions of self-sufficiency, in which the transcendent principle is seen as embodied within the individual person. Such systems are essentially non-theistic, although they may also include a formal recognition of the community or state god(s). Toynbee sees examples of the idolization of the self-sufficient philosopher in Indian philosophy (in which the prime example would be the Sâmkhya school, for which the individual is an eternal self-sufficient monad), in Hînayâna Buddhism's ideal of the extinction of all desire, in the idea of *apatheia* cultivated by the Stoics and Epicureans, and in the Confucian goal of incorporation of the traditional social virtues.[62]

The worship of human power, whether in the form of the state or of the individual, proves ultimately spiritually insufficient, particularly when confronted with the fact of evil and suffering in the world. The parochial community inflicts suffering upon others in its drive for power; the ecumenical empire imposes peace with the sword; the self-sufficient philosopher can preserve self-sufficiency only at the cost of repressing sympathy and love for fellow-creatures. The disillusionment with all human idols leaves open the way for the development of the higher religions, those which rise above the worship of humanity as well as the worship of nature.[63]

Such religions in fact have arisen in particular social situations. Toynbee insists, however, that they are not *produced* by the social milieu, but by encounter with the Absolute Reality, the mystery of the Holy. Nevertheless, a particular social context is the condition of possibility of the human developments which allow the higher religious formulation of that encounter. Specifically, the religions of the deification of the ecumenical community or of the self-sufficient philosopher are characteristic of the "dominant minority" in a society (so, e.g., Confucius, a literatus; Plato, a citizen in a society based on slavery; Gautama, the son of a prince). The founders of the higher religions, by contrast, tend to arise from the dominated majority in disintegrating societies; and the catalyst for their spiritual revolution is a social time of troubles, in which the imposed values of the community are called into question.

[So, for example, prophetic Judaism and Zoroastrianism arose among those uprooted in the 8th and 7th century B.C. by Assyrian militarism and the "Völkerwanderung" of the central Asian nomads. The transformation of the Hînayâna to Mahâyâna Buddhism, and the subsequent influence on the Hînayâna itself, as well as the emergence of transcendent theistic Hinduism, began about the second century B.C., among peoples uprooted by Greek and Central Asian invasions of India. Christianity was founded among the peoples uprooted by Macedonian and Roman militarism and social revolution. Islam arose in the disintegrating remnants of the old Roman Empire.[64]]

The higher religions represent the high point of the evolution of religion, and they tend to share certain fundamental characteristics which differentiate them from their predecessors. (1) They recognize as the supreme object of human worship a transcendent Being, God or the Absolute. (2) They are universal in scope, anticipating salvation for all humanity. (3) They manifest some kind of organization, conceiving salvation as a collaboration of humanity with the Supreme Reality in which the problem of evil is addressed by some kind of self-sacrificial suffering for the sake of others.

By these criteria, we may enumerate seven higher religions which are still alive: Hînayâna Buddhism, Mahâyâna Buddhism, Hinduism, Parseeism (modern Zoroastrianism), Judaism,[65] Christianity, and Islam.

IV. GOD'S WORD IN HUMAN WORDS — THE INDIC-SINIC RELIGIONS

"Om. I am the Lord, in no wise different from him, the Brahman."

Daily prayer of the twice-born Hindus

"I go to the Buddha as my refuge. I go to the Law as my refuge. I go to the Order as my refuge."

The Refuge Formula, recited at every Buddhist shrine

The progress of our considerations thus far has brought us to affirm the existence of a divine self-revelation, consisting of a transcendental immediacy to God which is at the same time mediated or made categorical by human history. The most explicit part of the thematization of man's realization of revelation is found in the history of religion. That history, judged by the criteria of our anthropological presuppositions, shows not equality and uniformity, but significant breakthroughs to higher forms.

We have furthermore asked whether revelation in its categorical form should be considered an unending asymptotic progression, or whether there may be a "special" categorical revelation, a sign or symbol system in which God's self-gift is humanly present in a final, triumphant and definitive way.

If such a special categorical revelation exists, it will come to us in accord with the human capacity (what Lonergan calls the "probabilities"[1]) for receiving it. Our next step, therefore, is to examine the highest thematic forms to which religion has attained as a human collaboration in transcendence.

THE THEMATIZATION OF REVELATION IN THE HIGHER RELIGIONS

We have already noted the major criteria by which the "higher" religions are distinguished and have considered Toynbee's schema of the circumstances in which they arose: as systems of worship/transcendence created, adapted, or adopted by the internal proletariats in "second generation" civilizations.[2] The Babylonic civilization brought about the conditions for the rise of Zoroastrianism and Judaism; the Syriac for Islam; the Indic for Hinduism and Hînayâna Buddhism; the Sinic for Mahâyâna Buddhism (including Zen Buddhism) and Neo-Taoism; the Hellenic for the worship of Isis and Cybele, Mithraism, Christianity, Manichaeism, and Neoplatonism.[3]

Of these a number have disappeared or been absorbed—particularly in the West, where the eventual triumph of Christianity assured the elimination of its earlier rivals in the late Hellenistic world. There remain today four major "families" of related traditions: the Buddhist, comprised of the Hînayâna (or "small vehicle"), the Mahâyâna (or "great vehicle"), Tibetan (Tantric) Buddhism (sometimes referred to as the "Vajrayâna"—the "Thunder" vehicle), and Zen; the Zoroastrian/Judaeo-Christian, including Judaism, the three major forms of Christianity (Orthodox, Protestant, Catholic), and the Parsees, the remnants of the religion of Zoroaster; the Hindu, comprising many different schools; and the Islamic, whose major divisions are the Sunnah and Shî'ah forms.

The simple enumeration of the major religions in the modern world makes it apparent that a thorough examination of them would be a complex and lengthy task. Its complexity would be increased by the fact of plurality *within* religions; for each of them has developed in time, has received influences from other traditions (some of the major lines of influence are indicated in the schema below), and has generated different schools of interpretation and practice. Furthermore, there coexist within each religion different levels and kinds of participation, differing centers of gravity and emphasis, as well as various degrees of appropriation on the part of the individual adherent (so that a particular individual might find more kinship in belief and attitude with members of another tradition than with some others who are nominally of the same religion).[4]

There are therefore a number of ways in which the study of religions might validly be approached. One might approach a religious tradition through its theology and its sacred writings. On the other hand, one might get a very different picture if one looked at the same religion in its lived practice: its spirituality, cult and rituals, the practices and tenets of the ordinary adherent. Yet again, one might see a religious tradition through its organization, its structures and officials, or through its history, its interaction as a community with society, its sociology, politics, etc.

It is clearly impossible for a study like ours to undertake even a cursory examination of all these aspects. Yet despite the enormous complexity of the higher religions, it is clear that each major religion has a "classic"

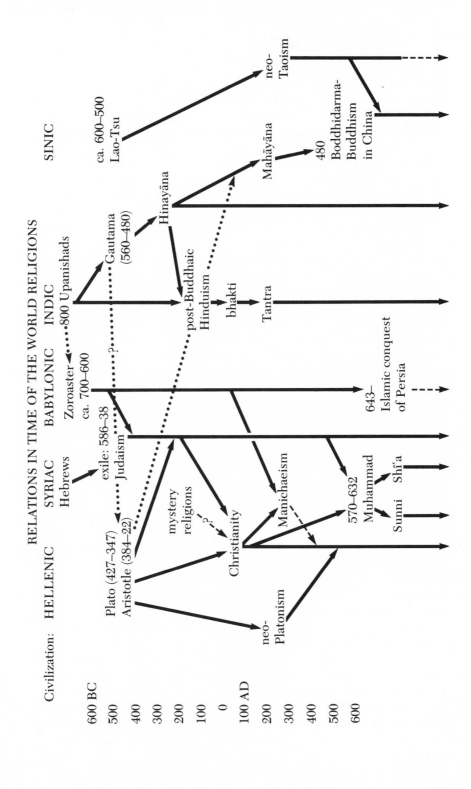

RELATIONS IN TIME OF THE WORLD RELIGIONS

Civilization: HELLENIC SYRIAC BABYLONIC INDIC SINIC

600 BC
500
400
300
200
100
0
100 AD
200
300
400
500
600

Zoroaster
ca. 700–600

800 Upanishads

Hebrews
exile: 586–38
Judaism

Plato (427–347)
Aristotle (384–22)

Gautama
(560–480)

ca. 600–500
Lao-Tsu

mystery
religions

Christianity

Manichaeism

neo-
Platonism

570–632
Muhammad
Shí'a
Sunni

643–
Islamic conquest
of Persia

Hinayāna

post-Buddhaic
Hinduism

bhakti

Tantra

Mahāyāna

480
Boddhidarma-
Buddhism
in China

neo-
Taoism

form which contains something in its approach and attitudes that identifies it, distinguishes it from other kinds of religion, and serves as the basis of the tradition which perdures in the different variations. The significant aspect of that classic form may consist not so much in the specific doctrines and practices of a religion, on which there may be considerable difference, but in a more basic conviction which is taken for granted and lies behind all the conflicting views. (Christians, for example, may differ among themselves on the status of Jesus, on the structure of the Church, on the place of the Scriptures, or on the precise nature of redemption; but nearly all Christians will think of the ultimate Reality as being in some sense personal, will accept that there are such realities as sin and salvation, and will see the latter as being intimately connected both with divine grace and with significant human acts in history, both of these in some way culminating in Jesus. It is precisely these common suppositions which set Christian religion apart from a Hindu or Buddhist tradition.)

Our effort here will be an attempt to discern the "classic" contribution of each great religious tradition to the thematization of revelation, while recognizing that this in no way represents an adequate treatment of the concrete religions. (Our attempt will therefore be similar to Tillich's "typological" approach and to van der Leeuw's phenomenology of religions,[5] in which he discerned certain "ideal types" exemplified in the existing world religions. At the same time, we note that in practice, every living religion is a syncretism of higher and lower forms, and of different types or tendencies within these forms.)

More specifically, we shall take as our interpretative key William James' statement that the essential core of every religion consists in two elements: a problem, and its solution by contact with some higher power. Moreover, our own philosophical analysis has uncovered two major aspects of the problem: the meaning of human existence, and the fact of evil. We shall therefore ask of the major traditions of the higher religions:

(1) What is the problem? What kind of anthropology and theology is presumed? What is the setting out of which this religion arises?

(2) What is the solution? What is revealed about the meaning of human existence and the problem of evil? What is the higher power involved? Who is the agent of "salvation," and how? What is the meaning of "conversion," or the achievement of transcendence? What existential imperative is given to earthly life, and what is its ultimate goal?[6]

We shall first present an overview in two chapters of the major forms of the great religions; in the following section we shall then consider their points of convergence and divergence.

As already noted, our overview will be restricted to the "higher" religions, that is, those which (1) go beyond the worship of nature or of man to recognize an *ultimate* being or power: what we have called "God," or the Absolute, (2) have a world-consciousness or universal directedness, in accord with the need of a "solution" to the universal existential dilemma of man, and (3) take recognizable historical form, manifesting some kind of organized collaboration of people among each other and with God.

It is generally recognized that there have been three great "types" of civilization and culture: the Indian, the Chinese, and the Western (which is an amalgam of Middle Eastern and Hellenic influences). The great religions, although they have expanded beyond their original contexts, have in general developed and formulated their language and symbols primarily within one of these cultural spheres: Hinduism and Hînayâna Buddhism in the Indian, Mahâyâna Buddhism as an Indian transplant in the Chinese, Zoroastrianism, Judaism, Christianity and Islam in the Western. In the present chapter we shall consider the Indic and Sinic forms of religion; in the following, the Western.

THE INDIC AND SINIC RELIGIONS

The great religions originating in the Indian subcontinent all share a common basic world-view. They presuppose that the earthly condition of humanity is *samsâra:* the "round of existence," bondage to an endless cycle of births, lives, deaths, and rebirths in new forms. From this bondage we need to be liberated (although there is some difference in emphasis on what exactly the liberation is from, and even more difference on how the goal of liberation is conceived). All likewise agree that this world as we experience it is not (ultimately) real, that it has some aspect of "illusion."

The overcoming of the illusion of *samsâra* reveals the Absolute which already in reality pervades and is All. In this regard the Indic religions tend to be what van der Leeuw calls "religions of repose," rather than religions of "unrest" or of action.[7] The "Holy" of Otto is seen especially as *fascinans.* There is an emphasis on mystical experience, the experience of peace, of union with the ultimate reality, even now. For this reason there is a tendency to monism or pantheism in the theoretical forms of the Indic religions. God or the Absolute is experienced as already "All." In popular religion the pantheistic tendency is reinforced by a strong admixture of the remnants of nature worship.[8]

The character of Indian religion was substantially changed when it was transplanted, in the form of Mahâyâna Buddhism, into the Chinese civilization. Although the Mahâyâna probably had its origins in northern India (possibly even with some Hellenic and Persian influence), its major diffusion and principal later developments occurred in China and its

sphere of cultural influence (including especially Japan). The incorporation of much of the spirit of Taoism, as well as the adaptation of Buddhism
to the less metaphysical and more pragmatic, existential, social and humanistic Chinese character and language,[9] gave to the Mahâyâna and its
offshoots, like Zen, a radically different mentality from that of the originating Indian world-view. In particular, the doctrines of *saṁsâra* and the
unreality of the world are transformed into a more positive stance toward
humanity and present existence, while the notion of "liberation" and the
tendency to monism are attenuated by a stronger sense of relationship and
plurality, and Chinese pragmatism injected a more active element into the
mystical spirit inherited from India.

Hinduism

Of all the great religions Hinduism is perhaps the most difficult to deal
with in a summary way, for over its three-thousand-year history it has presented myriad forms. M. Dhavamony lists as its main forms: Vedism, Brâ-
manism, classical Hinduism, Sectarian Hinduism, Medieval Hinduism,
Modern Hinduism, and Contemporary Hinduism.[10] Even within these
forms it is difficult to define, for "the beliefs and practices of the Hindus
differ greatly from one period of history to another, and within a given
period, from one region to another, and within a given region, from one
class of society to another."[11] Furthermore, Hinduism tends to be highly
syncretistic, incorporating within itself even movements and ideas contradictory both to each other and to its own prior doctrines. There are nevertheless certain central ideas which tend to underlie and synthesize the
various forms.

First of all, Hinduism in all its forms is a "salvational" religion, with
clear teachings on a human problem, on liberation from the problem, and
on the realization of man's ultimate meaning in God or the Absolute. All
of these doctrines, furthermore, are thought by the various schools to be
based upon an infallible Revelation, expressed in the accepted Scriptures.[12]

The greatest degree of consensus lies in the definition of the problem
or dilemma which besets the human situation, and in the conviction of the
need and possibility of salvation (*moksha,* = release, liberation, escape,
or its synonym *mukti,* = release, deliverance; both from the stem *much,*
= let go, let loose, set free).[13]

We have already mentioned the idea of *saṁsâra,* the cycle of rebirth.
It is joined with the notions of *mâyâ,* the force which produces "illusory"
or finite existence, and *karma,* the "universal law of immanent retribution,"[14] according to which every action has necessary and inescapable

consequences within the world, leading to a chain of rebirths in higher or lower states as reward or punishment.

The whole misery of existence due to *saṁsāra* is called *kleśa* (= pain, affliction, distress). Five kinds of *kleśa* are enumerated: ignorance (*avidyā*), egoism (*asmitā; asmi* = "I am"), desire (*rāga*) or attachment to pleasure, aversion (*dvesha*) or aversion to pain, and the tenacity of mundane existence (*abhiniveśa*) or the will to continue in life.[15] These are the "hindrances" or impairments which appear in the psychic part of man (*manas*) and prevent or restrict the appearance and realization of the true Self (*ātman*).

It is presumed by practically all Hindus that the *ātman* is eternal and immortal and in some way intrinsically one with ultimate Reality (*Brahman*). The most basic problem of existence in the world of *saṁsāra* is that the true nature of the Self is hidden. The most basic of the "hindrances," then, is ignorance (*avidyā*). This is conceived not merely as the absence of knowledge, but as a positive tendency to mistake things for what they are not,[16] in particular, to mistake the empirical and psychic self for the real Self and the empirical world of *māyā* for Reality. Ignorance is thus the ultimate cause of all misery, for it leads to the other forms of *kleśa*. For all Hindus *moksha* is primarily escape from this ignorance.

Ignorance causes egoism (*asmitā* as above, or *ahaṁkāra*, from *aham* = "I" and *kara* = doing, making, causing). The Sanskrit words mean both "self-consciousness" and "selfishness," for the mistaking of the phenomenal individual ego for the real Self is what causes greed, pain, and the desire for earthly life. *Moksha* is thus also conceived as liberation from egoism and its consequences.[17]

It may also be said that *moksha* signifies salvation from sin, but this is not to be conceived in the full Christian sense. Sin for Hinduism is primarily *adharma*—conduct which goes against *dharma*, the order of the universe (which is therefore also the fundamental moral law). *Adharma* includes both physical evils and bad actions.[18] It includes the primitive notion of sin as the breaking of taboo or ritual laws, as well as the notion of offending the gods by acting against their will. The concept, however, remains hazy and undeveloped; it is subordinated to the more general evil of "egotistic desire,"[19] so that ignorance rather than perversion of will remains the fundamental evil,[20] and liberation is not so much from sin as from the human condition as such.

The "problem" for Hinduism may then be stated summarily: ignorance (*avidyā*) causes "I-making" (*ahaṁkāra*), or egoism, the mistaking of the phenomenal self for an ultimate reality; this in turn produces desire (*kāma*), leading to actions which have necessary and unavoidable consequences (*karma*); this chain of acts and consequences produces bondage to empirical existence in a wheel of rebirth (*saṁsāra*).

With regard to the "solution," while all Hindu systems agree that salvation consists in the human spirit's attaining its true status,[21] there is a basic divergence in the conception of *moksha* between the "absolutist" and the theistic forms of Hinduism. The former represents the view of humanity, reality, and salvation contained in the majority of texts of the *Upanishads* and developed by the philosophical commentary ("Vedanta") of the Advaita school. Upanishadic soteriology is above all intellectualist; it is centered on the overcoming of the blindness of *avidyā* (ignorance) by insight into the true nature of the Self, *ātman*. This true nature is the identity of *ātman* with *Brahman*, the ultimate reality:

> He who consists of the mind, whose body is subtle, whose form is light, whose thoughts are true, whose nature is like the ether, whose creation is this universe, who cherishes all righteous desires, who contains all pleasant odors, who is endowed with all tastes, who embraces all this, who never speaks, and who is without longing—He is my Self within the heart, smaller than a grain of rice, smaller than a grain of barley, smaller than a mustard seed, smaller than a grain of millet; He is my Self within the heart, greater than the earth, greater than the mid-region, greater than heaven, greater than all these worlds. . . . He is my Self within the heart, He is that Brahman. (*Chhāndogya Upanishad*, III. xiv. 2–4).[22]

Salvation consists in the realization of the identity of the true Self with an Absolute in which there is no duality, individuality, or time, an absolute stasis in pure consciousness and bliss.[23]

In theory, the final absolute status of the Self may be interpreted in a pluralist or a "monist" (non-dualist) way. For the Sāṁkhya school and its practical counterpart, Yoga, the process of disengagement from bondage leads to the freeing of the spiritual subject from matter; it attains to pure consciousness, without objects, silent, alone, peaceful, and eternal.[24] An infinite number of such self-subsistent monads exists eternally, with no communion between them. In practice, however, the Sāṁkhya school, along with Yoga, has been absorbed into the Vedānta. The indestructible life-monad is interpreted as a particle of the one Brahman, essentially identical with it.

> Thus, with one bold stroke, the transcendental monism of the Vedic Brāhman doctrine of the Self is reconciled with the pluralistic life-monad doctrine of the dualistic, atheistic Sāṅkhya; and so the two teach-

ings now are understood in India as descriptions from two points of view of the same reality.[25]

For "absolutist" Hinduism, *moksha* consists in the overcoming of the illusion of *mâyâ;* it is not a moral accomplishment in or through history, for the reality of salvation is present *always;* its realization is like waking from a dream.[26] All that is needed is the putting aside of the illusion of individual selfhood; one then realizes that *âtman* is identical with universal *Brahman*. The primary means of attaining this insight is through asceticism (which is nothing but the *practice* of the conviction that the empirical world is "unreal"). The ideal is to become a *yogin* or *yati* (= ascetic). Salvation is self-conquest; the only savior is one's Self.[27]

[The "gods" in the Sâmkhya system are merely "highly favored beings" who live in delight; for this very reason they are not transcendent, but involved in *samsâra*, and are inferior to the accomplished *yogin*.[28] The Yoga school sometimes encourages devotion to Îśvara, the personal God, who is regarded as a special "soul" or monad, but this is merely a means to attain concentration.[29] The non-dualist Vedânta also condones such devotion as a means; but it is regarded as an inferior way, still within the bounds of illusion, for those who are unable to tread the path of knowledge.[30]]

While the "absolutist" Upanishadic tradition, especially as interpreted by the Advaita Vedânta, has had enormous influence in philosophy (and is not infrequently what Westerners identify simply as "Hinduism"), it is far from being the prevailing Hindu view of salvation. As S. G. F. Brandon notes:

> If Hinduism thus contains what is probably the most thorough-going and sustained attempt to provide a working philosophy of life in which the individual is directed to work out his own salvation mainly by intellectual effort, it also affords the most significant proof of the inability of such a discipline to meet the spiritual needs of the average man.[31]

From the first or second century B.C., largely in response to the challenge posed by Buddhism,[32] the *bhakti-mârga*, or "path of devotion" (i.e., to a personal God), continually increased in importance. From at least the twelfth century, it has been the central current of Hinduism.[33] The *bhakti* movement sees *moksha* as escape from the world of rebirth by union with God—usually Vishnu (frequently in his appearance as Krishna) or Śiva, understood as the one transcendent God.

The theistic interpretation of salvation accepts the Upanishadic state-

ment that *âtman* and *Brahman* are one; but it takes this to mean that the
individual human soul is an emanation from God, of the same "essence,"
but having a separate conscious existence and being indestructible.[34]
Theistic Hinduism likewise devalues the world as being evanescent; it is
mâyâ in the sense of not being the *ultimate* reality. Nevertheless Hindu
theism rejects the idea of the world's complete falsity. Still, what separates
Śaṅkara, for example, from the theists is not so much his view of *mâyâ* (for
as we have seen, Śaṅkara holds that the world is not Being, but neither is
it absolutely non-being; it is what Western philosophy calls contingent
being). It is rather his contention that there is no distinction between the
liberated soul and the Absolute (or *Îśvara, as* the Absolute).[35] For the
theists, even in divinization the soul is not annihilated, but remains in loving relation to God.[36] This means that for the theist, being in the world
takes on value, for it is the sphere of striving toward God. The theistic
interpretation of *moksha* affirms the reality of freedom, love, personality,
community, history, and moral obligation, because they are the means of
relating to the Lord and thus attaining liberation.

It is in the *Śvetâśvatara Upanishad* that there emerges for the first
time a personal God who is superior both to the world and to the changeless eternal Reality of *Brahman-Nirvâna*[37] (the latter term having evolved
under the influence of Buddhism). The high point in the scriptural revelation of the transcendent personal God, however, occurs in the *Bhagavad-Gîtâ*, which for this reason in R. C. Zaehner's estimation "ranks as the
most significant sacred text in the whole history of religions."[38] While the
Sâṃkhya-Yoga and Advaita schools teach that devotion to *Îśvara* is a lower
way to transcendence, the *Gîtâ* teaches exactly the opposite:[39]

> Beyond the Unmanifest [the primal Nature of the Sâṃkhya system]
> there is another Unmanifest [masculine gender]; this is He who does not
> fall to ruin when all contingent beings are destroyed.
>
> Unmanifest is He, surnamed "Imperishable" [i.e., Brahman]: this,
> men say, is the highest way and, this once won, there is no more re-
> turning: this is my highest home.
>
> But that highest Person is to be won by love-and-worship (*bhakti*)
> directed to none other. In Him so all beings subsist; by Him this uni-
> verse is spun (8:20–22).[40]

When Arjuna explicitly asks which are spiritually higher, those who
serve God or those who revere the Imperishable Unmanifest, Krishna (the
human manifestation of Vishnu, the supreme God) answers:

> Those I deem to be most integrated who fix their thoughts on Me and
> serve Me, ever integrated, filled with the highest faith (*śraddha,* =
> trust, confidence).

But those who revere the indeterminate Imperishable Unmanifest, unthinkable though coursing everywhere, sublime, aloof, unmoving, firm,
     who hold in check the complex of the senses, in all things equal-minded, taking pleasure in the weal of all contingent beings, these too attain to Me (12:2–4).

Krishna, for the *Gîtâ,* is both identical with and above *Brahman,* the Absolute.[41] The goal of the Self "becoming *Brahman,*" attaining *Brahma-nirvâna,* is taken for granted; but this is not the ultimate goal.[42] Beyond these (and *a fortiori* beyond the lower union with the gods in "heaven," which remains on the level of *karma*[43]) is a participation in God's mode of existence:

By worship-of-love (*bhakti*) addressed to Me, none other, Arjuna, can I be known and seen in such a form as I really am: so can my lovers enter into Me (BG 11:54; *cf.* 6:29; 18:55, 65).

For the theist, this goal is far beyond any melting into the undifferentiated One; and Râmânuja dismisses the selfish cultivation of one's own soul as "fit only for those who do not know how to love."[44]
     For Hindu theism, God is not only the goal but also the agent of salvation. Only he can bring the human person to knowledge and union with himself. He does so by revealing himself and his love (BG 18:64–66) and by bestowing His grace (*prasâda*) (BG 18:56, 58). For many Hindus of the Vaisnava (worship of Vishnu) tradition, the supreme revelation takes place in the *avatâra* or human manifestation of God in Krishna. The worship of Śiva as supreme God recognizes no "incarnate" form, but developed (particularly in south India) a powerful love mysticism. The chief means of salvation is the realization of God's love for humanity and the human self-surrender in return:

The ignorant think that love and God are two
different things; they do not know that love is God.
After knowing that love is God,
they remain possessed of love which is God.[45]
The Lord is love; he forms the body of love outside.
He is love before and after his actions outside;
as the Lord of mystics, he resides within love;
the supreme Real; He is the help of those who love Him.[46]

The reaction of humanity to God's self-revelation of love is *bhakti,* loving devotion, and *śraddha,* faith. (The followers of Râmânuja, the chief philosophical theorist of theistic Hinduism, divided on the question of grace and works. The "monkey school" held that God alone saves, but man must do his part—just as the mother monkey saves her children from danger by carrying them on her back; but they must hang on to her as she jumps. The "cat school" held that man's position is analogous rather to the kitten, which must simply go limp to be carried in its mother's mouth.[47])

In general, the *bhakti-mârga* (path of devotion), although it is supreme, is expected to involve also the way of knowledge (*jñâna-mârga*) and the way of action (*karma-mârga*). The latter involves fulfilling the duties of one's caste, for this is *dharma*, right order. In the *Bhagavad-Gîtâ* Krishna does not eliminate the caste system (as Buddhism did, at least in principle), but reaffirms it; but in contrast to the Upanishads, theistic Hinduism did offer salvation in this life (i.e., without having to be reborn in a higher state) to women and to the lowest castes.[48]

Hînayâna Buddhism

Hînayâna Buddhism[49] is the form of the Buddhist tradition which represents the closest link with the early forms of Buddhism and with the historical Buddha, and is the religion of modern Sri Lanka and most of Southeast Asia (Burma, Thailand, Cambodia, Laos; Vietnam follows the Mahâyâna tradition).

For all Buddhists, but especially for the Hînayâna, the life of the Buddha constitutes an indispensable starting point. Although all the written biographical sources date from some five hundred years after the Buddha's death, and are compilations which mix legend and myth with historical recollections, a basic factual outline may be gleaned from them. Gautama (a brahmin clan name) Siddhârtha (his given name: "he whose aim is accomplished") Śâkyamuni (sage of the Śâkya tribe) lived, according to modern scholars, between 563 and 483 B.C.[50] in northern India (or perhaps Nepal). He was born of a noble family and spent his youth in luxury. At the age of twenty-nine he had a conversion experience (precipitated, according to the legends, by encounters with old age, disease, and death) and made his "great renunciation." Leaving home and family, he studied meditation and performed austerities. He found these of no avail, however, and left his companion ascetics. He journeyed to Gaya in present-day Bihar and there, seated under a Bo tree in meditation, he received enlightenment in the year 528 B.C. From this point on he was an Arhat ("worthy one"), the Tathâgata ("the one who has attained thus-ness") and the Buddha ("the enlightened one"). For the remaining forty-five years of his life, he dedicated himself to teaching the way to nirvâna. He had many disciples, whom he organized into a monastic community (the Saṁgha).

At the age of eighty, he died and, in accord with his teachings, definitively entered nirvâna.

The core of the Buddha's message is explicitly (and indeed exclusively) concerned with the human problem and its solution. He calls his solution the Middle Way, because it avoids the extremes of the pursuit of pleasures, on the one hand, and painful asceticism on the other:

> There are two ends not to be served by a wanderer; What are these two? The pursuit of desires and of the pleasure which springs from desire, which is base, common, leading to rebirth, ignoble, and unprofitable; and the pursuit of pain and hardship, which is grievous, ignoble, and unprofitable. The Middle Way of the Tathâgata avoids both these ends. It is enlightened, it brings clear vision, it makes for wisdom, and leads to peace, insight, enlightenment, and Nirvâna (*Samyutta Nikâya*, 5.421ff).[51]

While it is not possible to isolate the original doctrines of Gautama from later additions and interpretations, so as to formulate an archaic Buddhism,[52] scholars believe that we may safely attribute to the historical Buddha at least the sayings known as the Four Holy Truths, which are the foundation of the whole of Buddhist teaching.[53] These truths set forth the fact of suffering or sorrow (*duhkha;* Pâli *dukkha*);[54] its source; the solution; and the way of achieving that solution:

> This is the Noble Truth of Sorrow. Birth is sorrow, age is sorrow, disease is sorrow, death is sorrow; contact with the unpleasant is sorrow, separation from the pleasant is sorrow, every wish unfulfilled is sorrow—in short all the five components of individuality[55] are sorrow.

> And this is the Noble Truth of the arising of sorrow. It arises from craving, which leads to rebirth, which brings delight and passion, and seeks pleasure now here, now there—the craving for sensual pleasure, the craving for continued life, the craving for power.

> And this is the Noble Truth of the stopping of sorrow. It is the complete stopping of that craving, so that no passion remains, leaving it, being emancipated from it, being released from it, giving no place to it.

> And this is the Noble Truth of the Way which leads to the stopping of sorrow. It is the Noble Eightfold Path—right views, right resolve, right speech, right conduct, right livelihood, right effort, right mindfulness, and right concentration (*Samyutta Nikâya, loc. cit.*).

The elements of the Eightfold Path are traditionally divided into three groups (the "Threefold Training"): wisdom (*prajña*) = right views and right resolve or intention; morality (*śîla*) = right speech, right conduct, right livelihood; concentration (*samâdhi*) = right effort, right mindfulness, right concentration.

Also thought to stem from the Buddha is the analysis of the interdependent causes of bondage to the world of *samsâra*. This Buddhist expansion of the theory of *karma*, the law of moral cause and effect, is called the circle of "inter-dependent co-arising" (*pratîtya-samutpâda*):[56]

> Ignorance is the cause of the psychic constructions; hence is caused consciousness; hence physical form; hence the six senses; hence contact; hence sensations; hence craving; hence attachment; hence becoming; hence rebirth; hence old age and death with all the distraction of grief and lamentation, sorrow and despair. This is the arising of the whole body of ill (*Majjhima Nikâya*, 1.256ff).

Since aging and dying in turn cause ignorance, the twelve preconditions (*nidâna*) of dependent co-arising form a wheel, the wheel of life, the eternal circle of bondage to *samsâra*.

The Buddha concludes that the principal causes of bondage to suffering are craving or desire (*tṛshṇâ*) for life, and the ignorance (*avidyâ*) that ultimately gives rise to it. The radical cure, then, is the elimination of all desire by means of the knowledge of the Four Noble Truths.

There are three important developments of the Buddha's teaching which are crucial to the Hînayâna view of the problem of salvation and its solution. On the cosmological level, there is the doctrine of impermanence (*anitya;* Pâli *anicca*); on the anthropological level, the doctrine of "no soul" or "no self" (*anâtma;* Pâli *anatta*); on the theological level, Hînayâna atheism.

The doctrine of impermanence (*anitya* from *a-* = not, *nitya* = constant, perpetual, eternal; hence *anitya* = transient, temporary, uncertain) stems from the Buddha's insight into the nature of *samsâra* and the "interdependent co-arising" of all things. It is attributed to the Buddha in the Pâli scriptures:

> Whether Buddhas arise, O monks, or whether Buddhas do not arise, it remains a fact and the fixed and necessary constitution of being, that all its constituents are transitory [*anitya*] (*Aṅguttara-Nikâya*, 3.134).

> Impermanent, alas! are all compound things. Their nature is to rise and fall. When they have risen they cease (*Digha-Nikâya*, 2.198).[57]

Anitya means simply that the world is constantly and completely changing; there are no permanent "substances" or beings in it. This doctrine has several important consequences. First, it is the source of the doctrines of *anâtma* and atheism, which we shall consider shortly. Second, it leads to an epistemological nominalism: since there are no real or permanent substances in the world, the names we use are only useful conventions to designate the presence of certain "constituent parts" (which themselves are changing); they do not "refer" to any real *thing*.[58] Third, *anitya* leads to craving or desire, for we wish for permanence and being, and hence cling to things; this in turn leads to universal suffering (*duḥkha*), since nothing in the world is permanent or can satisfy us. Fourth, the impermanence of the world leads us to seek *nirvâṇa* (Pâli *nibbâna*), an escape from the transient and impermanent world of suffering.[59]

The notion of *anitya* immediately implies the absence of any real "self" or soul in man:

> Whether Buddhas arise, O monks, or whether Buddhas do not arise, it remains a fact and the fixed and necessary constitution of being, that all its elements are lacking in a self. This fact a Buddha discovers and masters, and when he has discovered and mastered it, he announces, teaches, publishes, proclaims, discloses, minutely explains, and makes it clear, that all the elements of being are lacking in a self (*Anguttara-Nikâya* 3.134).[60]

Of course we must speak of the "self," but this is simply a convention to indicate the presence of certain conjoined phenomena, namely the five *skandhas* (Pâli *khandas*): body, sensations, perceptions, psychological dispositions, and consciousness.[61] There is no "self" or "soul" to be found apart from or "behind" these conjoined phenomena.

The Hînayâna *anâtmâ* doctrine seems to intend to deny (1) that the phenomenal "ego" (with its cravings and illusions) is ultimately real, (2) that there is a "soul" or *âtman*, conceived in a dualistic manner (as it seems to be in Upanishadic Hinduism) as something unchanging and permanent, unconditioned, separate from and behind the phenomena of worldly selfhood, and (3) that any finite thing exists *in itself*, i.e., independent of the rest of reality (like the monads of the Sâmkhya system). On the other hand, it would seem that the *anâtmâ* doctrine is not to be understood as a simple phenomenalism in the manner of David Hume; for the Hînayâna, despite its polemics against the idea of the "self," implicitly affirms a genuine spiritual reality in man which is the "subject" of ethics and which enters *nirvâna*. One early Hînayâna school, the *Pudgalavâda* ("Personalists") explicitly held that there exists a "person" (*pudgala*) who is neither identical with nor different from the five *skandhas* (somewhat as Aristotle's "soul" is neither identical with nor separable from prime matter), who is the subject of knowledge, who is reborn, and who enters *nirvâna*.[62] Although this doctrine was judged unorthodox by the conservative Theravâda school, it shows that many early Buddhists were not content with a completely negative doctrine. Even the orthodox tradition explicitly denied that the dispersal of the *skandhas* (either at death or on entering *nirvâna*) constitutes annihilation[63]—although they were unwilling to say exactly *what* is not annihilated. Furthermore, orthodox theory holds that the phenomena of human psyche and consciousness are held together by a mysterious (and real) force, *prâpti*, to form a pattern (*samtâna*) which marks them as belonging to a particular "self." As A. L. Herman points out, it is difficult to see how this differs, except verbally, from the affirmation of a real substantial self:

> What more could one ask for in such a psychology than to have an individuating principle, the samtâna of patterned desires, together with a force that keeps the pattern in existence as traces capable of being recollected through memory? . . . The Hînayâna doctrine of self as a process comes perilously close to the Pudgalavâda doctrine of self as a person.[64]

We may take the Hînayâna position, then, as a polemic against egotism and dualism, but an implicit affirmation of the reality of a spiritual principle in man. (This affirmation will become more explicit in the Mahâyâna.)

Another consequence of the *anitya* doctrine is Hînayâna "atheism." Early Buddhism presents a doctrine of salvation in which God or the gods do not figure at all.[65] Modern historical scholarship, as well as knowledge of living Buddhism, however, shows that the nineteenth-century scholars who thought they had found there a purely rational, utilitarian and godless approach to life were mistaken.[66]

The word "God" may be used in at least three senses: (1) personified forces or powers of the world: the gods of polytheism; (2) the personal creator of the world: Hindu *Brahmâ* (masculine); (3) the transcendent ground of existence, whether conceived as personal, impersonal, or supra-personal: Hindu *Brahman* (neuter). Hînayâna Buddhism takes for granted the existence of the Hindu gods; they are, however, irrelevant to the attainment of nirvâna, and, being themselves involved in *samsâra*, are inferior to a human *arahant*. Hînayâna Buddhism is an "anthropocentric" religion in holding that nirvâna can be achieved only by a human being. The gods are highly placed in the round of reincarnation, but in order to achieve *nirvâna* they must be reborn as humans. For the same reason the Hînayâna is not interested in the personal creator, Brahmâ. In this sense it is "atheistic"—in the context of early Hindu popular theism.

It could not be said, however, that Buddhism denies God in the third sense: a transcendent Absolute. As Geoffrey Parrinder notes, "It used to be maintained that early Buddhism was atheistic, but it is now realized that there was no generally accepted belief in a supreme God for the Buddha to deny."[67] The Buddha apparently gave no consideration to the metaphysical notion of Brahman developed in the Upanishads.[68] On the other hand, early Buddhist texts speak of "becoming Brahman" as a synonym for liberation into *nirvâna*.[69] Thus the "atheism" of the Hînayâna is rather a denial of the relevance of the polytheistic pantheon than a rejection of the Absolute.[70]

At the same time, Prof. Conze perhaps goes a bit too far in claiming that "when we compare the attributes of the Godhead as they are understood by the more mystical tradition of Christian thought, with those of Nirvana, we find almost no difference at all";[71] for there is no hint of a personal or dialogical relation with *nirvâna a fortiori*, there is no conception of divine "intervention" to aid us to salvation.

The "solution" in the Hînayâna tradition is presented conceptually in a negative way. "*Nirvâna*" (*nibbana*) itself signifies "blown out" or "extinguished," like a flame:[72] "the going out (*nibbana*) of the lamp itself was the deliverance of the mind" (*Therîgâtha*, 116; *Dîgha-nikâya* II, 157); "the steadfast go out (*nibbanti*) like this lamp" (*Suttanipâta*, 235).[73] But this statement must be understood in the light of the pre-scientific physical conceptions of the time. "Fire" was thought to be an element, indistinct but latent in all things, especially in those used for fuel. When burning, it is in a state of manifestation; when "blown out," it "goes home" to its primal unmanifest state.[74] Therefore Buddhists insisted from the beginning that "extinction" is not the same as "annihilation," even though it means a disappearance from the phenomenal world. The one who has entered *nirvâna* may be spoken of as having "gone home":

> "What do you think about this, sire? When some flame in a great burning mass of fire goes out, is it possible to point to the flame as being either here or there?"
> "No, reverend sir. That flame has ceased to be, it has disappeared." [Literally, "it cannot be designated"; "it has gone to non-designability."]
> "Even so, sire, the Lord has attained Nirvana. . . . The Lord has gone home. It is not possible to point to him as being here or there" (*Milindapañha*, 70–73).[75]

Nirvâna means true spiritual happiness, but absolutely unconditioned—that is, not dependent upon states of mind or any causes whatever.[76] The condition of the *Tathâgata*, therefore, seems to be parallel to what the Upanishads describe as the union of *âtman* with *Brahman*. For this reason, it cannot really be spoken of; for all our categories, including selfhood and even existence and non-existence, stem from and refer to *saṃsâra*, the world of "interdependent co-arising." The Hînayâna tradition emphasizes the absolute transcendence of *nirvâna*; it is not "immanent" in the world of *saṃsâra*.[77] "None of what is here can be carried over there."[78] *Nirvâna* is therefore ineffable.

This is one reason why the *dharma* is presented in the Hînayâna tradition as a practical message rather than a conceptual or dogmatic one. The Buddha aims at liberation, and does not speculate on metaphysical matters which do not immediately lead to it. In the famous "parable of the arrow" (*Majjhima-nikâya* I, 426ff) the Buddha pictures the person engaged in metaphysical questioning as one who has been shot with a poisoned arrow, but who refuses to have the wound attended before finding out who shot the arrow, what it is made of, where the materials came from, and dozens of other things. Such a person, says the Buddha, will die. Better simply to attend to removing the arrow. This is what the Buddha's doctrine does; it tells us what the problem is and how to reach its solution, *nirvâna*; it leaves aside all that is not "useful" for this goal.

Theoretically, *nirvâna* can be attained even during life. The Buddha has entered into *nirvâna* "without basis"—at death, he was liberated from all conditions and becoming whatsoever. But even in life one may experience *nirvâna* "with the basis still remaining": i.e., all attachments to the world are cut off, but one still experiences the world through the senses.[79] It appears that in early Buddhism it was expected that upon hearing the *dharma* one could become an *arahant* immediately and easily within one's lifetime; as the tradition developed, however, the ideal was thought more and more difficult to attain, so that it would ordinarily require a long series of rebirths.[80] This in turn has led, in Buddhism as in Hinduism, to a double conception of salvation, with a more immediate as well as an ultimate goal. Theoretically, the goal is *nirvâna*, but in practice most modern Theravâda Buddhists (even among the monks) hope rather by accumulating good *karma* to attain a happy rebirth in this world.[81]

There is also a certain ambiguity about the place of the Buddha as "savior" in the Hînayâna. In theory, it is up to each individual to attain *nirvâna* alone. The Venerable Walpola Rahula, head of the *Saṅgha* in Sri Lanka, writes:

> A man has the power to liberate himself from all bondage through his own personal effort and intelligence. . . . If the Buddha is to be called a "savior" at all, it is only in the sense that he discovered and showed the Path to Liberation, Nirvâna. But we must tread the path our-

selves. . . . According to the Buddha, man's emancipation depends on his own realization of the Truth, and not on the benevolent grace of a god or any external power as a reward for his obedient behavior.[82]

This statement reflects the teaching of the scriptural texts:

You yourself must make the effort; the Tathâgatas do but point the way (*Dhammapada*, 276).

Everyone is his own protector; what other protector could there be? (*Dhammapada*, 160).

Dwell in such a way that you are an island and a refuge to yourselves, and do not seek any other refuge (Dîganikâya).[83]

Yet the first step toward salvation must be faith in the Buddha as the revealer of the *dharma;* only Buddhas attain enlightenment without receiving the *dharma*-message from another, and later theory holds that even they must have heard it in earlier lives from another Buddha.[84] All forms of Hînayâna Buddhism hold that guides are necessary, and every Buddhist takes "refuge" in the Buddha and the *Saṅgha* (community), as well as the *dharma*. Within two hundred years of the Buddha's death, the Mahâsâṅghika school was attributing to him super-human attributes; while even within the orthodox Theravâda he is called *Bhagavad* (= Lord; the title by which Hindu *bhaktas* call the personal God) and *devâtideva* (god above gods);[85] and even the oldest Pâli texts endow him with qualities like omniscience and infallibility which are considered divine in the monotheistic religions. In practice, his followers seek not only *nirvâṇa,* but union with the Buddha himself.[86] Even if those are right who consider "original" Buddhism to have been a philosophy of life, there can be no doubt that Hînayâna today is religious in its attitudes and practices.

With regard to the means toward salvation, it is clear that although Hînayâna Buddhism has a number of theoretical similarities to non-dualist Hinduism, it is in the concrete much less a religion of "repose" than the latter. It is true that attaining *nirvâṇa* is ultimately a matter of intellectual illumination or wisdom, and therefore depends upon the practice of meditation and mental transcending of the world. Buddhist meditation ("right concentration"), however, is built upon a practical program of right-mindfulness, which implies a thorough knowledge of the world of *karma*.[87] For the Buddha, knowledge of the problem is essential to arriving at the solution. Furthermore, the entire training in concentration depends upon knowing the right way and practicing morality. The Buddha's eightfold path gives a practical method of striving toward salvation, in which conduct and the taming of desire (but without the extremes of asceticism, which the Buddha rejected) play an important part.

Moreover, the Pâli canon states unambiguously that the Buddha's motive in teaching *dharma* was compassion—even if this creates some theoretical difficulties with the doctrine of the ultimate insubstantiality of all selves, with the need to extirpate all connection with *saṁsâra*, and with the command to self-reliance. His followers are exhorted to follow him in this compassionate attitude toward all things. (For the Mahâyâna, as we shall shortly see, this becomes the crucial turning point of an entirely new doctrine.) Practically, the doctrine of salvation by enlightenment following upon right conduct opened up the way for Buddhism's break with the caste system and for the admission of women to the *Sangha*.[88]

Finally, Hînayâna Buddhism is a highly anthropocentric religion. Despite the doctrine of rebirth (which may take place in the realm of the animals or the gods), human destiny and action has the central place, for it is only as a human being that one can practice virtue and acquire wisdom, and so become an *arahant*. (Even those who attain *nirvâna* from the heaven of the gods can only do so on the basis of their merit as human beings in previous lives.[89])

Mahâyâna Buddhism

Buddhism arose as a way which emphasized self-reliance, and retains much of its early emphasis in the surviving Theravâda form of Hînayâna. In its major developments, however, it was quickly transformed from a fairly austere philosophy of life, centered on monasticism, to a widespread lay religion with intense devotion to a merciful Savior, so that van der Leeuw characterizes the Mahâyâna[90] form of Buddhism as the "religion of compassion."[91]

We have seen already that the devotional movement called *bhakti* was beginning to take hold in India two centuries before the birth of Christ. This same movement which created Hinduism as we now know it was also a major influence in the transformation of Buddhism.[92] Already by two centuries after the Buddha's death the Mahâsângika sect was exalting him to a kind of divine status. Contrary to the "orthodox" doctrine which held that Buddha was essentially an ordinary human being who had achieved the ultimate state, the Mahâsângikas proclaimed that he had an infinite "body" and endless life and power, that his activity did not cease upon his entry into *nirvâna* but that he educates tirelessly, and that he creates "manifestation bodies" which appear in different worlds at the same time.[93] From these ideas, combined with the increasing power of the *bhakti* movement and—according to some scholars—the influence of

Greek thought *via* Iran, the Mahâyâna developed. This school was to become the major form of Buddhism in northern Asia, and in its spread through China, Tibet, and Japan it would eventually absorb many elements from non-Indian sources—especially from Taoism in China—to produce later forms (Zen and Tantric Buddhism) even farther removed from the original orthodoxy.

It is first of all the scriptural canon which decisively divides the Mahâyâna from the Hînayâna. The former accepts as canonical a number of *Sûtras* written or redacted (in Sanskrit)[94] between 100 B.C. and 600 A.D. which claim to expound a "secret doctrine" given by the Buddha himself but hidden until it could be favorably received. (This is quite contrary to the doctrine of the Pâli scriptures, in which the Buddha explicitly states that he teaches everything openly and to all, and denies that he holds anything back.[95])

These doctrines announce a new and higher way to *nirvâna* (indeed, a higher form of *nirvâna*) than that of the *arhat:* the way of the *bodhisattva*, the being (*sattva*) of enlightenment (*bodhi*). The *bodhisattva* is one who has determined not merely to follow the Buddha, but himself or herself (for *bodhisattvas* can be female) to become a Buddha, and, furthermore, who has vowed not to enter *nirvâna* until all other beings have been led to *nirvâna* as well.

The Mahâyâna agrees with the Hînayâna in the fundamental conception of the problem (*samsâra*) and its ultimate solution (*nirvâna*), but the explication of the human situation that produces the problem (anthropology and cosmology) and of the way to attain the ultimate goal (theology and soteriology) differs considerably.[96] A quotation from the beginning of one of the great Mahâyâna scriptures, the *Lotus Sûtra* (*Saddharma-Pundarîka:* "the lotus of the true teaching [*dharma*]"), composed some time in the first century A.D., will give some indication of the profound nature of the difference. The Lord Buddha in this passage addresses his disciple Sâriputra (who was noted for his wisdom)[97] in the presence of a vast throng of *arhats* and other disciples:

> By means of one sole vehicle, to wit, the Buddha-vehicle, Sâriputra, do I teach creatures the law; there is no second vehicle, nor a third. This is the nature of the law, Sâriputra, universally in the world, in all directions. . . . And those creatures, Sâriputra, who now are hearing the law from me, shall all of them reach supreme, perfect enlightenment. In this sense, Sâriputra, it must be understood that nowhere in the world a second vehicle is taught, far less a third.
>
> Yet, Sâriputra, when the Tathâgatas . . . happen to appear at the decay of the epoch, the decay of creatures, the decay of besetting sins, the decay of views, or the decay of lifetime; when they appear amid such

signs of decay at the disturbance of the epoch; when creatures are much tainted, full of greed and poor in roots of goodness; then, Sâriputra, the Tathâgatas . . . use, skillfully, to designate that one and sole Buddha-vehicle by the appellation of the threefold vehicle. Now, Sâriputra, such disciples, Arhats, or Pratyekabuddhas who do not hear their actually being called to the Buddha-vehicle by the Tathâgata, who do not perceive, nor heed it, those Sâriputra, should not be acknowledged as disciples of the Tathâgata, nor as Arhats, nor as Pratyekabuddhas. . . .

The Chief of the world appears in the world to reveal the Buddha-knowledge. He has but one aim, indeed, no second; the Buddhas do not bring over (creatures) by an inferior vehicle. . . .

It is but my skillfullness which prompts me to manifest three vehicles . . . for men (occasionally) have low inclinations, and might perchance not believe (us when we say), Ye shall become Buddhas. . . .[98]

As we have seen, to become an *arhat* was the ideal of the Hînayâna. To this was added the notion of the *Pratyekabuddha* ("private Buddha"), those who attained enlightenment alone. In this passage, however, the Buddha condemns the *arhat* ideal. There is in reality only one way to supreme *nirvâna:* the way of the *bodhisattva*, i.e., the one who will become a Buddha. The teaching of the way of becoming an *arhat* is now called "an inferior vehicle"; it was taught by the (historical) Buddha only because people were so degraded that they could not understand the true way. (This is an example of the important Mahâyâna concept of "skill in means" [*upâya* = approach, expedient, stratagem]: the Buddha or his disciple adapts the message to the capacities of the hearers; he uses whatever means will work to effect conversion on whatever level possible.)

The *Lotus Sûtra* tells us that five thousand monks, nuns, and lay devotees, all *arhats*, were too proud to hear the Buddha's new message and left the assembly, whereupon he states:

My congregation, Sâriputra, has been cleared from the chaff, freed from trash; it is firmly established in the strength of faith. It is good, Sâriputra, that those proud ones are gone away.[99]

So is the Hînayâna dismissed.

The new ideal proposed by the Mahâyâna *sûtras* is that of the *bodhisattva*. This term had already existed in the Hînayâna, meaning simply one who is destined for eventual enlightenment. In the Mahâyâna, however, it comes to mean a future Buddha ("enlightened one") who reaches perfection but who, driven by compassion, purposely *puts off* entry into *nirvâna* in order to aid other beings to salvation. It is this selfless compassion for all beings which makes the *bodhisattva* superior to the *arhat* and brings him to the true *nirvâna:*[100]

The Lord: "What do you think, Sâriputra, does it occur to any of the Disciples and Pratyekabuddhas to think that 'after we have known full enlightenment, we should lead all beings to Nirvâṇa, into the realm of Nirvâṇa which leaves nothing behind'?"

Sâriputra: "No indeed, Lord."

The Lord: "One should therefore know that this wisdom of the Disciples and Pratyekabuddhas bears no comparison with the wisdom of a Bodhisattva. What do you think, Sâriputra, does it occur to any of the Disciples and Pratyekabuddhas that 'after I have practiced the six perfections,[101] have brought beings to maturity, have purified the Buddha-field, have fully gained the ten powers of a Tathâgata. . . after I have known full enlightenment, I shall lead countless beings to Nirvâṇa'?"

Sâriputra: "No, O Lord."

The Lord: "But such are the intentions of a Bodhisattva . . ." (Pañcaviṁśatisâhasrikâ 40–41).[102]

The *bodhisattva*, having arrived at perfection and complete knowledge, sees the misery of countless beings on the plane of *saṁsâra* and determines: "I shall become a savior to all those beings, I shall release them from all their sufferings" (*Ashtasâhasrikâ*, XXII, 402–404).

The means by which the *bodhisattva* saves is the creation of a "Pure Land" or heaven into which creatures are reborn, and from which they can attain *nirvâṇa* without further rebirth (in this the Pure Lands differ from the heavens of the gods). Devotees reach this heaven by means of the *bodhisattva*'s "grace": the *bodhisattva* bestows on the faithful the merit (*punya*) which the *bodhisattva* has gained by spiritual acts.

The doctrine of the "turning over" (*parinâmanâ*) of merit is remarkable in that it seems to contradict the law of *karma*, or at least to hold that there is a more powerful *karma* which can overcome the earthly form.[103] Mahâyâna theory explains that the *bodhisattva* reaches a stage where there is no longer any proportion between acts and the merit they acquire; the good *karma* of truly spiritual acts has no limit. At the same time, when the highest stages of the *bodhisattva* career are reached, the *bodhisattva* has no personal need of merit, as pure disinterested acts have no karmic effect; thus the *bodhisattva*'s inconceivable merit is "stored" to be dedicated to others.[104]

The *bhakta*, or devotee, must have faith in the *bodhisattva* and desire to be reborn in his or her Pure Land kingdom. Faith in the *bodhisattva* is in continuity with the Buddhist ideal of driving out egotism; for faith eliminates all self-reliance, and absolute dedication—aided by the *bodhisattva*'s wonder working power to transform minds[105]—is meant to produce a new self.[106] (It is notable, however, that here salvation is achieved not by the extirpation of all desire and attachment, but by love and longing.[107]

There is some dispute in theory over whether salvation requires good works as well as faith; Indian Mahâyâna tended to presume that moral conversion and conduct are necessary, while the most extreme form of Pure Land Buddhism in Japan preaches salvation through faith, regardless of conduct.[108]

The doctrine of the Pure Lands accompanies an enormous expansion of Buddhist cosmology. Early Buddhism had an anthropocentric view: the earth with its four continents and assorted heavens and hells above and below, was the center of the single universe. Mahâyâna teaching, however, now held that just the *immediate* universe is composed of one billion such worlds, and that this universe is only one among universes "as numerous as the sands of the Ganges."[109]

There is a similar expansion in the objects of worship or devotion. While Hînayâna teaching had always recognized that there were other Buddhas besides Gautama, it had centered its attention on the latter as the teacher for our world. In the Mahâyâna, not only is the Buddha Gautama exalted to new heights, but he is associated with—and sometimes eclipsed by—other Buddhas and *bodhisattvas* whose earthly lives are placed in a mythological past. In India, Gautama retained preeminence until the advent of Tantrism; in China and Japan, the celestial Buddha Amitâbha (short form: Amita, whence Chinese A-mi-to, Japanese Amida) became the focus of devotion.

Among the *bodhisattvas* there are several who became the center of cult. The earliest was Maitreya, who is to be born as a Buddha in the future; as he is now in the heaven of the gods, awaiting earthly rebirth, he is available and can be prayed to (unlike Gautama, who in the early orthodox view has become "extinct" in *nirvâna*—although, as we shall see, this idea was later modified). Mañjusri is revered as a *bodhisattva* who vowed to remain in *samsâra* until *all* beings have been saved; since he will infallibly one day become a Tathâgata, it is implied that eventually every living being will be saved—"a rare eschatological statement in the Buddhist tradition."[110] Avalokitesvara (Chinese Kuan-yin, Japanese Kannon) begins as a *bodhisattva* attendant on Amitâbha, but is transformed in devotion into an omnipotent, omnipresent being. It is said that Avalokitesvara had been a Buddha in past life, but did not enter *nirvâna*—thus being superior to the Buddhas who did so. (In China, the originally male *Avalokitesvara* eventually changes sex, and Kuan-yin is revered as a female *bodhisattva*—in popular devotion, the female deity.[111])

Eventually there arose a certain confusion of the status of Buddhas and *bodhisattvas*. In theory, a *bodhisattva* is one who *will be* a Buddha, i.e., enter *nirvâna*, but has put off this final stage. But some of the texts state that *bodhisattvas*, although they remain in *samsâra* to save others, have *already* reached *nirvâna*, and have appeared as Buddhas in past lives. Even more significantly, it is claimed that Gautama the Buddha did *not* become "extinct" by entering *nirvâna*. In the *Lotus Sûtra*, Gautama states:

> "The truth is that many hundred thousand myriads of koṭis [= tens of millions] of Aeons ago I have arrived at supreme, perfect enlightenment. By way of example, young men of good family, let there be the atoms of earth of fifty hundred thousand myriads of koṭis of worlds; let there exist some man who takes one of those atoms of dust and then goes in an eastern direction fifty hundred thousand myriads of koṭis of worlds further on, there to deposit that atom of dust; let in this manner the man carry away from all those worlds the whole mass of earth, and in the same manner . . . deposit all those atoms. . . . However numerous be those worlds where that man deposits those atoms of dust and where he does not, there are not, young men of good family, in all those hundred thousands of myriads of koṭis of worlds so many dust atoms as there are a hundred thousand myriads of koṭis of Aeons since I have arrived at supreme, perfect enlightenment. . . .
>
> When, however, the Tathâgata, who so long ago arrived at perfect enlightenment, declares himself to have but lately arrived at perfect enlightenment, he does so in order to lead creatures to full ripeness and make them go in. . . .
>
> The Tathâgata who so long ago was perfectly enlightened is unlimited in the duration of his life, he is everlasting. Without being extinct, the Tathâgata makes a show of extinction, on behalf of those who have to be educated. And even now, young men of good family, I have not accomplished my ancient Bodhisattva-course, and the measure of my lifetime is not full. Nay, young men of good family, I shall yet have twice as many hundred thousand myriads of koṭis of Aeons before the measure of my lifetime be full. I announce final extinction, young men of good family, though myself I do not become finally extinct. . . . I was not completely extinct at that time; it was but a device of mine, monks; repeatedly am I born in the world of the living (*Saddharma-Puṇḍarîka*, XV).

Here we find the remarkable claims being made that the Buddha has existed, and has been in the state of Buddhahood, always (for although the language of "attaining" enlightenment is kept, the inconceivable numbers of aeons is a virtual or "material" way of saying eternity); that he is, and remains forever, a *bodhisattva*, remaining in relation to *saṁsâra* for the salvation of the world; that his apparent entry into *nirvâna* was merely an exercise in "skill in means" (*upâya*) to bring ignorant people to salvation; and that he becomes incarnate in the world repeatedly as savior! To the

Hînayâna's "ascending" Buddhology (the man Gautama is exalted to the highest sphere of being) is now added a "descending" Buddhology (the eternal Logos becomes flesh).[112]

In short, the *Lotus Sûtra*'s doctrine about the Buddha is strikingly parallel to the doctrine of Vishnu's *avatâra* proclaimed in the *Bhagavad-Gîtâ* (IV. 1–10); and it is difficult to escape the conclusion that the Buddha here is, like Vishnu, the absolute, transcendent and loving God of theism: "So am I the father of the world, the Self-born, the Healer, the Protector of all creatures" (*Saddharma-Puṇḍarîka* XV. 21; cf. *Bhagavad-Gîtâ* IX. 17, 18: "I am the father of this world, mother, ordainer . . . true home and refuge").

Despite the fact that it still avoids the word "God," which is associated with anthropomorphic and mythological ideas, the Mahâyâna acknowledges the existence of what a transcendental philosophy means by that word: the Absolute, the spiritual ground and goal of human spirit.[113] While the Hînayâna tends to be pre-theistic and trans-polytheistic, the Mahâyâna tends to be both theistic and polytheistic—and also philosophically pan(en)theistic.

The Mahâyâna explicitly affirms the existence of the Absolute (*asamoskṛta:* literally, the Unconditioned) which enters into relation with humans (see, for example, the *Diamond Sûtra*, 7).[114] It also accords divine status to the Buddha Gautama, and also to a plurality of other Buddhas and celestial *bodhisattvas*.[115] This apparent (and devotional) polytheism is reduced to metaphysical monotheism by the doctrine of the "three bodies" (*trikâya*) of the Buddha.[116] There is first the "appearance body" (*nirmâna-kâya*), the physical body of the Buddha on earth. It is a created appearance, and is "illusory" in the same way that all phenomena are (see below); but by the same token, it is as "real" as any other human body, is subject to the same physical laws and ills, and goes out of existence at death. Secondly, there is the "enjoyment body" (*sambhogakâya*): the transcendent body of the Buddha(s) in the bliss of *nirvâna*. It is beyond sensation, but can be seen by the *bodhisattvas* and can be communed with by humans. It is different in each of the Buddha heavens. Finally, and most importantly, there is the "Dharma-body" (*dharmakâya;* perhaps "Truth-body" would be a close approximation). It is the ontological origin of all the other "bodies"; it alone is ultimately Real, and is the metaphysical One; thus it is the same for all Buddhas. This is why the Lord can say in the *Lankâvatâra Sûtra*, "I am all the Buddhas of the past";[117] in the Dharma-body, the *Tathâgatas* are all one and the same; they differ only in the forms which are manifest to different beings.

One further step brings this transcendental theism to pan(en)theism: since the material world is *anitya*, impermanent and merely phenomenal, and all spiritual beings will eventually reach *nirvâṇa* and Buddhahood, it follows that in an ultimate perspective the Dharma-body is the *only* reality, and is *our* inmost nature also, which is exactly the conclusion reached by the idealist philosophies of the Mahâyâna. (It will be noted that this solution is curiously similar to the Hindu non-dualist system of Śaṅkara, in which the highest Brahman, the One, is manifest through *mâyâ* as Îśvara and as individual souls.)

We have now arrived at the second fundamental divergence of the Mahâyâna from the Hînayâna tradition, which consists in the philosophical revolution from a common-sense realism to transcendental idealism. The Mahâyâna concluded that there exists an ultimate and absolute reality, which can be known by us although it cannot be described or spoken of: this is the final "Buddha nature." The implications of this affirmation are developed in the two central Mahâyâna schools of philosophy: the Mâdhyamika (from *mâdhya*, "in the middle") and the Yogâcâra (= "practice of yoga") or Vijñaptimâtra (= "consciousness only"; from *vijñâna* = consciousness, *mâtra* = nothing but).[118] These are the complementary philosophies of "emptiness" and of Absolute Mind.

The great master of the Mâdhyamika school was the south Indian Nâgârjuna (second century A.D.). Expanding upon the doctrine of *anitya*, he used a brilliant dialectical method to show that all possible positions on the reality of the world lead to absurdity.[119] He concludes, therefore, that everything whatsoever is relative and dependent, having no reality of its own; furthermore, all human concepts (including those of the Mâdhyamika itself) are inadequate to knowing the truth. There is in reality nothing corresponding to the ideas of birth or death, annihilation or persistence in being, unity or plurality. All that we can finally say is that everything is *śûnya*, "void" or "empty"—or, in the more familiar term of Indian philosophy, all is *mâyâ*, "illusion."[120]

The doctrine of *śûnya* leads to a startling conclusion: if all is illusion, then in reality there is not only no empirical world or self, but there is no Buddha, and no *dharma*, either. Since all distinctions belong to the sphere of *mâyâ*, the distinction between bondage and liberation also falls:

> There is no difference at all
> Between *nirvâṇa* and *saṁsâra*.
> There is no difference at all
> Between *saṁsâra* and . . . .
> Between the two we cannot find
> The slightest shade of difference. . . .
> Since everything is relative,
> What is finite and what is infinite?
> What means finite and infinite at once?

What means negation of both issues?[121]
What is identity, and what is difference?
What is eternity, what non-eternity?
What means eternity and non-eternity together?
What means negation of both issues?
Bliss consists in the cessation of all thought,
In the quiescence of plurality.
No reality was preached at all,
Nowhere and none by Buddha!
(*Mâdhyamika-śastra* of Nâgârjuna, ch. XXV).[122]

Since all distinctions are relative, so is the distinction between *sam-sâra* and *nirvâna*. These are not to be thought of as two realms or realities; they are the *same* reality, from two standpoints. We must therefore not cling to any concept whatsoever: not even to those of *nirvâna*, the Buddha, *śûnyatâ* (emptiness) or relativity itself. Since we cannot know anything as real, there is nothing to grasp at; we should therefore simply "let go."[123] This insight becomes crucial to the further development of the Mahâyâna, and forms the cornerstone of Zen.

Although Hindus saw the Mâdhyamika school as a sort of nihilism, it seems rather that *śûnya* or the "Void" is rather to be seen as the Absolute, the One which transcends all thought or description[124]—the same, in fact, as the *nir-guna Brahman* of the Vedânta, which is ultimately the only Real-ity, immanent in all things. For the Mahâyâna, that Reality is the ultimate nature of the Buddha, which is also the "this-ness" or "such-ness" (*tathâtâ*) of everything:

> No coming or going of the Void is known, and that which is void is that Tathâgata. . . . For the Tathâgata is not from other things, and that which is the Suchness of these things, and that which is the Suchness of all things, and that which is the Suchness of the Tathâgata is this one Suchness. There is no duality of Suchness (*Ashtasâhasrikâ*, ch. 31).[125]

The Mâdhyamika school is primarily interested in the dialectical na-ture of our *thought* about the Absolute described in the Mahâyâna *sûtras* as the "Void." It therefore does not develop (although it presumes) the notion of the Absolute as Consciousness.[126] The Yogâcâra school, on the other hand, which came to dominate the Mahâyâna increasingly after the year 500 A.D., is characterized above all by its doctrine of *citta-mâtra* (= "thought alone"),[127] which holds that the only final Reality is Absolute Mind.

Yogâcâra distinguishes three kinds of "nature" or "essence" (*svabhâva* = "own being"): illusory being, in which things appear as objects, distinct from others; conditioned being, where the dependence of beings on others is recognized; fully real being, in which all is one single undifferentiated "suchness," which is Mind[128] (again like the Upanishadic Brahman). This final reality can be experienced by the practice of yoga meditation, in which we attain the inmost self, which is identical with the Absolute. Salvation is therefore found in turning away from objective and external being toward inner being.[129]

In each person the Yogâcâra distinguishes three levels of consciousness. There are the six sense-consciousnesses (inherited from early Buddhism); above these is mind (manas), called the "witness consciousness": it is the observer, the "I." Finally, there is the "store-consciousness" (âlayavijñana). It is beyond phenomenal consciousness and the ego. In it are planted karmic "seeds" which give rise to experience. It is also the "womb of Buddhahood" (Tathâgatagarbha): it is the Buddha-nature present in us, which seeks Buddhahood.[130] In the last analysis, then, the store-consciousness is an emanation from the ultimate reality, the absolute consciousness which is the Dharmakaya of the Buddha,[131] and is in some sense identical with it.[132]

It would seem that the Mahâyâna, while avoiding the word "God," has introduced transcendental theism into Buddhist thought, and likewise, while avoiding the notion of âtman, it has reintroduced a transcending self.[133] It has likewise transformed the notion of nirvâna. The aim of the bodhisattva is now the nirvâna which is "not permanently fixed," i.e., which does not exclude samsâra.[134] The bodhisattva, having realized the non-duality of all things (Lankâvatâra Sûtra, II.28), can no longer be defiled by the world, and has no reason to escape from it. Even in the Hînayâna, as we have seen, nirvâna is not to be interpreted in a nihilistic sense. Nevertheless, early Buddhism so emphasized the transcendence of the goal that nothing positive could be said of it; it has nothing in common with the here and now. The Mahâyâna, on the other hand, emphasizes the continuity between present existence and the ultimate goal, either in the notion of the Pure Lands (which for many effectively replace nirvâna as the goal) or more radically in the philosophic doctrine of the non-duality of nirvâna and samsâra.

The theoretical and practical development of the Mahâyâna in China brought it ever farther from its Indian roots. To the Chinese mind the doctrine of rebirth, instead of epitomizing the problem from which we must seek salvation, appeared as an affirmation of the survival of the soul after death. The fourth and fifth centuries A.D. saw Chinese Buddhist writers, having put aside the abstruse "anatta" doctrine, actually defending the immortality of the soul against the naturalism of the Confucians.[135] The Lotus Sûtra was by far the most popular scripture in China; it was its positive, personal and joyous doctrine, inculcating a strong hope for salvation, which appealed to the Chinese and won over a majority of the population to Buddhism by the fifth century.[136] By this time also the notion of a Buddha-nature residing in all sentient beings had been developed and set forth (especially in the *Mahâparanirvâna sûtra*), and was understood in China to imply a real eternal self which will persist even in *nirvâna*, as well as the eventual salvation of all creatures.[137] Combined with the worship of the *bodhisattvas* and celestial Buddhas and the admixture of elements from native religion and philosophy, these features gave to Chinese Buddhism the appearance of a polytheistic or even theistic religion.

The Mahâyâna perhaps reaches its culmination in the synthesis with Taoism which was accomplished in China, from the eighth century onward, in the schools of "meditation" (*dhyana*; approximated in Chinese as *Ch'an*, which becomes Japanese *Zen*). Ch'an Buddhism was in part a reaction against the over-systematization which eventually plagued the Mahâyâna: the means of salvation became so multiplied that the goal itself was lost.[138] For this reason Ch'an was distinctly anti-traditionalist in many of its practices. It was also very much a product of the Chinese mind,[139] and in particular of the philosophical current of Taoism. At the same time, it is in strong continuity with the *prajña* tradition, and takes for granted the monist metaphysics of the Mahâyâna *sûtras*. It is, in fact, a practical exercise in the oneness which these teach.[140]

Ch'an Buddhism (and its descendant, Zen) is in fact characterized by an aversion to theory and an emphasis on direct, immediate insight. It is empirical in its outlook, and attempts to effect a direct transmission of Buddhahood. The southern Ch'an (the northern school died out) typically looked for sudden enlightenment. This does not mean that no preparation was needed, but rather that enlightenment is an act of the Absolute, and thus is outside time; it is beyond the reach of anything we can do.[141] For this reason, enlightenment and salvation are sought in the perfectly ordinary and inconspicuous aspects of daily life; it is there that the Buddha nature is suddenly and paradoxically revealed.[142]

The Mahâyâna interprets the "conversion" experience, like the Hînayâna, above all in terms of the transcending of egotism.[143] There are three principal ways in which this is accomplished: (1) by faith in the graciousness of the *bodhisattvas*, ultimately of Being itself; (2) by insight into the "emptiness" of all things, which shows that there is nothing to cling to; when one lets go of everything, one can then find the Absolute as the "suchness" of all things and of one's self; (3) by compassion for all beings, in imitation of the Buddha's compassion. The Mahâyâna necessarily has less emphasis than the Hînayâna on moral striving or on a "way" of salvation, for it recognizes the paradox: a desire for *nirvâna* is itself a desire which stands in the way of *nirvâna;* hence one must simply let go. The "letting go" occurs in faith and/or in the doing of things which have no goal, but are done for their own sake: meditation, devotion, the practical tasks of everyday life.

V. GOD'S WORD
IN HUMAN WORDS —
THE WESTERN RELIGIONS

THE PERSIC-SEMITIC-HELLENIC RELIGIONS

The four great Western religions, although all having their origins in the Middle East, have all attained their classical forms through interaction with Greek civilization. Judaism, Christianity, and Islam may properly be called "Western" religions even in a geographical sense, since their major areas of diffusion have been Europe, Africa, and the Americas (although all three also retain a significant presence in the Near and Middle East, and Islam is also a major force in Asia). Zoroastrianism alone remains geographically removed from the Western world with which it is associated by ideas. More significantly, all four great religions (including Zoroastrianism, through the Greek conquest under Alexander) share the same inheritance from the Greeks, particularly in the sphere of philosophy, which in each case made a major contribution to the formulation of revelation.

Judaism, Christianity and Islam are of course also intimately related through a line of "descent": Christianity from Judaism, Islam from both. There is also convincing evidence that this line may be continued backward to include Zoroastrianism as well, insofar as Judaism in its formative period seems to have received a number of its most significant concepts through contact with the official Zoroastrian religion of Persia during and after the Exile.

The four great Western religions are even more closely linked in their common world-view than the Oriental religions. Just as the latter share presuppositions regarding the human condition in *samsâra*, so Zoroastrianism, Judaism, Christianity and Islam share a basic position of prophetic monotheism, with the anthropology that it implies.

The theological stance of monotheism holds that the ultimate transcendent Reality, the supreme Being, is unique and "personal"—i.e., is the ultimate source and exemplary embodiment of the personal qualities in humanity: intelligence and freedom. Monotheism implies paradoxically the simultaneous affirmation of the absolute transcendence of God and of his relatedness to humanity through our conceptions of him. These conceptions or images therefore must be continually purified by reference to the reality always beyond them. Typically the monotheistic religions implicitly express this fact in calling God by a "proper name": that is, a name which tells us nothing about God, but which is simply the means by which the Absolute is present in being able to be invoked.[1]

By "prophetic" in this context is meant that God is experienced as being in some sense "over against" or personally differentiated from his creatures, revealing himself to them and demanding of them an active response. While it would be an over-simplification to qualify the Indic-based religions as "mystical" and the Persian and Semitic as "prophetic" (for elements of each type are found in both), there is certainly a difference in emphasis which corresponds to this division. While the Oriental religions tend to find the Divine as the most profound "Self," found by an inward movement, the Western faiths more typically find God as the holy "Other"; while the former tend to be (with the qualifications we have already noted) what van der Leeuw calls "religions of repose"—i.e., union with the divine is already a reality, which needs only to be recognized— the latter tend to be "religions of unrest," in which unity with God is something to be striven for and accomplished, especially by a relation to the world and others epitomized in ethical norms.

Central to the monotheistic religions is the notion of creation: it insists upon the distinction of the world from God (even though that distinction itself may be seen theologically as "within" God) and its utter dependence upon him. The distinction of the world from the divine has important consequences: it allows for the "secularization" of the world as a consequence of the insight that the earth is humanity's sphere of creativity; it provides the "space" in which God can reveal himself as "Other," as "Thou" to the human being; it implies human responsibility in freedom for becoming, within the world, what God reveals as our destiny, and thus valorizes history; and it permits the formulation of the notion of sin as radical rebellion of freedom resulting in separation from God. Judaism, Christianity, and Islam, then, all emphasize the place of human freedom and the need for human activity to transform the world according to God's "will." Contrary to the Indic belief in an eternal world of rebirth, this view sees human life as created out of nothing and ending its connection with the world in death.[2] Furthermore, the world itself, having been created by God from nothing, has a purpose to serve and a limited time in which it may be accomplished. Thus an existential urgency is given to human existence which is largely lacking in the *saṁsâra-nirvâṇa* traditions.

While we shall deal with Judaism and Christianity as distinct religions, it should be kept in mind that the Judaeo-Christian tradition is in many ways a unity, not only because of the derivation of Christianity from Judaism, but also because of the fundamental similarity of the two religions on the most basic issues touching our subject. Indeed, from our point of view Christianity may be considered the "universal" form of Judaism—that is, the form in which the religion of the Jewish people becomes a world religion. (The relation of Judaism to Christianity in some ways parallels that of Hinduism to Buddhism. Both Hinduism and Judaism are "ethnic" religions, tied to a particular people. Hinduism, with few exceptions, has never fared well outside India, largely because of the difficulties of transplanting the caste system. Judaism has survived and expanded in diaspora, but remains essentially connected with a single "people"—one is Jewish by descent—and, for some at least, with a particular nation. Both generated daughter religions which broke with these ties and brought the originating religious insight into a wider context. Mahâyâna Buddhism, through the mediation and incorporation of Chinese thought, became the universal form of Hinduism; Christianity, through the mediation and incorporation of Hellenic thought, became the universal form of Judaism.[3])

Our exposition of the Judaeo-Christian tradition will be brief and schematic, both because a familiarity with this tradition is presumed, and because a great deal of the relevant material has either already been treated or (in the case of the specifically Christian message) will be dealt with at length in the last chapters of this book.

Zoroastrianism

Among the surviving higher religions, the religion of Zoroaster is the least known and least widespread. It survives today only as the faith of the Parsees, who form a small (and persecuted) minority in their original homeland, Iran, and a somewhat larger diaspora centered mainly in India, where their ancestors fled to escape earlier Muslim domination.[4] At one time, however, Zoroastrianism was the official orthodoxy of the great Persian Empire, and as such played an important role in world and religious history, including that of the biblical religions. It was Ahura Mazdâ, the Wise Lord, the God of Zoroaster, who inspired Cyrus, the King of Kings, to send those other great monotheists, the Jews, home from their exile in Babylon.[5]

It was also the religion of Zoroaster which first introduced a number of ideas which have had a significant effect on both the Judaeo-Christian tradition and Mahâyâna Buddhism:[6] the notion of linear time and salvation history (also "discovered" by the Hebrews), the devil, the myth of the eschatological savior, optimistic eschatology, the resurrection of the dead, the last judgment, angels, and possibly some of the great Gnostic myths.[7] Above all, the religion of Zoroaster gave to the world the first and most powerful systematization of a dualistic theology and a view of salvation as a cosmic struggle of good against evil.[8] Some later dualisms (Zervanism,

Mithraism, Manichaeanism) are directly traceable to Zoroastrianism; others (the doctrines of the Bogomiles and Cathari, for example) are probably indirect descendants.

Unfortunately, comparatively little is known of early Zoroastrianism. Most of the *Avesta*, the principal sacred book, has been lost, and what remains contains many linguistic difficulties, so that translations are frequently tentative at best. The dates of Zarathushtra (to give him his Iranian name—"Zoroaster" is the version given by the Greeks) are impossible to determine with certitude. Zoroastrians place him in extreme antiquity— some six thousand years before Christ;[9] the Greek historians give a date several thousand years before Christ; modern scholars differ enormously, the favorite estimates being: 1700–1500 B.C.;[10] tenth or ninth century B.C.;[11] eighth or seventh century B.C.;[12] sixth or early fifth century B.C.[13] The latest possible date seems to be immediately before the establishment of the Persian Empire by Cyrus; this would accord with a Sassanid tradition which puts Zarathushtra's life two hundred and fifty-eight years before Alexander.[14]

Although the details of Zarathushtra's life are unknown, the crux of his message can be clearly discerned in the *Gathas*, a part of the *Avesta* which stems from his preaching. Prior Iranian religion was of the same family as that of the Aryan invaders of India; it seems to have seen the world in terms of a contention between good and evil, both stemming from a single high god who is primary among many deities. Zarathushtra accepts the idea of contention, but rejects the notion that both good and evil can come from the same divine source—and therefore also rejects the idea that evil should be accepted with resignation (as in the worship of Nature, expressed in polytheism). Instead, he proclaims one supreme God, Ahura Mazdâ ("the Wise Lord"), who is the author only of goodness and good order (*Asha*—later *Arta*).[15] The other gods he either qualifies as evil spirits (the *daêvas*) or assimilates into his monotheism by making them quasi-personified attributes of God (the six *Amesha Spentas*—the "Holy Immortals").[16]

The origin of evil then is attributed to another spirit, who from the beginning is opposed to goodness, whose nature is "the Lie" (*Drug* or *Druj*, implying not only untruth, but chaos: everything opposed to *asha*, right order):

> Now to eager listeners will I speak of the two Spirits Mazdâ did create. . . .
> Now, these are the two original Spirits who, as Twins, have been perceived (by me?) through a vision. In both thought and speech, (and) in deed, these two are what is good and evil. Between these two the pious, not the impious, will choose rightly.

Furthermore, the two Spirits confronted each other; in the beginning (each) created for himself life [on the one hand] and nonlife [on the other], so that in the end there will be the worst existence for the followers of the Lie, but the best Mind for the Righteous.

Of these two Spirits, the deceitful chose the worst course of action, while the most beneficent Spirit . . . chose Truth, as also do those who believingly propitiate Ahura Mazdâ.

Between these two Spirits the daêvas did not choose rightly at all . . . they chose the worst mind. Then, all together, they ran to Wrath with which they infect the life of man.

. . . Thus did the Holy Spirit speak to the Destroyer: "Between us neither thoughts, nor wills, nor words, nor teachings, nor beliefs, nor deeds accord; our inner selves and souls are quite apart" (*Yasna* 30:1, 3–6; 45:2).[17]

It is clear in this text that Zarathushtra's dualism is not absolute or "symmetrical"; that is, there is no anti-God on the level of Ahura Mazdâ. Rather, both of the Twins, the Spenta Mainyu (= Holy or Beneficent Spirit) and the Angra Mainyu (= Destroying Spirit) stem *from* Ahura.[18] Furthermore, they differ from each other not by nature, but by *choice*. It is *ethical* dualism which is central to Zarathushtra's thought, and it is notable that he immediately draws attention to the "existential imperative" for the hearer to choose the good. It should also be remarked that the Indo-Iranian language in which the *Gathas* are written had a special verb form (the "injunctive") which was used for the mythic expression of timeless, ever present truths. Thus, the choice which was made "in the beginning" is also being made *now*, and we must decide which side *we* will take.[19]

The idea of humanity's freedom and responsibility is central to Zarathushtra's message: "we freely choose the path we tread" (*Yasna* 31:11). The ethical message is intimately tied to a spiritual and theological one; by our choices we determine our relation to Ahura Mazdâ. The experience of intense personal relationship with God is strikingly present in the *Gathas*. God reveals himself, and we respond to his revelation by our free choice. Ahura Mazdâ is the transcendent God, without mythological connections to the earth; he is irrelevant to the fulfillment of everyday wants.[20] The relationship to such a God can only take place at a level of religious experience where humanity's own transcendence is realized at a high level.

Eliade notes the "urgency and existential tension with which Zarathushtra questions his Lord."[21] Over and over in the *Gathas* we hear the refrain: "This I ask thee: speak to me truly, O Lord!"[22] Zarathushtra presumes to question Ahura Mazdâ, for he is confident of his friendship:

"Ahura, to Thee do I appeal as lover to the beloved; teach me how I may be one with Thee in perfect bliss" (*Yasna* 46:2)

"To Thee as sacrifice Zarathushtra brings the very life and being of his self—to Mazdâ thoughts of love and their first fruits . . . faithful obedience to Thy Law" (Yasna 33:14).

"Thus may I realize Thee as the First, and also Last, O Mazdâ, in my mind, as Father of all Love" (Yasna 31:8).

The "passionately personal"[23] relationship of Zarathushtra to God stands as a prime example of the turn to interiority which characterized the religious revolution of the "axial period."

The intensity of Zarathushtra's religion could not be maintained for long after his death, however, and the period of the Achaemenids, while it saw the enthronement of Ahura Mazdâ as the supreme God of the Persian Empire, provided the opportunity for the restoration of the power of the Magi (the priestly caste of the Medes) and the rehabilitation of much of the Old Iranian religion, now under the guise of Zoroastrian monotheism. The "Younger Avesta" (i.e., that part of the Avesta written in a language later than Zarathushtra's) was composed during this period, and reintroduces the cult of the traditional gods (among them Mithra, who was to become the center of a major mystery religion of the Roman Empire), now officially subordinated to Ahura Mazdâ.[24]

The next great stage of Zoroastrianism was the renewal and theological systematization which took place under the Arsacid and Sassanid dynasties (226–642 A.D.). This period witnessed a return to the spirit of the Gathas, as opposed to the "paganizing" of the Yashts.[25] The Pahlavî (a dialect of Middle Persian) books, the classical formulation of Zoroastrian doctrine as a metaphysical dualism, although partially written after the Muslim conquest, are based upon the re-established religion of the sixth century, which in turn is based upon the dualist orthodoxy established in the fourth century (under Shâpûr II).[26] (It was probably also in the sixth century that the present redaction of the Avesta itself took place.[27])

The essential message of Zoroastrianism remains the same: "The original word of the Good Religion is that all good comes from the Creator and that no evil comes from Him" (Dênkart).[28] But this message is now systematized into a full-blown metaphysical dualism and theory of sacred history. In the beginning of the first world era (each of which lasts three thousand years), Ahura Mazdâ, now called Ohrmazd, encounters his negative counterpart, Ahriman,[29] and creates the everlasting ideal prototypes of his creation:

Ohrmazd was on high in omniscience and goodness: for infinite time he was ever in the light. . . .

Ahriman, slow in knowledge, whose will is to smite, was deep down in the darkness: he was, and is, yet will not be. The will to smite is his permanent disposition, and darkness is his place. . . .

Between them was the Void. . . .

Ohrmazd, in his omniscience, knew that the Destructive Spirit existed, that he would attack and, since his will is envy, would mingle with him; and from the beginning to end he knew with what and how many instruments he would accomplish his purpose. In ideal form he fashioned forth such creation as was needful for his instrument. For three thousand years creation stayed in this ideal state, for it was without thought, without movement, without touch.

The Destructive Spirit, ever slow to know, was unaware of the existence of Ohrmazd. Then he rose up from the depths and went to the border whence the lights are seen. When he saw the light of Ohrmazd intangible, he rushed forward. Because his will is to smite and his substance is envy, he made haste to destroy it. Seeing valour and supremacy superior to his own, he fled back to the darkness and fashioned many demons, a creation destructive and meet for battle. When Ohrmazd beheld the creation of the Destructive Spirit, it seemed not good to him—a frightful, putrid, bad, and evil creation: and he did not revere it. Then the Destructive Spirit beheld the creation of Ohrmazd and it seemed good to him—a creation most profound, victorious, informed of all: and he revered the creation of Ohrmazd.

Then Ohrmazd, knowing in what manner the end would be, offered peace to the Destructive Spirit, saying, "O Destructive Spirit, bring aid to my creation and give it praise that in reward therefor thou mayest be deathless and unageing, uncorrupting and undecaying. . . . " But the Destructive Spirit cried out, "I shall not go forth, nor shall I any more give aid to thy creation; nor shall I give praise to thy creation nor shall I agree with thee in any good thing: but I shall destroy thee and thy creation for ever and ever; yea, I shall incline all thy creatures to hatred of thee and love of me." And the interpretation thereof is this, that he thought Ohrmazd was helpless against him and that therefor did he offer peace. He did not accept but uttered threats. And Ohrmazd said, "Thou canst not, O Destructive Spirit, accomplish all; for thou canst not destroy me, nor canst thou bring it about that my creation should not return to my possession" (*Bundahishn*, 1:1–10)[30]

Ohrmazd realizes that he must fix a limit to his struggle with Ahriman, and they agree to do battle for nine thousand years. Ohrmazd knows that the first three thousand would be spent according to his will (Paradise); the second three thousand would be "in mixture" and in struggle; in the last three thousand would come the climax of the battle, and Ahriman would be defeated (*Bundahishn*, 1:11–13). Thus sacred history comes into being: time is created and given direction and purpose.[31]

Ahriman had already begun the struggle by his primal envious Lie (i.e., that he did not revere Ohrmazd's creation, and would turn it against him); Ohrmazd responds with the *Ahunvar*, the Word of Truth (the principal prayer of the Zoroastrians). It sets forth his power, revealing the whole course of history and his own final victory; at this the Destructive Spirit is stunned and falls back into darkness. While he lays temporarily crushed, Ohrmazd creates the world, starting with the Holy Immortals and spirits, including the *Fravahrs*,[32] the spiritual souls of all human beings, then proceeding to matter. He makes first the sky, then water, earth, plants, cattle, and finally Gayômart, the Blessed Man. Meanwhile, Ahriman in the darkness fashions spiritual beings in his own likeness (*Bundahishn*, 1:11–27).

It is to be noted that the Zoroastrians, unlike other dualists (particularly the Manichaeans and Gnostics), hold that matter is the creation of Ohrmazd, and as such is totally good. Ahriman can create other spirits like himself, but he cannot create matter. Zoroastrian feeling about the material world is completely positive; the words for "good, holy," and "productive, bounteous" are related.[33] The body is made of the same "substance" as the soul; it is not an inferior kind of being. As Eliade remarks, Zoroastrianism represents "the most rigorous and most daring religious valorization of matter that we know of before the Western chemist-philosophers of the 17th century."[34]

Ohrmazd next prepares for the struggle with Ahriman by consulting with the *Fravahrs*. He asks if they would be willing to become incarnate in the world to do battle against the Destructive Spirit; for only by their free collaboration can Ohrmazd be assured of final victory.

> And the *Fravahrs* of men saw by that omniscient wisdom that they would suffer evil from the Lie and Ahriman in the world, but because at the end (which is the Final Body), they would be resurrected free from the enmity of the Adversary, whole and immortal for ever and ever, they agreed to go into the material world (*Bundahishn*, 1).[35]

In its doctrine of "Genesis" Zoroastrianism has already disposed of several of the major problems or mysteries which beset theistic religion. There is no problem of theodicy, for God is in no way responsible for evil; there is a co-aeval evil principle, to whom God is completely opposed. God is not, at the beginning, infinite or omnipotent; he must become infinite and omnipotent through his conquest of evil. There is no mystery of the motive of creation; Ohrmazd creates the world and humanity for the simple reason that he needs them in his struggle against Ahriman. There is no problem of unmerited human suffering: for humanity freely chooses, from the start, to enter the world and to undergo suffering at the hands of Ahriman in order to aid in his subjection.

For three thousand years, the Zoroastrian creation story continues, Ahriman remained helpless, while the primal Man, Gayômart, along with the primal ox or bull, lives in peace on earth. At the end of this time, Ahriman attacks. His entry to the sphere of Ohrmazd's creation is somehow aided (although the texts are unclear exactly how) by a figure named "the Whore": a primal female who cohabits with Ahriman.[36] Ahriman's attack brings death to Gayômart, and intermingles evil with the goodness of creation throughout its whole extent, creating the state of "mixture" (gumê-ciśn).[37] At the same time, he has fallen into Ohrmazd's trap, for he is now within the sphere of earth, bounded by the impregnable fortress of the sky: he cannot escape.

From Gayômart's union with the Good Mother, Earth, springs the first human pair, Mashyê and Mashyânê.[38] In them humanity "falls": for they accept Ahriman's claim to have been the creator of the earth, and blasphemously offer him worship.[39] By this "lie" humanity betrays its maker. From this point, the battle continues through the third three thousand year period. Each human who comes into the world must freely choose sides in the cosmic battle in which the earth has become the battlefield. Humanity properly belongs to Ohrmazd, however, for he is its father, as the Good Mother Earth is its mother; to choose evil is treason.

The final three thousand year period of history begins with the birth of Zarathushtra, whose soul, created in the second period (like all human fravashi), now comes to earth to bring the "Good Religion," the earthly form of Ohrmazd's wisdom.[40] After Zarathushtra's death, every thousand years a savior (saoshyant) will appear, born of his seed, culminating in the Sôshyans, who will be the agent of the resurrection of all humanity and the final destruction of Ahriman.[41]

The resurrection will be the last phase of salvation history. For each person, however, there is also an individual judgment at death. At the "Bridge of the Separator" (Cinvato paratu) each soul is confronted with its own conscience (dâenâ, one of the constituents of human nature)[42] in personified female form; for the good, the form of a lovely maiden:

> The soul of the righteous seems to be among plants, and to be inhaling fragrant odors. . . . There appears to him his own Conscience in the form of a Maiden, beautiful, radiant, white-armed, robust, fair-faced, erect, high-breasted, of stately form, noble-born, of glorious lineage, fifteen years old in appearance, as beautiful in form as the most beautiful of creatures. And the soul of the righteous addressed her, asking: "What damsel art thou . . . ?" Then to him his own Conscience gave answer:

"O thou good youth of good thought, good word, good deed, of good conscience, I am the Conscience of thine own self. . . . Lovable as I was, thou didst make me more lovable by thy good thoughts, thy good words, thy good deeds, thy good religion; beautiful, thou madest me still more beautiful; desirable, still more desirable" (*Hâdôxt Nask*, 7–14).[43]

For the evil, however, conscience appears as an ugly and decrepit whore:

The soul of the wicked spoke thus: "Who art thou, than whom, among all the creatures of Ohrmazd and Ahriman, I never saw any uglier . . . filthier, and more stinking?" To it she spoke thus: "I am thy bad deeds. . . . It is on account of thy will and actions that I am ugly and vile, disgusting and diseased, decrepit and of evil complexion . . ." (*Artâh Virâz Nâmak*, 13–15).[44]

The good are then led across the bridge to heaven, while the evil fall to hell. (It is to be noted that for Zoroastrianism the myth of the ordeal at the end of life has been transformed to a moral judgment; it is a person's works which determine the outcome, not any skill or magic or ritual.[45])

Heaven and hell, however, are not the ultimate realities. At the end, Sôshyans raises up the bodies of all, through the power of Ohrmazd (who answers the obvious objection against physical resurrection, declaring: "Behold! If I created what had not been, why should it be impossible for me to recreate what once was?" [*Bundahishn*]).[46] All re-embodied humans must now pass through an ordeal of molten metal, as the earth is consumed and purified in Ohrmazd's fire. For the saved it will be like a bath of warm milk, but for the damned it will be torment. This torment, however, is also purification; in the end, all are united with Ohrmazd, as he himself makes up for what is lacking to their goodness:

Whoso (on earth) had not performed the sacrifice nor ordered a *gêtô-khrît* ("earthly redemption") nor given clothing in alms to those who deserved it, (will stand) there naked, and Ohrmazd will perform sacrifice on his behalf and the Spirit of the Gâthâs will provide him with raiment.[47]

Ohrmazd and his good spirits will finally defeat and destroy Ahriman and his creations;[48] all human beings, the allies of God, are saved, body and spirit; and the material world, now purified of the mixture of evil, will become immortal.

It is apparent from this outline that Zoroastrianism is above all an ethical religion. It sees existence as "relentless struggle,"[49] a continuous bat-

tle of good against evil in which humanity has the central place. Its emphasis is always on human choice. There is, in a sense, no "salvation"—
i.e., by another; although Ohrmazd and his "angels" help and inspire, each human being is responsible not only for his or her destiny, but also for contributing to the defeat of the "Lie." Indeed, it is in a sense humanity which saves God; for the all-good but originally finite Ohrmazd can only become infinite by eliminating evil; and without the help of the righteous, this could not be accomplished:

> "For if the mighty Frawashis of the Righteous had not given me support, in that case the animals and men which are the best of the (various) species would not have been mine. Power would have been the Lie's, dominion the Lie's, material existence the Lie's" (*Yasht* 13).[50]

The means by which humanity advances the struggle against evil is by the practice of The Religion (*Dên*), i.e., Zoroastrianism, which consists in good thought, word, and action. It is a code of order. It is also one of strong affirmation of human life and of the material world. No religion, Zaehner notes, has ever so strongly opposed asceticism and monasticism (and especially celibacy): for strong human life is necessary to defeat Ahriman and reclaim the world. Fruitfulness is virtuous, sterility is vice. The strong, positive virtues of agriculture are emphasized: it is necessary to make the earth strong and fruitful, and thus to resist the Enemy, the author of disease and death.[51]

The "wisdom" which is the core of Zoroastrian ethics is above all reasonable behavior, moderation, common sense. There is no mysticism in Zoroastrianism; the light of reason is Ohrmazd's thought.[52] Sassanid Zoroastrianism explicitly adopted the ideal of the "golden mean" from Aristotle as the summation of its ethics.[53] One should enjoy the world, as a preparation for heaven. Lamentation and sorrow are the inventions of Ahriman; joy is a positive duty, and one of the ways of defeating him. The creation account states: "To help the sky (Ohrmazd) gave it joy, for he fashioned joy for its sake: for even now in the mixed state creation is in joy" (*Bundahishn* 1:21).[54] The traditions state that Zarathushtra was born into the world laughing. Zoroastrian worship was imbued with this same spirit. The sage Âdhurbâdh, considered the arbiter of orthodoxy, counseled: "On the day of Ohrmazd drink wine and make merry." "On the day of Rashn (the god who judges the soul at death), life is gay: do, in holiness, anything you will."[55]

A "catechism" explains the meaning of "faith" for the Zoroastrian: freely taking the part of Ohrmazd. The Zoroastrian is to be a friend, child and collaborator of Ohrmazd, not (like the worshipers of Varuṇa, Yahweh, and Allah) his slave or servant.[56] As the creature and child of Ohrmazd, one must affirm without doubting:

> "I have come from the unseen world, nor was I (always) of this world. I was created and have not (always) been. I belong to the gods, not the demons, to the good, not to the wicked. I am a man, not a demon, a creature of Ohrmazd. . . . My mother is Spandarmat (the Earth), and my father is Ohrmazd. . . . To perform my function and to do my duty means that I should believe that Ohrmazd is, was, and evermore shall be, that his Kingdom is undying, and that he is infinite and pure; and that Ahriman is not, and is destructible; that I myself belong to Ohrmazd and his Bounteous Immortals. . . . "

It also specifies what is meant by good thoughts, good words, good actions:

> "My first duty on earth is to confess the Religion, to practice it, and to take part in its worship. . . . My second duty is to take a wife and to procreate earthly offspring, and to be strenuous and steadfast in this. My third (duty) is to cultivate and till the soil; my fourth to treat all livestock justly; my fifth to spend a third of my days and nights in attending the seminary and consulting the wisdom of holy men, to spend a third of my days and nights in tilling the soil and making it fruitful, and to spend (the remaining) third of my days and nights in eating, rest, and enjoyment."[57]

The sacrifices and rituals of Zoroastrianism (of which there were many)[58] were intended to advance the purification of the world by recreating in one's self and one's ambient the purity that preceded the "mixture" of evil in the world.[59] Purification was also achieved by means of a kind of sacramental penance, with confession to a priest and performance of expiation. The communal dimension was significantly present: one was to be repentant not only for one's own sins, but also for *others'* sins committed *against* oneself.[60]

In worship it was especially important to participate in communion with the physical world and its spiritual guardians; therefore the Zoroastrians celebrated above all festivals of creation. Humanity must love the creation: earth, water, fire, and animals. Fire especially was considered related to Asha, the Beneficent Immortal who personifies Righteousness; for goodness is embodied and symbolized in Light.[61]

Zoroastrianism produced several offshoots which were much more directly influential on Western religion than this humanistic and world-affirming creed itself. One was Mithraism, the mystery religion of the

Roman legions in the early centuries A.D. In it, Ahriman was apparently a power who had proper dominion over humanity, and seems to have been identified with finite Time, which controls our destiny. Mithra serves as a savior-god who brings salvation through a cosmic sacrifice.[62] More significant was the religion of Mani, a self-proclaimed Babylonian successor to Zarathushtra (also to the Buddha and Jesus), who was executed by the Persians in 276 A.D. Manichaeanism inherited the idea of the universe as a struggle of good against evil, and human life as the effort to disentangle the good, symbolized by light, from the evil darkness. In very un-Zoroastrian fashion, however, it identified evil with matter, and taught liberation by asceticism, especially in sexual matters.[63] Most significant of all, however, were the apparent borrowings of Judaism, through which the positive message of the Zoroastrian heritage has entered permanently into the structure of Western religion.

Judaism

The ancient Yahwist religion of the Hebrew people[64] was limited in its conception of salvation. The human being was considered an enlivened (en-spirited) body, whose real existence ended at death; although there was an idea of a shadowy existence in *sheol*, this was not conceived as a positive state of being, nor as any kind of union with God. As with most primitive religions, therefore, the focus of religious connection with the higher Power was the attainment of benefits in this world: life and prosperity. Furthermore, at least for the "official" Yahwism which is transmitted in the Bible, the major emphasis is on the nation, rather than the individual.[65]

The earthly focus of Yahwist thought is seen in the Hebrew terms used to express "salvation": these are all based upon the idea of extending help in danger, protecting from evil, or freeing.[66] Especially important is the notion of giving victory (*yasha'* and derivatives, whence *yeshu'ah* [God gives victory, God saves; hence the name "Jesus"] and *hoshi'ah-nna* ["Hosanna" = "give victory"]). Yahweh is above all a leader in battle (indeed, it was this quality which permitted the triumph of Yahwism over the agricultural and other cults which were a continual temptation for the Hebrews); he gives battle against the human enemies of the Hebrew confederation as well as against the demonic spiritual powers which were thought to cause sickness and other evils.

Yahweh is the exclusive and omnipotent savior. So overpowering was the Israelite experience of Yahweh that he ultimately absorbed all other powers, so that even evil powers had their source in him; it is Yahweh who sends trials upon people, who hardens their hearts, who is responsible for the afflictions which beset humanity, as well as for deliverance from them. Israel experienced the sacred as Power, and that Power as an awe-full and inscrutable will.[67]

The help of God is to be attained by faithfulness to his will as expressed in his covenant with people he arbitrarily chooses as his own. The primary response of his people must be trusting him, obeying his commands, and worshiping him according to the rituals he prescribes. God in turn will be faithful to his people; he will reward the good and punish evil-doers. (The question of the suffering of the innocent and the prosperity of the wicked does indeed arise, and is expressed with particular power in the Book of Job; but the ultimate answer which early Hebrew religion can give, even in Job, is submission to the majesty of God.)

The notion of the covenant is given new and deeper meaning by the prophets, who criticize merely external religion and insist upon a change of heart, which expresses itself in concern for social justice and care of the needy and oppressed. At the same time that monotheism is purified and the transcendence of God is recognized in new dimensions, there is a deepening sense of personal encounter with him, and his nature begins to be seen increasingly in terms of love, forgiveness and compassion.

In the period during and following the exile many of the sacred Scriptures were given their final redacted form, and Judaism officially became a "religion of the Book"; transcendent monotheism was firmly established, and the doctrine of creation formulated. At the same time, there was no normative form of Jewish belief; vastly different interpretations co-existed, both in the diaspora and in Israel,[68] as is witnessed by the New Testament. The religious problem of salvation is therefore conceived in different contexts. First, and in continuity with the ancient religion, salvation was sought in the restoration of Israel as a nation, under the Messiah, the king who would establish universal peace and God's rule on earth. Second, the influence of the Hellenistic world led to a greater concern for the eternal fate of the individual and to a possible solution to the problem of retribution; the person begins to be conceived in many circles in a Greek way (although modified by the Jewish idea of creation)[69] as an embodied soul or spirit who after death meets God and receives the reward of life's conduct. Third, there is a projection of the idea of political salvation to a cosmic dimension, with speculation about the end time developing the concepts (possibly borrowed from Persia) of a dualistic struggle between good and evil, a final resurrection of the dead for judgment, and eschatological salvation by a transcendent Savior (ideas which also became associated with messianic expectations).[70]

Following the Roman destruction of the temple (70 A.D.) and repression of Judaism (135 A.D.), only two major forms of Jewish belief survived, both of them having Pharisaic roots: the sectarians who proclaimed that the messianic expectations had been fulfilled in Jesus, who had by 135 already significantly expanded into the Gentile world and who became known as Christians; and the Jewish continuation of the Pharisees. The original Jewish-Christian community was quickly outnumbered by Gentile believers, and in Palestine was effectively eliminated by the Roman repression. Among the successors of Pharisees, from the year 70 until about 200 A.D. the foundations of "normative" Judaism were set. The canon of the Scriptures was formulated in 90 A.D., with a few books added in 135 A.D.; the triumph of Pharisaic Judaism was symbolized by the inclusion of the Hellenistic "wisdom" writings. Concepts such as the resurrection now become part of normative Jewish faith.

During this time the *Mishnah* ("repetition"), a compilation of oral tradition, was written. The *Mishnah* ignores the hope for imminent Messianic salvation and the apocalyptic speculations which were widespread in the previous (and to some extent contemporary) period. The notion of Messianic salvation is replaced by the ideal of the sanctification of life by obedience to the law.[71] The Messiah is relegated to the end of time, and the Messianic belief is transformed into an a-historical force: the Messiah's coming is the goal, but this goal is to be reached by Israel's standing beyond the vicissitudes of history. By submitting to whatever happens (in particular, the rule of the Gentiles), Israel will win the reward of God's rule through his Messiah. Salvation, then, depends upon sanctification, which is attained through obedience to the patterns of holiness given in the Torah.[72]

The *Mishnah* in effect completes and extends to all Jews the code of behavior established by Leviticus for priests and Levites. Although they might be living among and under Gentiles, in their own homes Jews are to have the same standards as the officiants in the (now non-existent) temple. This ritual purity assures the separation of Israel from the rest of humanity, and sets it apart for its essential task of becoming holy, in imitation of God's holiness and in obedience to his revelation.[73]

In the absence of a Jewish state and of the temple, the synagogue became the chief center of Jewish religious life, and the rabbi its chief authority. The *Talmud* ("teaching") was composed by the addition to the *Mishnah* of the commentaries (*Gemara*) by the rabbis. The Palestinian *Talmud* was edited between A.D. 220 and 400; the Babylonian *Talmud* between 200 and 650. The latter is recognized as the authentic source of the teachings of rabbinic or classical Judaism to this day.[74] It continues the central theme of the *Mishnah:* the sanctification of Israel by obedience to the *Torah* will bring about the coming of the Messiah and God's final rule.[75]

The problem of salvation is then reduced, on both the universal and the individual scale, to the problem of Israel's faithfulness or unfaithfulness to God. For the individual, the obstacle to salvation is sin (unfaithfulness, disobedience to the law). Although Judaism never developed a notion of "original sin" in the sense taught by Christianity, the rabbis did see humanity as living in a "fallen" world, influenced by conflicting "drives" toward good and evil. The *Torah* reveals what is truly in conformity with God's will, and establishes the pattern for living in such a way that evil is avoided. Sin, when it occurs, is overcome by repentance and expiatory suffering. Although divine grace plays a part, it is conceived simply as an aid to the sinner's own repentance. By living life in the world faithfully, interpreting it in the light of the divine and sanctifying its every aspect, the Jew prepares for the life to come, and the Jewish people as a whole prepare the coming of the Messiah.

Although rabbinic or Talmudic Judaism remains the norm for all subsequent Jewish orthodoxy, several later movements had a major impact upon Jewish thought and life. In the ninth and tenth centuries, Judaism absorbed through the mediation of Muslim culture the philosophic inheritance of Greece and the method of reconciling faith and reason. The culmination of medieval Jewish philosophy was reached in Moses ben Maimon or Maimonides (1135–1204), whose works on exegesis and metaphysics (especially the *Guide for the Perplexed*) are still much esteemed.

The heritage of Gnostic thought entered Judaism in the esoteric mysticism of the *Kabbalah*. God is here conceived as the *En-Sof* (the Infinite or Endless), Being without attributes, from whom there emanate ideal qualities (the *Sefiroth*—in concept somewhat similar to the *Amesha Spentas* of Zoroastrianism) which mediate between God and world. For Kabbalism, theogony and cosmogony are identical; that is, God becomes himself in the becoming of the world. The sin of Adam is conceived as a cosmic rupture which affects God himself; the aim of the Jew is to restore God's presence (the *Shechinah*) to the *En-Sof* from which it was alienated.[76] After the expulsion of the Jews from Spain (1492), Kabbalism became more popular and was integrated with Messianism. Human life is conceived as exile, and humanity is seen as menaced by its own corruption and the corruption of the world.

The major development in Kabbalism stems from Isaac Luria (1514–1572). Luria's great contribution was the doctrine of *Tsimtsum* ("retreat" or "withdrawal"): in order to create the world, God, who is the All, must make room for the world by emptying a region of himself. The creation is thus a kind of exile of God from himself.[77] Luria also saw the primal Adam as a universal being who before the fall embraced the whole cosmos, existing in ideal state. By his fall, matter was created and the light of Adam's divine nature was broken into the many sparks which are individual souls.[78] Luria taught a doctrine of metempsychosis after death; this was seen as being in reality the transmigration of the single soul of the cosmic Adam. Humanity's purpose, through continued reincarnations, is the *Tik-kun:* the restoration of ideal order, by which man will achieve the enthronement of God in his kingdom.[79]

The tradition of the *Kabbalah* was furthered in the movement of Hasidism. Its founder, the Rabbi Israel Baal Shem Tov ("Master of the Good Name"), intended to make the Kabbalic teachings accessible to the common people. The chief characteristic of Hasidism was the development of the idea of the *zaddik* ("holy man"), who alone is capable of perfect union with God; others must simply follow his rule. The *Torah* and *Kabbalah* were relegated to second place, the example of the saints and guidance of the *zaddik* being primary. Hasidism emphasized self-abnegation, loving humility, the expiation of sin, and awareness of the divine Presence, as well as faithful adherence to the law (as interpreted by the *zaddik*). Hasidism survives still, but in somewhat modified form, having moved closer to orthodox practice.

With the European Enlightenment, a Reform movement began within Judaism. It rebelled against Talmudic orthodoxy, and attempted to make Judaism a universal creed, no longer tied to a single nation. In the contemporary world, religious Judaism exists in many forms and with a variety of interpretations of humanity and its salvation: from resurgent nationalist messianism, centered in the state of Israel, to highly supernaturalist (and sometimes anti-nationalist) pieties. Attitudes toward the law and traditions also vary widely. What unites all religious Jews, however, is the belief in the unity and the goodness of God and of his creation, so that humanity's salvation is found not in flight from the world, but in its transformation toward God's kingdom. Human involvement in the world, in creativity and in the struggle for social justice, is therefore crucial to God's solution to the human dilemma.

Islam

Islam is the youngest of the great world religions, and probably today the most vital and growing. It is the conscious heir of both Judaism and Christianity, and claims to be their prolongation and fulfillment.

More than any other religion, Islam reveals its nature in its scripture, the *Qur'an.* Classical Islam is the "religion of the Book" *par excellence.* The mainstream of Islamic thought has consistently held fast to a fundamentalist interpretation of revelation: the *Qur'an* is the infallible word of God, spoken to his Prophet Muhammad in Arabic so that humanity can understand it (Sûrah XII.2);[80] it is the reading (qur'an = lecture, reading) of a tablet eternally preserved in heaven and revealed on earth through Muhammad. It is itself considered a wonder, and constitutes the proof of its own genuineness (XI.13).

Muhammad (ca. 570–632 A.D.) according to tradition received this revelation from God through the angel Gabriel. The text of the Qur'an was written down from his sayings—perhaps during his life, certainly within a short time after his death. The essential message is simple: there is but one God (Allah),[81] who is Absolute; humanity is called upon to recognize him and follow his law. The bulk of the Qur'an consists in the repetition of these truths, along with a concrete exposition of the commands which humanity must follow.

The center of Muhammad's message is the absoluteness of Allah:

> Say: He is Allah, the One.
> Allah, the eternally Besought of all!
> He begotteth not or was begotten.
> And there is none comparable to Him (CXII).[82]

> [He is] the Originator of the heavens and the
> earth! When He declareth a thing, He saith unto
> it only: Be! and it is (II. 117).

> Allah is the Light of the heavens and the
> earth (XXIV. 35).

Muhammad preaches an absolute monotheism: Allah is the only God; the unpardonable sin is to worship other gods, or to associate others with him:

> Your God is one God; there is no God save Him,
> the Beneficent, the Merciful (II. 163).

> Lo! Allah pardoneth not that partners should be
> ascribed unto Him (IV. 116).

> Unto Him is the real prayer. Those unto whom
> they pray beside Allah respond to them not at
> all, save as one who stretcheth forth his hands
> toward water that it may come unto his mouth,
> and it will never reach it (XIII. 14).[83]

Muhammad affirms the validity of the revelation of Allah to the Jews and Christians; Muhammad's is the last of a series of covenants, in the line of those made with Noah, Abraham, Moses, the Prophets, and Jesus (XXXIII. 7). Jesus is given particular honor; he is the Messiah promised to Israel, and the greatest of the prophets before Muhammad. But Christians are mistaken in attributing divinity to him or calling him God's Son:

> The Messiah, Jesus son of Mary, was only a messenger of Allah. . . . So believe in Allah and His messengers, and say not "Three" [i.e., the Christian Trinity]. Far is it removed from His transcendent majesty that He should have a son (IV. 171; cf. V. 46, 72–75, LVII. 27).

> Lo! the likeness of Jesus with Allah is as the likeness of Adam. He created him of dust, then He said to him: Be! and he is (III. 59).

> He [Jesus] is nothing but a slave[84] on whom We bestowed favor, and We made him a pattern for the children of Israel (XLIII. 59).

This same judgment is attributed to Jesus himself (miraculously speaking as an infant!):

> Lo! I am the slave of Allah. He hath given me the Scripture and hath appointed me a Prophet. (XIX. 30)

Jesus indeed is said to have predicted the coming of Muhammad (who is associated by Muslims with the Paraclete promised by Jesus):

> Jesus the son of Mary said: O Children of Israel! Lo! I am the messenger of Allah unto you, confirming that which was before me in the Torah, and bringing good tidings of a messenger who cometh after me, whose name is the Praised One (LXI. 6).[85]

As for Muhammad himself, he is also a slave of Allah (II. 23), a messenger, like those who have gone before (III. 144). He is, however, Allah's final messenger, not only a prophet, but the "Seal of the Prophets" (XXXIII. 40), the final prophetic revelation. He is the "friend" of Allah, as are all the righteous (VII. 196). This is the limit of intimacy between creature and Creator. Although Allah is closer to each person than the jugular vein (L. 16), he remains utterly transcendent. The *Qur'an* not only denies the sonship of Jesus, understood in the sense of his divinity, but refuses the notion of such intimacy with Allah as is implied even in the wider notion of humans as his "children":

> The Jews and Christians say: We are sons of Allah and His loved ones. Say: Why then doth He chastise you for your sins? Nay, ye are but mortals of His creating (V. 18).

> It is not meet for the Beneficent that He should choose a son. There is none in the heavens and the earth but cometh unto the Beneficent as a slave (XIX. 92–93).

The final and proper relation of the human to Allah, the true religion, is "The Surrender": *Al-Islâm* (III. 19; V. 3). (The corresponding verb is *aslama*, "to surrender or submit"; *muslim* is the participle of the verb; hence *muslim* = "those who make the surrender."[86])

The making of the surrender to Allah's will is itself a gift from him (XLIX. 17). So absolute is Muhammad's conception of the uniqueness of the divine power that everything whatsoever—good or evil—must ultimately be ascribed to Allah's will. Human disbelief and disobedience are thus also the product of his inscrutable decree:

> As for the disbelievers, whether thou warn them or thou warn them not it is all one for them; they believe not. Allah hath sealed their hearing and their hearts, and in their eyes there is a covering. Theirs will be an awful doom. . . . In their hearts is a disease, and Allah increaseth their disease (II. 6, 7, 10).

> And though We should send down the angels unto them, and the dead should speak to them, and We should gather against them all things in array, they would not believe unless Allah so willed (VI. 112).

> Allah sendeth whom He will astray, and guideth unto Himself all who turn [to Him] (XIII. 27; cf. XIV. 27).

> And whomsoever it is Allah's will to guide, He expandeth his bosom until the Surrender, and whomsoever it is His will to send astray, He maketh his bosom close and narrow as if he were engaged in sheer ascent. Thus Allah layeth ignominy upon those who believe not (VI. 126).

> He whom Allah leadeth, he indeed is led aright, while he whom Allah sendeth astray—they indeed are losers. Already have We urged into hell many of the jinn and humankind (VII. 178, 179).[87]

Even the revelation itself is a means of misleading many (II. 26). Furthermore, there are adversaries to salvation. The fall of the devil (*Iblîs*, from the Greek *diabolos*) through pride is described several times in the *Qur'an;* he becomes the enemy of humanity, leading toward sin:

And We created you, then fashioned you, then told the angels: Fall ye prostrate before Adam! And they fell prostrate, all save Iblîs, who was not of those who make prostration.

He [Allah] said: What hindered thee that thou didst not fall prostrate when I bade thee? [Iblîs] said: I am better than him. Thou createdst me of fire while him Thou didst create of mud.

He [Allah] said: Then go down hence! It is not for thee to show pride here, so go forth! Lo! thou art of those degraded.

He [Iblîs] said: Reprieve me till the day when they are raised (from the dead).

He [Allah] said: Lo! thou art of those reprieved.

He [Iblîs] said: Now, because Thou hast sent me astray, verily I shall lurk in ambush for them on Thy Right Path. Then I shall come upon them from before them and from behind them and from their right hands and from their left hands, and Thou wilt not find most of them beholden (unto Thee).

He [Allah] said: Go forth from hence, degraded, banished. As for such of them as follow thee, surely I will fill hell with all of you (VII. 11–18; cf. XV. 28–43).[88]

As is already clear from the above, the temptation of humanity takes place by Allah's desire:

Thus have We appointed unto every Prophet an adversary—devils of humankind and jinn who inspire in one another plausible discourse through guile. If thy Lord willed, they would not do so; so leave them alone with their devising (V. 113).

The implication is a positive predestination from Allah not only to salvation, but also to damnation:

And if We had so willed, We could have given every soul its guidance, but the word from Me concerning evil-doers took effect: that I will fill hell with the jinn and mankind together (XXXII. 13).

Not only on the plane of salvation, but also in earthly life Allah's will is all-determining: Allah gives life and causes death (III. 156); he gives laughter and weeping (LIII. 43, 44); no calamity befalls us except by his leave (LXIV. 11); nothing at all happens to us, except what he has decreed (IX. 150); one should not even say, "I shall do a certain thing tomorrow," without adding: "if Allah wills" (XVIII. 24–25). The message of the *Qur'an* is unequivocal: *all* is from Allah (IV. 78), and "Allah doeth what he will" (XIV. 27).

At the same time, paradoxically, the second great message of the

Qur'an is human responsibility. Muhammad's mission is to proclaim an urgent call to conversion and ethical behavior, and to warn of impending judgment; a mission which makes no sense if humanity is not capable of acting freely. In fact, it appears from literary analysis that one of Muhammad's principal concerns was to combat the "fatalist" concept of life which was prevalent in his environment.[89] It is stressed that Allah has sent his messengers to all people (XVI. 36), and that he never punishes without sending a messenger to warn people to repent (XVII. 15). Despite the deterministic cast of many Qur'anic sayings, therefore, human responsibility is in practice assumed. Along with the message that Allah determines all things comes his command to act righteously. Each person is entirely responsible for his own actions, and must be judged for them by Allah. It is notable that there is no priesthood in Islam, no intercession for others (this is somewhat mollified in Shi'ite Islam; see below); each person stands alone before Allah in full responsibility. There is no relying on the merit of anyone else; each person must achieve salvation by personal effort. This is the "bad news" (LIII. 36) which Muhammad brings for sinners; they must know

> That no laden one shall bear another's load,
> And that man hath only that for which he maketh effort,
> And that his effort will be seen
> And afterward he will be repaid for it with fullest payment (LIII. 38–41; cf.
>   VI. 165; XVII. 15; XXXV. 18).

How can humanity be responsible, if everything is determined by Allah? This question is not answered by the *Qur'an*, and has exercised Muslim theology for centuries. But both assertions are plain in Mohammed's teaching. Indeed, immediately after affirming that every occurrence, good or evil, is from Allah (IV. 78), the *Qur'an* goes on to say in the very next verse: "Whatever of good befalleth thee, it is from Allah, and whatever of ill befalleth thee it is from thyself" (IV. 79).

A great proportion of the *Qur'an* is devoted to the concrete formulation of the ethical demands of surrender to Allah. The subjects covered range from universal ethical precepts to the norms for divorce and the duties of everyday life. Social justice and concern for others form a large part of this teaching; along with belief in and worship of Allah alone, they are the primary emphasis of the *Qur'an*.

> Righteous is he who believeth in Allah and the Last Day and the angels
> and the Scripture and the Prophets; and giveth his wealth, for love of
> Him, to kinsfolk and to orphans and the needy and the wayfarer and to

those who ask, and who sets slaves free; and observeth proper worship and payeth the poor-due. And those who keep their treaty when they make one, and the patient in tribulation and adversity and time of stress. Such are they who are sincere. Such are the God-fearing (II. 177).

From the *Qur'an*'s teaching (as concretized through the *hadîth*, the tradition of the Prophet's practice) are derived the five "pillars" of Islam, the duties of every Muslim. They are: First, the repetition of the brief creed: *"la ilaha illa Allah; Muhammad rasul Allah"*—"there is no god but God (Allah); Muhammad is the Prophet of God." Second, prayer at five specified periods of the day. Third, giving alms. Concretely, this takes the form of the payment of the poor-due or tax (*az-zakâh*), a property tax for the relief of the poor. This duty is much stressed in the *Qur'an* (for example, II. 110, where it is placed next to worship). Fourth, fasting during the month of Ramadân (II. 183). Fifth, a pilgrimage (*hajj*), for all who are able, to Mecca, the seat of the original sanctuary of Allah. The *Qur'an* also imposes a duty of warfare for the faith and for his people (*jihâd*):[90]

Warfare is ordained for you, though it is hateful unto you; but it may happen that ye hate a thing which is good for you, and it may happen that ye love a thing which is bad for you. Allah knoweth, ye know not (II. 216).

Whoso fighteth in the way of Allah, be he slain or be he victorious, on him We shall bestow a vast reward. How should ye not fight for the cause of Allah and of the feeble among men and of the women and the children who are crying: O Lord!. . . . So fight the minions of the devil (IV. 74, 75, 76; cf. IV. 95).

It is made clear, however, that the strivings of humans in no way benefit Allah; he is entirely independent of his creatures (XXIX. 6).

Although the *Qur'an* is replete with commandments and prescriptions, the legalistic spirit is tempered by an understanding attitude toward circumstances and human weakness: "Allah would make the burden light for you, for man was created weak" (III. 28). Exceptions are frequently conceded, even to important regulations; when a person is driven to an objectively sinful act, "lo! Allah is Forgiving, Merciful" (XVI. 115 and *passim*).

Although much space is given to the regulation of everyday affairs, the emphasis is upon an ethical attitude and on what today would be called "social justice." On the other hand, there is little of the idea of bearing others' burdens; it is presumed that Allah gives to each what he deserves or needs.

Muhammad did not break with the institution of slavery, but he made the freeing of slaves a virtue. Likewise, he did not undo the inferior position of women—indeed, the *Qur'an* plainly states that the male is above the female (II. 228, IV. 34)—nor did he abolish polygamy and concubinage; but he made an important step forward in proclaiming that women have rights "similar" to those of males (II. 228); they are also promised the same heavenly reward (IX. 72).

Although there are passages in the *Qur'an* which denounce bitterly the religious opponents of Islam, there are also passages which recommend tolerance, especially to the other "People of the Book," i.e., Jews and Christians, leaving differences in the hands of Allah:

Had Allah willed He could have made you one community. But that He may try you by that which He hath given you (He hath made you as ye are). So vie one with another in good works. Unto Allah ye will all return, and He will then inform you of that wherein ye differ (V. 48).

Unto each nation have We given sacred rites which they are to perform; so let them not dispute with thee of the matter, but summon thou unto thy Lord (XXII. 67).

Lo! Those who believe, and those who are Jews, and Christians, and Sabaeans—whoever believeth in Allah and the Last Day and doeth right—surely their reward is with their Lord (II. 62).

The Last Day and the Judgment form one of the most frequent themes of Muhammad's preaching. The dead will be raised—for Allah, who created all from nothing, can bring alive again what has died (XIX. 66–67)[91]—and all will receive the fruits of their actions on earth. There are vivid descriptions of the sufferings of hell; but more frequent and lengthy are the descriptions of the delights of Paradise, which is imagined in a thoroughly material way:

They will be honored
In the Gardens of delight,
On couches facing one another;
A cup from a gushing spring is brought round for them,
White, delicious to the drinkers,
Wherein there is no headache nor are they made mad thereby.
And with them are those of modest gaze, with lovely eyes . . . (XXXVII. 40–48; *cf.* IX. 72; XIII. 35; XVIII, 32; XXII. 23; XLVII. 15; LVI. 12–40).

For Islam the religious "problem" and its "solution" are both concerned with the practical ordering of human life in the world. As we have seen earlier, the classical problem of theodicy can hardly be raised in Islam; for God is beyond all questioning.[92] The problem lies entirely with humanity: we are alienated from God. Although in every way dependent upon him, humans forget God, and live as though the world were an independent self-standing reality. The forgetfulness of God—reinforced by the seduction of the devil—is the root of sin and alienation ("Lo! Man is verily an ingrate" [XXII. 66]).

The solution to this situation is given by God himself, who addresses our forgetful being and demands that we remember that he exists and that he alone is God; we are to recognize our being as coming from him and returning to him.[93] Salvation consists in complete submission to this revelation and in making the fact of God's absoluteness the central and guiding insight of life. Concretely, this means that we must make the world God's in practice, by establishing in earthly institutions and community the moral order revealed by him.

It follows that Islam is above all a religion of ethical involvement with the world and its structures: a *political* theology. The Muslim Islamic scholar Fazlur Rahman calls it the "major characteristic" of Islam to establish a Community (*Umma*) of the Faithful, expressing their belief in the divinely ordained pattern of human conduct (*shari'a*) through human institutions, backed by government.[94] Islam has nothing corresponding to "the Church" because *all* of human existence must be brought under the institutionalized rule of God's revealed law; there is no possibility of independent "sacred" and "secular" realms.[95] Islam has therefore constantly insisted upon establishing itself as a political power, even if it does not necessarily impose belief in its creed, because it considers itself the repository of the revealed will of God, which must be worked out in the concrete structures of human life.[96] It is not sufficient that the message of the *Qur'an* should be proclaimed; it must be effectively implemented, for only then is it truly God's infallible message.[97] God's message and law must not merely enter human history; they must triumph in history:

> A God to whom it is, in the final analysis, indifferent whether He is effective in history or not is certainly not the God of Muhammad and the Qur'an. If history is the proper field for Divine activity, historical forces must, by definition, be employed for the moral end as judiciously as possible. . . . The Islamic purpose must be achieved, as an absolute imperative, and for this not only preaching but the harnessing of social and political forces is necessary.[98]

A consequence of the idea that God has revealed his will for human society has been the predominance, in the mainstream of orthodox Islam, of law (*sharî'a*) over all other aspects of religious life. The *Qur'an*, literally interpreted, is of course the first source of knowledge of God's will. The law is also interpreted through *sunna* (literally "trodden path"), the tradition based upon the Prophet's way of acting (largely transmitted in the *Hadîth*, writings which purport to trace oral revelation back to Muhammad himself); through *ijma*, consensus—first of the companions of Muhammad, second of the living community, and finally, if the others are silent, through *ijtihâd*, personal reflection.[99]

Given the fundamentally political character of Islam, it is not surprising that its major religious division—into the Sunni and Shî'a sects—had its basis in political differences. When Muhammad died, Abû Bakr, the father of his favorite wife, Aisha, was elected Caliph (= "successor," i.e., to the Prophet). A strong party, however, favored 'Alî, the husband of Muhammad's daughter Fâtima, and father of the Prophet's only surviving grandsons, Hasan and Husayn. 'Alî was overlooked again in subsequent elections, and was finally assassinated in 661. His son Husayn, having taken up the claim to the caliphate (the older Hasan having renounced his rights), was massacred, with most of his family, in 680. These events precipitated the schism in Islam. The widespread discontent of non-Arab Muslims with the Arabic caliphate (which under the Umayyad dynasty became increasingly irreligious) found expression in adherence to the cause of the family of 'Alî. These partisans became known as the Shî'a (*shî'a* = "party," i.e., of 'Ali), while those who remained faithful to the caliphate were termed the Sunnah (= tradition).[100]

While the immediate cause of the schism was political, there was already from the beginning a theological conflict as well. Shi'ism arose at least partly from the desire for a more-than-human savior.[101] The Shî'ites tended to idealize and glorify the person of Muhammad, raising him to a super-human level. His family shared in the same process of glorification. This was the reason why the leadership in Islam must remain in the Prophet's family. Furthermore, the deaths of 'Alî and Husayn were looked upon as martyrdom, and there was introduced to the Shî'a what would become its most salient characteristic: the "passion" motif, a belief in a kind of salvific suffering of God's elect (an idea influenced by Christianity, and in contrast to the triumphalism of orthodox Sunni theology).[102] 'Alî and his successors became known as Imâms—a term originally referring to the one who led public prayer (the caliph), which in the Shî'a came to designate the supreme political and religious authority.[103]

The development of Shî'ite theology was largely a function of its political failure and of its absorption of ideas from the original religions of its non-Arab (especially Persian) adherents: Christianity, Manichaeanism, Zoroastrianism, and even Buddhism.[104] When the line of 'Alî ran out, there developed the idea of Muhammad al-Mahdî, the "Guided One of God," a quasi-divine personage who will appear at the end of time to establish God's rule. For the majority of Shî'ites, the Mahdî is identified with the "hidden Imâm," the last descendent of 'Alî, who disappeared but will return.[105] This eschatological doctrine, in which the influence of Christianity and Zoroastrianism is clearly perceived, becomes the hallmark of Shî'ism.

The persecution of the Shî'ites by the orthodox led to the formulation of the principle of "dissimulation of belief"; at first merely a practical means of escaping persecution, it became a theological principle by being applied to 'Alî, who purportedly hid his knowledge of his divine right to the caliphate, and finally to God himself, who hides the true (esoteric) meaning of the Qur'an,[106] including the doctrine of the Imâms. The esoteric hermeneutic of the Shî'a required masters who would reveal the true meanings of the Scripture; these masters were of course especially the Imâms.

The position of the Imâm was progressively exalted, so that belief in the Imâm became a third principle of faith, along with belief in God and his Apostle (Muhammad). The adoption of the Neoplatonic concept of emanation, combined with the analogy of God as Light (which appears in the Qur'an: XXIV. 35), made the Imâm an epiphany of the primal Light, intermediary (along with Muhammad) between God and humanity, and the ultimate human being. In the most extreme sects, he is conceived as an actual incarnation of God.[107] This doctrine allows in principle for the discovery of entirely new dimensions in Islam, not contained in the revelation to Muhammad—contrary to the fundamental orthodox tenet that Muhammad is the Seal of the Prophets, the last revelation.[108] This conclusion is actually reached in the more extreme (Ismâ'îlî) Shî'ite sects.[109] At the same time, the Shî'a also exalted Muhammad, conceiving him as perfectly sinless (an idea which entered orthodoxy), and inventing for him a miraculous biography.

The Shî'a differs from the Sunna in not recognizing ijma' (consensus) as a principle of orthodoxy; it appeals instead to the authority of the Imâm, who is held to be sinless and infallible in all matters.[110] Unfortunately, there is much disagreement on the identity of the Imâms, resulting in a proliferation of sub-sects. On the other hand, the principle of consensus (along with a fundamentalist attitude to the Qur'an) has allowed the Sunna to be remarkably cohesive.[111] Similarly, the Shî'a has kept open the "door of ijtihâd" (personal interpretation of dogma and law), which has been closed in Sunni Islam since the tenth century.[112] One correlate of this is that most Shî'ite Muslims reject the doctrine of predestination, which figures prominently in Sunni teaching, and affirm human freedom.[113]

The Shî'a survived for centuries in a more or less underground existence until the Ṣafavid dynasty, following the Turko-Persian wars, made it the state creed of Persia. The Islamic world was then divided in a way parallel to the roughly contemporaneous division of Europe into Catholic and Protestant by the principle *cujus regio, ejus religio*. This situation still obtains, for the most part, today, with Shîites forming the majority in the former Ṣafavid areas of Iraq and Iran and being strong in Pakistan, while the Sunna predominates elsewhere.

Despite the significant divergences between the sects, some Shî'a ideas entered into orthodox Sunni Islam: for example, the veneration of the house of the Prophet and the concept of the Mahdî. Much more significant, however, was the power which Shî'ite ideas exerted indirectly, through influence on the mystical movement known as Ṣûfism.[114]

Along with the schism of the Shî'a, Ṣûfism must rank as the most significant development to affect Islam. While the main emphasis of Muslim theology and spirituality is social and political, its foundation is universally acknowledged to lie in the prophetic consciousness of Muhammad, which is based upon the Prophet's "mystical" experience of the Absolute.[115] Alongside and in tension with the socio-political institutions of Islam, which take their root in Muhammad's doctrine, a piety grew up which sought to imitate rather the Prophet's experience, and emphasized the personal and mystical dimensions of faith.

The origins of Ṣûfism can be traced to a pietistic-ascetical reaction against the overly legalistic and external character of early Islam. For two centuries, Ṣûfism (the term derives from *ṣûf* = "wool," from the coarse clothing worn as a sign of asceticism) remained spontaneous and individual. In reaction against the over-politicization of Islam (and the attendant power struggles), certain Muslims sought holiness in isolation and interiority. The Qur'anic doctrine of trust in God was expanded to imply renunciation of the world. (It is probably not accidental that the early home of Ṣûfism was in Khorasan, in northeast Persia, where Buddhist influence had been strong.[116]) This ascetical movement grew and, located in a crossroads of cultures, absorbed ideas from many sources: Christian, neo-Platonic, Gnostic, Manichaean, Jewish, Zoroastrian, and Buddhist, as well as being influenced by (and influencing) developing Shî'ism.[117]

Within two hundred years of the Prophet's death, Ṣûfism had become a recognizable type of life; by the eleventh century it had become a religion within a religion, with many organized orders or brotherhoods. It was the prime source of the intense missionary activity among the Turks, in India,

Central Asia, Anatolia, and Africa.[118] It was above all a religion of the un-educated masses, offering a piety of the heart and meditative techniques (including singing and dancing) to attain direct union with God. In contrast to the distant and abject relation to God implied by official Islam, it em-phasized the notion of *walâyat*, divine friendship.[119] It venerated holy men, believed in miracles, and developed a cult of saints and a concrete focus for piety in visits to their tombs. It insisted on complete submission to the authority of a *shaykh* or spiritual master (*gûru*). Sûfi Islam became a religion of intercession, mediators, and grace. It was also willing, in its missionary activity, to make compromises with the religious beliefs of con-verts, leading to new non-Arabic interpretations of Islam. At the extreme, it approached both Hindu monism and the Christian idea of incarnation. It also served at the same time as a protest movement against the official state religion and the despotic rulers with which it was associated.[120]

Perhaps the most dangerous aspects of Sûfism, from the orthodox point of view, were its tendency to monism and its emphasis on *ma'rifa* (= "gnosis"). The first transformed the Qur'anic moral doctrine of the unity and omnipotence of God into a pantheism in which God is the *only* being, and the world an emanation from him.[121] The goal of devotion, then, is to attain *fanâ* (= "absorption" or "annihilation"): the replacement of human attributes with the divine[122]—an idea which sounds suspiciously like the *nirvâna* of the Hindus and Buddhists. The correlative notion of *ma'rifa* holds that God is ultimately knowable only by an inner intuitive certitude—thus constituting an authority outside and independent of rev-elation in the *Qur'an.*

The doctrinal dangers of the Sûfi movement were recognized both by the authorities of orthodoxy (the doctors of Qur'anic law) and by members of the movement. At the same time, the appeal of Sûfi piety, interiority and personal sanctity and the insufficiency of legalist piety were increas-ingly felt even within the strongholds of orthodoxy. On both sides there-fore, there were efforts at rapprochement. The synthesis was achieved by the great theologian al-Ghazâlî (1058–1111).

Al-Ghazâlî nearly single-handedly provided the intellectual frame-work which saved orthodox, fundamentalist Islam and at the same time permitted the absorption of the energies of Sûfism. His contribution was threefold. First, he provided a devastating critique of philosophy. Islam in the early Middle Ages had inherited the rich intellectual tradition of Hellenic civilization and of Hellenized Christianity, and had produced a series of brilliant philosophers, culminating in the great Ibn Sînâ (Avi-cenna). Unfortunately, these intellectual developments led to clashes with orthodox theology and literalist Qur'anic faith. Hence, Islamic philosophy, "having failed to satisfy orthodox requirements . . . was denied the passport to survival."[123] It was al-Ghazâlî who dealt the death-blow. In his work *The Incoherence of the Philosophers* he attempts a point-by-point refutation of the teachings of the great philosophers, exposes their inner inconsistencies and disagreements with each other, and shows their incompatibility with Islamic faith. Henceforth the place of reason in Islam was to be at the service of orthodoxy; independent philosophy was replaced with theology.[124]

Al-Ghazâlî's second great contribution was to "purify" Ṣûfism and so make it acceptable to orthodoxy. Himself a devoted Ṣûfi, he showed that, cleansed of un-Islamic elements and correctly interpreted, Ṣûfism could be completely orthodox, while at the same time adding new spiritual life and vigor to the faith. He laid down the hermeneutic principles which allowed an orthodox interpretation of the piety of interiority. His third contribution was related: he reconstituted Islam by synthesizing the spirituality of Ṣûfism into an orthodox Qur'anic theology.[125] Islam was saved from a radical split between popular piety and official doctrine, and was immeasurably enriched by the addition of a religion of love and personal relationship to the ethical and legal structure of orthodoxy.

In al-Ghazâlî's orthodox interpretation, mystic experiences are valid, but are only the first moment in a total experience, in which there is a return to the world and the ethical values of the *Qur'an*—on the model of Muhammad himself. Against Gnostic tendencies, al-Ghazâlî insists that while the mystic *experience* is valid, it gives no *content* to religion beyond what is given in the external revelation of the *Qur'an*. The ecstatic claims of unity (or even identity) with God made by Ṣûfi mystics are to be taken as "non-responsible" statements, made in a state of spiritual intoxication.[126] In other words, such statements are disclaimed on a theological level, but at the same time they are permitted to stand on the religious and emotive level as a kind of spiritual hyperbole or poetry. They are also counter-balanced by an emphasis on sin and the need for purification—ideas common to orthodoxy and the mystic way. Thus dogma is saved, while the spiritual energy of devotionalism is gained. Ironically, the reconciliation of Ṣûfism with Sunni orthodoxy strengthened the position of Sunni Islam at the expense of the Shî'a, for by allowing an affective devotion to Muhammad and to 'Alî, and by claiming the Imâms themselves as authorities, Ṣûfism undercut much of the appeal of Shî'ism to the masses.[127]

Among the ideas which mainstream Islam absorbed from the Ṣûfi movement was intense devotion to Muhammad himself. He was provided with a miraculous birth and had miracles attributed to him (quite in opposition to his own statements recorded in the *Qur'an*); he was turned to for help in times of need; he became, in effect, the virtual mediator between God and humanity.[128] Even such ideas as Muhammad as the primal light, existing before Adam, and through whom God creates the world, which if taken literally would seriously compromise God's uniqueness, could be accepted by Sunni theology as correct "eulogistic" statements of the honor due the Prophet.

Despite the synthesis achieved by al-Ghazâlî, however, Sûfism was not entirely absorbed into orthodoxy, and Gnostic and monist forms of mysticism (as for example the system of Ibn al-'Arabi, 1165–1240) kept reappearing from time to time. Nevertheless, Islam has on the whole succeeded both in absorbing new forms and in remaining remarkably true to its foundations. In the modern period it has been characterized by several reform movements which have attempted to purify it of accretions and return even more radically to the original tradition. Moreover, in all but the most extreme of its sects it has always been faithful to the simple originating insight of the Absoluteness of God and the imperative of humanity's complete submission (*islam*) to him.

VI. A FINAL WORD OF GOD? THE DIALECTIC AND CONVERGENCE OF RELIGIONS

In the year of the death of King Ozias, I saw the Lord Yahweh seated on an exalted throne; the train of his robe filled the sanctuary; Seraphim were above him, each having six wings: two to cover its face, two to cover its feet, and two with which to fly.

And they cried aloud to each other in these words:

"Holy, holy, holy is Yahweh Sabaoth.

His glory fills all the earth."

The foundations trembled at the voice of him who cried, and the temple was filled with smoke. I said:

"Woe is me, I am lost;

for I am a man of sinful lips,

I live in the midst of a people of sinful lips,

and my eyes have seen the King, Yahweh Sabaoth."

Is 6:1–5

[The father said to his son:] "Place this salt in water and then come to me in the morning."

The son did as he was told.

The father said to him: "My son, bring me the salt which you placed in the water last night."

Looking for it, the son did not find it, for it was completely dissolved.

The father said: "My son, take a sip of water from the surface. How is it?"

"It is salt."

"Take a sip from the middle. How is it?"

"It is salt."

"Take a sip from the bottom. How is it?"

"It is salt."

"Throw it away and come to me."

The son did as he was told, saying: "The salt was there all the time."

Then the father said: "Here also, my dear, in this body, verily, you do not perceive Being; but It is indeed there.

Now, that which is the subtle essence—in it all that exists has its self.

161

That is the True. That is the Self. That art thou. . . . "

Chhândogya Upanishad, VI. 13:1–3

Our examination of the classic formulations of revelation in the higher religions has taken place not only with the recognition that all are expressions of God's self-manifestation, but also in the light of the question of whether there are grounds for affirming a "special" categorical revelation of God in history: a final and definitive human expression and presence of God's "solution" being achieved through human collaboration. Christianity and Islam both explicitly claim to be such a special revelation, and in at least some forms of each of the remaining higher religions there can be found implicit indications of a similar claim—if not to be God's final word, at least to represent a higher form of truth, a synthesis of the truths present elsewhere.

Before we turn to an examination of the Christian claim, we will attempt to encapsulate some of the more striking divergences and convergences manifested in the human response to and formulation of God's self-revelation.

THE DIALECTIC OF RELIGIONS

There are of course significant differences in the cultural forms and "languages" in which each religion finds its primary expression. Even those which are not tied to a particular people or place (as Hinduism is to India or Judaism to the Jews) tend to take on a certain emotional, intellectual and aesthetic coloration from their cultural ambience(s).[1] (Of some this is of course much more true than of others; for Islamic orthodoxy, the *Qur'an* can only be read in Arabic, and Sunni Islam remains closely tied to the Arabian ethos, while Christianity and Mahâyâna Buddhism, for example, have subsisted in multiple and very diverse cultural expressions.) However, although the aesthetic-symbolic dimension is clearly important to the formulation of the conversion experience, our interest at this point must be more centered on the differences in the interpretations of reality which are symbolized than on the specifically aesthetic, psychological and cultural differences expressed in the symbols themselves.

On the level of interpretation of existence it is clear that there are divergences among the higher religions which are substantial, and cannot be reduced to cultural or linguistic differences. It will perhaps be helpful to set forth the general lines of these differences. Of course it must be borne in mind that each of the characteristic interpretations in our classifications may be found, to some degree, in each of the religious traditions, that there are syncretistic combinations of the "classic" forms (e.g., the religions of Mani, combining elements of Zoroastrianism, Buddhism, and Christianity), and that exceptions may be found to each of our generalizations. It is only a question here of discerning predominant forms.

First of all, there are several variant (although sometimes partially overlapping) conceptions of the Absolute or ultimate Reality. One radical position holds that the Absolute cannot be represented at all in terms taken from our present experience of being. This position is characteristic above all of Buddhism, but it plays an important role in the Advaita philosophical school of Hinduism, and is to some extent present in all mystical and metaphysical traditions, insofar as the Absolute is recognized as completely transcendent.

A second position holds a monist interpretation of the divine: the Absolute is in reality the *only* being, so that all that is—including evil—is ultimately identical with the primal Real. Philosophical Hinduism is the prime foremost example of this position; it is found also in the idealist forms of Mahâyâna Buddhism, in Taoism (and hence in some forms of Zen thinking), in the more extreme Jewish, Christian and Muslim mystics, and in Hellenistic neo-Platonic thought.

The third major position is monotheist: the ultimate reality is represented as (a) personal and self-revealing Being, distinct from the world and creator of it. The great monotheistic religions are Judaism, Christianity, and Islam, but, as we have seen, the majority of Hindus are also monotheistic, and the term might also be applied in a wide sense to some forms of Mahâyâna Buddhism. For the theist, the existence of evil is a real metaphysical problem, for it seems to challenge either the omnipotence or the goodness of God, both of which must be affirmed.

Finally, there is a dualist representation of the ultimate, in which being is seen as irreducibly metaphysically divided into good and evil. Only Zoroastrianism among the great religions consistently holds this theology, but it manifests itself in heretical forms of Christianity, as well as in the syncretistic religion of Manichaeanism. The existence of evil is explained in this system, but the unity of being is compromised.

There are also differing views on the source of knowledge of right relation to the Absolute. Theist traditions tend to think in terms of revelation and inspiration by God, while the monist and apophatic traditions rather speak of "enlightenment" from within the individual (compare the prophet Isaiah standing before the thrice-holy and totally other God with the Upanishadic invitation to the insight, "That art thou . . ."). Like the distinction between "prophetic" and "mystical" religions, however, this difference between religions of revelation and of enlightenment must not be over-emphasized. All the great religions have both "prophetic" and "mystical" dimensions; all have scriptures which are believed to be derived from a supra-human source; all find their message concretely mediated by revered human teachers (we shall return to this point at length below). Revelation, except in the most fundamentalist and literalist interpretation, must come through the mind of its receiver (categorical revelation as "achievement"), while enlightenment is experienced as somehow "given" from a transcendent source.[2] Concretely, the Buddha acts in a prophetic manner, and the *Saṅgha* receives his word as revelation; Muhammad acts like a mystic, and the *Ummah* interprets the inspired revelation at least partly in the light of inner experience; the Zen adept receives instruction under absolute obedience to a master, and the Christian believes in the Spirit which blows where it will.

Nevertheless, the difference in focus and emphasis is certainly significant, and points to wider differences in the interpretation of salvation itself. The three Hindu "ways" of salvation—salvation through knowledge (*jñāna-mārga*), through works (*karma-mārga*) and through faith (*bhakti-mārga*)—occur in all the great religions, but again there are significant differences in the centers of gravity. Hînayâna Buddhism and Advaita Hinduism (and some of the philosophical forms of the Mahâyâna) probably represent the extreme position on salvation through knowledge, or enlightenment: there is no real *achievement* of salvation, merely an insight into reality as it already and always is. Zoroastrianism, Judaism and Islam all center on salvation through works, the former perhaps most radically, in that God himself as well as the world must be "saved" through struggle against evil. All the world religions, however, insist upon "works of the law" to some extent, even if the law's function is in theory merely pedagogical. Salvation by personal relation—grace and faith—is typical of Christianity, Mahâyâna Buddhism, and theistic Hinduism. In each of these, as we have seen, the question arises whether salvation is through grace (faith) *alone*, or whether there is also a human contribution or achievement involved.

The different "ways" of salvation are signs of different answers to the question of what humanity is and how the world is related to our final goal. It is a characteristic of religion in general to maintain that the world, as it now is, is not ultimate, that there is something wrong. There are fundamentally distinct ways of perceiving the nature of and solution to that wrongness, however. One current sees salvation in the denial of the world, and sees the truest nature of humanity as not belonging to it. The Buddhist doctrine of "no-self" and the Hindu identification of the real self with "âtman" tend to imply a negative evaluation of the world and of human engagement in it. If "nothing from here may pass over to there (i.e., nirvâṇa)," then the world is in the last analysis valueless to salvation, if not actually a hindrance to it. Furthermore, according to the theory of *karma*, all suffering within the world is just, for it was merited in previous existences. The answer to the human dilemma is an altogether different kind of existence. Practically, these religious traditions typically and logically stress asceticism and exalt the monastic life.

At the opposite extreme, the Zoroastrian-Jewish-Islamic view sees the human being as intrinsically involved with the world, and the kingdom of God as being in continuation with present existence. The doctrines of creation and of the resurrection of the body are symbolic of this continuity, even when the latter is combined with a notion of a separable "soul." These religions emphasize moral activity and conformity to the law of God. They condone enjoyment of the world and are suspicious of asceticism and monasticism (this is of course especially true of Zoroastrianism; some forms of both Judaism and Islam have developed ascetical practices, usually under the influence of other traditions). Suffering and evil are to be opposed; they originate not with God, nor with the world, but with the misuse of freedom.

A third current attempts a synthesis of the two antitheses, affirmation-denial: it affirms that salvation is attained through the world, that humanity is essentially spirit in the world, and at the same time that the world must be transcended and transformed. There is a necessary tension between the already, here-and-now, and the not-yet, beyond. In Christianity and some forms of Mahâyâna Buddhism (especially Zen) this attempted synthesis seems to reach its highest formulations. In these religions asceticism has a place, but is meant to be balanced by the "sacramentality" of the world. (In Christianity, for example, monasticism and celibacy have played a large part, but it is marriage which is considered a sacrament.) Suffering and evil are considered opposed to God or the Ultimate Real. They originate in sin (Christianity) or in misdirected craving (Buddhism), and are to be opposed by loving and compassionate self-sacrificing action, in imitation of the nature of ultimate Reality itself.

THE CONVERGENCE OF RELIGIONS

It will already be apparent that despite very major differences the great world religions develop largely according to similar patterns and are in agreement on a number of important points. Can we then speak of a convergence of the great religions? Do they, on the whole, point in the same—or a similar—direction?

To state that the higher religions converge on some very fundamental points seems easily justifiable. There do seem to be insights and spiritual attitudes interpreting the ultimate reality of human existence which occur with some regularity in the higher religions and seem typical of them—i.e., of a formulation of religious insight which includes world-consciousness and the worship of a transcendent principle beyond nature and humanity. Beyond such fundamentals, however, it is difficult to see how one could speak of an objectively verifiable convergence; the voices of the world religions form at best (in the words of St. Francis de Sales, adopted by Zaehner as the title of his study) a "concordant discord." To extricate from that discord a common directedness toward some central expression of revelation is to make a judgment on what that revelation is. Given the many diversities even within the individual religious traditions, it would seem inevitably to involve employing a principle of selectivity by which those aspects of religions are judged significant and valuable which point in the direction of one's own interpretation of existence.[3] Such a process, however, is quite legitimate, so long as we admit what we are about. We have in fact explicitly formulated a principle of selectivity in our anthropology and metaphysics; we have likewise already formulated a view of the problem to be addressed by religion and a heuristic structure of the solution. It is these which give the interpretive key which we shall apply to the data of religious phenomenology.[4]

Without yet specifying the categorical content of revelation, we have reached the conclusion from existential experience that any "solution" to the human dilemma must be a form of "conversion" which includes being in love with God in an absolute way and collaborating with others in history to overcome evil and sin. In the light of this anticipation, we may discern in the higher world religions a certain convergence toward a religion of love. Conversion, or transformation of the subject, takes place on the three levels of morality, intellect, and religion.

Moral conversion is expressed in the practice and formulation of an ethic of love, both of God and of others. All the great religions recognize the "golden rule" of human behavior: that of recognizing in each person a value equal to one's own. Although there is a wide disparity in formulation, all religions tend to become in practice religions of love. This means as well the affirmation of the value of personal being, essential equality of all persons, the building of community, and human responsibility in freedom for one's own existence, for the world, and for others.

On the intellectual level, conversion is expressed in the tendency to seek an understanding of existence which is in accord with the transcendental experience of "being in love." This means the affirmation of both the reality and the relativity of finite being, in the world and in persons, and the affirmation of God as the absolute and holy Mystery of Being. The Absolute is affirmed, furthermore, as being (in some sense) "personal" or supra-personal: in any case, the foundation of our own experience of person, consciousness, freedom and love. The relation with the Absolute is seen as analogous to the unity of persons—in themselves, and/or in dialogue with each other: that is, as personal unity (the Absolute as the final "self" of all selves) or as communion. Intellectual conversion also implies, therefore, a "metaphysical" view of being:[5] the world is more than meets the eye (Lonergan's "already out there now real"); values and ideas are (in some way) realities, not a mere by-product of material existence.

It is of course obvious that these tendencies toward a religion of conversion as absolute being in love exist in tension, on all levels, with the limitations of transcendence and with human failure to be converted, which, as we have seen, are also part of the concrete phenomenon of religion. Thus there are very varied degrees of success in the achievement and formulation of transcendence. In particular, one can point to religious phenomena on the moral level (the Hindu caste system, Judaic legalism, Christian exclusivism, Moslem militancy) and on the intellectual level (inadequate conceptions of God, of the world, of humanity) which implicitly oppose the dynamism of transcendence as love. Moreover, there is frequently a disparity between formulations and actual performance, in both directions: actions do not live up to formulated ideals, and, on the other hand, conceptual structures are not adequate to the strivings of conduct. Our contention, however, is that a religion of love, with all that it implies, is the implicit goal toward which the higher religious formulations tend, that it achieves significant expression in the world religious types we have surveyed, and that once it is formulated explicitly, it can be recognized as a goal even where it conflicts with existing structures.

On the religious level, conversion tends to expression as what we have called "mediated immediacy" to the Absolute or God. There are naturally differences of accent; some religious traditions stress the immediacy of God, some the mediation of God through creatures. Both aspects, however, come to some kind of expression in all the world religions. Immediacy to God is sought in mysticism; the mediation of God is sought in savior figures and revealers.[6] As we have already seen evidence of both of these tendencies in our outline considerations of the major religious traditions, it will suffice here to consider a few important points concerning immediacy and mediation, with several examples of each. (It goes without saying that there can be no attempt here to provide an exhaustive exposition of these two themes.)

Immediacy to God: Mysticism

*This Soul of mine in the heart is Brahman, and when I go from here I shall
merge into it.*

Chhândogya Upanishad, 3:14

> *There is not a private meeting of three
> but God is a fourth in it,
> nor of five but he is a sixth,
> nor of a lower number than that, nor a higher,
> but he is with them wherever they may be.*

Qur'an 58:8

*I know a man in Christ who, fourteen years ago—was it in his body? I do
not know; was it outside his body? I do not know, God knows— . . . this
man was transported up to the third heaven. And this man—was it in his
body? was it without his body? I do not know, God knows—I know that
he was transported to paradise and that he heard ineffable words which
it is not permitted to repeat.*

2 Cor 12:2–4

> *May all be one,
> as you, Father, are in me and I in you;
> may they also be one in us,
> so that the world may believe that you sent me.
> I have given them the glory which you gave me,
> that they may be one as we are one:
> I in them and you in me,
> so that they may be perfectly one,
> and that the world may know that you sent me
> and that I have loved them as you have loved me.*

Jn 17:20–23

Some kind of mysticism is found in all the higher religions. It is not
infrequently seen as the major point of convergence of all religions. Indeed, it is sometimes claimed that all mystical experience is fundamentally
the same, and surpasses all confessional differences and religious diversity.
On this view, the "message" or "content" dimension of religion would simply be an inadequate description of one basic religious experience, which
is met in its purest form in mysticism. The content, that is, is seen as a

secondary interpretation, posterior to and separable from the originating experience.

There is of course a truth in this position: the unity of the "object" of transcendental experience (God) and the sameness of the fundamental conditions of receptivity in the subject will necessarily mean that there is a basic similarity in all mystical experience (and, for that matter, in its formulations as well). However, this does not justify the claim that all mystical experience is simply the same. Such an assertion overlooks several important points.

First: it overlooks the epistemological conditions of human experience, which are such that several different kinds of experience may have a similar structure. There are many different non-thematic, pre-conceptual experiences. They are all similar in being non-thematic, but this does not mean that they are the same experience, or an experience of the same thing. Not all pre-thematic experience is experience of the transcendent; nevertheless, descriptions of such experiences will have something in common with descriptions of transcendent experience, simply because both kinds are non-verbal and pre-conceptual, and must be expressed (if at all) in words and ideas taken from the same thematic sources.

Moreover, there are different levels of experience of the transcendent. We may distinguish, for example, between the experience of the *Vorgriff* of being (the "natural desire for God") and the experience of what we have called "transcendental revelation." Furthermore, within the latter we may distinguish between the experience of God's self-gift as an *offer*, bearing an invitation to respond (Rahner's "supernatural existential"), and that same invitation as accepted (experience of "grace") or rejected (experience of sin, the void; the infinite experienced as absent). All of these are experiences of the "infinite," but, although they are clearly existentially related and interwoven, they are not simply the same experience. None of these is simply available to introspection, nor adequately thematizable; for this reason, they cannot be adequately distinguished by reflection or language. Nevertheless, it cannot be presumed that all discourse about transcendental experience refers to the same aspect of such experience. A person may indeed have an existential experience of "transcendental revelation"; it does not follow, however, that this is the referent of *every* transcendental experience. The fact of plurality in our own being ("concupiscence") means that our experience, even if it is "of" an existential unity, may "advert to" only a particular and incomplete (hence "abstract") aspect.

Second: the claim that all mystical experience is the same overlooks the interrelatedness of experience and interpretation.[7] It is true that "transcendental revelation" is logically "prior" to its categorical expression, but existentially the two are inseparable. One does not "have" an experience, and "then" interpret it; there is some level of interpretation (although not necessarily the final level) *implicitly* operative in the very "having" of experience.[8] Furthermore, our prior and habitual interpretations not only direct our experiences, but *constitute* them on the level of *meaning*, so that they are not mere unappropriated "data," but are genuinely "experienced" data.[9]

Third: the claim that mystical experience is all the same overlooks the factual differences in the descriptions of mystical states, as well as in the explanation of their meaning—differences which occur not only between different religious traditions, but within traditions.[10]

R. C. Zaehner insists that there are at least three distinct mystical states: (1) the "pan-en-henic" state, in which all creaturely existence is experienced as one, and the one is seen in all; (2) the state of pure isolation of the (uncreated) soul or spirit; (3) the state of absorption of the self into God. The first of these constitutes "nature" mysticism, which Zaehner characterizes as a descent into the Jungian collective unconscious. It is typified by a kind of consciousness which precedes individuality. Zaehner speculates that it may also be consciousness in the manic state of the manic-depressive psychosis.[11]

The second form consists in a contemplation of the isolated self: one's own spirit is seen as "infinite" and absolute. The Sâṁkhya-Yoga system is the prime example of such "solipsistic" mysticism, centered on the experience of one's own spirit,[12] but it was known also to Christian mystics, who consider it a lower and "natural" form of mystical consciousness: Ruysbroeck speaks of it as the soul's natural rest in itself, prior to any love for God; Richard of St. Victor describes it as the contemplation of the self as God's image, as distinct from the contemplation of God.[13] It originates in what Martin Buber calls the "pre-biographical unity" of the spirit. Insofar as it remains enclosed in the self, it is, for Zaehner, a "mystical dead-end."[14]

The third form of mysticism is theistic: the mysticism of love. The spirit, even though "lost" in God, remains in some way itself, for love requires mutuality. Theistic mysticism is therefore characterized by an experience of union rather than of simple unity.

In the terminology we have adopted from transcendental philosophy, these three forms of mysticism may be seen as three mediations of the immediacy of God: (1) Mediation by the "pure notion (Rahner's *Vorgriff*) of Being," i.e., the dynamism of mind toward all that is, with emphasis on the *objective* pole of consciousness. This kind of experience centers on the unity and "givenness" of being; it corresponds to Kant's transcendental idea, "the world." (2) Mediation by the pure notion of Being, with emphasis on the *subjective* pole of consciousness. This experience centers on spirit itself as *quoddamodo omnia* ("in some way, everything"—Aristotle's phrase for the infinite openness of consciousness); it corresponds to Kant's transcendental idea, "the soul." (3) Mediation by the pure notion of Being, focusing on the *goal* of the dynamism. This experience centers on the distinction between the transcendent goal and the categorical subject. It corresponds to Kant's transcendental idea, "God."

Each of these may also be an experience of "grace" or of God's transcendental self-revelation, which cannot be adequately distinguished in reflection from the "natural" infinity of the transcendental dynamism.

Mysticism—on one or more of the levels described—abounds in practically all the great traditions. (Zoroastrianism is perhaps an exception; even here, however, the intimate relation of the Prophet with Ahura Mazdâ may be seen as an example of love-mysticism.) We shall draw attention to only a few examples, making no pretense at a comprehensive overview.

Hinduism perhaps shows most clearly the different varieties of mystical experience/theology. The philosophical "monism" of the Upanishads points to the unity of the (real) Self, âtman, with the essence of all things, *Brahman:* "That art Thou." It seems to point to a pre-personal, unconscious unity of the All. In its major interpretation, however, in the Advaita school, the Ultimate (*Brahman*) is presented as Consciousness, and the relation of all things to it is spoken of as "non-dual" (*a-dvaita*) rather than "monist." As we noted above in our discussion of Śaṅkara, there remains some ambiguity about the absoluteness of the denial of the personal self. It is clear that the personal self is not *ultimately* real, and belongs to the sphere of *mâyâ;* yet there is some question whether it is ever simply annihilated in identity with God (as Śaṅkara's Hindu opponents claimed, denouncing him as a "secret Buddhist"). The *bhakti* hymns and prayers of Śaṅkara give rather a different impression from his purely philosophical writings, and are open to a more theistic interpretation:

> O Lord (Vishnu), even after realizing that there is no real difference between the individual soul and Brahman, I beg to state that I am yours and not that you are mine. The wave belongs to the ocean and not the ocean to the wave.[15]

We have already made mention of the soul-mysticism of the Sâṁkhya-Yoga tradition; each soul is a monad, eternal and distinct from all others. The goal of yoga is to reach pure, isolated objectless consciousness. (In the Yoga schools, one may be encouraged to *use* devotion to a god—considered one of the eternal monads, among the others—to help concentration, but this is considered merely a device.) This doctrine is in a general way parallel to that of the Jains.

Finally, there is a strong and widespread (although sometimes neglected by scholars) tradition of Hindu theistic mysticism. The *Bhagavad-Gîtâ* is its great monument. Râmânuja, as we have seen, gives philosophical formulation to a doctrine of mystical union with God which is at the same time differentiated (*"viśishtâdvaita"* = "qualified non-dualism"). On the more popular level, the *Bhâgavata Purâna* abounds with tales of Krishna as the divine Lover and Beloved, and develops an erotic mystical symbolism centered in his union with Râdhâ, representing the soul. The southern Indian *Śaiva Siddhânta* perhaps represents the culmination of Hindu theistic mysticism, teaching salvation as union with the personal God, and the love of God as the key to all religious experience.

Modern reformers and renewers of the Hindu tradition have generally represented a theistic approach to mystical union. The great Devendranath Tagore (1818–1905) expressed his rejection of a monist interpretation of Hinduism:

> Śankarâchârya has turned India's head by preaching the doctrine of Monism: the identity of God and man. Following his teachings, both ascetics and men of the world are repeating this senseless formula, "I am that Supreme Deity."[16]

His son, the Nobel prize winning writer Rabindranath Tagore, expressed in his poetry the mysticism of love, which needs distinction for the sake of communion:

> Let only that little be left of my will
> whereby I may feel thee on every side,
> and come to thee in everything,
> and offer to thee my love every moment.[17]

The mysticism of Buddhism is diverse and also difficult to classify, both because of the diversity and because of the negative language so frequently employed. Hînayâna Buddhism, with its lack of a concept of God and its theoretical denial of the soul (at least as an independent, substantial entity), encourages the practice of meditation as conducive to the attainment of *nirvâna*, but this concept is undefined enough to permit multiple interpretations. Mahâyâna Buddhism, especially in the "meditation" school (Ch'an–Zen) which developed from the *śûnyavâda* or doctrine of the "Void," tends to a more definitely positive interpretation of *nirvâna*.

Modern Zen writers like Suzuki are willing to identify the Zen experience with the experiences of Western mystics and to speak of its object (with qualifications) as God.

We have seen that the Ṣûfi tradition in Islam expands the Qur'anic vision with perspectives borrowed from non-Arabic sources. At its extreme limits, Ṣûfism approached the monist mysticism usually associated with absolutist Hinduism. The doctrine of *fanâh* or mystic extinction, although it could be interpreted in a moral sense as the "getting rid" of the sinful self and leaving the self in the image of God, often seems closer to an expression of pantheism. One of the greatest Muslim mystics, Hussain ben Mansur al Hallaj, wrote daring lines like these:

> I have become He whom I love,
> and He has become myself.
> We are two spirits in one body,
> when you see me, you see Him.[18]

For his statement, "I am the Real" ("*anâ al'Ḥaqq*"—the last being one of the names of Allah) al Hallaj was executed in 922. His heritage, however, continued in Islam. Despite the reconciliation worked out by al-Ghazâlî,[19] Ṣûfi mysticism continued to be attracted by monist doctrines. The great Spanish Ṣûfi Ibn al-'Arabi (1165–1240) taught that intuition is the only valid mode of cognition; that the Absolute is in itself transcendent, nameless, and without qualities, but becomes self-conscious through the generation of the world; that humanity is therefore an offshoot of the divine essence; that evil is a necessary part of the self-manifestation of God, and that there is no eternal punishment for sin; and that there is no *becoming* one with God, for (as Śaṅkara also taught) in reality we are *already* divine.[20]

Judaeo-Christian mysticism on the whole tends to be a mysticism of love and therefore to preserve the distinction between God and creation. The profound immediate experience of the divine found in the prophets, for example, also emphasizes God's absolute transcendence. The introduction of Greek elements into the tradition, especially in Christianity, allowed for the metaphysical formulation of an immediacy to God which preserved his transcendence and at the same time permitted a mysticism of "participation." Both Christianity and Judaism (in the Kabbalah) also gave rise to mysticisms which approached pantheism, but in Christianity the doctrines of the creation, incarnation and grace already encompassed so immediate a relation with God, while preserving the priority of love, that truly monist mysticism remained marginal.

The Mediation of God: "Incarnation"

The Blessed Lord said:
Unborn am I, changeless is my Self, of all contingent beings I am the Lord! Yet by my creative energy I consort with nature—which is mine—and come to be in time.
For whenever the law of righteousness withers away and lawlessness arises, then do I generate Myself on earth.
For the protection of the good, for the destruction of evildoers, for the setting up of the law of righteousness I come into being age after age.

Bhagavad-Gîtâ 4:6–8

The Lord said:
I roused many Bodhisattvas and established them in Buddha-knowledge. I brought myriads of myriads of beings, endless, to full ripeness in many myriads of aeons . . . repeatedly am I born in the world of the living.

Saddharma-Puṇḍarîka 15:3, 7

In the beginning was the Word,
and the Word was with God
and the Word was God.
He was in the beginning with God.
Everything was made through him,
and nothing came to be without him. . . .
And the Word was made flesh
and dwelt among us . . .

Jn 1:1–2, 14

Just as all the great religions teach the possibility of an intimate nearness of God to the individual, all also envision the need of some degree of external mediation of his presence. In a general way, all religions have a dimension of mediation insofar as all depend upon religious language, rituals, and symbols to communicate their message. Such mediation, however, may be conceived merely as the means of bringing the individual *to* the personal mystical experience, and so remain extrinsic to the experience itself (although, if the claim we have made in the last section is correct, the elements of interpretation can never be completely separated from experience, and hence the "message" to some extent implicitly conditions even mystical experience). We shall concentrate, however, on the more profound and intrinsic kind of mediation in which the mediator not only is the means to the experience of God's presence or self-revelation or salvation, but in some sense embodies that experience. We shall see that we may discern a tendency to the en-humanization of God's presence and work in savior figures who mediate salvation for others and "incarnate" the divine in the world.

Hinduism once again provides the clearest examples of the "incarnational" principle outside of Christianity. For all orthodox Hindus there is first of all a mediation of the Absolute in the scriptures: the *Vedas* are considered an eternal text whose earthly form (even to the sounds of the words) is literally and vocally inspired. There is also a strong sense of mediation in the *gûru* or teacher, who is to be treated by the disciple as a revealing god. Most important from our point of view, however, is the doctrine of the *avatâra* ("descent"; from *ava* = down, and *tri* = cross over, attain; hence *avatri* = descend into, appear; *avatâra* = descent, incarnation) of the gods, or of God, to earth in finite form.

A number of the gods are said to appear in finite avatars, but the doctrine is especially associated with Vishnu and Śiva, who are (respectively) for their devotees simply God, the Absolute. We have already encountered Vishnu's avatar, Krishna, as the central figure of the *Bhagavad-Gîtâ*.[21] There it is explicitly stated that Vishnu, who is the supreme Brahman, comes to birth in the world many times for the salvation of its creatures (IV:6–8; see introductory quotation to this section), even though many do not recognize his presence: "For that a human form I have assumed fools scorn me, knowing nothing of my higher state—great Lord of contingent beings" (IX:11). Salvation is to be attained through devotion to the person of Krishna, the finite manifestation of the personal God (Vishnu).

The interpretation of the *avatâra* doctrine naturally differs according to the anthropological positions of the various philosophical/theological schools. It must be borne in mind to begin with that Hinduism in general assumes that *every* human being is in some sense an "incarnation" (and reincarnation) of a divine principle (*atman*). For Śankara, every soul is eternal and ultimately identical with the Absolute spirit. The Lord—i.e., the personal divine manifestation of Brahman within the sphere of "illusory" being—in the avatar assumes a "shape," by his creative-illusionary power (*mâyâ*). The worship of such shapes of the *ishta-devatâ* (the god of one's choice) is helpful, but they are not ultimately Real. Râmânuja, as we have seen, considers the personal God (Vishnu) to be identical with Brahman. In his avatars, he does not abandon his own nature, but assumes forms "similar" to those of his creatures. Madhva holds that individual human selves are real, separate, and dependent on God. The avatars are *parts* of God's nature, while human souls are merely reflections of God.

Both before the *Gîtâ* (in the Epics) and after, other avatar stories are told. The *puranas* list some twenty-two avatars of Vishnu which have become part of common Vaisnava belief. Aside from Krishna, the most important is that of Rama, the hero of the epic *Ramayana*. Here the "incarnation" of Vishnu is conceived in a materialistic fashion: one-half of his divine nature becomes human in Rama, one-quarter in his brother Lanksmana, and one-eighth in each of two other brothers. Later Hinduism introduced yet more avatars, associated with historical figures. The most influential was the teacher Caitanya (born 1486), the inspiration of the Krishna movement familiar to the modern world. Caitanya was considered a reincarnation of Krishna, who is the supreme God Vishnu. He was also thought to reincarnate Krishna's spouse, Râdhâ, who was likewise a manifestation of Vishnu. The love of these two—both ultimately divine—is meant to serve as the model for the loving devotion (*bhakti*) by which we are saved.

Geoffrey Parrinder enumerates twelve major characteristics which summarize the major features of the avatar doctrine.[22] (1) The avatar is "real"—i.e., an actual body. There are, however, different interpretations of what "reality" in the finite world is. Furthermore, the human body of a divine avatar may be quite unusual; Krishna in the *Bhagavad-Gîtâ* is described as having four arms, and later Krishna devotion (incorporating a theme from the *puranas*) adds that his body is shining blue.[23] (2) The human avatars (as we have seen, there are also non-human ones) take human birth through ordinary parents. Although there are frequently mythological and material elements in the popular accounts (v.g., in the *Vishnu Purâna* Krishna and his brother come from two hairs from Vishnu's body), the mode of human conception is normal. (3) The lives of the avatars intermix human and divine elements; while they have some human limitations, they perform miracles and manifest extraordinary powers (some versions are of course much more mythological than others). (4) The avatars, like all human beings, finally die. (5) There are possibly historical reminiscences of historical heroic figures behind some of the avatars, especially Krishna and Rama. (6) The avatars are repeated—as the *Gîtâ* says, whenever righteousness declines, God takes birth for the salvation of his creatures. (7) The character and behavior of the avatar are considered examples for human conduct. (8) The avatar comes with a mission to fulfill: to establish *dharma*, the law of righteousness and order. (9) For *bhakti* Hinduism, the avatar is not pure illusion; *mâyâ* is interpreted as the divine creative power. (10) The avatar is the bringer and guarantor of divine revelation. Although this is not the only way God is known, the avatar is conceived as a special messenger and savior.[24] (11) What is revealed is the personal and loving God, calling humanity to relationship with him. (12) The God of the avatars is a God of grace, who takes the initiative in salvation.

The mediation of the relation to the Absolute also takes several different forms in the Buddhist tradition. In its original form, Buddhism seems to have come close to being a religion of complete self-sufficiency. Nevertheless, several levels of mediation of the way to *nirvâna* appear. The three "refuges"—Buddha, Dharma, Sangha—already represent a mediation of salvation through community, scripture, doctrine, revelation, and a personal guide. Although each person is theoretically to reach *nirvâna* by personal effort, the Buddha's vow and career implicitly introduce an element of mediation by his person. Even in Hînayâna Buddhism, the Buddha himself is venerated, and there is a desire for communion with him.

In the Mahâyâna, the aspect of mediation is so pronounced as to become, in many instances, primary. An intense devotion to the scriptures is typical of almost all Mahâyâna sects. It is true that the *Sûnyavâda* and its offshoots in Ch'an and Zen Buddhism tend to downplay the role of mediation; since the "Void" is the only final Reality, salvation (if such a term is appropriate at all) occurs through an immediate insight. Some forms of Zen, in reaction against the excesses of the devotional schools, devalue all mediations, including the scriptures and the Buddha himself ("if you meet the Buddha, kill the Buddha . . ."). Nevertheless, even here the coming to enlightenment is mediated by strict discipline, traditional techniques, dogmas, and above all the person of a master, who is, if not the "revealer," at least the indispensable guide to enlightenment.

The more widespread and popular forms of the Mahâyâna, however, are founded in devotion to real saviors: the Buddhas and *bodhisattvas*. As we have already seen, the *Lotus Sûtra* teaches a doctrine of incarnations—or perhaps better, avatars—of the Buddha. This idea is systematized in the *trikâya* ("three bodies") doctrine, according to which the one transcendent Buddha-nature becomes manifest in the many Buddhas and *bodhisattvas* both in their glorified heavenly bodies and in "appearance" bodies which are born on earth. On a philosophical level, this doctrine fits with the absolute Idealism of the major schools; since everything finite is simply "appearance," the human aspects of the Buddha are also. There is at the same time, especially on the more religious level, a kind of "Docetistic" tendency in operation; the Buddha, for example, is said to have had an immaculate and virginal birth, and his (human) body to have been "made of mind."

The Buddha in the Mahâyâna is clearly seen as a transcendent revealer and savior. Furthermore, as we have already seen, the doctrine of the merit of the *bodhisattva* clearly inculcates the notion of salvation through the mediation of an Other, who is (or will be) incarnate as a human being. The "incarnational" tendency in Buddhism reaches its extreme point in the Buddhism of Tibet, where the Dalai and Panchen Lamas were taken to be continual reincarnations respectively of the *bodhisattva* Avalokiteśvara and the buddha Amitabha, and as such to have supreme spiritual and temporal rule in Tibet.

Islam, as we have seen, is characterized by belief in the uniqueness and transcendence of God. There is a strong opposition in orthodoxy to any immediacy of God in the sense of "immanence" (as in Hinduism). The transcendent God relates to humanity through the mediation of his revelation, which is contained in the *Qur'an*, revealed (through angels) to his prophet or apostle, Muhammad. It is the Word, in the Book of God, which mediates his presence. Similarly, there is a strong opposition to any mediation of God other than his revelation; there is no *person* between the individual believer and God. Nevertheless, both of these forbidden doctrines—immanence and personal mediation—arose in Islam, both separately and in conjunction, and had important influence. We have already noted the tendencies of Ṣûfism toward immanentism. We shall now see that there was an almost equally strong tendency to a theology of personal mediation of salvation.

The influences which led in this direction were varied. We have already considered briefly the origins of Shî'ite messianism, in which the heroes 'Alî and his descendants, the Imâms, were exalted to super-human status. The neo-Platonic doctrine of emanationism, influential on philosophers and mystics alike, posited the Logos of God as an intermediary between the One and the creation. At the eastern reaches of early Islam, in Persia, contact was made both with the Zoroastrian idea of the Sashoyant, the hidden descendant of Zarathushtra who is to come at the end of history, and (indirectly) the Indian *bhakti* movement, expressed in both Hindu devotion to the avatars and Buddhist devotion to the saving *bodhisattvas*. Finally, the very vehemence of the Muslim polemic against the Christian idea of incarnation brought the latter into particular prominence, and allowed it to exert a significant (if subliminal) influence even on those who rejected it.

The idea of a human mediator was quite naturally associated above all with Muhammad, secondly, in the Shî'a, with his descendants, 'Alî and his family, and, finally, with an eschatological figure, the Mahdî.

The respect for Muhammad as God's final prophet grew, especially in Ṣûfi circles, to veneration and personal love. He began to be thought of as the model of human behavior, the perfect human being, the intercessor at the day of judgment. In Muslim gnostic and neo-Platonic speculation, he was regarded as the Perfect Man who unites the macro- and micro-cosmos: even the goal of creation itself! In one tradition, God is portrayed speaking to Muhammad: "If thou hadst not been, I would not have created the spheres"; and in an Indian Ṣûfî text: "From the Empyrean to that which is beneath the earth, everything seeks My satisfaction, and I seek thy satisfaction, O Muhammad!"[25] Bêdil, a Persian poet from Sind, wrote that at Muhammad's death, "he became united with HE [Allah]; the difference in between disappeared," while other Ṣûfîs of Sind developed the theory of the pre-existent Reality of Muhammad.[26]

From a kind of "adoptionist" theology of Muhammad's union with God some thinkers—notably the famous al-Hallaj—passed to a theory of emanation and/or incarnation. Islamic theology had developed the notion of *hulûl* to describe both the relation of the soul to the body and the Christian doctrine of the incarnation of God in a human being—the latter, of course, being rejected. Al-Hallaj uses this term, in connection with neo-Platonic Logos theory to describe the relationship of God to Muhammad. He teaches that the Light of Muhammad is the divine Logos, hypostasized and separated from the Godhead. (He goes on to apply the same notion to the relation of God to the faithful in prayer: each person becomes an "incarnation" of the divine spirit; he looks to Jesus as an example of this.) Al-Hallaj was judged heretical and executed; but his teachings show how far Islamic devotion to the Prophet could stretch.

We have already noted in the section on Islam how the same kind of gnostic and emanationist ideas were applied in the Shî'a to 'Alî and Ḥusayn, who because of their violent deaths became suffering saviors as well. Similar reverence was extended to the Imâms. While such ideas never became the beliefs of the majority of Muslims, they were and remain the doctrines of a sizable minority, and exercised a potent influence on popular devotion throughout Islam.

Finally, either through Shî'ism or Ṣûfism (or from the first, through the second) there entered into Moslem belief the expectation of the second coming of Jesus and of an eschatological "savior" figure, the Mahdî. While the latter was only "divinized" in Shî'ite thinking, orthodox Islam as a whole adopted Messianism as a part of its creed.

THE CHRISTIAN CLAIM

I recommend, therefore, above all, that you make petitions, prayers, supplications, acts of thanksgiving, for all people. . . . This is what is good and pleasing to God our Savior, who wishes that all should be saved and come to the knowledge of the truth. For God is one; one also is the mediator between God and humanity, Christ Jesus. . . .

1 Tim 2:1, 3–5

There is no doubt that not only all heathens, but also all Jews and all he-
retics and schismatics who die outside the church will go into that ever-
lasting fire prepared for the devil and his angels.

Fulgentius of Ruspe, *De Fide ad Petrum*, 38, 79

The human person—every person without exception—has been redeemed
by Christ, because Christ is in a way united to the human person—every
person without exception—even if the individual may not realize this fact.
"Christ, who died and was raised up for all"—for every human being and
for all human beings—"can through his spirit offer man the light and the
strength to measure up to his supreme destiny!"

Pope John Paul II, *Redemptor Hominis*

We undertook our examination of comparative religious phenomenology in response to the question raised by Rahner's theory of transcendental and categorical revelation. Having affirmed the existence of
a divine self-revelation, consisting of an immediate relation to God which
is at the same time mediated or made categorical in history, we were
led to ask: What is the relation of the various categorical expressions/
interpretations of revelation to each other and to God's transcendental
self-revelation? Is revelation always "general," or does there exist a
"special" normative or final expression of our relationship to God? Having eliminated the possibility that all expressions of revelation are entirely equal, we were left with the two possibilities of (1) a continuing
dialectic/complementarity of religions, reaching no final form, or (2) the
existence of a "special" revelation, either in the present or the future,
whose relation to general categorical revelation is as yet undetermined.
We turned to the classical types of higher religion represented by the
great world religions as epitomizing the highest and most explicit formulations of revelation. We have found that the structure of revelation
as "mediated immediacy" to God is verified in each of them,[27] but that
there is a divergence on the nature of both the immediacy and the mediation. In regard to the latter, in particular, there exists a conflict, for
several traditions claim that there can be no final mediation, while several others claim to embody such a final form.

Principles of Discernment

If we are to make any judgments concerning the conflicts, as well as the consensus, of religions, we must do so on the basis of explicit and methodically founded principles. We have already explicitated the principles which serve as our basic hermeneutic and criterion of judgment. They are drawn from our fundamental vision of human existence, or anthropology, joined with our existential experience of conversion; these together yield a heuristic "anticipation" of God's salvific word.[28] While these principles cannot determine *a priori* the content of the specifically religious formulation of revelation, any such revelation must at least be in continuity and complementarity with them (remembering also that philosophical positions may also be a categorical expression of the achievement of transcendence in response to God). A religious formulation will be judged a positive achievement of categorical revelation insofar as it affirms, expresses, broadens, deepens and expands the values and transcendent possibilities of our humanity, insofar as we are living a transcending and converted existence. These values and possibilities are precisely what are formulated in a transcendental anthropology.

RECAPITULATION OF ANTHROPOLOGY

These elements were formulated in our first volume, and have already been summarized above in our first two chapters. It will perhaps not be amiss, however, to recall them briefly here, this time joining together the anthropological presuppositions with the heuristic anticipation of salvation. In doing so we will note that the conclusions of our anthropology, drawn from Lonergan and Rahner, correspond closely to the "anthropological constants" set forth by Edward Schillebeeckx as the "system of coordinates of man and his salvation."[29] Our anthropological conclusions may be summarized in six statements:

1. Humanity is that being in which the transcendent process of the world comes to self-knowledge, subsuming the finality of matter into the realm of consciousness and meaning, on the levels of performance and formulation. (Schillebeeckx, numbers 1, 5: being human means relationship to corporeality, nature and the environment. Bodiliness is constitutive of humanity: need for integration of reason, temperament, imagination, freedom, instinct, love, etc. There is a mutual relationship of theory and practice.)

2. The human being is free spirit, who by intelligent freedom (love) constitutes transcendence toward being and the good, in the context of history and community. (Schillebeeckx, numbers 2, 3, 4: being human involves other people; the human is directed toward others, in I-Thou and I-he relationships. Being human is connected with social and institutional

structures. Human beings and their cultures, norms and values are conditioned by non-uniform conditions of history and geography. This implies
the necessity of "critical remembrance" of human history and its great traditions.)

3. The human is a finite spiritual being who listens for a possible further dialogue with God, in fulfillment of our basic desire for knowledge
and love; in Rahner's terminology, to be human is to be a "hearer of God's
word." (Schillebeeckx, number 6: humanity has a religious and "para-re-
ligious" consciousness: "utopian" consciousness as the expression of hope
for the future; basic faith as the ground for hope; permanent religious orientation.)

4. Humanity seeks salvation (and authentic human existence) in
God's "answer" to the problem of evil, with its dimensions of moral impotence (concupiscence), the "social surd," and personal sin.

5. Humanity exists in an existential dimension which goes beyond
our abstract "nature." Existentially we are called to find salvation as a gift
in a higher collaboration of love with God and others. (Schillebeeckx, number 7: humanity is an irreducible synthesis of the anthropological constants.)

6. Existentially, humanity finds salvation in being in love with God
in an absolute way, usually with a thematic expression in "religion."

The formulation of our anticipation of the nature of salvation, or God's
"answer" to the human dilemma (Lonergan's "heuristic structure of the
solution"), is based upon the principle that the solution will fit the problem, and therefore must correspond to the order of the world and the basic
structures of human being. We can therefore anticipate certain elements
which salvation will include, even before we have concretely identified it
in history. These elements may also be formulated in six statements:

1. God's salvific action is an "existential"—i.e., it is not "added on"
to an already complete world, but is the (hidden and transcendent) actual
order of the world. It is therefore universal and permanent in extent.

2. Salvation must occur in humanity, by introducing some further dimension of higher integration to existence in continuity with our basic dynamism toward being and the good. Such a higher integration must meet
the fact of evil and provide a means of making it into a potency for good.
Because it leaves lower levels intact, it will leave humanity responsible
and free, and therefore must come to us through our intellect and consent.
Because it is in accord with the actual world-order, it must come about
through emergent probability, i.e., it will be historical and progressive.
For this reason we can expect that there will exist not only the full realization of the means to salvation, but also emergent trends toward it, in
which it becomes effectively probable in history.

3. The new dimension in humanity will include a new integration of
freedom—therefore a new depth of love—and a new integration of intellect in search of truth. Because our being is historical, this must take place

in collaboration with others. Salvation may therefore be described as a "higher collaboration" of humanity with God and others in pursuit of truth and love.

4. Humanity must collaborate in salvation; it will be a human achievement as well as a divine gift. We must recognize and accept God's action. We must also enter into the dynamism of salvation and further its progress by becoming part of it. Because human freedom remains intact, our collaboration will include sin; but it will finally be "holy" because it is ultimately God's work, which cannot fail. As a human collaboration, salvation must necessarily have some societal-institutional dimension.

5. Salvation must integrate not only freedom and intellect, but also human sensitivity and other areas of consciousness, i.e., it will have an aesthetic dimension, expressed in myth, symbols, images, etc. Indeed, it is to be expected that the symbolic level will have priority and be the normal level for our apprehension and expression of God's "word," since humanity lives primarily on this level.

6. Salvation will partake of the mystery of God and his freedom, and therefore will have a nature and content beyond what can be heuristically formulated—especially if God's answer is in some sense "supernatural," going beyond a mere solution to the problem of evil and bringing humanity beyond its "nature."

Existentially, we are already experiencing salvation or the invitation to it; it finds its foremost expression in "religious conversion," which means a love of God "in an absolute way" and an inclusion of our neighbor and the world in the dynamism of that love.

To the extent that these principles genuinely formulate and correspond to our lived experience and performance as subjects, they give us a standard or criterion by which we may interpret existence. At the same time, the foregoing is not the only valid expression or formulation of the "anthropological constants" or the "heuristic structure" of salvation. Their foundation is on the level of performance, not on the level of concept. Therefore we are obliged always to be ready to reformulate and advance our positions, and revise those formulations which run counter to actual performance. This is only possible if we continually advert to our actual performance as transcending and converted persons, and genuinely understand the referents of our own and others' thematizations of that performance. Hence the need for dialogue, whose basis is to be found in the common experience of subjectivity called to transcendence.

On the basis of our transcendental anthropology, then, we may discriminate among the various implicit and explicit views of humanity expressed in the religious traditions. All the great religions express the structure of a mediated immediacy to God, but their recognition of this structure on the level of formulation may conflict or correspond to varying degrees with the basic performance of conversion and with its foundation in the transcending subject. Those religious positions must be affirmed which accord with and advance transcendence; those must be rejected or revised which conflict with it.

In accord with our transcendental-existential analysis, those religious positions will be judged more adequate which more clearly thematize the mediated immediacy to God in terms of personal being and the value of love; that is, those positions which affirm that the experience which mediates what the Absolute is, and how humanity contacts that Absolute, is above all the experience of free affirmation of the other in personal dialogue. The structure of mediated immediacy, which is revealed in transcendental analysis to be the condition of possibility of a human reception of God's self-revelation, is the structure of personal being, and the culmination of personal being is revealed as inter-personal love. This implies that religious formulation will be true to the dynamism of conversion insofar as it recognizes the primacy of the personal and the conditions for its realization. Those conditions include the reality (and also the relativity) of the finite world and of history as the necessary locus in which transcendence is realized.

We have contended that there is a convergence of religions toward the ideal of love. We are now furthering that claim with the thesis that religions are true to their own most basic dynamism insofar as they explicitly recognize this ideal and its conditions of possibility, and provide a grounding for them by uncovering the personal experience of God revealing himself in the existential imperative to engagement with our neighbor in love—i.e., in the experience of "being in love with God in an absolute way," expressed in the mediation of the unconditional love of neighbor.[30]

In summation, therefore, our anthropological criteria point toward religion which is:

(1) centered in personhood and love;

(2) historical as well as transcendental (i.e., sees human transcendence as realized through engagement in history);

(3) conscious of the problem of salvation, particularly as it exists in personal freedom (sin);

(4) capable of progression, in accord with the dynamic and incomplete nature of every formulation, hence open to dialogue with other religious formulations, and able to expand its own through them;

(5) able to subsume or synthesize the whole of human experience, including its lower levels;

(6) holy: i.e., an actual sign, in practice, of conversion and transcendence (this dimension must include not only conversion from sin, but also

opposition to suffering and a positive commitment to the advancement of human existence);

(7) communal: manifesting a mediation of the experience of God in community and structures;

(8) transcendent: engaged in the world, but in such a way as to point "beyond" it or to reveal its "groundedness" and goal in God.

If we are to affirm the existence of a "special" categorical revelation, either as a fact or as a possibility, among the world religions (or as a projected convergence of them), we must expect that it will include these elements, and will also manifest a content which goes beyond what we have anticipated.

Application of Anthropological Principles to World Religion

It would seem that a critical point of division both within and among the world religions lies in the way in which inner-worldly history is regarded. We may note within each tradition a certain tension between world-embracing and world-escaping tendencies. While in theory these may be regarded as the first two parts of a Hegelian triad, to be synthesized in a notion of "world-transcending," and while it is true that every religion, insofar as it is a religion of love, does in practice accomplish such a synthesis, reaching the transcendental in and through the categorical and historical, nevertheless it is also true that religious formulations are not all equally explicit in their affirmation of history as the locus and means of encounter with the Divine.

It has become a commonplace to observe that the Occidental religions differ from the Oriental precisely on this point. While we must bear in mind that there exist exceptions and counter-tendencies (on both parts, and in both directions), on the whole this generalization is borne out by the phenomenology of religions. While all religions implicitly affirm historical being insofar as they affirm, in practice, the value of person and love, the explicit formulation of the spiritual validity of human history is particularly Western. The common Hindu-Buddhist presumptions concerning *saṁsâra*, rebirth, and the iron law of *karma* (with the caste system it implies, at least for Hindus); the predominantly intellectual nature of both the problem and its solution in these systems; the tendency to idealism and monism—all militate against a full and explicit realization of the intrinsic historicity of the human person and the human relationship with God. It is for this reason that van der Leeuw characterizes the Oriental religions as "religions of repose," tending to emphasize mysticism, while the Western religions manifest "unrest" and even in their mysticism tend toward engagement with others and the world.

Of course, the "discovery" of history, even as the locus of human relation to the Absolute, is not limited to religion; categorical revelation includes as well the achievements of philosophy, ethics, and culture in general. The existential value of history may be said to have been discovered by the Chinese and Greek humanist and ethical traditions; it found expression in Confucian philosophy and law and in the Greek tragedies of the classical period. Nevertheless, it achieved there no significant connection with the explicitly religious dimension. In the Greek world, the insight had to await the Judaeo-Christian tradition for religious expression. In China, Mahâyâna Buddhism provided only an incomplete vehicle for the expression of historical religiosity. (We have pointed out, on the other hand, that it was precisely the historical and this-worldly character of native Chinese insight which permitted the Mahâyâna to be transformed, in some of its manifestations, into a religion of compassionate engagement with the world, including even a kind of "eschatological" directedness to history. Nevertheless, these tendencies run counter to the basic presupposition of the cyclical nature of *saṁsâra,* and the *bodhisattva* doctrine gives a mythological rather than historical anchoring to engagement with the world.)

It is the prophets of Israel who are generally credited with the religious valorization of history[31]—although it would seem from modern studies that the honor must be shared with the Zoroastrians, if not with Zarathushtra himself. It should be noted that what was "discovered" in these religions was not (as one sometimes hears) the idea that God is "involved" in history, in the sense of "intervening" on behalf of his people; such notions are common even to primitive religions.[32] What was significant was rather the conviction that (in contrast with the mythic, cyclical view of time) history itself has purpose and direction, and (in contrast with a purely "transcendental" anthropology) is not only the "locus" but the means of salvation: human engagement in the world and with others has an eternal relevance and validity. For Zoroastrianism, indeed, creation and history are *the* means invented by God to achieve his own final victory over primordial evil; hence every aspect of the world, and particularly human freedom, has value and is involved in a "salvation history" whose triumphant end is to be brought about by human decision. Furthermore, the world itself, in its final purified state, will constitute the eternal kingdom of Ahura.

The Jewish prophets came to a similar vision of the value of history through the notion of God's chastisements of Israel for its unfaithfulness. Historical events have value in themselves, insofar as they are determined by God; history (i.e., the reversals in Israel's fortunes) is to be interpreted as a message from God. Hence revelation is conceived as occurring not in mythic sacred time, but in real historical time, at particular moments and through historical events.[33] "Historical facts thus become 'situations' of man face to face with God and, as such, acquire a religious value that nothing thitherto could bestow on them."[34] History is furthermore directed to an end in which time itself is "saved."[35] Even when these notions are "demythologized" and purified of anthropomorphisms, historical action retains its existential aspect as the irrepeatable "dialogue" of humanity with God. In effect, the religious discovery of history is the discovery of humanity as historical, precisely in our relation to God, and hence the affirmation of the value of becoming, of plurality, of the historical uniqueness of personality, and consequently the break with the myth of recurrence and the uniformity of being. In Rahner's language, the categorical is explicitly affirmed as the essential mediation of the transcendental.

A corollary to the Zoroastrian-Israelite view regards the problem of evil. Whatever may be the origin of evil (Zoroastrianism: a primordial metaphysical fact; Israel: a consequence of sin and/or trial from God), our response to it must be the same. If history is the mediation and realization of the eternal, then it becomes crucial for humanity to take action to oppose evil and suffering and to build the "kingdom of God" within the world.

[Arnold Toynbee regards the "Jewish-Zoroastrian" and the "Hindu and Hellenic" as the two major tendencies in the history of religions in the effort to transcend human self-centeredness and so relate to the higher conception of God. The Hindu and Hellenic traditions do so by means of a cyclical and astronomical world-view, in which humanity is placed in a cosmos of such infinity and/or repetitiveness that the here-and-now—and hence the individual ego—loses value. The danger of this view is that while it eliminates self-centeredness, it also seems to deprive history, or even finite existence, of meaning. The Absolute becomes transcendent in such a way that it has no relation to this world. There is the further danger (as Whitehead also points out) that such a world-view may react to the problem of suffering by the cultivation of indifference (as is seen in Stoicism and in Hindu asceticism).

The Jewish-Zoroastrian tradition, on the other hand, counters human egotism by creating a non-recurrent, linear view of history, governed by a supreme personal Being. History is seen as a dialogue with God, and human being is seen as essentially relational. On this view, human involvement in the world, and especially in response to the problem of suffering, is crucial. The danger of this tradition, however, is that while it gives historical existence value and meaning, it carries the risk of falling back into the same self-centeredness—or group-centeredness—which it is the function of religion to counter: it may end up placing the earth at the center of the cosmos, and a "chosen people" (i.e., my group or tribe) at the center of the earth. While the Hindu and Hellenic view holds the danger of making the Absolute utterly dissimilar to humanity, this view holds the danger of remaking God in humanity's image (the constant temptation of Israel, repeatedly condemned by the prophets).[36]]

The Zoroastrian-Israelite religious valorization of history was taken up and amplified by Christianity and Islam. But while the latter remains (at least in its classical orthodoxy) within the confines of the Judaic understanding of salvation history, Christianity radicalizes the idea in its doctrine of the incarnation, and achieves a kind of higher synthesis of the historical and transcendental religious tendencies.

We have seen that Zoroastrianism, Judaism, and Islam all claim to be a "special"—and in the case of Islam, final—categorical revelation from God. What is unique in the case of Christianity is that it claims final and universal validity, and bases its claim on belief in the incarnation: that is, on the doctrine that in Jesus, God himself enters history in a unique and irrepeatable way for the salvation of humanity. The notion of a "descent" of God is common in the Hindu and Buddhist traditions, but it is there presumed that the avatar or "incarnation"[37] of God is repeated many times (or, for certain theologies, is actually universal). Christianity is alone in affirming a single, unique presence of God, tied to a definite historical person and events. Christianity thus presents a unique position on both immediacy to and mediation of God: for God is immediately present to the believer (the "indwelling of the Holy Spirit"), and this transcendental immediacy is connected directly with an external mediator (Jesus), who in turn is, in his categorical human existence, the presence of God. Thus for Christian faith the "achievement" of categorical revelation by humanity finds in Jesus its definitive expression, for it is identical with God himself revealed in human existence. At the same time, the humanity of Jesus is not simply a human "appearance" in which the transcendent is gloriously manifest; it is true human being, which therefore achieves transcendence through an absolute act of self-giving toward God, expressed in the absolute love of neighbor. The revelation of God in human form is the revelation of the "loss" and "finding" of self in absolute love. Thus the Christian idea of incarnation is inseparable from the concrete life and self-sacrificing death of Jesus, and the validating of these through the resurrection. Through the doctrine of the incarnation, Christianity presents itself as a synthesis of transcendental immediacy to the Absolute (as is emphasized in the Oriental religions) and revelation in and through history (as is emphasized in the Western traditions). God is revealed through person in history, but the true meaning of person in history is absolute self-gift to the transcendent God, expressed in the love of neighbor. The eschatological goal of history (immediacy to God) is thus seen as already (proleptically) present in the resurrection of Jesus, and to be lived by the Christian in the world as a continual "death" to self and "rising" in the life of absolute love of others.

As we have already noted, Christianity is not unique in being a religion of love or in declaring that the pattern of self-sacrificial love of the world is revelatory of the nature of the Absolute. In particular, as Toynbee writes, Mahâyâna Buddhism approaches the "incarnational" insight:

> It will be seen that the Mahâyâna and Christianity have two institutions in common. Instead of kicking against the pricks of Suffering, they both accept Suffering as an opportunity for acting on the promptings of Love and Pity. And they both believe that this ideal is practicable for Man because the trail has been blazed for Man by a Supreme Being Who has demonstrated his own devotion to the ideal by subjecting himself to the Suffering that is the necessary price of acting on it. . . . The Christian-Mahâyânian way of life also surmounts another previously unsurmountable dilemma. It makes it possible for the Universe to have significance without at the same time making it necessary for this significance to depend upon the Universe's centering round the Self. On the Christian-Mahâyânian road the significance can be found in self-sacrifice for the sake of other living beings and for the love of a Supreme Being who is the centre of the Universe because He is Love as well as Power.[38]

Buddhism, transformed by Hellenic (in the origins of the Mahâyâna) and Chinese (in its development) influences, becomes, like Christianity, a religion of love. The great difference between the traditions is in the connection of the revealing insight with history: for the saving Buddhas and *bodhisattvas* of Mahâyâna Buddhism are mythological beings, and their "incarnations" mere appearances, while Jesus was an historical human being who gave not merely his doctrine but his life. In Buddhism, moreover, there remains a certain tension between the performance of religion as personal and historical, and its official formulations, which support an a-historical immediacy to the Absolute. The same kind of remarks may be made, *mutatis mutandis*, of the *avatâra* traditions of Hinduism. It seems justified to say, then, that Christianity is the religion of the personal and historical revelation-mediation of God *par excellence*, representing the historical culmination of the tendencies toward a religion of mediated immediacy and of love which we have found in all the higher religions.

Ernst Troeltsch and the "Absoluteness" of Christianity

The judgment we have reached thus far coincides approximately with the conclusion reached by Ernst Troeltsch in his famous inquiry concerning the "absoluteness" of Christian religion.[39] A brief summary of Troeltsch's position and comparison with our own will allow us to formulate the stage we have arrived at in our question concerning a "special" categorical revelation.

Although he inherits the notion of Christianity as "absolute religion" from Hegel, Troeltsch begins by rejecting an idealist (Hegelian) "evolutionary" justification of the absoluteness of Christianity, as well as a "supernaturalist" apologetic. He proposes instead that we may arrive at a "principle of normativeness," based upon metaphysics, which will formulate the goal of all religion. Such a principle for Troeltsch is to be found in the positive evaluation of human *person* and of transcendent values. (We have reached a similar conclusion by a somewhat parallel method: beginning with a metaphysical anthropology, we have heuristically anticipated the divine "solution" to the human dilemma; comparing the formulations of that solution in the higher religions, we have pointed to a convergence toward a mediated immediacy to God in a religion of love; such a mediated immediacy is the structure of human person as "spirit in the world."[40])

On the basis of this method Troeltsch examines the history of religions and concludes that Christianity is the highest point of expression of his normative principle and the point of convergence of religious striving. Among the world religions, "Christianity is in actuality the strongest and most concentrated revelation of personalistic religious apprehension."[41] It is the only complete break with nature religion (cf. Toynbee's analysis of lower religions as worship of nature or of man), and the only consistent depiction of the "higher world" as "infinitely valuable personal life." It renounces the world only insofar as it is superficial and evil; it affirms the world insofar as it is both *from* God and *leads to* God.[42] For this reason it takes seriously history, interpersonal dialogue, communal morality, and the human project in the world.

Likewise, Christianity affirms that the human qualities which we call "personal" are not only not illusory, but reflect (albeit imperfectly and analogously) the nature of ultimate Reality itself. For Troeltsch, the contrast between a personal or impersonal conception of the Absolute, and the consequent model for human behavior, is decisive:

> It is necessary to make a choice between redemption through meditation on Transcendent Being or non-Being, and redemption through

faithful, trusting participation in the person-like character of God, the ground of all life and of all genuine value. . . . The higher goal and the greater profundity of life are found on the side of personalistic religion.[43]

All the great religions, according to Troeltsch, share (at least to some extent) four great sets of ideas: the ideas of God, the world, the soul, and a "higher life" beyond the world. The fourth of these (which corresponds to our idea of "salvation") is attained or actualized in and through the first three. Each of these ideas, for Troeltsch, attains its highest formulation in Christianity.[44]

Troeltsch goes on to examine some of the restrictions in the various forms of religious consciousness when judged by his normative principle. Non-Christian religions in general tend to narrow the understanding of God by identifying him with or placing him within Nature.[45] In primitive religions, the absoluteness of God is limited by narrowness of vision; God's reign is restricted to the tribe or group; outside of it, other gods rule (i.e., in Toynbee's terminology, the "lower" religions have a limited, non-universal frame of reference).[46] Among the higher religions, the mystical religions (which Troeltsch calls the "non-Christian religions of redemption") remain at the level of a "naive" conception of the Absolute, as the obscure foundation of religious feeling or experience.[47] The human being, in the mystical and non-historical religions, is understood as one who *is* rather than as one who *becomes*, through self-surrender and ethical conduct. There is no positive meaning given to the divine nature[48] (and hence, on an anthropological level, no positive meaning given to humanity as spirit).

In the religions of law, on the other hand, there is really no redemption, for humanity is left to rely on its own strength. Zoroastrianism and Judaism, in particular, attain a high level of consciousness as ethical and rational religions, but they remain legalistic in structure. Judaism besides is tied to a particular people, and is thus not universal.[49] In Islam—also considered a religion of law—universality is likewise lacking, salvation being restricted (in theory) by the doctrine of predestination and (in practice) by the *Qur'an*'s canonizing of "Arab idiosyncrasies."[50] As against all the religions of law, the religion of Jesus is the freest and most inwardly oriented means of reaching the Absolute.[51]

Troeltsch concludes, then, that Christianity is the "culmination point" and "convergence point" of all the developmental tendencies in religion, and the focal synthesis of all religions.[52] In the terminology which we have been using, Troeltsch sees Christianity as synthesizing the immediacy of God and his immanence, as stressed in Oriental religion, with God's transcendence and the necessary mediation of the world, as taught in the Zoroastrian-Judaic traditions.

Although we would perhaps wish to introduce more *nuance* in the treatment of the world religions, and would emphasize more strongly the positive continuity between them and our basic anthropology, we find that our own conclusions at least in a general way parallel Troeltsch's.

Where does this leave us with regard to the question of "special categorical revelation" and the Christian claim that Jesus and the community of his Spirit represent the definitive revelation of God in history? Has Troeltsch in fact demonstrated the "absoluteness" of Christianity? Walter Kasper writes:

> The attempt of Ernst Troeltsch to establish the absolute character of Christianity by proofs drawn from comparative religion was doomed from the start. All that could be shown in such a way was that the world's religions converge to some extent upon Christianity; and that approach, by reducing Christianity to the level of historical phenomena—that is, to the relative—necessarily emptied Christianity's absolute claim of all real content.[53]

Indeed, Troeltsch reaches the conclusion that Christian faith is *not* absolute, but is "normative," i.e., for the individual and for all of religion up to the present.[54] But because Christianity is an historical phenomenon with all the intrinsic limitations of such, and because, by its own teachings, revelation is historical, it is not impossible that there will be a further and higher revelation than the Christ in the future.[55] Troeltsch concludes that we cannot possess the Absolute *in an absolute way* within history.[56] We can discover, by historical examination, that nowhere does there exist a greater revelation of God than in Christianity—thus far; we can even see in Christianity the fulfillment of the religious strivings of humanity, but we cannot extrapolate this normativeness and convergence to the future.[57]

Troeltsch recognizes, however, that such a position is not satisfactory for the person who puts faith in Jesus; Christian faith affirms with certitude that the Christ is the radical and definitive revelation of God—the norm not only for the present, but for the future as well.[58] At the same time, he cannot see a means of arriving at such a point by means of the philosophy of religions. He therefore places the burden of the question of the *absoluteness* of Christianity within faith. This leaves unresolved, however, the fundamental question of whether it is reasonable to *make* such an act of faith (i.e., in Jesus as absolute savior) to begin with.

Furthermore, it is notable that by the end of his life Troeltsch had significantly revised his earlier position, and finally renounced even the claim of "normativeness" for Christianity.[59] Instead, he concludes that religious values are so conditioned by culture, and cultures so diverse and relative, that it is impossible to judge one religion superior to the others. Truth has many cultural and religious expressions, and "the question of their several relative values will never be capable of objective determination, since every proof thereof will presuppose the special characteristics of the civilization in which it arises."[60] At best, Christianity can be normative for a person of Western culture.

Troeltsch's modification of his views and the reasons for it must be taken seriously. Indeed, they coincide with our warnings concerning the limitations and relativity not only of every particular philosophical or religious "formulation," but more fundamentally of every "language" or symbol system. At the same time, there seem to be two bases for going beyond Troeltsch's relativism. These are embodied in the two aspects of method which we have named "transcendental" and "dialectical." A transcendental method takes its starting point not from concepts or formulations, but from the performance of the subject. It attempts to reach those basic structures of human being which are prior to and the condition for *all* formulations whatsoever. In this sense, it provides a trans-cultural starting point for philosophical/anthropological reflection. This is not to say that its expression is trans-cultural; like all formulations, that expression is linguistically and culturally conditioned. Likewise, even experiences themselves already bear an interpretive coloring. But there is something in human being which is common to all humans and is more fundamental than their different languages and symbols; it is precisely this foundation which provides the "deep grammar" for all languages and symbols, for it is the basic structure of our being able to symbolize at all. Transcendental method allows a reference to the very conditions of human experience and language themselves, and hence provides the possibility of a cognitional theory and a metaphysics (and hence an anthropology and philosophy of religion) which are in principle "verifiable" by any subject.

It is this possibility which gives rise to the second aspect, dialectic. Transcendental method does not immediately provide a trans-cultural language, but it provides a basis for comparison of languages, concepts, judgments with each other and with their common foundation and conditions of possibility. It allows cross-cultural dialogue which has some hope of reaching conclusions and judgments—even though the process may be long and tentative and call for many complex revisions of thought along the way.

In short, the diversity of cultures and religions does not mean cultural or religious isolation. It is possible and necessary (as contemporary religious studies are increasingly realizing[61]) to enter into a genuine dialectic of religious positions. This of course presupposes first of all an understanding of other cultures and religions, which is itself a major undertaking; but our modern experience has shown that such understanding is not so difficult as it may have seemed to Troeltsch, and that there is perhaps more ground for agreement among the great religions—at least on some fundamental matters—than he imagined, and that where agreement is not possible, there is yet a possibility and a basis for dialogue concerning our different judgments.

In this perspective, despite his later reservations, there is still validity to what Troeltsch accomplishes in his earlier work: he establishes clearly the prior need for criteria of judgment concerning religious validity; he finds the primary criterion in the notion of the person; he compares the relative merits of religious traditions, and finds supremely personal religion in Christianity. It is true that the very concepts used—for example, "person"—are themselves culturally conditioned, but this does not per se invalidate the criteria or the judgment. It does mean that such concepts and criteria must (1) be given a basis in a subjectively "verifiable" philosophy of human being, and (2) must be open to correction through confrontation and dialogue with other positions. It is exactly this which we hope to have accomplished in transcendental/dialectical reflections.

Insofar as our methods and conclusions here have been (up to this point) generally parallel to Troeltsch's, we hope to have achieved not by any means a "demonstration" of Christianity, but only a preliminary step toward a rational judgment of the credibility of the Christian claim. The affirmation of a *relative* uniqueness of Christian religion and the possibility of seeing it as a convergence-point of world religions does not mean that Christianity can claim to contain or synthesize all that is positive in categorical revelation; in this sense Troeltsch's later position is certainly correct.[62] However, if this affirmation is established on the basis of clearly explicitated criteria and can be accepted on a personally appropriated basis, it will open the way to a further step in reflection on the validity of the Christian claim, and on what it does mean for the relation of Christianity to the rest of revelation. If it cannot be so accepted, it forms the basis for furthering the dialectic by confrontation with other positions. At the very least the making of such an affirmation clarifies some of the basic issues involved in religious judgments and allows for dialogue and personal decision concerning them.

[It is also worth noting that the relativist position which Troeltsch arrives at, although it does not coincide with the claims of orthodox Christian doctrine, does correspond with the understanding which many modern Christian believers have reached—more or less unreflectively—with regard to their own faith. In the light of increased contact with and more sophisticated knowledge of other religions, and under the influence of the general atmosphere of relativism which accompanies the scientific world-view, a good many Christians seem to discount the absolutist dogmatic claims of the creed, or to interpret them in a merely "symbolic" or eulogistic, "poetic" sense. Christianity and its doctrines are valued for their "aesthetic" qualities; the Christian faith is embraced because it is the best option available, and best symbolizes a Western person's attitudes with regard to God, neighbor, and world. But the truth of its formulations about Jesus as God's final revelation and "incarnation," their definitiveness for the future and for others outside our culture, seem to many to represent immodest and presumptuous claims, beyond our possibilities of affirmation. Ironically, at the very same time that biblical and dogmatic literalism have become massive popular movements, among educated people a "demythologized" Christianity which discounts any literal meaning to the absoluteness (hence also the divinity) of Christ seems to have become a widespread phenomenon, and without any direct contact with the scholarly or theological movements in a like direction.]

These observations bring us back precisely to the project we have undertaken here: that is, an examination, on the grounds of "foundational" theology, prior to dogmatic affirmations, of the credibility of the Christian claim. For Christianity, in its classic expression, it is not sufficient that Jesus be recognized as the ultimate revelation of God "so far," or for a particular culture; he is rather affirmed to be completely normative, for all time: the definitive or "eschatological" manifestation of God. Of course, this must not be taken to mean that Christian religion is an *absolute* presence of the Absolute in history—i.e., a pure immediacy to God. Nothing categorical is simply identical with the transcendental or Absolute. The Christian claim is, however, that in Jesus there is present the definitive *mediation* of the transcendental—so much so that this mediation belongs to the nature of God himself. This is what is said in the doctrine of the divinity of Christ.

The question which remains for us, then, is: If we can accept Christian belief as the supreme expression of personalist religion, the highest revelation of our own humanity in its relation to God, and (in some sense) the convergence point of the most genuine strivings of world religion, is there reason to go further, and to affirm that in Christ there has occurred a definitive, "special" categorical revelation, a unique and final "word" of God to humanity?

VII. JESUS THE CHRIST AS GOD'S WORD

In the history of the Universe, in so far as human insight has been able to probe the mystery of it so far, we can see events that have been decisive and therefore significant: the successive geneses of our galaxy, our sun, and our planet; the epiphany of Life on this planet; the epiphanies of the Vertebrates, of the Mammals, of Man. These are all instances in which a particular creature has, in fact, served as the instrument or vehicle for a decisive event at a particular point in Space-Time. If it is not incredible that the Earth may have been singled out circa 2,000,000,000 B.C. for becoming a home of Physical Life, it is neither more nor less incredible that Abraham may have been singled out circa 1700 B.C. at Ur, or Israel circa 1200 B.C. at the foot of Mount Sinai, for becoming a vehicle of God's grace to God's creatures. If it is not incredible that the first Adam may have been created, circa 1,000,000 or 600,000 B.C., at some point, not yet located by pre-historians, on the land-surface of this planet, it would be neither more nor less incredible that a Second Adam may have become incarnate in Galilee at the beginning of the Christian Era.

Arnold Toynbee, An Historian's Approach to Religion

Death reigned from Adam to Moses, even over those who had not sinned by a transgression similar to that of Adam, who was the prefiguration of the one who was to come. But there is no comparison between the fault and the gift. If, through the fault of one, the multitude died, how much more have the grace of God and the gift conferred through the grace of one man, Jesus Christ, been profusely spread upon the multitude.

Rom 5:14–15

If our procedure thus far has been valid, we have arrived at a point where it is credible to think of Christianity as the religion of "mediated immediacy" *par excellence*, the culmination of the personalist trend in religious understanding. It may thus be said to have a certain relative "normativeness," in that it contains and expresses certain insights which are indispensable to a higher understanding of what it is to be human.

The question remains: Are there grounds to think that in Christianity we meet a final, definitive, "special" revelation of God in history? Is the claim of Christianity itself to "absoluteness" founded? This question cannot be settled simply by an examination of Christianity as a religion; it turns us to the center of the Christian claim, that is, to Jesus himself.[1] In this chapter we shall summarize Karl Rahner's justification of faith in Christ, as formulated principally in his synthetic work, *Foundations of Christian Faith*, under the categories of transcendental and categorical Christology. In the next chapter we shall attempt a critical reflection on this justification and its implications, and subsequently we will undertake a re-examination of the relationship of Christ and Christianity to the world religions in the light of our conclusions.

THE AFFIRMATION OF JESUS THE CHRIST AS ESCHATOLOGICAL SAVIOR

Rahner's attempt to establish rational grounds for the affirmation of a "special" and definitive categorical revelation in Jesus may be divided into two major steps: (1) the formulation of the notion of an "absolute saving event," and (2) the identification of the "absolute saving event," manifest in history, with Jesus: the event of his life, his person, his message and his living memory in community.

Rahner thus divides his presentation into two mutually complementary "moments": a "transcendental Christology" (representing the *a priori* anthropological basis for belief in Christ), and a "categorical Christology" (representing the historical motives of credibility). Rahner insists that these two moments exist in mutual dependence. In particular, the transcendental moment is not to be thought of as the product of pure *a priori* reasoning; it "arises in fact only subsequent to and because of a historical encounter with Jesus as the Christ."[2] Nevertheless, this moment is logically prior, in that it examines the existential-ontological conditions of possibility, in humanity, both for the event of Christ as a final self-revelation by God and for our recognition and acceptance of that event. The historical moment then examines the facts concerning Jesus to confirm, in the light of the transcendental ontology-anthropology, the actuality of his fulfilling the conditions.

Transcendental Christology

The expectation of an *"absolute* saving event" means the hope for a salvific revelation from God which brings about an *immediacy* to him, in the mediation of the world; God speaks to us a final and definitive "word," which is in and for the world, but points beyond it; in this final word, the value of our present existence is not lost, but is "subsumed" into an eternal value. This in turn presumes the affirmation of the essential value of history for the human person and for our salvation, and the consequent expectation of salvation *in* and *for* the world (and not simply *from* the world), i.e., the affirmation of the continuing mediation of the world in our relationship to God, even at its highest existential point.

Thus Rahner's transcendental moment of Christology is in effect an anthropology, formulated through several steps of a transcendental reduction/deduction. In this analysis of the structure of Rahner's argument we will attempt first of all to give Rahner's own formulation, and secondly to bring out the parallels with Lonergan's transcendental analysis of the "heuristic structure" of the "solution" to the human dilemma and with the language we have used in our own anthropology.

Rahner presents his transcendental Christology in five statements:

(1) A transcendental anthropology reveals humanity as essentially open to God—even in those aspects of existence which are marked by incompleteness and failure:

> Man is understood as the existent of transcendental necessity who in every categorical act of knowledge and of freedom always transcends himself and the categorical object towards the incomprehensible mystery by which the act and the object are opened and borne, the mystery which we call God. This is true in all of the dimensions of his existence: his knowledge, his subjectivity, his freedom, his interpersonal relations, his relationship to the future, and so on. It is also true of the hiatus characteristic of each of these dimensions individually and of all of them taken together, the hiatus between the unity which is sought after ("reconciliation") and the plurality which is ever present.[3]

(2) Our own transcendence expresses itself in the hope that God is in actuality freely revealing himself to us, "speaking" a word of dialogue to us and inviting our response; furthermore, reflection shows that this hope itself is only possible if God's self-gift inspires it:

> Man is understood as someone who dares to hope . . . that his existence is borne by this all-pervasive mystery not merely as the asymptotic goal and the dynamism of an infinite movement which always remains within

the realm of the finite. He hopes rather that this mystery gives *itself* as the fulfillment of the highest claim of existence for the possession of absolute meaning and of the very unity which reconciles everything. Consequently, the finite, the conditional and the plurality which we are inescapably does indeed remain, but nevertheless it participates in the infinite itself, in the unity of the fullness of meaning, in a Thou who is absolutely trustworthy. . . . In order for *this* movement to be possible, it must already be borne by the self-communication of its goal as the dynamism towards it, a self-communication of God which is at the same time the real essence of grace and of the process of transcendental and universal revelation.[4]

(3) Because human existence is both transcendental and historical, the self-communication of God and the hope of it are necessarily mediated historically. This self-communication of God through the categorical necessarily implies a dynamism in which the categorical expression is always exceeded by the reality of God as goal:

God as he is in himself can be present revealing himself within the realm of the categorical (and without this neither is there any transcendental presence of God for us) only, first of all, in the mode of *promise*, promise as the ongoing transcendence of the categorical which affirms the starting point of hope and its categorical goal merely as a stage of hope in the absolute sense, affirms it as the mediation of revelation, and hence also negates it as not identical with the real goal of hope; and, secondly, in the mode of *death* as the most radical event of that negation which belongs to the very nature of every historically mediated revelation, and which becomes absolute in death because nothing categorical can any longer be hoped for.[5]

(4) On the basis of our existential hope for a communication of God himself in history, we expect and look in history for an absolute saving event:

This most courageous act of hope searches in history for that self-promise of God which loses its ambivalence for the human race as such, becomes final and irreversible, and is the end in an "eschatological" sense. *This* self-promise of God can be understood *either* as fulfillment in an absolute sense, that is, as the establishment of the "kingdom of God"; *or*, if history continues, as a historical event within history which is of such a nature that it makes the promise itself irrevocable without bringing the history of the entire world as a whole to the culmination of complete fulfillment.[6]

(5) The absolute saving event implies an absolute human savior, that is, a person in whom the absoluteness of salvation is manifest, for only a human subject's free acceptance of God's gift of himself as our absolute Future can be the historical manifestation of a final and victorious self-giving by God. This free acceptance must be made complete in death; yet by its nature it will also be and show that eternal validity, that triumph over death, which attainment of God as our absolute Future implies:

> The categoricality of God's irreversible offer of himself to the world as a whole, which allows this irrevocable offer to be present historically and which mediates to us the hope which corresponds to *this* offer, can only be a man who on the one hand surrenders every inner-worldly future in death, and who on the other hand in this acceptance of death is shown to have been accepted by God finally and definitively. For an offer of God to a *free* and "exemplary" subject can be shown in a categorical way to be *irreversibly* victorious and eschatologically final only by the fact that it is actually accepted by this free subject. We are presupposing here the anti-individualistic conviction that, given the unity of the world and of history from the viewpoint of both God and the world, such an "individual" destiny has "exemplary" significance for the world as a whole. Such a man with this destiny is what is meant by an "absolute savior."[7]

It is clear that Rahner's "transcendental Christology" is simply a restatement and expansion of his basic existential-ontological anthropology which we summarized in our first chapter and integrated with Lonergan's idea of a "heuristic structure" of God's "solution" to the problem of evil. It will perhaps help to clarify Rahner's thought further if we once more restate it in these terms:

(1) Humanity is oriented to a saving relationship with God which is anticipated in the structure of our existential being. This implies that:

(a) we are essentially open to and made for the eternal, i.e., for God; humanity is an "obediential potency" toward God;

(b) the structure of human being is that of "spirit in the world"; we must become in history, through freedom, what will be our eternal validity before God;

(c) we confront in ourselves existentially the dilemma of evil and sin;

(d) we may and do expect from God a saving event in history which corresponds to our need for salvation.

(2) Existentially, we are already within God's "solution"; we experience it above all in our capacity for "being in love with God in an absolute way" (which also implies an absolute love of neighbor and an absolute hope for ourselves—even in the face of death—and the world). From these experiences, and in the light of the religious formulation of a claim to an abso-

lute mediation of God in history—above all in Christianity—we may formulate the notion of an "absolute saving event." We look for the existence of such an event in history as the categorical achievement and confirmation of our transcendental experience of being in love in an absolute way.

(3) We may intellectually "anticipate" (heuristically and existentially, in the light of religious history) the structure of such an absolute saving event, by examining the problem it solves, the nature of humanity which is to be saved, and our own experience of salvation actually operative in our lives. A definitive saving event or final, victorious categorical expression of being in love with God in an absolute way must be:

(a) *immediacy* to God—in which human being-toward-God is really confirmed by God's gift of himself; the saving event can only be definitive or absolute if it consists in the self-gift of God, for any merely human achievement of the finite categorical revelation of God is by its very nature provisional;

(b) *mediated* by historical being, even while it points toward an eternal validity or absolute Future which transcends history; the saving event can only be definitive or absolute for humanity if it is historical, for nothing purely transcendental can be definitive for humanity on earth (because of the very nature of our being as spirit-in-world).

Furthermore, unless the absolute saving event is to mean the end of history altogether in the establishment of God's "kingdom," it must consist in a movement toward the absolute Future in which that Future is already present, validating and confirming the dynamism of the movement. It must therefore have a definitive historical moment, appearing as a special ("eschatological") categorical revelation which is the sign and reality of God's definitive victory over sin and its consequences, and not merely as the "mixed" reality of humanity's approach to God. Because salvation for humanity must occur *in* humanity, and must be a freely embraced transformation of human freedom, the absolute saving event must be *personal;* it must consist in (at least)[8] one person whose life and death (as the final moment of absolute abandonment to God) manifest and are the victorious grace (self-gift) of God in history. Such a person would be the sign of the fact that *our* (ambiguous and incomplete) experience of grace is validated by God as his definitive, absolute self-gift, overcoming all ambiguity and incompleteness. As the sign and exemplar of universal salvation, this person may be called the "absolute savior."

Categorical Christology

The categorical moment in Rahner's Christology may be divided into three major statements: (1) Jesus' eschatological claims implicitly present him as the "absolute savior" anticipated in the transcendental moment; (2) the resurrection of Jesus—in the light of his life and teaching, as well as of our anticipation of an absolute saving event—attests to the truth of this claim; (3) the affirmation of Jesus as "absolute saving event" is the equivalent of what the Christian tradition affirms as the mystery of the incarnation and the divinity of Christ. In Rahner's presentation each of these statements is the conclusion of the examination of the New Testament data in the light of the transcendental human horizon which serves as the hermeneutical presupposition. We shall briefly summarize Rahner's process of thought, bearing in mind that Rahner intends to present only a summary of the minimal claims about Jesus that may be accepted by modern exegesis. Because Rahner's treatment of the life and mission of Jesus is little more than an outline, an attempt will be made here to "flesh out" the presentation with material drawn from the conclusions of other recent summaries of New Testament research.[9] These are not presented as definitive, but merely as representing responsible modern scholarship. The reader is referred to the notes for bibliographical citations of more complete treatments.

JESUS' ESCHATOLOGICAL CLAIM

First: implied in Jesus' self-understanding (as revealed in the New Testament accounts), in his message, and in his actions is his identity with God's absolute and definitive self-communication to humanity.

Jesus' message centered on the coming of God's kingdom: the eschatological age, the reign of God, was being fulfilled; the transition from the old age to the new was not to take place in some indeterminate future, but was immediately at hand.[10] Although it is difficult for modern exegesis to determine exactly Jesus' position—whether he preached a "consistent" or a "realized" eschatology, or whether even in his message there was a tension between the two—nevertheless it is clear that he insisted that *now* was the time for decision regarding God's kingdom, and that a change was to come (at least) in the immediate future.

God's "kingdom" signifies the complete sovereignty of God's gracious love. Jesus not only proclaimed its coming, but saw himself as intimately connected with that love and with its arrival for us. He addressed God as his Father ("Abba") in a unique and distinctively intimate way;[11] he was conscious of divine inspiration, and indeed presented himself as the eschatological prophet, the man of the Spirit of Isaiah 61:1f;[12] he identified himself—at the very least functionally, and with some probability personally—with the "Son of Man" of Daniel 7:13.[13] All this implies that Jesus experienced in himself the radical and victorious offer of God to him, and saw it as valid for all. For this reason the kingdom was connected with the proclamation of Jesus precisely as *his* proclamation.[14]

Jesus' claim is also made through his actions. While the miracles of Jesus are significantly reduced by modern scholarship, there can be no doubt that the miracle tradition has an historical core, representing (at the least) the memory of Jesus as an exorcist and healer.[15] It is not our intention here to discuss the modern theological meaning of "miracle" or the philosophical horizon for the credibility of such events;[16] it suffices for our purpose to note that for the Scriptures, the acts which we call "miracles" are "wonders" and "signs": signs namely of the arrival of the kingdom of God and the ending of Satan's power on earth. The healings of Jesus represent the penetration of God's rule into the physical world, and the integration of all things in his love (the "peace" [*shalom*] which typifies God's kingdom). They are therefore an eschatological phenomenon: the miracles of Jesus show that *in him* the kingdom, God's final relation to humanity, has come.

Other aspects of Jesus' behavior likewise testify to an unprecedented claim. Even while remaining within the bounds of Judaism, he broke with the law,[17] in particular the sabbath restrictions and the commandments of ritual purity, and this "religious radicalism" is explained as the consequence of a new immediacy of God. He did not teach in the manner of the rabbis, commenting on the law, but placed himself above it, claiming even the power to countermand, on his own authority, what every Jew took for the word of God himself (Mt 5:21ff: "it was said . . ." [i.e., God commanded] "but *I* say . . ."). Unlike the prophets, Jesus did not claim a special "oracle" from God; his own relationship with the Father was his mandate for proclaiming the eschatological morality. He therefore implicitly claims by his preaching to be God's own final word.

The meals of Jesus contain a similar implication.[18] In them he shows his solidarity with social and religious outcasts, who are nevertheless loved by the Father. Every meal, in the Jewish context, was a sacred activity and signified fellowship with God. This aspect was intensified with Jesus, for whom the eschatological fellowship (the "banquet" of the kingdom of God) was symbolized in table fellowship. This gives the particular significance—in the eyes of his contemporaries, the element of scandal (Mk 2:15–17; Mt 9:10–13)—to Jesus' eating with sinners: by doing so, he implicitly claimed the power to take sinners into the eschatological fellowship with himself and with God, i.e., the power to forgive sins. This signifies an unprecedented claim to a divine prerogative (Mk 2:7).

Jesus' call of his disciples to follow him likewise bespeaks an extraordinary claim.[19] Unlike the disciples of the rabbis, Jesus' disciples did not choose him; he chose them, and commanded their obedience, even to the leaving behind of everything for his sake. They were not to become teachers, but were to share Jesus' own fate and authority.

Similarly, Jesus called upon every person to make a choice,[20] a final decision, for or against God's coming reign, and this decision was explicitly linked to acceptance or rejection of Jesus himself (Mk 8:38). As people act toward Jesus, so will the Son of Man, the eschatological savior-judge, act toward them. Jesus thus presented himself as (at least) functionally identical with the Son of Man. It is in relation to Jesus that the final choice regarding God was to be made. That Jesus understood his own preaching as the radical and *final* call of God is implied in his imminent expectation of the arrival of the kingdom.[21]

Finally, Jesus faced his own death with resolution, as something required by faithfulness to his mission and thus as God's will. He therefore accepted his death freely, and deemed it (at least) the death of a prophet. Possibly Jesus also saw in his acceptance of death a more positive soteriological significance as a "sacrifice" which would in some manner bring about the arrival of God's kingdom. He maintained his extraordinary claim even in dying, trusting in his filial experience of God even in apparent abandonment.[22]

In summary, Jesus' message, his person, and his actions all imply an unprecedented claim to be God's final, eschatological word to humanity. Jesus presents himself as having a nearness and solidarity with God which are beyond those of any other person, to the extent of claiming a "functional identity" with God in presuming to speak for him, forgive sins, call to conversion, serve as the standard for eschatological judgment, etc. In short, "he is God's Kingdom, God's word, and God's love, in person."[23] Thus the implied claim of Jesus is, in Rahner's terms, equivalent to that of being God's "absolute saving event."

THE VALIDATION OF JESUS' CLAIM: THE RESURRECTION

The second major step in Rahner's categorical Christology regards the resurrection of Jesus. The resurrection is central to the affirmation of Jesus as "absolute saving event," for it not only attests to the credibility of Jesus' claim, but also is the necessary completion of the conditions which make Jesus the "absolute savior."

Before the resurrection may be used as an argument for the absoluteness of revelation in Jesus, however, it must be shown that the resurrection itself is credible. The historical witness to the resurrection is believable only if there is a preliminary horizon in which the occurrence of such an event is admissible at all. As Wolfhart Pannenberg points out,[24] the scriptural statements about Jesus' resurrection are formulated within the horizon of "apocalyptic," in which the resurrection is seen as intrinsically connected with the (imminent) end of the world and final judgment. This horizon, however, cannot be assumed to be totally acceptable, or even accessible, to a modern person, not only because of the foreignness of the symbolic context of apocalyptic, which may give it the appearance of mythology, but above all because of its cosmological assumptions, combined with the obvious fact that the expected end of the world did not take place and does not to us appear imminent (at least from supernatural causes).

If the idea of resurrection is to have meaning today, we must first determine whether there is some core to the apocalyptic expectation which, separated from its mythic trappings, can remain valid for us. This question can only be decided in the light of our view of what humanity's final expectation can be. Rahner therefore attempts to formulate the horizon of credibility for the occurrence of an "eschatological" event—the resurrection of Jesus—independently of the apocalyptic eschatological expectation of the Scriptures. Here again Rahner's argument is based upon the mutual interrelationship of the transcendental and categorical moments.

Horizon of Credibility of the Resurrection

Such a horizon of credibility is provided by Rahner's transcendental anthropology. In the light of this view of humanity and of our existential relation to God, the resurrection may be seen not as a brute fact, an extraordinary and arbitrary miraculous intervention which remains extrinsic to our experience, but rather as the fulfillment of our own deepest hopes. This horizon provides a necessary principle of interpretation if the resurrection is not to be misunderstood in a mythological or materialistic sense. Insofar as humanity is perceived as transcendent toward God, awaiting an absolute saving event, and looking for such an event in history, the resurrection of Jesus may be recognized as precisely the fulfillment of that implicit expectation. Rahner therefore presents the expectation of an absolute saving event as an *a priori* horizon of credibility for the resurrection. This expectation may be formulated more generally as (1) our hope for *our own* resurrection, and (2) more explicitly as our hope for an absolute saving event which, with regard to human death, must be manifest as victory and overcoming in God. Although these two formulations in reality express the same thing, the first emphasizes more the positive aspect of salvation as *for* eternal life; the second emphasizes salvation as *from* evil, death, and sin. The latter has already been the subject of discussion in earlier sections. We shall therefore concentrate, in our resume of Rahner's thought, on the first point, which is already implied in his anthropology, but is here explicitly related to the notion of resurrection.

Rahner begins with the Heideggerian insight that the human is a being who lives facing death; our consciousness is implicitly formed by the knowledge that we must one day die, that biological, psychological life will come to an end. Yet transcendental anthropology also shows that the human being is "spirit": our conscious being is on a level which presupposes and arises out of biological life, but which cannot simply be reduced to the latter. Even in present life, our real "self" is more than the interplay of physical-psychic elements. Because spirit or conscious selfhood is a higher synthesis than biological life, it is possible to conceive an existence of the self which is not tied to this particular (continually changing) physical reality which is "my" body. (This does not imply that spirit could then be unrelated to matter altogether, as a disembodied pure "soul" in the Platonic sense; it only means that the end of this biological system which is now my body does not necessarily and per se mean the end of the self or of conscious being.)

Furthermore, it has been shown that human conscious being is a dynamism toward the eternal: a final and definitive mode of being. Reflection reveals that this kind of being cannot be a simple continuation of the earthly form of life. As Dante saw, an unlimited and therefore ever-incomplete earthly life, an eternal temporal succession with no hope of ending, would be hell, for it would mean permanent desire, without hope of completion. (As we have seen, the horror of unending time, with no way out, is also a central feature of Indic religion's aspiration to "*nirvâna*," being "blown out."[25]) We desire an end, a finality, a completion to life, which by definition must be found outside life itself.

Moreover, the dynamism which constitutes us as spirit is ultimately a drive toward and desire for God. Human nature is "a natural desire to see God" which existentially reveals itself as oriented to an intimacy with God which is *immediate*;[26] no other end can satisfy the infinite longing and openness of human transcendence; as Augustine prayed, "Thou hast made us for Thyself, and our hearts are restless until they rest in Thee." But to know God *in himself*, immediately and in a definitive way, means by definition a form of communion which transcends the mediation of creatures.[27] Even now the experience of "mediated immediacy" to God points beyond the limits of spatio-temporal existence, or "life" in the world as we now know it.

The human desire of an "afterlife," therefore, is in its essence a desire for the divine and the eternal; and eternity is not a "continuation" of temporal existence, but a new mode of being. With respect to temporal existence, death is the end of the human person; the existence which arises out of death is not a further openness to progression, but is rather fulfillment, *being* in a final and definitive way. Eternity should not be imagined, therefore, as existence over an unendingly long time (which, again, is a concept at which, if taken seriously, the human mind rebels); it is rather the mode of being of spirit and freedom *outside* time. Because we now exist in time, which necessarily conditions our thought (cf. the Thomistic–Aristotelian doctrine of knowledge through the "phantasm," and the principle that "there is nothing in the intellect that was not first in the senses"), it is literally impossible for us to *imagine* eternity. But imagination is not the criterion of reality; true judgment is. We can think and affirm as real what we cannot imagine—as both transcendental epistemology and modern physics agree.

Nevertheless, Rahner holds that we do already have some degree of *experience* of what is meant by the eternal; for it is the definitive mode of being of spiritual freedom, and we do experience ourselves as spiritual and free. The concept of eternity is meaningful to us as the final validity of what is already the deepest reality of our being. Every genuine act of love is a kind of pre-apprehension of eternity (as the poetry even of romantic love intimates). In particular that kind of love which we have identified with "religious conversion"—"being in love in an absolute way," expressed in the absolute love of neighbor—holds an experience of the eternal, within time and the world; for in such an act we experience a determination of our freedom whose motivation and meaning already go beyond the spatio-temporal world. In this kind of experience we are engaged in creating a new step in evolution, beyond that of *bios*, adumbrating Teilhard's "point Omega." Anyone who has performed such an act, says Rahner, has *eo ipso* experienced and affirmed a hope for the eternal—even if on the level of conceptual formulation it may be ignored or denied.[28]

It follows that every person, insofar as we are faced with the existential choice of love or its denial, is implicitly presented with the decision to affirm or deny hope for the eternal, for being in its definitive sense. The "fundamental option" of a human being implicitly entails a stance toward the eternal.

The hope for eternity, furthermore, understood in the light of Rahner's anthropology, is a hope for "resurrection." The human is a constituted being; we are not pure spirit, but "spirit-in-the-world," spirit as the higher synthesis of matter, which cannot be "left behind" in the higher integration. Even our definitive, eternal being must be in relation to what is philosophically called "matter": i.e., the principle of potency. Human spirit is never pure act, pure spirit; it is always, even in its final state, the spiritual determination *of* the non-spiritual, non-self-aware: matter. Again, the form of this relation in eternity cannot be imagined. But we can

affirm that what becomes eternal is the human person, and not merely
some "part" of the person (as sometimes seems to be implied in the idea
of the "immortal soul").

Moreover, even when spirit as eternal is no longer "in" the world, the
world remains "in" it; that is, the human historical relation to the world
perdures in the spiritual reality (self-determining freedom) it has produced. What finite spirit eternally *is* is what it has *become* by its being in
the world. Therefore, although the spatio-temporal world itself is not eternal (in the theological sense; the physical "eternity" of the world is not in
question here, and cannot be philosophically excluded[29]), our free being-
in-the-world and human action on the world are decisive for our eternity;
only by our being in the world can we become a freedom (selfhood) which
is eternally valid. This is so because human spirit is essentially dialogical;
it attains itself not simply in itself, but in an outward movement toward
the other.

Rahner concludes, then, that insofar as our hope for eternity is precisely a hope for the eternal validity of the *person*, with its essential relatedness to matter (potency) and to others, we may call this hope a hope for
"resurrection"; for "resurrection" (as the term is used in the Christian
Scriptures) is precisely an image-word which signifies the eternity of the
whole historical person, in all its aspects.[30] (We must of course avoid a
mythological notion of resurrection as a continuation or resumption of spatio-temporal life; the symbolic character of the "resurrection of the body"
is misunderstood if it is taken as a statement about the physical "stuff" of
our present existence. What precisely eternal or resurrected life means in
terms of the *form* of the relation of spirit and matter cannot be determined
or imagined.[31])

Rahner concludes, therefore, that every human being has a transcendental experience of hope for "resurrection." This hope is either accepted
or rejected in our fundamental attitude toward existence, insofar as we opt
either for "faith" or for despair and sin, for "being in love absolutely" or
for closing the self off in egotism. If this hope and anticipation of a definitive fulfillment of personal relational being in God is accepted and is formulated within an anthropology of human being as spirit in the world, then
we arrive at an explicit "eschatological hope," and we are led to inquire
whether a sign of its fulfillment by God has been concretized in history.
Thus the first element of the horizon for the credibility of Jesus' resurrection is formulated as our transcendental hope for *our own* resurrection.

The second element of this horizon of credibility is formulated as our
hope for a saving event from God. Existentially, we not only hope for fulfillment of our being in eternal validity with God, but we concretely look
to that fulfillment as *salvation* from our present human dilemma. As we

have analyzed it, the salvation we anticipate has two basic aspects: (1) a "solution" to the problem of evil and sin; (2) a higher form of life, corresponding to our existential orientation to absolute love. Each of these aspects also implies an anticipation of "resurrection."

Insofar as death is existentially the result of sin and evil (for death appears not simply in hope as the moment of entry into human completion in the eternal, but also in anxiety as the moment of complete self-loss, concupiscence, and alienation), salvation must be a triumph over death; since the "solution" must come to us in our actual condition, it cannot simply abolish death, but must turn death itself into a source of life. In anticipating salvation, then, we look not only to a confirmation of our hope for a final destiny beyond death, but also for a victory over death as the source of alienation during life—a victory which allows us not only to die finally in the ending of life, but which allows us to "die" to sin and to self *in* life, in order to live in truth. In anticipating salvation as "resurrection," then, we anticipate it likewise as salvific death.

Finally, God's salvific word to humanity goes beyond being a "solution," and becomes the principle of a new form of life, a sharing of the absoluteness of God's own life of love. Through reflection on religious conversion we can formulate the expectation of an *absolute* saving event: God's gift of himself in history. In life, this gift must appear personally as the absolute savior, God's "real symbol," his absolute categorical revelation. But this event and person (like every human being) must also exist in a final state, beyond death, and in this aspect, the "absolute saving event" coincides with what we have called "resurrection," seen now in its aspect of "exaltation" or "glory": the absolute fulfillment of God's historical "other" in union with God.

In summary, then, the elements of the existential philosophical anthropology which we have gleaned from Rahner and Lonergan become the horizon within which the credibility of the resurrection of Jesus is given. Our hope for our own resurrection, or eternal validity; our hope for salvation as the solution to evil and sin; our hope for an absolute saving and divinizing presence of God in history—these allow us to see the resurrection of Jesus not as an arbitrary miracle, but as the paradigm of human destiny beyond death, as the sign of victory over sin on earth, and as the final glorious state of God's self-revelation.

Historical Grounds of Credibility

Given the transcendental horizon of expectation of a "resurrection" as God's sign of his triumphant self-gift in history, there remains the task of showing why it is credible to affirm that such an event has in fact taken place in Jesus of Nazareth. While a thorough discussion of the historical evidence concerning the resurrection of Jesus would be a lengthy and complex task, the main elements are quickly summarized:

(1) Jesus presented himself as God's eschatological messenger; his life and message show him to have been an inspired prophetic figure, and corroborate his claim. It is not *a priori* unthinkable that in him the "resurrection," the historical sign of God's victorious self-gift, occurs.

(2) It would seem that we must accept as a positive historical fact that the tomb in which Jesus was buried was found empty some days after his burial.[32] The narrations concerning the empty tomb stem from the Jerusalem tradition; given the proximity of the tomb itself, and hence the opportunity of direct verification or falsification, such a claim could never have been sustained if it were not factual (this is not to deny that the resurrection accounts as we now have them contain irreconcilable contradictions; it only means that the core affirmation of all the accounts is true). Furthermore, in all the accounts the first and principal witnesses to the empty tomb are women; as the word of women would not be accepted as competent testimony in the Jewish context, this constitutes a strong argument for historicity (since the Church would not have invented a story in which the primary witnesses could not be admitted). Moreover, the Jewish polemic against the resurrection never denies the fact of the empty tomb, but disputes rather *how* the tomb became empty. This, of course, is the central point. The empty tomb in itself proves nothing; the question is: Why was it found empty? The answer to this question is not established by any direct historical evidence (in the canonical accounts, no one saw or claimed to see the event of the resurrection); different interpretations of the empty tomb are therefore possible (see Mt 28:11–15; Jn 20:15).

(3) The witness of the disciples of Jesus answers the question of how the tomb became empty by reporting experiences of Jesus, now alive with a new kind of life; in these meetings with Jesus, there is an experience of God. We must note the insistence of the New Testament witness on the reality and the centrality of this message (see 1 Cor 15:14). Furthermore, the quality of the testimony is enhanced by the fact that the witnesses themselves adopted from the first a critical and reserved attitude. The cross signified for them the apparent failure of Jesus' mission and message; the initial reactions to the claim of the resurrection experiences, or even to the experiences themselves, include disbelief (Mk 16:14; cf. Jn 20:24ff), doubt (Mt 28:17), scoffing (Lk 24:11), resignation (Lk 24:21), fear and dismay (Lk 24:37). In short, the sobriety and reserve of the witnesses assures that they are not enthusiastic or possessed fanatics.

Nevertheless, these same people, who had shortly before abandoned the living Jesus, and who after his death were cowering in hiding, were transformed into courageous witnesses who were willing to give their very lives for the message they now proclaimed fearlessly. Something clearly happened to effect this transformation. Their own explanation is that they encountered God in the risen Jesus. Is this explanation believable? Rahner's conclusion is that in the light of the convergence of the factors we have examined—the transcendental horizon of hope for the resurrection; our own experience of supernatural life; the life and message of Jesus; the fact of the empty tomb; the quality of the witnesses—the explanation proffered by the New Testament is credible.

Meaning of the Resurrection

Once we affirm the occurrence of the resurrection of Jesus as the culmination of God's absolute self-revelation in history, it remains necessary to clarify more precisely what is meant by this "resurrection."

First of all it should be noted that the term "resurrection" alone does not suffice to describe the event which took place in Jesus (although it is, of course, the principal and "summarizing" symbol of that event). The biblical background to the idea of resurrection contains several diverse but overlapping elements: (1) resurrection as the presence of the person (either conceived simply as the person's "soul," in the Hellenistic context, or conceived as united with a new "heavenly" body—see 1 Cor 15:40) with God after death—i.e., the same reality signified by the "immortality of the soul"; (2) resurrection as "healing" by God, a restoration of life (especially in the case of the martyrs for faith—see 2 Mac 7); (3) resurrection as the eschatological life at the end of time.[33] It is clear that none of these suffices to express the reality of the "resurrection" of Jesus; indeed the term itself is used in the New Testament in a way which goes beyond its previous usage, and its intent can only be apprehended by the conjunction of other concepts, such as "exaltation."

For the New Testament, experiencing Jesus as "resurrected" means experiencing the truth of certain realities: (1) Jesus' eschatological claim is vindicated, despite the apparent contradiction of the cross. Jesus has (as he claimed) a unique position in the coming of God's kingdom, for Jesus now lives the life of the kingdom (hence the ambiguity of the "body" of Jesus after the resurrection; he does not simply "return" to life, but enters wholly into a new form of life). (2) The kingdom proclaimed by Jesus has in fact begun, *in him* (this represents a theological advance over the earlier expectation that Jesus would soon *bring* the promised kingdom to earth). (3) Jesus shares in the very power of God; he is "ascended" to God and is "seated at God's right hand"; Jesus is the Messiah, the King, since it is in him that the kingdom is established. (4) Jesus is transformed by God's "Spirit," and sends this same Spirit upon his followers, i.e., the reality which took place in Jesus' resurrection, the sharing in God's power, becomes available to humanity. While Jesus is completely transformed by the Spirit (Paul: the Lord has *become* Spirit [= Mt.: "all power has been given" to him]), we are partially transformed, and share in the power of the kingdom, which we experience as the forgiveness of sin and a filial relation to God. (5) Jesus gathers a Church, through his Spirit; those in whom the power of the eschatological kingdom is active form community with Jesus and among themselves, in his active memory.

The notion of the experience of Jesus' resurrection, then, should not be confined to the reception of certain visions and auditions which indicate an external reality (i.e., what has happened to Jesus); it also includes an experience of transformation of the subjects themselves, so that the conviction of Jesus' vindication, etc., is internally grounded in a transcendental encounter with God. (Although this fact is perhaps obscured by the fact that Christian theology, following the liturgically-motivated schema of Luke's Gospel, tends to separate Jesus' resurrection, ascension, and sending of the Spirit, we should reflect that all of these are in fact aspects of the one reality of Jesus' glorification by God; to experience them is to experience the "resurrection." This perspective is apparent in John's Gospel, where the entire sequence takes place on Easter. Expanding upon this perspective one may rightly see—as John does—the death of Jesus as related as well; for the resurrection is the manifestation of the true significance of Jesus' death itself.)

In Rahner's terminology, then, the resurrection fulfills and completes the conditions of Jesus as "absolute savior," i.e., the absolute saving event in its eternal validity and power (not only *for* Jesus, but also *for us*). Like all humans, Jesus had to die; but because he is the presence of God's kingdom, his victorious self-revelation, that death was also exaltation, the definitive historical event in which death is shown to be overcome. Until the resurrection, the absolute saving event was not fully present (even in Jesus); the kingdom was yet to come, the divine self-revelation and corresponding human transformation were not complete. With the resurrection, Jesus has entered the kingdom, and the eschatological reality has begun definitively and with eternal validity.

The reality of the resurrection furthermore necessarily includes the transformation of others in connection with Jesus; that is, faith in the resurrection is an intrinsic element in the resurrection itself, for the resurrection means the historical and salvific *victory* of Jesus' message, which is identical with his claim as absolute savior. The resurrection therefore must not simply "happen," but must be known and produce in others an entry into the absolute and victorious saving event. (In this sense Bultmann is right to say that Jesus was resurrected "into the *kerygma*."[34])

The resurrection, then, both attests that Jesus is the "absolute saving event" and culminates that event itself.

The third major statement of Rahner's categorical moment of Christology is that the affirmation of Jesus as "absolute saving event" is the equivalent of what the Christian tradition affirms in the doctrines of the incarnation and the divinity of Christ.

In explaining why this is so, Rahner returns once again to the nature of an *ultimate* or definitive act of self-revelation by God: the only *absolute* saving event must be identical with God himself, in history. No mere prophet or religious genius could be God's ultimate revelation or self-gift; for each such revelation is always capable of further progression and higher integration. If God posits a *definitive* saving act, it cannot have the same provisional character as "general" categorical revelation; it must have a different relation to God than any other saving and revealing event in the course of history. The absolute saving event could not simply be a particular and supreme instance of the history which we carry forward under God's grace and guidance; it must rather be God's own history. Otherwise, it would remain provisional. Only if posited by the divine freedom can this event be irrevocable, absolute, "eschatological."

Rahner concludes, then, that God's gift of himself, in order to be definitive and also manifest in history, must consist in his own reality, not only in its origin, but precisely in its historical, created character; and it must also, at the same time, be completely human—for salvation in order to be *for* humanity must be accomplished *in* humanity. Therefore, in order for Jesus to be God's eschatological revelation—as he implicitly claimed, and as the resurrection attests—the man Jesus must belong to the essence of God.[35]

Unity of the Transcendental and Categorical Moments

The credibility of the Christian claim in Rahner's method is neither deduced purely from transcendental reflection nor induced purely from categorical data; it is precisely the interaction and convergence of the two—the conditions of possibility of existential experience and the concrete evidence of history—which allows the affirmation.

Only the knowledge of the actual event of Christ makes possible the transcendental deduction of an "absolute savior." On the other hand, only such a transcendental, anthropological moment can give a rational context

to the eschatological claims of New Testament religion. Thus the eschatological *context*—without which the Christian claim makes no sense—is
not accepted arbitrarily, but is shown to correspond to and interpret our
existential experience of God. Of course, Rahner's formulation of the content and interaction between the two moments is not the only possible
one; we have, in fact, tried to show that it corresponds in its general lines
with Lonergan's "heuristic anticipation" of God's "solution" to the problem of evil; it is also similar to Schillebeeckx's procedure in *Jesus: An Experiment in Christology* and to Tillich's in his *Systematic Theology*. The
process is open to further amplification and revision, but the basic method
of combining historical argumentation with philosophical presuppositions
seems crucial to a responsible modern justification of belief.

Rahner notes, finally, that the whole process outlined takes place in
the context of faith,[36] in the sense of *fides qua creditur*—i.e., the person's
engaged relationship with God and his saving presence in history (or what
we have named "religious conversion"), even if this relationship exists only
in an interior and unreflexive manner.[37] As Lonergan remarks, the identification of God's solution is a part of the solution itself; the achievement
of responsible affirmation of special categorical revelation is itself a part of
categorical revelation, and is therefore God's gift. For this reason the appropriation of the process demands personal involvement and attention to
the interior data of our existential relation to God. At the same time, it
does not per se demand explicit Christian faith, and thus remains accessible, in the context of dialogue, to other believers and seekers.[38]

THE "EXISTENTIELLE" CHARACTER OF THE ARGUMENT

The verification of the claim that Jesus is the absolute savior involves
not only an existential process of thought, but an existentielle engagement:
that is, it demands and depends upon our participation. The process is not
merely objective: salvation "is found" in Christ; it is experiential, subjective: I (we) find salvation in Christ—I am (we are) saved by Christ. Such
an assertion is verifiable only insofar as it is lived. This implies that the
"demonstration" of the truth of Christian faith is not something objectively
graspable, but is rather a reality which the inquirer must be part of; we
discover God's "solution" by being actively engaged in it; we are ourselves
a sign of its truth, a part of the mediation of the divine love.

The elements of the solution to the human dilemma—the integration of life as free spirit in the world (wholeness and "holiness"); the
forgiveness of sin (healing and peace); a new and higher form of life in
love (the orientation to communion with God and all others)—must be
found in us. (This is simply an instance of Lonergan's "principle of con-

tingent predication"[39] or Rahner's anthropological reduction of theological statements: to say that "God saves" is exactly equivalent to saying that humanity is saved, that salvation is a reality in the world.) The fact that we are sinners means that the verification of salvation in us is not "objectively" perfect; it takes the form of witness and signs, which may also be anti-signs. This is true both of the individual and of each community of salvation.

The "verification" of salvation is therefore also a task of living out a "saved" form of existence. To the extent that I do not *live* the life of love, the existence of a finite mediation of absolute love is thrown into doubt; its credibility is lessened, both for others and for myself (for my own response to God is the first witness of the credibility of salvation). Rahner points out that the existence of the whole history of salvation depends upon the existence of an absolute event of salvation. The converse is also true: the absolute salvific event could not be such if it did not in fact epitomize a whole history of salvation. The existence of general categorical revelation is the condition of possibility of a "special" categorical revelation; for the latter is nothing other than the unique instance of the former in which God's self-revelation is totally accepted and victorious.

To reiterate in other terms: if Christ is resurrected, then we must experience the reality signified by resurrection; for Christ's resurrection is the definitive victorious moment and sign of that salvation which is an existential of all human existence. The inverse is also true: if we do not live the experience of resurrection, then we have no right to affirm the resurrection of Christ. Our living of this experience, however, is not a mere fact; it is also a demand for "achievement" on our part—at least in the sense of the acceptance of God's love as the principle of transformation of our lives.

The affirmation of the resurrection of Christ is (as we have seen) intimately tied to the affirmation of his eschatological mediation, his "ascension" and the sending of his Spirit to the Church in transforming power. In order for the affirmation of the resurrection to be made honestly and responsibly, that transforming power must be experienced as real, operative, verifiable in experience, and must be connected with the anamnesis of Christ—the "dangerous memory" (Metz) which provokes transformation. Christ can only be acknowledged as savior if salvation actually takes place through Christ, and can be seen to do so. Thus the life of the Church and of the individual Christian forms a vital part of the credibility of the Christian claim, and the identification of the "solution" in Christ involves an existentielle involvement in that solution.

Further Reflections on Rahner's Christology

The crux of Rahner's Christology, from an apologetic point of view, appears to lie in the affirmation in the transcendental moment of an *absolute* revelation of God in history. This affirmation of absoluteness is expressed in various ways: as the hope for a non-asymptotic self-gift of God; as the expectation of a "special" or eschatological categorical revelation; as the listening for a personal "word" of dialogue from God, as distinct from the many "words" *about* God; as the claim of an imperative to love "in an absolute way." Such an absolute nearness of God can by no means be deduced *a priori* from the "nature" of humanity, of God, or of a "solution" to the problem of evil; the affirmation, then, depends upon a matter of existential fact. Do we, existing in the world, have an experience which can be identified (in the light of the universal religious claim to intimacy with God, and especially the Christian claim) as *immediacy* to God himself? (When we say "immediacy" in this context, we mean of course an immediacy which is beyond the mediated immediacy of Absolute Being as the ground of all experience whatsoever, the immediacy by which we "participate" in being, and which grounds the world precisely *as* finite or distinct from God.) We have already touched upon this point in several places; we must now restate the same lines of thought in the light of the implications which are here being drawn.

In itself, the notion of salvation or revelation by God leaves open an infinite range of possibilities. Because God is both free and personal, a history of his relation to humanity is potentially endless and always open to advance; any revelatory event within history would be conditional, capable of being superseded by further events or "words" about God. A salvation/revelation history which remained within the natural mediation of the world would be one in which no event could be definitive or ultimate. There could be no "absolute" relation to God or "absolute" religion; at best some religion might have for its time a kind of relative normativeness of the sort affirmed by Troeltsch.

This would mean that God remains ever and absolutely transcendent to history, "outside" the finite and categorical world by that distinction ("within" his own Being) which is the act of creation. God, the Absolute, would not be found "within" the sphere of the relative (although the relative, of course, is always found "within" his absolute Being). We would have no experience of God "in himself," but only of God as mediated by his world. God would be (solely) the ever-receding "horizon" of all experience and of the self and world. With regard to the finality of human life, this would mean either that (1) humanity is not made for immediacy with God, and all human fulfillment consists of infinite progress within the sphere of creation, or that (2) humanity is made for immediacy with God, but the world is irrelevant to it; such immediacy can only begin beyond the world, in an escape from the world; at best, the world would be a preparation for it, at worst, an obstacle to it.

We have discerned, however, within the formulations of universal religion, the claim to an immediacy of God which is at the same time relevant to and mediated by the world. This claim reaches its culmination in the Christian affirmation that God enters history. But to say that God enters history (if this is not to be reduced to a mere mythological assertion, where God's "entry" is conceived as taking place simply at a discrete external "point" of space-time, but remaining extrinsic to human subjectivity per se) must mean that God enters *our* history: that we are radically capable of and called to the experience of immediate intimacy with God; that at least some persons have experienced that intimacy, in which God himself is heard to speak the supreme word, "I love you dearly" (*Bhagavad-Gîtâ*, XVIII:64), in which God's own "Spirit" is the spirit within us, crying in reply "Abba"—"Father!" (Rom 8:15).

The issue therefore is whether this is so: whether the concept of an *absolute* saving event corresponds to our actual experience. Each person must ask: Do I experience an *immediacy* to God—to the absolute mystery of love—already now, in my actual finite condition? Do I have the experience of a "mediated immediacy" of the Absolute: a movement or dynamism toward God in himself, in which God is already present as the goal?

Since these are questions regarding experience, one person cannot answer for another; each must decide individually. Nevertheless, Rahner believes that we can point to instances which, if they can be affirmed as belonging to our experience, signify and imply the kind of mediated immediacy to God which is in question. We have already considered several of the limit experiences which Rahner cites as evidence of our reception of a gift of God himself in history.[40] We shall here attempt a brief recapitulation and reflection.

First of all, it must be admitted that our minds resist the idea that any mere part of a larger whole (such as an individual's life, or the history of humanity) can be normative for that whole, and therefore it is difficult to admit that any particular experience could be absolute or normative for all experience. Nevertheless, it is clear that we have experiences of *relative* uniqueness or definitiveness, in which a particular moment of experience transcends its limitations and becomes in some way universal.

A first example may be found in truly great art or music: any individual work is limited in its context, is dependent upon others, conveys meaning in a particular kind of symbols; nevertheless, there are works which transcend their own times and symbolic systems, and attain a kind of universality. The greater such a work is, the more its particularity, the "once," becomes a universality, "for all." The conditioned and individual becomes universal, and not by the negation of its conditioned character, but precisely in its particularity.

On the interpersonal level, an example is found in the experience of real personal love. The true act of love involves a "giving" or dedication of the whole of one's existence to the beloved, in whom the lover sees qualities of absoluteness, and who therefore becomes the lover's whole "world." Yet this occurs with regard to an other who is in se limited, who is not the only possible love of one's life, who does not in fact possess every lovable quality. The beloved other, even while retaining a relative and partial character, becomes the "sacrament" of the whole, including even God.

A third example is drawn from the experience of facing our own death. The existentielle awareness of our mortality and of the radical aloneness of dying brings with it the opportunity of recognizing the uniqueness of each one's existence; it brings to the fore the experience of subjectivity. In this awareness, furthermore, each of us faces the moment of radical and absolute answerability for life. Other lives and other deaths might be possible for others; in theory, they might have been for me; but, in fact, it is one unique moment of death, culminating one particular life, which, in all its relativity and lack of necessity, will be my point of contact with the Absolute.

The absoluteness of the demands of conscience provides a fourth example. In every act in which we exercise moral responsibility on its deepest level, our relationship to God is mediated. Yet every such act is merely a finite and relative decision; it can never be completely good or totally free. In se, any such act is merely a part, a moment of life; yet it so mediates the whole that a person can be obliged to sacrifice the entirety of life itself to that part: one can be obliged to die for conscience.

All of these various relative experiences of absoluteness in unique and definite historical circumstances point to the paradox of the existential situation: we experience the normativeness and even absoluteness of values in this world—i.e., in a relative, finite condition which in itself cannot ground absoluteness. This is perhaps most easily seen in the summons to an absolute love of neighbor (and, by extension, commitment to the finite world as a whole). As we have seen, Rahner holds that an absolute love, bestowed radically and unconditionally on a human being, already implicitly affirms a definitive act of God identifying himself with humanity; for human beings are finite, relative, uncertain; we cannot of ourselves justify an absolute love, a full entrusting by another. Of themselves, human beings can only be loved with reserve, conditionally. If, then, we actually experience absolute commitment (or at least the imperative to such commitment), *in* the love of neighbor (or, in a wider context, in commitment to the world[41]), then this requires that the love of neighbor actually *be* the love of God, and this in turn requires that there be a unity of God and humanity *in history.* That is: if we have experienced a mediated immediacy to God in our personal history, then we must look in the history of humankind for a definitive ground, source, and sign of that mediated immediacy—a sign that God is in fact giving himself to humanity, and is thus found in our neighbor in a definitive way.[42]

Rahner's contention is that if there is a categorical revelation *of God*— i.e., if God actually gives *himself* to humanity in our finite history—then there must be a special or absolute moment of such a revelation; otherwise, revelation in history would not actually be God's gift of himself, but only a provisional and endless series of human approximations to God; he would remain the "asymptotic" goal of history, but would not be reachable within it. But our actual experience, for Rahner, indicates that God is reached within our finite condition; we must therefore seek his presence in some historical moment which confirms his absolute self-gift to humanity: i.e., we must seek the absolute saving event, which must be a personal union with God or an absolute savior. It is then the task of categorical Christology to show that such a sign and assurance has in fact taken place in Jesus.

We may restate Rahner's argument in yet another form. Our present existence in the world shows itself to be not merely the prelude and means to immediacy with God, but as already participating in such immediate intimacy. At the same time, our experience of intimacy with God is not "self-grounding," because our lives are always conditioned by failure, lack of openness, suffering and sin. Thus the mediation of the immediacy to God in our lives is always ambiguous. This is especially seen with regard to death; for we have not (yet) experienced, in our own persons, that triumph over death which must be a reality if God himself saves us by becoming present as the fulfillment of our finite existence.

Nevertheless, despite the ambiguity of our lives, we do experience an absolute *hope:* a confidence that our lives do mediate the presence of God. We therefore rightly expect and seek an historical witness, an incontestable historical presence of the mediation of God, where the ambiguity (especially of sin and death) is overcome, where we can see unambiguously the truth of our experience of absolute love, eternal validity, within human worldly existence, despite the fallenness and failure of our personal lives. Our sinfulness and imperfection would give the lie to the absolute value of personal existence, unless there exists in history an assurance of what we cannot verify simply and unambiguously in our individual and communal experience: that evil is definitively transcended into good, that death is overcome, and that therefore our hope for the world as the mediation of God is justified. Our own personal experience can give only a relative justification, conditioned by our struggle against sin and evil; but if we really experience God's presence *as victorious* in history, validating existence in the world, then there must be some point in history where that victory is completely real. Our relative experience of immediacy to God, victory over evil and death, points to and necessitates a definitive moment, a culminating revelation of God's salvific self-gift, an absolute or eschatological saving event. It is to this implicit expectation that the event of Christ, in his life, death, and resurrection, is shown to correspond.

VIII. SALVATION IN CHRIST

Have in you the same sentiments that were in Christ Jesus:
he, although his condition was divine,
did not cling jealously to divine status,
but he emptied himself,
taking on the condition of a slave,
and becoming similar to men.
Having behaved as a man,
he abased himself still further,
becoming obedient unto death,
even death on the cross!
Therefore God has exalted him,
and has given him the Name
which is above every name,
so that at the name of Jesus
every knee should bend,
in heaven, on earth, and in the underworld,
and every tongue proclaim
that Jesus Christ is Lord,
to the glory of God the Father.

Phil 2:5–11

Christology as the Culmination of Anthropology

Once it is accepted that there exists in history a "special categorical revelation" in which God's gift of himself is definitively and victoriously present in the person of the "absolute savior," a new and higher viewpoint is attained on the meaning of humanity, in which this immediacy to God can and does take place. The fact of the Christ-event means that humanity may now be defined not merely as an openness to God as absolute horizon, but as the potency (*potentia obedientialis*) for the incarnation. If Jesus is affirmed as God's self-expression in the world, then the humanity of Jesus—which is to say, the self-same humanity which is shared by every person—is the capacity for that self-expression of God. We have already

221

developed the anthropological position which holds that humanity is an unlimited orientation toward the Absolute Mystery. We may now state, with Rahner:

> If this indefinable nature, whose limit, that is, its "definition," is this unlimited orientation towards the infinite mystery of fullness, is assumed by God as *his own* reality, then it has reached the very point towards which it is always moving by virtue of its essence. It is its very *meaning*, and not just an accidental side activity which it could also do without, to be given away and to be handed over, to be that being who realizes himself and finds himself by losing himself once and for all in the incomprehensible. . . . Seen from this perspective, the Incarnation of God is the unique and *highest* instance of the actualization of the essence of human reality, which consists in this: that man is insofar as he abandons himself to the absolute mystery whom we call God.[1]

Because humanity is made for God, the human person attains full selfhood by belonging completely to God. This is what occurs in Jesus. Christology may now be seen to be the highest point of anthropology, while anthropology is the anticipation of Christology.[2] The "question" which is human existence is made possible only by the anticipation of the answer which is found in the Christ,[3] and this answer tells us what humanity finally is. The actual occurrence and identification of God's "solution" to the human dilemma, his "absolute saving event," reveals in the concrete aspects of humanity which cannot be anticipated heuristically, even though they are already being *lived* and thus "anticipated" in an unthematized or inadequately thematized way. (Thus for Rahner revelation in the Christ brings something new—even in content—to categorical revelation: it determines revelation in a way not otherwise possible by manifesting the concrete worldly form of God's absolute self-gift. Because of this, subsequent reflection is able to formulate such concepts as supernatural grace, resurrection, hypostatic union, etc.)

In the light of the Christ-event the human person may be defined as the potentiality to be God's self-in-the-other: the "possible otherness (*Anderssein*) of the self-emptying of God and the possible brother of Christ."[4] If Jesus is God's "word" or self-expression in the world, then all persons are the potentiality for and the imperfect realization of this self-expression, and the entire world—which is necessarily oriented toward the production of spirit as its final goal—is the "grammar" of God's possible self-expression.[5] The ultimate perspective on anthropology, in the light of Jesus, sees humanity as "that which comes to be when God's self-expression, his Word, is uttered into the emptiness of the Godless void in love."[6]

The "hypostatic union" is thus presented by Rahner as the culminating point of the Thomist metaphysics of "participation" (see above, Chapter I): it implies, as its condition of possibility, a certain intrinsic "partaking" of the divine being in all humans.[7] This is true first on the level of what humanity must *necessarily* be in order to be "spirit" at all, but there is also a further "divinization" of humankind implied in God's giving his very self as absolute gift, whose sign and culmination appears in Jesus the Christ. This "divinization" (of which the Greek Fathers of the Church speak, and which is already implied in the Johannine language about being "born from above"[8]) does not imply that all human beings have the *same* relation to God as the "absolute savior"; a "universal hypostatic union" (à la Spinoza) is ruled out as an existential hypothesis by the factual human condition of alienation and sin. Nevertheless, Rahner is able to speak of a "universal God-manhood inherent in the spiritual creature as such."[9]

The "hypostatic union" therefore is an intrinsic moment within God's giving of himself to all spiritual creatures; this gift, as Rahner stresses, must have a concrete tangibility in history as fully accepted by humanity and therefore triumphant as salvation:[10] that concretion is the incarnation, the existence of the absolute savior. The incarnation is not to be thought of as an absolutely higher level of existence, in which God's self-gift to humanity is surpassed; it is, rather, "a singular and unique moment in the universal bestowal of grace, which bestowal cannot even be conceived of without the hypostatic union of an individual person."[11] There is an intrinsic unity between the incarnation and the self-transcendence of human spirit—and of the whole material world which produces and is epitomized in spirit—toward God, in the dynamism of God's self-communication. Rahner thus emphasizes the continuity between "hypostatic union" and universal "grace": the active influence of God's self-gift or Word (Logos) on the human nature of Jesus is of the same kind as the influence of God on all free creatures.[12] Indeed, the hypostatic union is nothing other than the complete achievement of the deepest possibility of human existence.[13] What "happens" to the human being, Jesus, by virtue of his intrinsic unity with God, culminating in the resurrection, is of the same kind as what is the goal of *every* human being:

> The intrinsic effect of the hypostatic union for the assumed humanity of the Logos consists precisely and in a real sense *only* in the very thing which is ascribed to all men as their goal and their fulfillment, namely, the immediate vision of God which the created, human soul of Christ enjoys. . . . Prerogatives which accrue *intrinsically* to the human reality of Jesus through the hypostatic union are of the same essential nature as those which are also intended for other spiritual subjects through grace.

Christ as "Real-symbol" of God: The Point of Origin of the
Theology of the "Trinity"

The intrinsic connection between anthropology and Christology may
also be expressed in terms of Rahner's theory of "real symbol,"[14] for this
term corresponds exactly to the notion of "mediated immediacy." As we
have seen, the entire creation, which "participates" in God's being, may
be seen as God's expression of himself outside himself. The world is essentially oriented toward spirit, which is the highest possibility for the "appearance" of Being outside itself: the "symbol" or "sacrament" of God in
his "other," mediating his creative presence. Spirit is in turn intrinsically
oriented toward the possibility of God's free giving of himself in a more
immediate way. Such a self-gift and self-revelation of God for and in the
spiritual creature, however, must still be a mediated immediacy—i.e., it
still retains the nature of "symbol," the expression of the Subject in his
"other," but the "referent" of this symbolic reality is now God himself, in
his personal existence, rather than as the asymptotic horizon and source
of being.

This mediation of God's immediacy as self-gift, however, is imperfect
and distorted by the reality of evil and sin; the "sacramentality" or God-
symbolizing character of human history is limited and ambiguous. The
perfect symbol of God outside himself, therefore, will also be the expression of the "salvation" of human history: the victorious guarantee of the
reality of the entire "mediation" of God's presence. The self-expression of
God in his Other reaches its culmination in that spiritual creature in whom
human nature reaches its perfection as acceptance and expression of God's
self-gift in history: the "absolute" self-revelation of God or "absolute savior." This human being is the "real-symbol" *par excellence* of God giving
himself, expressing himself in his "other."

We may therefore speak of varying degrees of "symbol" or "sacramentality." The Christ (the special and final categorical revelation) may
be seen as God's ultimate real-symbol or "sacrament" in the world, while
the rest of humanity ("general" categorical revelation) participates in that
"sacramentality" to different extents, and the world itself is the symbol
or sacrament of God insofar as it exists for and points toward the production of finite spirit as God's other. Or, to use the terms somewhat
differently (and more in line with Rahner's usage, defining them "from
above"), we might say that humanity, as *potentia obedientialis*, is the
potential symbol of God himself (on the supernatural level), while the
absolute savior *is* that real symbol, and the sub-human world may be
regarded as the "language" in which the symbol is spoken, the material
of the "sacrament."

Rahner notes that it is from the recognition that "the man Jesus belongs to the essence of God" that the doctrine of the Trinity takes its beginning. In Jesus we experience God: in the concrete history of Jesus, God is present, as himself. Yet, at the same time, God remains always the ineffable and mysterious ground, the *origin* of what Jesus is. We are therefore led to distinguish the "Father" from the "Son" and arrive at the idea of the pre-existent Son as the eternal reality of the relation which is historically manifest in Jesus. Insofar as God has come, through Christ, as the salvation which divinizes humanity interiorly, he is called the "Holy Spirit." The distinctions within the "Trinity" refer in the first instance to the relation of God *to us*—i.e., the "economic" Trinity; but because God in history genuinely reveals *himself*, we can say that these distinctions must belong to what God is in himself (the "immanent" Trinity).[15]

Once the concept of the Trinity is formulated from the starting point of the presence of God's absolute self-gift in Jesus, and the latter is understood as God's "word," the expression or symbol of God in the world, the theory of symbol may be applied to the understanding of the divine Trinity. It cannot be known simply from reason that God must come to self-possession through self-expression or self-symbolization, as finite beings must;[16] for God is by nature the complete identity of knowing and being-known in absolute simplicity. But once it is known that God *does* in fact express himself *outside* himself, then the analogy of human consciousness, symbolizing itself in the "other" in order to come to self-possession in the act of free self-affirmation (love), may be applied to the divine life: first as it shares itself with us (the "economic Trinity") and second as it is in se (the "immanent Trinity"). God's internal self-expression in Logos and Spirit is then seen as the internal and necessary condition of possibility of his free external self-expression. On the basis of this understanding of the Trinity, one may then construct a Christology "from above." The divine Logos is seen as God's essential *ability* to express himself outside himself;[17] the Christ-event is seen as the actual free fulfillment of that capacity. From this point of view, one may even say that it is the incarnation which is the primal, and creation the derived, possibility:

> There can indeed always be the lesser without the greater, although the lesser is always grounded in the possibility of the greater, and not vice-versa. To this extent we can readily say: there could be men, that is, the lesser, even if the Logos had not himself become man. But we can and have to say nevertheless: the possibility that there be men is grounded in the greater, more comprehensive possibility of God to express himself in the Logos which becomes a creature.[18]

The Christ Event as Means of Salvation

From the foregoing it will already be clear how the soteriological function of Christ as "absolute saving event" can be understood. Jesus saves, in Rahner's view, not merely by performing some specific salvific act, but rather by what he *is*.[19] It is precisely by being the "real symbol" of God's victorious and loving self-presence, which is at the same time our definitive salvation (in biblical imagery, the "kingdom of God"), that Jesus is the cause (in the sense of "final," "exemplary" or "quasi-sacramental" causality[20]) of universal salvation. Christ is the means and mediation of God's loving and forgiving self-gift by being the culmination, the eschaton, of the history of that gift: "History hangs upon its own future and is mediated by it . . . it takes place in reference to its fullness and its victorious end."[21]

It is clear that in a metaphysical perspective there can be no question of some salvific act which "changes God's mind" from a hostile to a benevolent disposition to humanity. On the contrary, God's universal and absolute love is the source of all salvation. "We are saved because this man who is one of us has been saved by God, and God has thereby made his salvific will present in the world historically, really and irrevocably."[22] In scriptural language, the Father sends his Son for the salvation of the world. However, it may still be said correctly that Christ "effects" God's salvific will toward humanity, insofar as the goal of any action is its reason or cause ("final causality"). In the fullest perspective, the goal of God's salvific will is the entire history of salvation; but insofar as Jesus the Christ is the "highest and ultimate factor" in that history, he sustains and makes possible the whole, and may be called its reason and cause,[23] as well as its "quasi-sacramental" sign.

To assert the priority of God's salvific will, however, is not to deny that salvation is also *achieved* by us, and in a particular way by the absolute savior. According to the principle which is at the heart of transcendental metaphysics, human freedom and divine initiative are not in inverse, but in direct proportion: that is, the more we are responsible for our own acts, the more they are caused by God, the transcendental condition and goal of freedom itself. (Thus we have already seen that "transcendental revelation," the pure gift of God, becomes categorical in and through human achievement, which remains entirely *God's* self-gift.) Therefore, there can be no act of salvation by God which is not also a salvific act by the human person.[24] Jesus, as absolute bringer of salvation, had first of all to enact *his own* salvation; by doing so—i.e., by his lifelong active response to the Father in acceptance of his self-gift—he established in his person and in the world the irrevocable victory and victorious sign of God's love for all human history.[25]

We have seen in previous chapters that the notion of salvation is conceived in the great world religions in various ways, reflecting the different conceptions of the existential problem and of our ultimate goal. There are nevertheless basic similarities. We have already contended that there is a certain tendency to anticipate a "mediated immediacy" to God or the Absolute, and therefore to look toward an "incarnational" savior figure. There are also certain frequently encountered patterns of thought concerning the means of salvation. Thus salvation is seen as being effected through the *conquest* of evil by battle above all in Zoroastrianism, but also in apocalyptic Judaism, in Islam (in the idea of *jihad* or "holy war"), and in the secular religion of Marxism. Salvation occurs through *illumination* or the acquisition of special insight in Hînayâna and Zen Buddhism, in Vedânta Hinduism, and in Gnostic forms of Islam and Judaism. Salvation is made possible through *illustration* or moral example in both major forms of Buddhism, in Hinduism, in Islam, in Judaism and in Zoroastrianism. Salvation comes about through *mystical union* with a self-giving divine savior figure in *bhakti* Hinduism and in the Mahâyâna.

All of these ways of conceiving the "how" of salvation also occur in the Christian tradition. Already in the New Testament there are multiple descriptions and explanations of how Christ saves. Some are formulated on the imaginative level, using analogies from other areas of experience: thus salvation is accomplished by rescue, or our being freed from slavery; by the payment of ransom; by reconciliation of hostile parties; by "satisfaction"; by expiation, through sin-offering; by the "bearing" or "taking away" of sin; by legal aid before the court of God's justice; by victory over demonic powers. Other descriptions are more existential: salvation is achieved through our sanctification or justification; through the building of a new community; through the establishment of brotherly love and of freedom; through inner renewal and the granting of (new) life.[26] The subsequent tradition likewise elaborates the saving work of Christ in various metaphors and explanations. Christ is the "Victor" who battles and triumphs over the devil and his forces of evil (Irenaeus, Hippolytus of Rome, and many of the Fathers; a sub-theme is the idea of Christ as "physician," v.g., in Ignatius of Antioch); Christ is the divine philosopher who reveals the illuminating knowledge of God (Athanasius, Clement of Alexandria, etc.; the theme of Christ as philosopher is also common in early Christian art); Christ is the savior through his moral example for the transformation of our lives (in the Middle Ages, Abelard; especially in liberal Protestantism: Kant, Ritschl, Harnack, Sabatier, etc.); Christ saves by in-

corporating us into mystical union with him, and/or by sharing his supreme "merit" (the Platonic "incarnational" theories of redemption
through Christ's "assumption" of the whole of human nature: Irenaeus,
Athanasius, Gregory, Cyril, etc.; the theory of "the grace of the head"
communicated to Christ's total "body" in Aquinas; the theory of merit in
Gregory the Great, Anselm, Thomas Aquinas, and the Council of Trent).

The Christian tradition also contains another soteriological theory
which is not common in the other higher religions, but is frequently found
in more primitive religions: namely, the idea of the "propitiation" of God
by blood sacrifice, and/or the "satisfaction" of God's justice by vicarious
substitution of Christ as victim. These ideas are developed in their most
extreme form (penal substitution) by Luther and Calvin, but they are also
a part of the wider tradition (especially following St. Anselm[27]), and have
a basis in New Testament thought (in continuity with notions current both
in Judaism and the pagan world). The predominance of this idea of salvation through much of the Christian tradition has led to an emphasis on the
(suffering and) death of Christ as *the* salvific ("sacrificial") event.

The explanation of the salvific import of Christ through the notion of
"real-symbol" of salvation (and its correlative ideas of "sacramental" and
"final" causality) seems capable of "subsuming" all of the major images of
salvation into an ontological perspective, while eliminating the danger of
mythology which threatens some of the traditional images, especially the
last. (This is not to say, of course, that a metaphysical-theoretical theory
can *replace* those images; the realm of the symbolic/imaginative retains a
permanent validity, even within an ontological-existential level of explanation.) The idea of the efficacy of the "absolute saving event" for all humanity presupposes the essential unity of history and the solidarity of all
people among themselves and with the savior;[28] it explains the "mystical
union" of grace through the real union of participation in the sharing of
God's life, which has its culmination in the total Christ. It presupposes an
ontological framework, in which being is conceived as self-presence; thus
a new participation in the divine life must bring a new consciousness, and
salvation must essentially be revelation, or illumination. It insists as well
that salvation is both gift and accomplishment; and thus the savior is also
example (and even "exemplary cause") for the achievement of others, and
this achievement, both in him and in them, is the attainment of transcendence through the conquest of human inauthenticity and sin.

In this context the death of Christ is also seen to have particular significance—while it is related to his life and his resurrection, as well as to
the prior salvific will of God, in a way often neglected in the "satisfaction"
theory. The soteriological significance of Jesus' death stems from the fact
that for all humans, death is the point at which existence reaches its final

and definitive moment of self-surrender to God, whose love is the basis for that existence. As Rahner writes:

> The life and death of Jesus, or the death which recapitulates and culminates his life, possess a causality of a quasi-sacramental and symbolic nature. In this causality what is signified, in this case God's salvific will, posits the sign, in this case the death of Jesus along with his resurrection, and in and through the sign it causes what is signified.[29]

The affirmation of Jesus as "absolute saving event" and "real symbol" of salvation allows us also to complete the "identification" of God's solution to our plight, and so to attempt to answer synthetically the question of salvation as we first posed it: "What is God doing about the problem of evil?"

God's "answer" to the problem of evil (an "answer" which is not in fact a "response," but the existential order of the world's existence) is the gift of himself as our absolute future. This self-gift is experienced as the participation already in life of an immediacy to God, or the presence of his "Spirit" in us. This Spirit is conscious in us as the dynamism to absolute transcendence; it affects our human psyche and our apprehension of our own possibilities, allowing us to formulate the meaning of our lives in transcendent attitudes. It is experienced as "being in love" and being loved in an absolute way. This love is experienced forgiveness of sin (both received and to be given by us); it allows us, despite the relative, conditional and sinful character of the world, to live in absolute love of neighbor, in a collaboration of commitment to the world, and in hope for the future. It thus affirms the personal character of human life, and validates its eternal significance. Its dynamism leads to the achievements and formulations which constitute the history of salvation; these formulations anticipate the perfect accomplishment of salvation and present to the human community examples of self-sacrificial love and transcendent wisdom. In its culminating moment, God's self-revelation to humanity is manifest as an absolute reception of his love in Christ, whose cross and resurrection signify and guarantee the final triumph of love over every evil.

The Incarnation and the "Becoming" of God

Just as the affirmation of the incarnation brings to anthropology a new level of understanding, so too it allows us to advance our understanding of the nature of God; specifically, it allows new insight into the way in which God, the Unconditioned, may "become" or change. Rahner asserts that the incarnation reveals that the affirmation of God's immutability is a *di-*

alectical assertion; it remains correct only if we immediately add that God nevertheless can and does become something, in time.[30] In Lonergan's terminology, we may say that the affirmation of God in the Christ brings our "moving viewpoint" to a new and higher level of synthesis.

The affirmation of God's becoming does not contradict or replace the assertion of his immutability. Indeed, Rahner states that God can really become something in history precisely *because*—and not "although"—he is and remains infinite and unchanging.[31] That is, it is precisely the absoluteness of God which permits his immanence in his "other," freely posited by him. (For only if God is absolute and totally identical with his own being, with the fullness of being—which is to say, "immutable"—can the world be freely posited as *his* "other," and not as something *intrinsically* other than God of which he stands in need in order to attain his own fullness. Precisely because there can be no "whole" consisting of God-plus-world which would be greater than God himself, the reality of the finite and changing world can and must be the reality *of* God, and not simply an external reality added *to* God. God's absoluteness is the condition for his ability to give *himself* to the world, to "empty" himself in becoming what is not God.) Moreover, and in virtue of the same absoluteness, God's becoming "is not to be understood as a sign that he is in need of something, but rather as the height of his perfection. This perfection would be less perfect if he could not become less than he is and always remains."[32]

As we have already seen, Rahner explains the dialectical affirmation of God's immutability and historical becoming with the principle that "He who is not subject to change in himself can *himself* be subject to change *in something else.*"[33] (This statement is comprehensible and avoids being mere paradox only in the light of an ontological notion of "participation" and the analogy of being. At the same time, the latter do not give us positive insight into the essence of God, but confront us with the absolute Mystery and with the existential fact of our own existence as gratuitously given; thus we are faced with the ultimate Mystery of love.)

As has already been intimated in our earlier discussion of the relation of God to the world and again in our brief remarks on Christology, the changing or becoming of God in his "other," without change "in himself," may be expressed in terms of the theory of real symbol. In the process of self-symbolization the originating being constitutes its "other" outside itself as its sign, and in becoming one with that "other" realizes itself. A "real symbol" in Rahner's terminology is a being's self-expression in another for the sake of its self-possession in knowledge and love. The real symbol does not merely manifest this being and make it present, but *is* its reality. The originating being is related to its real symbol as its "form" or "formal cause" (in the case of God, "quasi-formal" cause).[34] (The prime example is the self-expression of human spirit in matter, constituting the human body;[35] in similar manner human consciousness realizes itself through the knowing of objects in symbols.) While finite realities *must* come to self-realization through self-exteriorization, because of the intrinsic plurality of finite being, God *freely* posits the world as his self-expression outside himself. The ultimate real symbol of God is the Christ-event, the incarnation; the humanity of Jesus is the *Ursakrament*, the "primal sacrament" of God, while all other creatures are less perfect sacramental signs.[36]

The world, therefore, both as creature and more especially as recipient of God's self-gift, is the sign or sacrament of God: it is thus God's being "outside himself." *In* this being-of-himself-outside-himself God has a history: the history we have referred to as "general categorical revelation," which is the gradual process of God-for-us (God-outside-himself) becoming fully identical with God-in-himself.[37] The identity becomes complete in the "absolute saving event" which is God's eschatological symbol.[38] "God-for-us"—i.e., God "outside" himself, God in humanity, engraced humanity sharing God's life—only becomes fully identical with God-in-himself when this sharing of God's very self reaches its eschatological point, which is begun and symbolized in Christ.[39]

The final identity, moreover, is not a simply an undifferentiated unity, but the union of love which is known to Christian theology as the Trinity and our participation in it. The affirmation of an absolute self-communication by God brings us to a new understanding of the assertion that God's inner being is Love. This must be affirmed first of all simply on metaphysical grounds, because God freely affirms (i.e., creates) the being of the other (the world, ourselves), and the free affirmation of another's being is nothing else than love.[40] In the light of the Christ-event (including the resurrection and the experience of the outpouring of God's life or "Spirit"), however, we assert that God gives not merely *our*selves, but also *him*self; God establishes his "other" so that that other may be united with him in the relation of dialogical love.

Finally, it may be noted once more that there is a certain similarity between "process" theology in general and the understanding of God's becoming presented here; at the same time it will be clear that the latter is differentiated from certain forms of "process" thought in that (1) our presentation insists upon the absoluteness of God as the all-encompassing condition of possibility for his self-giving to what is not himself, and (2) the final and full reality of God theologically expressed is seen not in terms of a bi-polar nature, but in terms of a Trinity of relations "within" the one absolute Godhead.

The "Absoluteness" of Jesus as Saving Event and Other Mediations of Salvation

It will be clear from the foregoing reflections that the notion of the "absolute saving event" as the real symbol and final cause of the whole order of salvation gives to Rahner's theology of God's self-gift a Christological and incarnational character even beyond what is generally found in the classical Christian tradition. Nevertheless, Rahner warns against the "primitive and naive" kind of Christocentricity which is sometimes observed in theology and even more in piety, which makes Christ the center and totality of our understanding of humanity and God. The "absoluteness" of Christ is frequently misunderstood in such a way as to lead to what Schillebeeckx calls a "positivism of revelation"[41]—as though to accept and understand the Christ event one did not need a horizon of understanding which is not simply identical with or given by the historical figure of Christ himself.[42] We therefore return in this section to re-examine the notion of the "absoluteness" of Christ as God's eschatological revelation in order to clarify what it does and does not imply, particularly in the light of recent questions which have arisen from the context of comparative religions and the ecumenical dialogue.

The absolute saving event, the union of God and humanity in the person of Jesus, is affirmed as the definitive mediation of God to human history. What is mediated is God: i.e., the incomprehensible Absolute. This means that there is no question of God's being "contained" or "comprehended" within the historical parameters of Jesus' life. The mediation of God's presence by a human being does not mean that God ceases to be God and becomes a finite phenomenon. The God revealed in Jesus remains—even to the humanity of Jesus—the Absolute Mystery. Jesus is therefore not to be thought of (as in certain Eutychian tendencies of Western theology) as the pure immediacy of the Absolute; rather, as a human being, he is the definitive historical *mediation* of that immediacy of God which is offered to every human being. The humanity of God in Jesus "neither is nor can be graced in itself with a closeness to God and an encounter with God which is essentially different from *the* encounter and self-communication of God which in fact is intended for *every* person in grace."[43]

It follows that, as mediation and sign, the humanity of Jesus is crucial to his status as "absolute savior." The "absolute saving event," seen from the point of view of its conditions in humanity, consists in humanity's radical acceptance of God's absolute offer of himself. The "incarnation," in other words, must be an "ontological" and not merely "ontic" reality; it consists concretely in the particular human life of Jesus, realizing and constituting itself in freedom, and facing death as the final abandonment into God's hands.

That which is united to God in Jesus—i.e., what mediates the immediacy of God—is the same reality which is in us as openness to God: the transcendental dynamism (*potentia obedientialis*) which constitutes us as spirit and person. In Jesus as "absolute saving event" the unity of that human dynamism with its goal manifests the eschatological validity of the dynamism itself, i.e., the eternal validity of human personhood. For every human person, however, the epitome of personhood is in our relation to God; so in Jesus it is his relation to God as Father, his "relational being," which is absolute. This relation is of course concretized and made categorical in Jesus' life, and secondarily in his teaching, but these are not simply identical with the relationship itself; they remain finite, conditioned and incomplete (even though they remain the expression and "sacrament" of the relationship, and as such attain the kind of normativeness associated with great works of art or of love, in which unique events take on a universal character without losing their relativeness).

What is "absolute" in Jesus' mediation of God, then, is not each particular element of his existence, taken separately, but rather the whole which is expressed and realized in them: i.e., the totality of his personal relation to the Absolute Mystery of God; and this relation reaches its fullness only in the resurrection—i.e., in an event which goes beyond the bounds of history and anticipates its end.

Thus Jesus as a human being does not exhaust every human possibility of positive relation to God and to others; he is rather the "exemplar" of how every such possibility is to be realized: i.e., in the dynamism of filial love. Therefore not all anthropology is simply contained within Christology; we must go elsewhere than to the Christ-event in order to know what humanity is and what we personally are called to be. There are many possibilities of being human that are not revealed in the historical person of Jesus, and therefore there are many modes of relating to God whose concrete form cannot take Jesus for their example or expression. (To cite only the most obvious case: Jesus was not a woman. The many possibilities of the specifically female aspects of humanity do not find in him a paradigm.)

It follows that to identify Jesus as the definitive or absolute saving event is not to say that the historical Jesus is the *totality* of the mediation of God or that his life and teaching exhaust God's self-revelation in history, so that the rest of categorical revelation would simply become superfluous. Even if we admit that wherever a revelation of God exists, it is "anonymously Christian," in the sense of anticipating the final revelation of God and partaking of the same unfolding of salvation which reaches its culmination in Christ, we must likewise admit that this does not make the revelation in Jesus the *complete* word of God, independent of the rest of revelation, nor justify a subsuming of all human experience into the specifically Christian content. As Hans Küng remarks, "Christian does not mean everything that is true, good, beautiful, human."[44] Moreover, the divine self-revelation in Jesus is not a presuppositionless and self-justifying event. There is much that must be revealed about God apart from Jesus in order for us to *come to* Jesus, and much that must be revealed about humanity apart from Jesus in order for us to *go from* Jesus to authentic living.

We have seen that Jesus in his resurrection becomes an "eschatological" reality; the resurrection is not the completion but the initiation of a process to be completed. As Pannenberg notes, the significance of Jesus' resurrection was originally bound to the idea that it constituted the initiation of the universal rising of the dead for the final judgment which was to come imminently with the world's end. Only in this context would the resurrection be the complete validation of Jesus' eschatological claim.[45] But the ending of the world and coming of the kingdom, as expected by Jesus and his earliest followers, did not in fact occur.[46] The meaning of Jesus' eschatological claim nevertheless remains valid for us, but within a different concrete (anthropological) horizon of interpretation from the "apocalyptic" expectations of the first century. Jesus' resurrection has the character of final or absolute revelation for us through connection with an ending and universal resurrection *still to come*.[47] The final divine confirmation of Jesus will occur, then, only at his return. Therefore, "when we speak today of God's revelation in Jesus and of his exaltation accomplished in the resurrection from the dead, our statements always contain a proleptic element"[48]—i.e., an anticipation of the future.

The resurrected Christ is not simply the known historical Jesus, but also the Lord whose coming we "await with joyful hope": the eschatological (and to that extent "unknown") total Christ, whose reality includes the whole of his ("mystical") body. The fullness of the meaning of the resurrection—and therefore the fullness of the meaning of the Christ as God's final "word"—is to be known only at the end of the world, when, as St. Paul puts it, God will be "all in all" (1 Cor 15:28). The process of history until the end constitutes "a part of that coming fullness, and this participation is an essential component of the eschatological reality and of Christ's resurrection itself. As we have seen, we could not say that Jesus was resurrected unless that event also produced the resurrection-faith of the disciples, the experience of the Spirit, and the community which sacramentalizes salvation.[49] As Bultmann put it: "The kerygma itself is an eschatological event."[50] In line with Rahner's thought, we may extend this idea to the entire history of general supernatural revelation/salvation, or the complete economy of "grace"; its categorical expression in universal religious experience is a "kerygma" without which the *total* eschatological event could not take place. The final and total "real symbol" of God, the "absolute saving event" in its fullness, includes a human participation in and reception of God's self-gift which transcends the limits of the earthly reality of Jesus (although that earthly reality remains for us, through the resurrection, the proleptic sign of the totality), and includes the totality of the human reception and realization of God's self-gift.

These considerations raise an important issue which has largely been neglected in the theology of the past but which is brought to the forefront in the modern encounter of world religions: if the "final cause" and "real symbol" of the economy of salvation must refer to the resurrected, eschatological reality of Christ, then what precisely is the relation between the *historical,* categorical Jesus and *universal* revelation/salvation history? More specifically: Does the affirmation of Jesus as the "absolute savior" imply *exclusivity*—or is it possible for the "absolute saving event" to be *plural* in its historical realization? In the light of the affirmation of universal transcendental revelation/salvation we may ask with Schillebeeckx: Does the historical Jesus finally become only the "symbolic point of reference of a kind of *mysticism of being?* Or is a *historical* event really the specific Christian access to God?"[51]

There is no doubt that the New Testament presumes an exclusive mediation by Christ. He is the one mediator (1 Tim 2:5); there is no other name by which people can be saved (Acts 4:12); he is the only-begotten Son (Jn 1:14), and no one can come to the Father except through him (Jn 14:6); while all have died in Adam, all live through him (1 Cor 15:21-22); he accomplishes the reconciling sacrifice once for all (Heb 9:12), etc.[52] As Schillebeeckx points out, already the Johannine writings combat the tendency to "λὐειν τὸν" Ιησουν (1 John 4:3), that is, any attempt to do away with Jesus of Nazareth in favor of a heavenly or spiritual Christ principle."[53] On the other hand, it can hardly be denied that the New Testament perspective is limited in its concerns, and hardly adverts to the modern problem of salvation outside Christianity.[54]

Rahner's Christology, as we have seen, affirms Jesus as the "unique and highest" instance of union with God,[55] but it is not immediately clear *why* Jesus must be unique. Rahner holds that the Christ event is intrinsically unsurpassable, that there is nothing new to be said by God after this revelation.[56] However, he insists that it is not the content of Jesus' message which is the ultimate revelation, "for God could also call forth and express in some other prophet the words which the man Jesus as the messenger of God says about God."[57] Jesus must be the self-expression of God in what he *is*, and not merely in what he says. At the same time, Rahner states that Jesus' person is intimately connected with his message; his proclamation flowed from (but did not exhaust) his interior experience of filial intimacy with God. Still, some have been led to ask: If the categorical message of Jesus is (at least in theory) accessible outside Christianity, (1) exactly what does explicit faith in Christ add to "anonymous Christianity" except the name "Jesus" as the symbol of what God is doing everywhere,[58] and (2) why must Jesus be the *only* absolute realization and symbol of this universal salvific act?

It is clear from Rahner's writings, especially on the Christian's existential relation with Christ,[59] that he does not consider Jesus merely a name pointing toward the infinite God, but a person to be loved in his concreteness. To the first question we may reply that for Rahner the Christ-event does bring about a determination of categorical revelation (and hence also of anthropology) which is not otherwise attainable. This new dimension of revelation is not contained simply in the message which Jesus proclaimed, but in the totality of his life, death, and resurrection (which includes the experience of his Spirit). If this is so, however, it should be in some way "verifiable" in the religious conversion produced by the Christ-event. We shall return to this point shortly.

The second and related question is perhaps more difficult to address. Rahner himself seems aware of the difficulty, for immediately after asserting that the closeness of God as salvation is present in Jesus and his proclamation in a new, unique and unsurpassable way, he adds that "it is not easy to say why this is so"—at least with regard to the pre-resurrection Jesus.[60] Again he asks:

> How . . . in the face of the Indian concept of the God-manhood of humanity as such, can the *uniqueness* of Christ's mediatorship be credibly proclaimed, unless one understands this uniqueness as that which gives the interdependence-in-salvation of all men its eschatological guarantee, its victory, its historical form and manifestation?[61]

But even if one does understand the mediatorship of Christ in the way that it has been presented here, why does this imply uniqueness? Certainly the affirmation of God's absolute presence in a human being does not per se imply a universal incarnation,[62] and the existential fact of sin and alienation militates against the idea of the "hypostatic union" with God of *every* human being; but could there not be *more than one* personal manifestation of God's completely victorious presence in history?

Rahner seems to imply that such a possibility cannot be ruled out by reflection, but only on the basis of faith:

When a person reflects upon the faith . . . this reflection might in the first instance understand faith in Jesus Christ merely as *one* abstract and conceivable possibility among others for coming to terms with life and death. But neither does reflection as such have to accomplish anything more than this: it grasps *this* possibility as given, as already actualized, and as salvific; it does not see any other and better concrete possibility. This is sufficient in order that, beyond the possibilities of reflection, the believer may allow himself to be grasped by the absolute claim of Jesus. It is *faith*, not reflection, which responds to this claim with an absolute and exclusive "yes."[63]

Certainly it is true that if a person finds a particular faith possibility actually salvific, and sees no better possibility, that person is justified in making an absolute faith commitment. But would one not have to say this of the Buddhist's or the Muslim's—or indeed the polytheist's—faith as well as the Christian's? If reflection can go no farther than providing a negative justification for the embracing of the specifically Christian claim, this may suffice for the believer, but it seems to eliminate the possibility of justifying that faith—in its specific content—to any other.

Furthermore, it is clear that the "yes" in faith to Jesus' claim must be absolute; but it is not immediately clear why it must be *exclusive*. Is it not possible, as Paul Knitter suggests, that the exclusivity associated with Jesus as God's final "word" is the product of the Jewish eschatological-apocalyptic mentality[64]—whose expectations were *not* fulfilled in Christ's resurrection—and therefore belongs to the culturally conditioned "medium" of the New Testament more than to its essential message?[65] Can the characteristic of exclusivity or uniqueness be derived independently of that apocalyptic medium, so that it belongs to horizon in which *we* may expect an absolute saving event?

Wolfhart Pannenberg believes that it can be so derived, from the notion of God's self-revelation:

The concept of self-revelation includes the fact that there can be only a single revelation. God cannot disclose himself in two or more different ways as the one who is the same from eternity to eternity. When someone has disclosed himself ultimately in a definite, particular event, he cannot again disclose himself in the same sense in another event different from the first. Otherwise, he has not disclosed himself fully and completely in the first event, but at most partially. Thus either there is always only a partial self-disclosure of God that is perceived under one-sided aspects, or there is in one instance a revelation that certainly is unique by definition, because a plurality again would abrogate its character as revelation.[66]

At first sight, Pannenberg's argument is reminiscent of Rahner's explanation of why there must be a definitive or final revelation of God if he is to reveal *himself* in history at all. Pannenberg seems to go farther, however, in claiming that this definitive self-revelation in history must necessarily be singular. We may wonder, however, whether this aspect of his argument is based on an equivocation. What does it mean to say that God—i.e., the Absolute Mystery—reveals himself "fully and completely" in a categorical event? Clearly there can be no categorical content which contains the totality of the divine reality. Must not God's ultimate revelation of himself reveal him precisely *as transcendent* to every categorical content? Does it not follow from our reflections on Rahner that the ultimacy of the absolute revelation consists rather in the personal relation to the Father which is manifest in Jesus? It is true, as Pannenberg says, that God cannot disclose himself ultimately "in two or more different ways"; there can be no question of reducing Jesus to one of a number of "avatars" of God, each revealing a different aspect of his personality. But does this mean that God cannot reveal himself *in the same way*—i.e., in the same relationship of human self-abandonment to the absolute love of God—in two or more persons?[67]

Furthermore, Pannenberg himself insists upon the proleptic character of Jesus' resurrection, the culminating point of his revelation of God. Does this not imply that the "full and complete" revelation is not simply contained in the historical life of Jesus, but is referred to an eschatological event in which the Christ is identical with but also transcends the historical Jesus both in his unity with God *and with other humans?* Does this in turn imply that the "cosmic" Christ may include other personal instances of the highest realization of the human possibility, perhaps unknown to us at present?

The expanded consciousness of modern people with regard to the physical universe sharpens this question. Science tells us that the universe is some fifteen billion years old, while our solar system came into being only two billion years ago. In the time between the "big bang" and the formation of our solar system, there was more than adequate time for the emergence of life, intelligence, and spirit in earlier generations of planetary systems than our own. It is quite feasible, from a scientific point of view, that entire worlds of intelligent beings lived and passed away before the earth was even formed. We cannot presume, therefore, that we are the only or the first spiritual beings in the universe. Furthermore, in the universe as it is now observable there appear to be myriad possibilities of solar systems with planets which might be the proper environment for life; and even on the hypothesis of an eventually collapsing and non-pulsating universe, galaxies will continue to exist for billions of years after the demise of the earth and the sun.

If other spiritual beings exist or existed or will exist in the universe, is it inconceivable that God may have willed to share with them his very life, as he does with us? And if this must be admitted as a possibility, is it to be excluded that an "absolute saving event" or "incarnation" may have occurred in those economies of salvation?[68] Paul Tillich already raised these questions and gave an answer in his *Systematic Theology:*

> In discussing the character of the quest for and the expectation of the Christ, a question arises which has been carefully avoided by many traditional theologians, even though it is consciously or unconsciously alive for most contemporary people. It is the problem of how to understand the meaning of the symbol "Christ" in the light of the immensity of the universe, the heliocentric system of planets, the infinitely small part of the universe which man and his history constitute, and the possibility of other "worlds" in which divine self-manifestations may appear and be received. . . .
>
> The basic answer to these questions is given in the concept of essential man appearing in a personal life under the conditions of existential estrangement. This restricts the expectation of the Christ to historical mankind. . . . At the same time, our basic answer leaves the universe open for possible divine manifestations in other areas or periods of being. Such possibilities cannot be denied. But they cannot be proved or disproved. Incarnation is unique for the special group in which it happens, but it is not unique in the sense that other singular incarnations for other unique worlds are excluded. Man cannot claim that the infinite has entered the finite to overcome its existential estrangement in mankind alone. Man cannot claim to occupy the only possible place for Incarnation.[69]

If one can agree with Tillich's position with regard to the universe as a whole, can one also extend it—as Paul Knitter for example seems to think possible—to human history on earth? If the absolute saving event is considered as God's irrevocable *sign,* and if a sign must carry significance *for* a particular group, is there sufficient plurality within human history to call for a plurality of such absolute signs? Is there anything to prevent such a plurality—given that the essence of what is signified, the absolute relation to God, must be the same? For the Christian, who acknowledges Jesus as the absolute savior, the question may be posed: Are the rest of the world religions related to the Christian revelation as the Old Testament is to the New—or can there be more than one "New Testament"?

Thus far we have been asking a speculative question about the possible plurality of personal realizations of the "absolute saving event." Following Rahner's Christology, which excludes a naive and implicitly monophysite identification of the humanity of Jesus with the divine, it is so far difficult to see, on purely theoretical grounds, why the Christ-event must of necessity be *unique* in history. We must also, however, ask the question of *fact:* Is there in fact evidence which would lead to the affirmation of another instance of the "incarnation"? Is there another claimant to the title of absolute savior?

The center of the affirmation of Jesus as the eschatological revelation of God is his resurrection. We may therefore ask: Is there evidence of another "resurrection" in history? ("Resurrection" of course is to be understood here not as revivification, but as the manifested fulfillment of our transcendental hope for eternal validity in God.) Paul Knitter again suggests that perhaps we may speak of the "resurrection" of others than Jesus. The experience of meeting the risen Christ, he points out, is explained existentially in terms of the inner state of the disciples, caused by God's action in Jesus (that is, it is not purely subjective). But, Knitter asks, does not the same kind of conversion experience occur in other religious contexts, in association with the continuance after death of other religious founders?[70] Is then the affirmation that the Buddha entered Nirvâna, for example, the equivalent of the affirmation of Jesus' resurrection?

It would seem that a distinction must be made. If we think of resurrection in terms of our transcendental hope, we may indeed expect and affirm that others have in fact attained it: i.e., have entered beyond death into the eschatological reality of the eternal validity of their lives with God. But the resurrection of Jesus is not merely what happened to Jesus after his death, his eternal validity; it is also the sign in history of that validity and its reason; it is the confirmation of Jesus' message and claim. It therefore has an intrinsic relation to its context: on the one hand to the cross, as the epitome of Jesus' self-abandonment to God, and on the other hand to the resurrection-faith of his disciples, as the historical effect of Jesus' exaltation (in this sense, as we have said, we may agree with Bultmann's assertion that Jesus is raised "into the kerygma" and that the kerygma itself is an eschatological event). We must therefore ask not merely whether others in history may have attained to eternal life with God—which we may hope and expect to be true—or whether this has produced conversion experiences, but also whether the interpretation of each such event, which is inseparable from the event itself,[71] is such that it manifests the "eschatological" or definitive relationship of humanity to God.

It would seem, then, that we are led back to the question of whether the Christ-event as a whole—including Jesus' message, in its intrinsic union with his life and death, as well as his resurrection, including its interpretive elements and transforming power for others—gives an interpretation of human existence which is definitive and unique in history, and therefore offers the inspiration for a unique and necessary contribution to human history.[72]

Various efforts have been made to identify such a unique interpretation based upon the Christ-event. Paul Tillich sees in Christianity the embodiment of the ontological principle of *participation*, as opposed to that of *identity* at work in Eastern religions. The former allows and encourages control over nature and an ideal of progress in the world; the latter prevents them.[73] The principle of participation leads to the Christian attitude of *agape* as the ideal form of love; the principle of identity leads to compassion. While *agape* "accepts the unacceptable and tries to transform it," compassion suffers the other's pain through identification. This, for Tillich, is a major form of love, "but something is lacking: the will to transform the other one, either directly, or indirectly by transforming the sociological and psychological structures by which he is conditioned."[74]

Others emphasize the significance of the cross of Jesus as the ultimate symbol of love, and/or as the revelation of sin and forgiveness. Whitehead remarks, in comparing what he considered the two supreme embodiments of higher religion: "The Buddha gave his doctrine for the world; but Christ gave his life."[75] Protestant theologians tend to emphasize that only the cross of Christ exposes and overcomes humanity's efforts at self-salvation.[76]

Our own examination of the question agreed that the Christ-event reveals elements of truth about the human situation which are either not present or not clearly thematized elsewhere. We have summarized these under the category of the "personal": the Christ-event is the revelation *par excellence* of the eternal validity of what constitutes the human being as person. This includes: the intrinsic relation of human spirit to the world; the infinite openness of spirit; the definitive quality of person as freedom, implying self-determination before God, and hence the reality of sin and the necessity of forgiveness; the primacy of *agapic* love; the reality of interpersonal dialogue; the meaning of death as self-abandonment to God in love.

At the same time, this does not mean that what is most specific to the Christian revelation is in no way contained in the other religious traditions, but only that in the Christ-event these elements reach for the first time a clarity and definitiveness of expression which is not attained elsewhere. (So, for example, Knitter points out that although Hinduism and Buddhism lack a concept corresponding exactly to "sin," the reality behind the notion is perhaps expressed in the concepts of *avidyâ* [= ignorance; Hindu] and *tanhâ* [= selfish craving; Buddhist].[77] Nevertheless, the Judaeo-Christian concept contains a personal and dialogical dimension which is not clearly present in the Eastern religions. Likewise, it must be admitted that the "religious radicalism" of Jesus—his break with the old law, etc.—which Rahner sees as the result of the "new" immediacy to God which he experienced,[78] has parallels in the similar breakthrough to religious and moral "interiority" in all the higher religions. It is the explicit connection of this breakthrough with a personal and filial relation to God which seems to set the Christian revelation to some degree apart.)

We should in fact not expect that the Christ-event will present a radically different revelation from what is found in higher religion in general. Just as the "hypostatic union," according to Rahner, does not make Jesus radically different from other human beings, but is rather the *fulfillment* of what every human person is called to, so likewise the categorical revelation in Jesus and his cause is not utterly new insight into the human situation, but rather the expression of precisely what all religion is striving to find and express. (It of course remains true that each tradition will express the truths of our relation to the Absolute in different contexts, not all of which are equally adequate, and each of which will have its own richness of particular concrete expression. As we have stated, the affirmation of a "definitive" or "absolute" revelation in Christ does not imply a *totality* of revelation, nor does it pretend that every aspect of our final relationship to God can be expressed in a single human context.)

Our understanding of what the "absoluteness" of the saving event in Christ means may be aided by a consideration of the "Adam" Christology of the New Testament, in particular of St. Paul.[79] Jesus is not to be conceived as an absolutely unique and separate case of the exaltation of humanity to divine status, but precisely as the new Adam, who initiates a divine form of life for *all* humanity. Jesus is God's final word precisely *as* "the first-born of many brethren" (Rom 8:29). To put this in classical theological terminology: the "hypostatic union" is unintelligible except in the light of the universal dimension of God-humanity known as "grace."

Might we not then explain the "uniqueness" of Jesus by using Teilhard's analogy of the "threshold"? The uniqueness and indispensability of the absolute saving event in Jesus would consist not in his being the only case of God's exteriorizing himself in humanity, nor in the historical unsurpassability of the categorical content of his earthly life, but in his embodying personally the "threshold" in which the victory of grace becomes a manifest and permanent factor in human history. Jesus is not necessarily the only instance of the "absolute closeness of God," but the resurrection of Jesus is the proleptic sign in (earthly) history of the finality of that closeness, its truth as victory. The resurrection of Jesus, in connection with its interpretive elements, is a "first" in history as a proclamation of God's victory, understood and manifest in a definite person. But what the resurrection manifests is not exclusive, but inclusive; Jesus becomes the "firstfruits" of the universal triumphant love of God (1 Cor 15:20-23; cf. Col 1:18; Gal 4:6).

In this perspective, might the "absoluteness" of Christ be better thought of as "indispensability" than "unsurpassability"? The latter carries overtones of a completeness which is indeed *proleptically* present in the Christ-event, but which may be misunderstood in a fundamentalist way as a kind of "positivism of revelation." The Christ-event is "indispensable" in that it manifests and sacramentalizes that personal relation to God which all are called to, and which must make its victorious appearance somewhere in history. The religion of the immediacy of God mediated by personal existence, therefore, appears as the goal of all religion, and in this way the religion of Christ may be said to be the "culmination" of religion. This does not necessarily mean, however, that every other religion must come to its fulfillment *through* Christianity, but only that each will be true to its own God-directed dynamism insofar as it incorporates—in its own language and symbols—the religion of "person" whose threshold in history appears with Christ.[80] (This does not of course exclude the possibility that it is precisely the interaction with Christianity which may be the catalyst to produce this incorporation; the contact with Christianity has in fact had an important role in the transformation of modern Hinduism and Buddhism. Likewise, it is to be hoped that Christianity may learn further dimensions of its own essence by contact and dialogue with the other faiths.)

In conclusion it may be helpful to summarize the major points this section has attempted to present. I have attempted to reconcile two affirmations which appear to be in tension, if not actually contradictory: on the one hand, the "absoluteness" of Jesus as God's "special" categorical revelation—conceived here as the indispensable "threshold" of personal religion; on the other hand, the legitimacy and independence of other approaches to the Absolute, even after the historical appearance of Christ. The key to the reconciliation, to my mind, seems to lie in the eschatological and proleptic nature of the resurrection as the culminating point of the Christ event and (hence) in the "sacramental" character of the Christian revelation. Whether this attempt has been to some degree successful must be left to others in this continuing dialogue to decide. For the moment it must suffice to present briefly the tentative conclusions and suggestions which seem to follow from our study:

(1) There seems to be no conclusive *a priori* reason to assert that the event of complete realization of the human essence in unity with God could not be plural in its personal manifestation; that is, it is possible to conceive of other "incarnations" of God's Word. This certainly appears to

hold for the universe as a whole, and for the earth, should *homo sapiens* be replaced by another species or higher "threshold" of life. It is therefore difficult to see why it should not be possible within the history of our race. This possibility does not seem to be excluded either by the classical doctrine of the "hypostatic union"[81] or by Christian confessional language about the uniqueness of Jesus.[82]

(2) In fact, however, Jesus appears to be the only *historical* figure who can be affirmed as the eschatological "real symbol" of God's triumphant love. The other great symbols of divine and personal love—v.g. the *avatârs* of Vishnu in Hinduism or the *bodhisattvas* of Mahâyâna Buddhism— though they represent a reality, do so through mythic, trans-historical figures. The resurrection of Jesus appears to be singular as an *historical* manifestation of God's eschatological unity with humanity. As John Cobb puts it, "so far as we know, Jesus is unique."[83]

(3) Even admitting the possibility of other (human) victorious self-manifestations of God in history, Jesus remains the "absolute saving event" in the sense of the indispensable "first," the threshold of humanity's entry into the sphere of divinization through grace, and the manifestation of this in the response of personalist religion, which remains the indispensable mediation of a higher consciousness of God. (This does not deny, however, that there may be other indispensable aspects of revelation which are also attained—perhaps even more clearly—outside Christianity.)

(4) The affirmation of Jesus as "absolute savior" includes the affirmation of the unity of *all* humanity with God, in the same relation of being "God's beloved child" (cf. Gal 4:6). All humanity is thus included in the relation of the "Trinity" as God's "word" or expression outside himself. This implies that our essential spiritual directedness is, like that of Jesus, toward the Father. Such a theocentric spirituality (in place of an exclusive Christocentric one) allows for a broader dialogue with other faiths.[84]

(5) The question of the extent of Jesus' uniqueness can remain an open question, to be asked in dialogue with others, even in maintaining an absolute *commitment* to Jesus as "absolute savior." As Knitter insists, we cannot and need not assert that there are no other instances of a fullness of God's victorious presence in history, at least until we have attempted to know and experience the affirmations of other faiths.[85]

(6) The burden of showing the credibility of Jesus' definitiveness rests upon the credibility and meaning of his resurrection, *and* on its transformative effect; that is, the credibility of Jesus as absolute savior is also an existential task and challenge for Christians. If Jesus introduces a new threshold in salvation history, then the "dangerous memory" of Jesus must actually be shown to have transformative power in the lives of his followers and for the world as a whole.

(7) Jesus does not simply "belong" to the Christian churches; Christianity can claim to share in the revelatory character of the Christ-event only to the extent that it is faithful to that event and its meaning. Furthermore, if Jesus is the "absolute savior," then there is a "searching Christology" oriented not only to the past, but to the future, and which may also reveal him in aspects which go beyond the historical memory. The "sacramentality" of the Church, therefore, must not be conceived as "over against" the other religions, surpassing and abrogating them, but rather as a dialogue which includes the "sacramentality" of human history as a whole, and of religious history in particular.

This last point brings us to a further topic, the relationship of Christian faith to other religions, which deserves to be treated, albeit briefly, in a separate section.

CHRISTIANITY AND WORLD RELIGIONS

There is no distinction between Jew and Greek: all have the same Lord, rich toward all those who call on him. Indeed, "whoever calls upon the name of the Lord shall be saved." But how can one call on him without first believing in him? And how can one believe without first having heard? And how can one hear without a preacher? . . . Thus faith comes from preaching. . . .

Rom 10:12–14, 17

The Christian faith is held today, as in the past, only by a minority of the human race; and it looks as though this minority may well be smaller rather than larger in the future. This thought casts a massive shadow over any assumption that it is God's will that all mankind shall be converted to Christianity.

John Hick: *God Has Many Names*

For most of Christian history, the relationship between the Church and other religions or systems of belief was conceived, on the Christian side, in fairly simple and unambiguous terms. The Christian attitude was not uniformly negative; especially in the early Church, there were many conscious borrowings from "pagan" sources, especially from the neo-Platonic philosophical schools, and the early Fathers developed a theory of the universal Logos which saw the same Word which was incarnate in Jesus as actively revealing God to the pagans as well. Later a more negative stance became common. Whatever the evaluation of the worth of other religions, however, the Christian's ultimate goal in their regard was the same: conversion to Christ and incorporation into the Church. From the conviction of the finality and necessity of Christ for salvation stemmed the remarkable and often heroic history of the Christian missions.

Today, several factors have emerged to challenge the traditional Christian understanding of mission. A new ecumenism has re-evaluated the notion that "outside the Church there is no salvation"; a perception has grown of the need of repentance for the de facto historical connection in recent centuries between missionary activity and European colonialism; increased and more sophisticated knowledge of other traditions has led to a more profound respect for their legitimacy as ways to God; certain doubts with regard to the "absoluteness" of Jesus have challenged the very theological basis of missionary activity. For various reasons and to various extents dialogue has begun to supplement or even to supplant missionary activity aimed at ecclesial conversion.

It is beyond the scope of this work to deal in detail with the entire complex of questions which are involved in the modern inter-religious situation.[86] Our treatment of the world religions has been typological rather than concretely phenomenological; as we have already remarked, for our purposes the concrete faiths (including the Christian faith) are too diverse and internally complex to be dealt with except in terms of classical forms, even if one restricts one's view to the higher religions. This does not mean, however, that such a treatment is adequate; on the contrary, it must point toward the necessity of the further step of encounter between religious traditions in their concrete form, which is to say in their actual believers. All we can hope to do here is to provide certain directions for such possible encounters by setting forth some of the implications of the foundational Christian theology we have developed here.

First of all, it is clear that on the basis of the theory of revelation/salvation we have presented, God's offer of himself is universally present and at work in all religion. Rahner is particularly clear on this point. In the light of transcendental revelation, it is possible for a person to attain salvation even where the salvific act (conversion, being-in-love in an absolute way) is not made thematic in religion, but it would be absurd to think that such salvific acts take place *only* where they are not so thematized.[87] It is necessary, then, to consider religious conversion, in its many forms, as the usual means in which transcendentality is mediated by historical experience and thus made categorically present.[88] The world religions, therefore, are to be considered as positive means of salvation—even though this does not remove the ambiguity of religion which stems from human sinfulness and concupiscence.[89] Furthermore, as we have seen, for Rahner all religious faith contains the "searching memory of the absolute savior,"[90] that is, a desire and expectation of the mediated immediacy of God in history. In this way (as in the Logos theory of the Fathers) the Christ is already present and active as a dynamism in non-Christian religions. (Rahner himself, however, restricts his attention to the interior faith of the *individual* non-Christian, rather than the social and institutional dimensions of the latter's religion: "What can possibly be said about the presence of Christ in non-Christian religions beyond his presence in the salvific faith of the non-Christian is a question for theologians doing the history of religion in an *a posteriori* way."[91] We have attempted here to supplement Rahner's theology by establishing at least the foundations of such an *a posteriori* approach.)

If we must admit, precisely in the light of the affirmation of Jesus as the "absolute saving event," that God calls people to salvation through the other world religions, it follows that we must admit as well the possibility that God calls *us* to salvation through those religions. That is, there may be aspects of God's total "word" which are to be learned from the achievement of conversion in other contexts and cultures than those which have been integrated into the Christian traditions. Christianity reads the Scriptures of Judaism as its Old Testament, and finds in them an anticipation of the Christ; should it not be possible, at the very least—leaving aside for the moment the possibility of a plurality of instances of God's victorious saving event—to find in the great world religions a greater depth and richness of the "searching" anticipation of the Christ?

Furthermore, religious conversion does not stand alone; it calls out for and is expressed in intellectual and moral conversion. The metaphysical and ethical systems which have grown out of others' conversion experiences may expand our understanding of our own, and may give us new possibilities of language to express the one mystery of salvation. The encounter with other ethical and social systems will also be an invitation to self-examination and self-purification; insofar as the Church is self-aggrandizing and self-centered it is not the Church of Christ, but a misrepresentation of God's saving event.

We have seen that there is a dialectic of basic positions on the nature of ultimate Reality and its relation to us. In each there is truth to be affirmed and advanced, as well as "counterpositions" to be reversed.[92] While it is impossible to anticipate the results of the actual encounter of religions in their complexity, our exploration of their classic forms already suggests certain contributions which the great religions can make to Christianity and vice versa.

From the Hebrew tradition Christianity has inherited a largely anthropomorphic image of God as a personal, moral being who stands apart

from or "above" the world. From the Hindu tradition we may learn to formulate a more integrated unity of religion and metaphysics.[93] The Hindu
vision of God's immanence may prove a corrective to the frequently ob-
jectivizing Western perspective and make a valuable contribution to the
theology of grace. When the Johannine Christ declares himself One with
the Father, the Hindu may ask: Is this so very different from the Vedân-
tin's *"aham Brahmasmi"* ("I am Brahman")?[94] If the Christian theology of
divinization and of "uncreated grace" is taken seriously, is there not a
sense in which the creature may find that our deepest being is identical
with God? From *bhakti* theology Christians may learn new ways of thinking about God's incarnation. "Even an elementary knowledge of *bhakti*
theology," Klostermaier writes, "will show at once that the Church's understanding of Christ would exclude the use of a term like *avatâra*"; but
in the Pancarata theology of the fivefold manifestation of God, *bhakti* presents categories in which the uniqueness of Christ can be preserved, while
emphasizing his continuity with the entirety of the world as God's self-
manifestation.[95]

Indeed, the Hindu philosophies of identity-in-difference have many
points in common with Rahner's theology of "real symbol," and the points
of connection may provide a fruitful source of reflection for the Christian
tradition. Christianity, for example, has generally rejected the understanding of the world as God's "body" as being offensive to his transcendence. In Rahner's theory, however, the world is presented as God's "self-
expression" or "symbol" outside himself, and, at the same time, the notion
of self-symbolization is exemplified by the "emanation" of the body as the
expression of the human spirit. It is not a very large step from here to the
affirmation that the relation between God and world is in some way analogous to the relation between soul and body. In that case, however, Rahner's way of thinking (along with certain forms of "process theology"),
based upon thoroughly Western metaphysical presuppositions, presents
certain significant affinities with the Vedânta system of Râmânuja, and the
exploration of this similarity might prove enlightening both in the Western
understanding of Vedânta and in the Hindu appreciation of the Christian
theology.

If we agree with Rahner's assertion that the word "God" is permanent
and necessary to our humanity,[96] we may learn particularly from Buddhism that this word must not be pre-defined nor simply identified with
any conceptual content. For Buddhists, "it is very difficult, if not impossible to make any positive statement at all which is not false and inadequate
owing to the mere fact of its being made."[97] This is particularly true with
regard to ultimate Reality. There is a grave danger of misconceptions if the
same kind of name which applies to something in the world is also given

to what is absolutely different from the world as ordinarily perceived and named.[98] On the other hand, Buddhism (like Hinduism, but perhaps even more radically), insists upon a transforming *experience* as the foundation of what we would call "religious conversion."[99] The Buddhist notion of "Emptiness" may serve as a corrective to a too-facile and simplistic "personalism" and the Western tendency to conceptualism.

The Buddhist disciplines of meditation and asceticism may remind Christians that while Christianity affirms the world, it affirms it as evolving toward a supreme value which is not simply present; what is eternally valid is not merely earthly life, but earthly life as transformed and integrated into the life of God. This means the transcendence and "negation" of lower values; concretely it calls for a certain renunciation of the "world" in its illusory character in order to reach it in its eternal God-centered reality.

A dialogue with Islam's insistence upon the absolute unity of God may bring about a re-examination of the idea of the divine Trinity, which in the understanding of many Christians is effectively a form of tri-theism. Rahner's critique of the modern notion of "person" applied to Trinitarian theology (as well as to the hypostatic union) is relevant here. The Muslim sense of the transcendent majesty of God and of absolute abandonment to him represents a fundamental ground of all spirituality. The category of "prophet" applied to both Jesus and to Mohammed probably corresponds to Jesus' own understanding of himself—possibly more closely than the designation of "Messiah" which has become associated with his name; a reflection on this category may increase our appreciation of the way in which the humanity of Jesus serves as absolute revelatory event.

It is clear that Christianity also has a major contribution to make to the other world religions, even if its claim to find in Jesus the highest expression of the "mediated immediacy" to God is not accepted by them. In particular, the Christian ideal of personhood, in which the attainment of God is intrinsically connected with responsibility for history and with inter-personal, dialogical love, offers a possibility of new depth to the Oriental religions. It has frequently been observed that "neither Hinduism nor Buddhism gives decisive motives for social transformation."[100] As Wendy Doniger O'Flaherty remarks, the doctrine of "illusion" could have been used to challenge the social system, but in fact it was not; instead, it was used to preserve the social status quo. For Hinduism, the moral drawn was uncomplaining acceptance of one's place in society; for Buddhism it was withdrawal.[101] In both cases, the fulfillment of *dharma* precluded commitment to social transformation. In contrast, the ideal of the "kingdom of God" has a revolutionary character not only for the individual, but for the social and historical context as well.

The Christian commitment to history also implies a process of demythologization and an existential interpretation of religious symbols. To the "automatic" working of *karma* it opposes the notion of personal sin and responsibility; to the chain of rebirth, the critical earnestness of a single life; to mythological savior figures, a concrete human life lived in self-abandonment to God; to a purely spiritual transcendence—which, because it attempts to go beyond the level of humanity, is in danger of sinking below it[102]—a human embodiment of the divine, grounded in the foundation of human personhood in God himself.

In these ways Christianity may serve, as Küng suggests, as a "critical catalyst" for the development of other faiths, within their own contexts.[103] Indeed, this has already begun to happen; the modern resurgence of Hinduism and Buddhism, and their renewed vitality in meeting the modern world, are in large measure due to the influence of their encounter with Christian ideas. (It is ironic, however, that the revolutionary ideal of the kingdom of God has reached much of Asia in the guise of the post-Judaeo-Christian philosophy of Marxism.) The Christian ideal of personhood realized in love—whether apprehended directly from Christian preaching or indirectly from its lasting effect on Western culture—has served to deepen and sharpen native religious ideals. (A prime example is the figure of Gandhi, whose inspiration for his love-centered and socially active but non-violent Hinduism was largely found in the Christian writings of Tolstoi.)

We have thought to find within all religions a basic tendency to become in practice religions of love. The Christian revelation offers a grounding for transcendence as love—in particular the absolute love of neighbor and commitment to the world—in its affirmation of God as Creator and as self-gift in history.[104] In Jesus it offers a supreme historical embodiment and symbol of this universal self-gift. Whether this historical embodiment can be acceptable as a primary religious symbol for other faiths is highly doubtful; nevertheless, what Jesus represents and "sacramentalizes" is the indispensable content of conversion, however it may be expressed. It is quite possible to conceive the various world religions co-existing in their plurality indefinitely; there is no reason to assume that a single world religion is a possible or necessary goal. On the other hand, it is clear that the kind of interaction envisaged here includes what Cobb calls the "mutual transformation" of religions; dialogue is not merely for greater understanding, but for the creation of new possibilities for all parties.

The idea that Christianity may and should advance through the integration of the revelations of other faiths should cause no difficulty to Christian faith. The history of Christianity—and of every religion—is one of adaptation and enculturation. Contrary to what W. C. Smith calls the "big bang" theory of religions—that each religion is essentially contained in its beginnings, and remains itself by faithful preservation of this core[105]—all religions are in great measure syncretistic. Even while proclaiming their own exclusive truth the religion of the Hebrews and of Christians surreptitiously and perhaps unconsciously borrowed constantly and extensively from surrounding culture and religion. In our own day it has become possible for us to be more aware of the universality of revelation and the interdependence of all humans in their search for God.

There is a further dimension to the call for Christianity to integrate within itself the positive elements of other faiths. As the modernization and secularization of the world continues, the traditional faiths are sometimes threatened with the possibility of extinction within their own originating cultures. In the former great centers of Mahâyâna Buddhism, China and Japan, that religion has been nearly totally eclipsed, in the one case by Marxism, in the other by secularism. The future of this form of Buddhism may be principally in the Christian and post-Christian West. The Christian churches would do a service to Christianity and to the world by consciously making themselves a new context for the Buddhist tradition—as the Church did, less consciously, for neo-Platonism. A Christianity expressed in terms of Buddhist wisdom or of Vedânta philosophy—alongside its Semitic and Greek inheritance—will be a Christianity enriched with a further dimension of Christ, and more capable of presenting itself as a sign of his salvation to the world.

NOTES

Abbreviations Used

CSM = Rahner, Karl (ed.): *The Concise Sacramentum Mundi* (New York: Seabury Press, 1975).

RH = *The Reason for Our Hope* (New York: Paulist Press, 1984)

TI = Rahner, Karl: *Theological Investigations* (New York: Crossroad, 1961–1980).

Chapter I: Has God Spoken?

1. Rahner, Karl: "Observations on the Situation of Faith Today" in Latourelle, René and O'Collins, Gerald: *Problems and Perspectives of Fundamental Theology* (New York: Paulist Press, 1982), p. 279.
2. *Loc. cit.*
3. Schillebeeckx, Edward: *Christ. The Experience of Jesus as Lord* (trans. John Bowden) (New York: Seabury Press, 1980), pp. 31ff.
4. See Lonergan, Bernard: *Method in Theology* (New York: Herder & Herder, 1972), chapters 10 ("Dialectic") and 11 ("Foundations").
5. See also the recapitulation of our anthropology below, chapter VI.
6. I believe that the difference between the position taken here and that of Schillebeeckx is only semantic. Schillebeeckx in his *Christ* speaks of suffering and evil as "not a *problem*, but an unfathomable, theoretically incomprehensible *mystery*" (p. 725). For him, a "problem" is something which we can objectify and set at a distance, while evil and suffering cannot be objectified; they involve each of us. I prefer to follow Lonergan in using the word "problem," giving it however a wider sense which includes the existential dimension to which Schillebeeckx refers, and to reserve the word "mystery" for the reality of God and his self-gift to humanity. Thus evil is a "problem," while *salvation* is a "mystery."
7. Chuang Tzu: *Basic Writings* (trans. Burton Watson) (New York: Columbia University Press, 1964), p. 43.
8. *Ibid.* p. 39f.
9. See O'Flaherty, Wendy Doniger: *Dreams Illusions and Other Realities* (Chicago: University of Chicago Press, 1984) for a detailed discussion of the different Indian interpretations of the "illusory" character of life.
10. For the Advaita, the question is not so much "How can evil exist in the light of the existence of God?" as "How can *anything* other than God exist?"
11. *Bhagavad-Gîtâ* II:19–20.
12. See Conze, Edward: *Buddhism: Its Essence and Development* (New York: Harper & Bros., 1959), pp. 192–197.

13. In Catharism, for example, or in the "followers of the free spirit" described by Ruysbroeck—see *ibid.*, p. 196.

14. The concept of "omnipotence" poses particular difficulties insofar as it is generally formulated in highly anthropomorphic terms. As we shall see, the concept as frequently used in religious language—i.e., the idea that God can by his will do absolutely anything—is highly problematic. Moreover, "power" per se is not a transcendental attribute. As used here, however, the term "omnipotence" stands simply for the transcendental attribute of God's absoluteness and total creativity with regard to the world.

15. See the Buddhist "parable of the arrow" (*Majjhima-nikâya*, I, 426ff.); text given in Eliade, Mircea (ed.): *From Primitives to Zen. A Thematic Sourcebook of the History of Religions* (San Francisco: Harper & Row, 1977), no. 282, p. 570f.

16. These categories are adapted from the doctoral dissertation of A. L. Herman: *The Problem of Evil and Indian Thought* (New Delhi: Motilal Barnarsidass, 1976), quoted in O'Flaherty, Wendy Doniger: *The Origins of Evil in Hindu Mythology* (Berkeley: University of California Press, 1976), pp. 2–3.

17. Lewis, C. S.: *The Problem of Pain* (New York: Macmillan, 1962), p. 95.

18. Juan de la Cruz: "Dichos de luz y amor," no. 62, in *Vida y Obras* (ed. Crisogono de Jesus, OCD, Matias del Niño Jesus, OCD, Lucinio del SS. Sacramento, OCD) (Madrid: BAC, 1964), p. 963.

19. For an overview of Hindu theodicy, see O'Flaherty, *Origins*.

20. Peter Berger in *The Sacred Canopy* (Garden City, N.Y.: Doubleday, 1969), p. 55f., calls this a "masochistic" theodicy in the sense that it places the blame for evil on man; we avoid the term, since it has bad connotations; although the free will explanation can be "masochistic" in the Freudian or Sartrian sense, it is not necessarily so.

21. Augustine sets forth his theodicy in his *De Civitate Dei*. It is based on Augustine's interpretation of Paul on Genesis, on writings of earlier Church Fathers, and on intertestamental literature, especially the book of Enoch; this in turn was probably influenced by Zoroastrianism in the Persian period.

22. *De Civ. Dei*, bk. XI, 11, 13; XII, ch. 9.

23. See Hick, John: "The Irenaean Theodicy" in Hick, ed., *Classical and Contemporary Readings in the Philosophy of Religion* (Englewood Cliffs, N.J.: Prentice-Hall, 1963) p. 511. Hick sees Augustine's as a pictorial presentation of the *problem*, but it must not be taken as a solution; I would say that there are elements of the solution that can be disengaged from the myth.

24. *Ibid.*, p. 515.

25. *Loc. cit.*

26. See above, under general types of religious theodicy: teleology.

27. Hick, *op. cit.*, pp. 516-17.

28. See *RH*, pp. 150ff.

29. The question "Why does not God create a world in which all choices are in fact good?" is a false question; see *ibid.*, p. 236f., n. 19.

30. See *ibid.*, pp. 177-183.

31. Lonergan, Bernard: *Insight* (New York: Philosophical Library, 1957) pp. 696ff; summarized in *RH*, pp. 191ff.

Chapter II: God Has Spoken

1. See *RH*, pp. 162ff.

2. See Lonergan, Bernard: *Insight* (New York: Philosophical Library, 1957), chapter XIX, which develops the essential points of Lonergan's "natural theology."

3. In Lonergan's procedure, being is defined in terms of cognitional acts; therefore in the affirmation of God's existence it is the note of intelligibility, rather than "being" which has priority. See *RH*, p. 141f.

4. *Insight*, p. 659f. Lonergan's use of the word "component" for the distinct aspects of the Idea of Being is unfortunate.

5. *Ibid.*, p. 660.

6. This explanation is in line with the Thomist principle that God has no "real relations" outside himself; that is, the relation of dependence (= being freely posited by another) which links the world to God is a "real" relation only on the world's side; on God's side there is no "real relation"—no dependence, contingency, or composition. It is necessary for the finite mind to think in terms of a relativity in God—a "relation of reason"—by virtue of the fact that we are unable to grasp the divine essence in its simplicity. As we shall see, this principle does not in fact exclude God's being "really related" to the world in the *modern* sense of the word "relation": that is, personal intersubjective love. It does, however, exclude a love proceeding from *need* ("eros") on God's part. (This in turn is expressed in the Scholastic principle that God creates "for his glory," i.e., for the participation in his being by what is "other" than himself. There is no *finis cui* of creation; God creates from pure benevolent, self-giving love; there is no self-seeking motivation.)

7. This question is sometimes posed in terms of three basic alternatives: at one pole, "pantheism," the doctrine that God is all, with its subset of monism; at the other pole, "classical theism," which is conceived as holding that God is totally "other" than the world; and, in between, "panentheism," which holds that everything exists "in" God. (See in particular Hartshorne, Charles, and Reese, William [eds.]: *Philosophers Speak of God* [Chicago: University of Chicago Press, 1953], pp. 1–25.)

It is first of all clear that each of these terms is susceptible of various definitions, and it is not clear that all those about whom they are used would agree with the characterization given. (In particular it is doubtful whether Hartshorne's characterization of "classical theism" actually applies to Thomas Aquinas, whom he takes as its principal representative. See Burrell, David B.: *Aquinas. God and Action* [Notre Dame, Ind.: University of Notre Dame Press, 1979], especially chapter 6. Burrell shows that Hartshorne's characterization of Aquinas is based on a neglect of historical context.)

Even if we accept these descriptions for the moment, however, it will be obvious from the above that such a posing of the problem is in any case inadequate from our point of view. The transcendental affirmation of God leads to the insight that (as in "pantheism") the Absolute is All, that is, the fullness of being, apart from whom there is nothing; and that (as in "theism") he is totally distinct from his creation, which he freely posits in being; and that (as in "panentheism") all exists "in" him. On the other hand, it equally affirms (as against "pantheism") that the contingent world is real, and really "other" than God, so that it can truly be related *to* him; but that (as against "theism") this otherness is "within" God; and that (as against "panentheism") there is nevertheless no intrinsic interdependence between God and creation. (One might also say that transcendental theism can affirm with Buddhist philosophy that God and world are both "nothing" [see Gómez Caffarena, José: *Metafísica Transcendental* (Madrid: Ediciones de la Revista de Occidente, 1970), pp. 317, 319], and, at the same time, that God and world are both positively affirmable in the analogy of being.)

8. Rahner, Karl: *Foundations of Christian Faith* (trans. William Dych) (New York: Seabury Press, 1978), p. 62.

9. This is simply an extension of the basic affirmation of transcendental philosophy that the pre-apprehension of the infinite (Lonergan's "absolutely unconditioned") is the condition of possibility of the affirmation of the finite (reaching "virtually unconditioned" judgments).

10. Rahner, *op. cit.*, p. 62; emphasis added.

11. *Ibid.*, p. 64. Note that this is another more positive way of stating the Thomist doctrine that God has no "real relations" outside himself.

12. *Ibid.*, p. 63.

13. It is of course true that on the level of imagination, one must use innerworldly images to present the divine being; however, transcendence in the image of finite "otherness" needs to be complemented by an image of "sameness" or immanence; and both need the correction of a level of theory which negates the finite content of the image, and a level of interiority which establishes the basis of speech about God in the subject's experience of transcendence.

Gómez Caffarena characterizes the simple otherness of God to the world as "mala transcendencia" (parallel to Hegel's "bad infinity"); see Gómez, *op. cit.*, p. 313. Rahner notes that this kind of misconception can lead to the (correct) denial of the existence of "God," for "*that* God really does not exist who operates and functions as an individual existent alongside other existents" (*op. cit.*, p. 63). Thus atheism and naive theism both harbor the same false notion of God. See also Küng, Hans: *Does God Exist?* (New York: Vintage Books, 1981), especially pp. 181ff.

14. In particular the "concrete realism" of Suarez, with its preference of the categories of causality over those of participation, seems to have suggested the extrinsicism of the world to the Absolute which has characterized much of postmedieval Thomism. More recent studies, returning to Thomas himself, have emphasized the importance of the Platonic element. See Gómez, *op. cit.*, pp. 295, 304f.

It is curious that the philosophy of St. Thomas on this point lends itself to such diverse and contradictory interpretations. As has been noted, Hartshorne and others consider Thomas the epitome of a "classical theism" which makes God a being alongside the world. On the other hand, there are Hindu intellectuals who consider Thomas' view of God as *actus purus* to be essentially the same view as that of the "monist" *Advaita Vedânta* (see for example the dialogue in Klostermaier, Klaus: *Hindu and Christian in Vrindaban* [London: SCM, 1969], p. 28.) Gómez sees Thomas' philosophy as what would today be called "panentheist" (*op. cit.*, pp. 317ff.), citing texts like *1 Sent.* 8, 1, 12 and *Summa Theologica* I, 8, 1; he sees figures like Meister Eckhart, Nicholas of Cusa, and Cardinal Rosmini as being genuinely Thomist in their inspiration.

15. Donceel, Joseph, S.J.: *The Searching Mind* (Notre Dame, Ind.: University of Notre Dame Press, 1979), p. 177.

16. *Esse divinum dicitur esse omnium rerum, a quo omne esse creatum effective et exemplariter manat (1 Sent. 8, 1, 12).*

17. Rahner, *op. cit.*, p. 62f.

18. The Western theistic traditions have consistently avoided applying the category of "material causality" to God's relation to the world; but this is what the image of "participation," taken concretely, implies. Eastern theists—Râmânuja, for example—have had no hesitation in using the categories of both material and formal causality for this relationship.

19. Gómez, *op. cit.*, p. 302.

20. Donceel, *op. cit.*, p. 200.

21. Gómez, *op. cit.*, p. 307.

22. Rahner, *Foundations*, p. 221. Rahner is speaking here in the context of God's becoming in the incarnation; but a world in which the incarnation can take place must already be God's expression of himself "in his other." We shall return to this idea in our discussion of the incarnation in chapter VI.

23. *Ibid.*, p. 222.

24. Wong, Joseph H. P., S.D.B.: *Logos-Symbol in the Christology of Karl Rahner* (Roma: LAS, 1984), chapter 2.

25. *Ibid.*, p. 92.

26. Gómez, *op. cit.*, p. 294.

27. Gómez, *op. cit.*, pp. 298, 302.

28. The expression is that of Franz Grégoire; quoted in Donceel, *op. cit.*, p. 186.

29. One might pose the question: If God's very being is necessary, and God in fact *is* related to the world, how can we see that relation as being other than necessary? Our knowledge of the freedom of creation stems from the fact that we experience our own being as non-necessary, i.e., contingent; since this being of ours is "of" God, there is something of God which he is not by necessity; it is therefore posited by him freely, in a way analogous to my own free acts of love, but without the element of need (i.e., a love of pure "agape").

30. Küng, Hans: *Menschwerdung Gottes* (Freiburg: Herder, 1970), p. 551 (my translation). As has been noted, God must always remain what we affirm in coming to his existence at all: the absolutely unconditioned horizon, the ground of the absoluteness of our own acts of judgment and love. A God who was intrinsically

in need could not be such a ground. As Tillich said of Bergson's conception of God as one who is dependent upon the openness of the future, a God who is "dependent upon an absolute accident" "cannot be the foundation of an ultimate courage. This God would himself be subject to the anxiety of the unknown. He would not be being-itself" (Tillich, Paul: *Systematic Theology*, vol. 1 [Chicago: University of Chicago Press, 1951], p. 275f). The same objection would seem to apply to any God who was intrinsically in need of creation.

31. Rahner, "On the Theology of the Incarnation," *TI* vol IV (trans. Kevin Smyth) (Baltimore: Helicon, 1966), p. 114. Emphasis added.

32. It will be clear that the position on God and the world outlined here has certain affinities with—and certain differences from—the "process" theologies associated with Alfred North Whitehead and his followers, in which God is conceived as having an absolute "antecedent" nature and a relative "consequent" nature. From the point of view of transcendental philosophy, Whitehead's religious extrapolation of his cosmology is problematic in some respects, especially in that there seems to be a more ultimate principle than God (namely, Whitehead's "creativity"). John Macquarrie suggests that if Whitehead's ultimate principle of "creativity" were incorporated into the divine being, one would have a Trinitarian vision (one not dissimilar to Hegel's). (See Macquarrie: *In Search of Deity* [New York: Crossroad, 1985], p. 151.)

Whitehead himself was in any case quite modest about his theological "suggestions" (see *Process and Reality* [New York: Macmillan, 1929], p. 405). We shall return to some of his ideas when considering how to understand God's activity in the world. Despite problems stemming from different starting points and epistemologies, the dialogue between transcendental and "process" theologies seems to hold the promise of fruitful mutual influence.

33. See Rahner, *Foundations*, p. 85.

34. Rahner, Karl: *Glaube als Mut* (Einsiedeln: Benziger, 1976), pp. 24, 27 (my translation). English version in *Meditations on Freedom and the Spirit* (trans. Rosaleen Ockenden, David Smith, Cecily Bennett) (New York: Seabury Press, 1978).

35. Rahner, Karl: *Do You Believe in God?* trans. Richard Strachan (New York: Newman Press, 1969), pp. 112–113.

36. Rahner, *Foundations*, p. 83.

37. In fact, this claim seems somewhat exaggerated. It is true that the Hebrews "discovered"—along with the Chinese and the Persians—a linear sense of history and along with it the "existential" quality of life and morality as lived definitively "before God." The notion of interventions of God in history, however, along with the idea of a "chosen" status of a particular people, while it may distinguish Hebrew religion from Greek philosophical thought, does not seem to be uniquely Hebraic, but to characterize many religions (including the Greek) particularly in their earlier and more anthropomorphic stages of expression.

38. Gilkey, Langdon: "Cosmology, Ontology, and the Travail of Biblical Language" in Thomas, Owen C. (ed.): *God's Activity in the World. The Contemporary Problem* (Chico, California: Scholars Press, 1983), pp. 31, 33, 36, 37. (Originally

appeared in *The Journal of Religion* 41 [1961], pp. 194–205. Citations will be according to Thomas.)

39. *Ibid.*, p. 40.

40. See Thomas, *op. cit.*, pp. 231ff. Our division of the positions will be seen to differ in some particulars, while it follows the general lines of Thomas's analysis.

41. *Ibid.*, p. 232.

42. Dilley, Frank B., "Does the 'God Who Acts' Really Act?" in Thomas, *op. cit.*, p. 53.

43. Bultmann, Rudolph, "The Meaning of God as Acting" in Thomas, *op. cit.*, p. 64. (Originally from *Jesus Christ and Mythology*).

44. Whitehead, Alfred North, *Process and Reality*, p. 404.

45. Whitehead, Alfred North, *Religion in the Making* (New York: Macmillan Co., 1926), pp. 88–90.

46. Whitehead, *Religion in the Making*, p. 88.

47. Whitehead, *Process and Reality*, pp. 407–411.

48. *Ibid.*, p. 407.

49. Whitehead, *Religion in the Making*, pp. 91–92.

50. Whitehead, *Process and Reality*, p. 406.

51. For a more complete discussion of a "process" view of divine causation, see Griffin, David R., "Relativism, Divine Causation, and Biblical Theology," in Thomas, *op. cit.*, pp. 214ff.

52. Thomas, *op. cit.*, p. 237.

53. Griffin, *op. cit.*, p. 124.

54. Hartshorne admits that contemporary scientific interpretations of the world, based on post-Einsteinian physics, seem to contradict his view of the ultimacy of time. See Hartshorne and Reese, *op. cit.*, p. 11.

55. The principal source for the summary presentation in this section is the excellent introduction of Sarvepali Radhakrishnan to Radhakrishnan (ed.): *The Brahma Sutra* (New York: Greenwood Press, 1969), pp. 28–39.

56. For the basis in Śaṅkara's epistemology and theory of causality, see Puligandla, R: *Fundamentals of Indian Philosophy* (Nashville: Abingdon Press, 1975), pp. 211ff.

57. *Loc. cit.*

58. Śaṅkara also holds that Atman, the ultimate "Self" is identical with Brahman; the distinction of the individual "I" belongs to the world of *mâyâ*. Yet he apparently also thought that this distinction is never completely lost, even in Nirvâna. See Radhakrishnan, *op. cit.*, p. 39.

59. It should be noted, as Rahner points out, that these two modes of experience of God are not adequately distinguishable on the transcendental level, but only *a posteriori*, in categorical reflection; for, on the one hand, spirit has in itself an unlimited horizon and, on the other hand, the self-communication of God in this life is incomplete. Mere transcendental reflection, therefore, cannot distinguish between the "natural desire for God" which is intrinsic to human being, and the "supernatural existential" which is from grace. See Rahner, *Foundations*, p. 130.

60. For a succinct summary of a transcendental metaphysical view of God and secondary causes, see Karl Rahner, *Foundations*, pp. 86-89; see also Lonergan, Bernard: "On God and Secondary Causes," in *Collection* (ed. F. E. Crowe, S.J.) (New York: Herder & Herder, 1967), pp. 54–67.

61. *Ibid., loc. cit.*

62. *Ibid., loc. cit.*

63. For a summary of this transcendental analysis, see *RH*, chapter V.

64. It is clear that we are speaking here of what is traditionally called "natural" revelation.

65. Vid. Rahner, *Foundations*, p. 87.

66. See above, p. 47f., and *RH* pp. 200–202 for examples of the manifestation of this transcendental experience.

67. See Rahner, *Foundations*, p. 87; also "Experience of Self—Experience of God" in *TI* vol. XIII.

68. Rahner, *Foundations*, p. 87. On humanity's transcendental "openness" as gift and achievement, see Lonergan, "Openness and Religious Experience," in *Collection*, pp. 198–201.

69. On the Rahnerian *reductio in mysterium* and Lonergan's "principle of contingent predication," see *RH*, p. 235, n. 52.

70. Rahner, *Foundations*, p. 89. Note that Bultmann uses the same example: "The Meaning of God as Acting" in Thomas, *op. cit.*, p. 62.

71. See Rahner, "Dialogue with God?" *TI* vol. XVIII.

72. See Lonergan, *Insight*, pp. 123–128; also, *RH*, pp. 28ff.

73. This conception of miracle which I have derived from an application of the idea of "obediential potency" to Lonergan's theory of "emergent probability" coincides in its essentials with Rahner's conception, which may be briefly summarized: every dimension of reality is constructed from lower levels to higher; the lower are "open" to the higher, in which they are "subsumed" (in the Hegelian sense). Matter and the biological are subsumed into the level of freedom, which therefore can be manifested in them without violating any of their laws. The " 'miraculous' is constituted by the fact that the higher order cannot be derived from the lower order in which the higher comes to appearance." It requires insight and involvement on the part of the subject to recognize the higher level in the lower, rather than reduce everything to the lower level. Rahner concludes with a definition of miracle close to our own:

> A miracle takes place in the theological nsense, and precisely not in the sense of a preternatural marvel, when for the eyes of a spiritual person who is open to the mystery of God the concrete configuration of events is such that there participates immediately in this configuration the divine self-communication which he already experiences "instinctively" in his transcendental experience of grace, and which on the other hand comes to appearance precisely in the "miraculous" and in this way gives witness of its presence. (*Foundations*, pp. 259–261).

74. *Cf. ibid.*, p. 259.

75. The great medieval Muslim theologian Ibn Sînâ (Avicenna; 980–1037) already advanced the theory that miracles are the "natural" effects of the power of mind over matter.

76. Note that "subjective" does not mean arbitrary or fictitious. The place of the subject is in the perception and appreciation of a transcendence which is *real*, and has a real ground in God.

77. Rahner, *Foundations*, p. 258.

78. See above, p. 66; Thomas, pp. 9, 232.

Chapter III: The Locus of God's Word

1. On the difficulty of capturing religious reality, see Samartha, Stanley J. (ed.): *Living Faiths and Ultimate Goals* (Maryknoll, N.Y.: Orbis Books, 1974), p. XV.

2. Dupré, Louis: *The Other Dimension* (Garden City: Doubleday and Co., 1972), p. 20.

3. James, William: *The Varieties of Religious Experience* (New York: Macmillan, 1961), pp. 45–46.

4. Durkheim, Emile: *The Elementary Forms of the Religious Life* (New York: Free Press, 1965), p. 52.

5. *Ibid.*, p. 56.

6. *Ibid.*, p. 62.

7. *Ibid.*, p. 63.

8. Wilson, Edward O.: *On Human Nature* (Cambridge, Mass.: Harvard University Press, 1978), p. 176.

9. James, *op. cit.*, p. 42.

10. Whitehead: *Religion in the Making* (New York: New American Library, 1960), p. 16.

11. Van der Leeuw, Gerardus: *Religion in Essence and Manifestation* (trans. J. E. Turner) (New York: Harper & Row, 1963), p. 681f.

12. James, *op. cit.*, p. 19.

13. *Ibid.*, p. 393.

14. Van der Leeuw, *op. cit.*, p. 679.

15. Montcheuil, Yves: "Le fait religieux, le besoin religieux" in Brillant, Maurice and Nédoncelle, M.: *Apologétique* (Paris: Bloud & Gay, 1948), p. 30.

16. Van der Leeuw, *op. cit.*, p. 680.

17. Dupré, *op. cit.*, p. 10.

18. James, *op. cit.*, p. 377.

19. Montcheuil, *op. cit.*, p. 30f.

20. *Ibid.*, p. 32.

21. Wilson, *op. cit.*, pp. 169–170.

22. *Ibid.*, p. 175.

23. *Ibid.*, p. 206f.

24. *Ibid.*, p. 185f.

25. James, *op. cit.*, p. 30.

26. The categories of "gift and achievement," "performance and formulation" are taken from Lonergan's "Openness and Religious Experience" in *Collection*, pp. 198–201.

27. See *ibid.*, p. 199.

28. Whitehead, *Religion in the Making*, p. 33.

29. Several examples of the limitations imposed on conversion by its available language are given in Rosemary Haughton's *The Transformation of Man* (New York: Paulist Press, 1967). See especially pp. 136–137, 147.

30. See especially the documents *Nostra Aetate* and *Lumen Gentium*. The Second Vatican Council marks the first time the Roman Catholic magisterium has officially taken such a positive position regarding salvation outside the (visible) Church—although it has always consistently rejected positions which would restrict God's universal salvific will or the universal efficacy of Christ's salvific work.

31. See, for example, the critique of ritual and sacrifice in Am 5:21ff.

32. On "emergent probability" see *RH*, p. 32f., and Lonergan, *Insight*, pp. 123–128.

33. On the "biases" see *RH*, pp. 177–181; *Insight*, pp. 191–203, 218–242.

34. Cf. the notion of "original sin." See *RH*, p. 182f.

35. Cf. Lonergan, *Insight*, p. 690f.

36. Rahner, art. "Revelation" in *CSM*, p. 1463.

37. In the following we shall use the word "religion" to stand for the thematic expression of categorical revelation. It is to be understood, however, that the word is used in its widest sense, and that the whole of human historical achievement is included as a "formulation" of conversion.

38. On the inevitability and necessity of such existential presuppositions, and on the possibility of their revision, see *RH*, pp. 73ff.

39. Pascal, *Pensées*, no. 433.

40. See *RH*, pp. 30–31.

41. On the notion of a "higher collaboration," see Lonergan, *Insight*, pp. 729–731.

42. R. C. Zaehner translation.

43. As Hans Küng points out (*Eternal Life?* [Garden City: Doubleday, 1984], pp. 46ff.) the temptation to attempt to capture the essence of religion in an evolutionary schema of thinking has been particularly strong in modern Western scholarship.

Even before Darwin's application of the idea to biology, the notion that development from lower to higher grades is the basic law of being had been propounded philosophically, notably in the system of Hegel. Comte and Spencer applied the idea to human culture and thought, including religion, and the Oxford cultural anthropologist E. B. Tylor gave classic form to the theory. He claimed that all religion evolves by a straightforward and uniform development from a primitive form. Because this evolution takes place at a different pace in different cultures, however, we are able to discern the religious characteristics of early humanity by observing surviving primitive societies. Tylor assumed that primitive religion must be pre-logical, and posited animism and magic as its primal forms. Taking this line of thought one step farther, James G. Frazer (in line with the ideas of Comte) postulated three stages of development: from an original magical world-view to religion proper, and finally to science, which eventually replaces religion as mankind matures.

We have seen already that the replacement of religion by empirical science has not in fact taken place; indeed, modern knowledge of ethnology shows plainly that the schemas of Comte, Tylor, Frazer, *et al.*, have no basis in history. On the level of the schema's content, animism, for example, has been shown not to be original, but a later, derived phenomenon. More importantly, modern studies not only find divergences from the schema in historical fact, but show that the kind of sequence assumed cannot be verified in any concrete case at all. Furthermore, the idea that there is a specifically "primitive" way of thinking which is pre-logical and qualitatively different from ours has been shown to be unfounded.

Although we may agree with Rudolph Otto in speaking of a kind of religious "a priori" in humanity, this consists simply in the fact that human beings share the same "nature," the same transcendental dynamism, and the same basic existential situation, and thus react to the experience of the "holy" within the broad parameters of these common factors. Naturally, then, there will be some parallels in religious developments in different societies and eras. But this by no means implies a uniform schema of development. On the contrary, what has been established empirically, as Küng says, is that religions have developed "wholly and entirely in an unsystematic diversity."

44. There are also many obvious developments in religions which do not necessarily represent progress to a higher form; in fact one can frequently detect periods of decline from an original inspiration. (For an interesting example, see "The arahant ideal in Theravada Buddhism" in *Journal of Religion*, June 1984.)

45. On the notion of a "classic" and its implications, see Tracy, David: *The Analogical Imagination* (New York: Crossroad, 1981), chapter 3.

46. Ayer, A. J.: *Philosophy in the Twentieth Century* (New York: Random House, 1982), pp. 2–3.

47. *Ibid.*, p. 3.

48. *Ibid.*, pp. 13–14.

49. On the differentiation of consciousness and the "realms" and "stages" of meaning which flow from it, see Lonergan, *Method in Theology*, pp. 81ff.

50. See *RH*, p. 193f.; Lonergan, *Insight*, p. 698.

51. Attempts have been made to extrapolate to a single primeval form of religion (animism, dynamism, totemism, even monotheism), present at the beginnings of humanity and from which all others would derive, either by evolution or degeneration, starting from either (a) the idea of a "natural religion," universally present in human conscience and reason, or (b) an evolutionary schema whose later developments are known historically. Both have been shown to be unfounded in the facts of religious history.

Nor can we get to a primeval religion by examining the beliefs and practices of surviving primitive societies. It is true that ethnology can find cultures that are arrested at the Upper Paleolithic stage of development and hence are, as Mircea Eliade calls them, "living fossils" (Eliade: *A History of Religious Ideas*, vol. 1 [trans. Willard R. Trask] [Chicago: University of Chicago Press, 1978], p. 24). But it must be remembered that such societies have as long a history as any modern group, even though that history might be unwritten and unremembered; it cannot be presumed that their present state is the same as that of our—or their—ancestors. Furthermore, the study of these societies reveals many differences between them. At best, we can find what Eliade calls "certain fundamental configurations" of religious behavior which will be common to all societies living at a certain phase of development and in the same circumstances. Human beings after all have the same physical and mental constitution, and it is to be expected that people having roughly parallel experiences will also have roughly the same parameters of possible responses. This is very far, however, from the positing of a single ancestral religion.

52. Whitehead, *Religion in the Making*, pp. 32–40. Whitehead presents the rationalization of religion as the last phase of religious evolution from ritual to emotion to belief and finally to rationality. Taken as an historical description, this must be qualified as at best an unproven hypothesis. Like other evolutionary schemas, it seems to presume that the psychological development of the individual from childhood to mature rationality parallels the cultural evolution of the race in general and of each particular religion. As we have noted, modern empirical studies of ethnology and the history of religion reject such an *a priori* assumption. Nevertheless, even if they do not *succeed* each other in the way Whitehead indicates, it is clear that these elements are important parts of all religions, and each may serve as a focus of a particular religion, just as any one of the four may be a stage in the religious development of the individual.

53. Toynbee, Arnold: *An Historian's Approach to Religion* (New York: Oxford University Press, 1956), pp. 18–19.

54. *Ibid.*, pp. 20–21.

55. Wilson, *op. cit.*, p. 174f.

56. Angelo Brelich, "Politeismo e Soteriologia" in Brandon, S. G. F. (ed.): *The Savior God* (New York: Barnes and Noble, 1963), p. 41.

57. Toynbee, *op. cit.*, pp. 21–22.

58. *Ibid.*, pp. 29–31.

59. *Ibid.*, pp. 29–37.

60. *Ibid.*, pp. 43–53. Toynbee notes that when artificial religions fail, they attempt to co-opt and adapt for their purposes a living religion to serve as a legitimation for the state—as Constantine did with Christianity.

61. *Ibid.*, p. 59.

62. *Ibid.*, pp. 59–70.

63. *Ibid.*, pp. 77–78.

64. *Ibid.*, p. 80.

65. Toynbee does not include Judaism as a higher religion because it remains fundamentally racial and thus "tribal" in character, and so lacks the characteristic

of universality. Christianity, for Toynbee, is Judaism in its "world" form. Although this idea in itself has validity, and has also been accepted by some Jews, it does not exclude the recognition of Judaism itself as a higher religion, particularly in its developments from post-Exilic times to the present. I therefore include Judaism as a higher religion in all senses of the word.

Chapter IV: God's Word in Human Words—The Indic-Sinic Religions

1. See *RH*, p. 193; Lonergan, *Insight*, p. 698.

2. See Toynbee: *A Study of History* (New York: Oxford University Press, 1962) vol. VIIB, p. 414.

3. See *ibid.*, table IV, pp. 772–773.

4. One interesting example is found in the anecdote recounted by Klostermaier about his religious dialogues in India: an educated Hindu of the Advaita school thought himself much closer to Klostermaier's Thomist Christianity than to the fundamentalist Hinduism of the Krishna devotees. See Klostermaier, *op. cit.*, p. 28.

5. Van der Leeuw, *op. cit.*

6. Cf. Herman, A. L.: *An Introduction to Buddhist Thought* (Lanham: University Press of America, 1983), p. 370, n. 23. Our schema roughly coincides with the five elements which Herman claims are identifiable in every religion: (1) the human problem which the religion attempts to resolve; (2) the chief cause of the problem; (3) the nature of the solution; (4) the way(s) adopted to reach the solution; (5) the law or ordering principle that guarantees that the ways will be effective.

Clearly the method we are using would not be an adequate approach for a study whose goal was to come to an understanding of each religion on its own terms; for in accepting the questions deriving from our anthropology as the key to our investigation, we risk neglecting aspects which do not conform to the same patterns of thought or questioning. (For a consideration of this aspect of methodology in comparative religious studies, see the introduction to S. G. F. Brandon, *Man and his Destiny in the Great Religions* [Manchester: University Press, 1962].) At the same time, for our present purposes some structure of comparison is necessary, and our questions are sufficiently generally formed to include the diversity contained in the higher religions.

7. See van der Leeuw, *op. cit.*, vol. 2, p. 605f. There is of course no pure form of either religion of repose or of unrest; both elements are found to some degree in practically all religions. There can be, however, as van der Leeuw points out, a strong preponderance of one or the other.

8. *Ibid.*, p. 605.

9. No small factor in the transformation of the Mahâyâna was the translation of its concepts into the Chinese language. While Sanskrit is a highly abstract and inflected language, capable of extreme subtlety and with many metaphysical concepts, Chinese is uninflected and eminently concrete, almost totally lacking in native metaphysical terms, but having an enormous capacity for expansion by the combination of designations for concrete realities and relationships.

10. Dhavamony, Mariasusai: *Classical Hinduism* (Roma: Università Gregoriana Editrice, 1982), p. 1.

11. *Ibid., loc. cit.*

12. On the Hindu notion of revelation and its relation to the scriptures, see *ibid.*, ch. 1.

13. In this section we shall include important technical terms in the original Sanskrit. Many of these terms have wide ranges of meaning and hence may be translated differently by Western scholars; hence a knowledge of the original terms is helpful in knowing exactly what concept is being dealt with.

14. On *karma*, as related to the problem of theodicy, see above, p. 30.

15. Dhavamony, *op. cit.*, p. 429.

16. *Ibid.*, p. 433; see also Zimmer, Heinrich: *Myths and Symbols in Indian Art and Civilization* (New York: Harper & Row, 1962), pp. 294ff.

17. Dhavamony, *op. cit.*, pp. 432–433.

18. *Ibid.*, pp. 430–431.

19. *Ibid.*, pp. 426–428.

20. Dhavamony, *Love of God According to Śaiva Siddhanta: A Study in the Mysticism and Theology of Śaivism* (Oxford: Clarendon Press, 1971), p. 79. As Dhavamony writes, even the greatest classic of devotion to a personal God, the *Bhagavad-Gîtâ*, does not know the deep humility of the repentant sinner. It is only among the monotheistic Tamil Śaivite mystics that something approaching the Christian notion of liberation from sin, as personal offense against God, develops. See *ibid., loc. cit.*, (cf. *Classical Hinduism*, p. 475f.) and Zaehner, R. C.: *Hinduism* (New York: Oxford University Press, 1966), p. 138.

21. Radhakrishnan, Sarvepali: *Eastern Religions and Western Thought* (New York: Oxford University Press, 1975), p. 21.

22. Nikhilananda, Swami: *The Upanishads* (New York: Harper & Row, 1964), p. 300.

23. Dhavamony, *Classical Hinduism*, p. 448; cf. Brandon, S. G. F.: *Man and His Destiny in the Great Religions* (Manchester: Manchester University Press, 1962), p. 325f.

24. For a brief treatment of the Sâṁkhya system, see *RH*, p. 46f.

25. Zimmer, *Philosophies of India* (Cleveland: World Publishing Company, 1956), p. 393; cf. Zaehner, *Hinduism*, p. 71; Radhakrishnan, *op. cit.*, p. 37, n.: the Sâṁkhya has practically the same account of the world of experience as the monist systems, "only a pluralistic prejudice which has no logical basis asserts itself, and we have a plurality of soul. When the pluralism collapses, as it does at the first touch of logic, the Sâṁkhya theory becomes identical with the pure monism."

26. For a fascinating study of the imagery of dreams and awakening in Hinduism, particularly in the Purânic period, see O'Flaherty, *op. cit.*

27. Van der Leeuw, *op. cit.*, p. 627.

28. Zimmer, *Philosophies*, p. 291.

29. Zaehner, *Hinduism*, p. 71.

30. There clearly are scriptural texts which speak of salvation through activity, as well as through knowledge. Śankara interprets these as dealing with two

different classes of people, while Râmânuja thinks that they apply to everyone, but at different times. See Dhavamony, *Classical Hinduism*, pp. 20–21.

31. Brandon, *op. cit.*, p. 330. Wendy Doniger O'Flaherty notes that "the attitude of the rank-and-file Indian toward the extreme form of the doctrine of illusion may be gathered from the fact that, in Telegu, the term 'Advaita' (i.e., the thought of philosophers from that school) comes to mean 'illogical behavior, upside-down or contrary to normal thinking' " (*op. cit.*, p. 117). It goes without saying that many Hindus remain in their religion on the *saṁsâric* plane, seeking not *moksha*, but earthly happiness from the gods or God. O'Flaherty remarks that Purânic Hinduism implicitly rejects the absolutist idea of *moksha*, while *bhakti* Hinduism explicitly does so (*ibid.*, p. 11).

32. Sivaraman, K. "The Meaning of *Moksha* in Contemporary Hindu Thought and Life" in Samartha, Stanley: *Living Faiths and Ultimate Goals* (Maryknoll, N.Y.: Orbis Books, 1975), p. 3.

33. Brandon, *op. cit.*, p. 331. For an overview of theistic Hinduism, see Macnicol, Nicol: *Indian Theism* (Delhi: Munshiram Manoharlal, 1968).

34. Brandon, *op. cit.*, p. 62.

35. Zaehner, *Hinduism*, p. 77.

36. *Bhakti* is both the goal (*sâdhya-bhakti*, perfected, attained devotion) and the means to the goal (*sâdhana-bhakti*, devotion directed to an end). Dhavamony, *Classical Hinduism*, p. 484.

37. Zaehner, *Concordant Discord* (Oxford: Clarendon Press, 1970), p. 110.

38. *Ibid.*, p. 117.

39. The position of the *Bhagavad-Gîtâ* is analogous to that of Christian theologians (v.g. Maréchal) who acknowledge a certain "natural" mysticism of Being, but place it on a lower level than the personal apprehension of God.

40. *The Bhagavad-Gîtâ* (trans. R. C. Zaehner) (New York: Oxford University Press, 1969).

41. Zaehner points out that all of the great Vedanta philosophers after Śaṅkara—Râmânuja, Madhva, Nimbârka, Vallabha, Caitanya—place the personal God above the unqualified Brahman. Zaehner, *Concordant Discord*, p. 158.

42. *Ibid.*, p. 121; Dhavamony, *Classical Hinduism*, pp. 457–458.

43. Sivaraman, *op. cit.*, pp. 5–6. Rebirth in heaven is the more immediate eschatology for most Hindus, but it is still within the sphere of *dharma*, and must lead finally to *moksha*, liberation from bondage to rebirth altogether.

44. Zaehner, *Hinduism*, p. 100.

45. *Tirumantiram* 257; quoted in Dhavamony, *Classical Hinduism*, p. 490.

46. *Ibid.*, 266; quoted *loc. cit.*

47. Dhavamony, *Classical Hinduism*, p. 491.

48. Zaehner, *Concordant Discord*, p. 136.

49. The term "Hînayâna" means "little vehicle," and is a name originally coined by Mahâyâna (= "great vehicle") Buddhists for those who refused to accept the new Sûtras (scriptures) and doctrines which arose in Northern India in the first centuries of the Christian era. The title carried a pejorative implication: not only was the older vehicle "small" in that it contained fewer means

of salvation, but also in the sense of being narrow and selfish, concerned with the individual's own salvation and rejecting the doctrine of the self-sacrificing boddhisattva (see below on Mahâyâna doctrines). Modern Theravâda Buddhists understandably dislike being classified as "Hînayâna." Unfortunately, there is no other convenient common name to designate the several conservative schools which resisted the Mahâyâna innovations. The Theravâda is the only form which still perdures; but it would be historically inaccurate to apply its name to the whole group of schools which included its ancestor. "Southern" Buddhism would likewise apply (with exceptions) today, but would not include the whole tradition; "Pâli" (the language of the earliest scriptures) Buddhism meets the same objection (some conservative schools had Sanskrit scriptures). Modern scholars therefore generally use the term "Hînayâna," but without intending any disparagement. See Herman, *op. cit.*, pp. 119, 128; Robinson, Richard H. and Johnson, Willard L.: *The Buddhist Religion* (Belmont, Cal.: Wadsworth Publishing Co., 1977), p. 212, n. 1.

50. Hînayâna Buddhists, however, generally prefer the dates 624–544 B.C. On the method of dating the Buddha's life, see Herman, *op. cit.*, p. 366, n. 6.

51. Translation from De Bary, William Theodore: *The Buddhist Tradition in India, China and Japan* (New York: Modern Library, 1969).

52. Parrinder, Geoffrey: *Avatar and Incarnation* (New York: Oxford University Press, 1982), p. 134.

53. In this section we shall include important technical terms where necessary both in Sanskrit and in Pâli. The latter is a vernacular derived from Sanskrit, and was the language of the earliest Buddhist scriptures. Later works, however, returned to Sanskrit; hence both languages are used by scholars in referring to the principal Buddhist concepts.

54. Robinson and Johnson, *op. cit.*, pp. 31–32, 45.

55. *Skhandas;* Pâli *khandas,* = "bundles" or "heaps"; they are: forms, sensations, perceptions, psychic dispositions, and consciousness.

56. Robinson and Johnson, *loc. cit.*

57. Both texts quoted in Herman, *op. cit.*, p. 108.

58. Herman, *op. cit.*, p. 158. The classic example of the use of the doctrine is in the non-canonical *Milindapañha,* 25–27.

59. Cf. ibid., pp. 108–112. It should be noted that the doctrine of *anitya* and its effects seems to presuppose that there is in man something which can only be satisfied by the real and eternal—in some way parallel to our idea of the unrestricted drive toward being, or "natural desire" of the infinite. Hînayâna Buddhism does not explicitly develop this idea; but the Mahâyâna does.

60. Quoted in Herman, *op. cit.*, p. 152f.

61. For further explanation, see *ibid.*, p. 155.

62. See Robinson and Johnson, *op. cit.*, p. 69f.

63. Brandon, *op. cit.*, pp. 340–341. See also Dayal, Har: *The Bodhisattva Doctrine in Buddhist Sanskrit Literature* (New York: Samuel Weiser, 1978), pp. 73ff. Dayal points out that there are texts which explain the continuity of reincarnation by stating that *vijñâna* (= consciousness), one of the *skandhas*, continues

after death and is reincarnated. Dayal suggests that *vijñâna* is the equivalent of the Western notion of "soul." This however does not explain what enters *nirvâna*.

64. Herman, *op. cit.*, p. 163.

65. For the different interpretations of the Buddha's silence on God, see *RH*, pp. 47–52.

66. See Parrinder, *Mysticism in the World's Religions* (New York: Oxford University Press, 1977), p. 54f.; also *idem, Worship in the World's Religions* (Totowa, N.J.: Littlefield, Adams & Co., 1976), p. 6f.

67. Parrinder, *Avatar and Incarnation*, p. 131.

68. Indeed, the Upanishadic teaching in his day was probably kept as a secret doctrine by the brahmin priest caste.

69. Parrinder, *Mysticism*, p. 56.

70. Parrinder calls early Buddhism "transpolytheistic" rather than atheistic. Parrinder, *Avatar and Incarnation, loc. cit.*, p. 56.

71. Conze, Edward: *Buddhism: Its Essence and Development* (New York: Harper & Brothers, 1979), p. 39.

72. The word derives from the prefix "*nis-*", which becomes "*nir-*" before soft letters, meaning "out, away," or "altogether" (emphasizing what follows), combined with *vâna* (contraction of *vâana*), the past passive participle from *vâ* (= "to blow"), meaning "blown." Hence *nirvâna*, = "blown out, completely extinguished."

73. Translations from Conze (ed.), *Buddhist Texts Through the Ages* (New York: Harper & Row, 1964), p. 92.

74. Robinson and Johnson, *op. cit.*, p. 69.

75. Conze translation. Conze points out that the same expression, "gone home," is used of the sun when it sets; the "enlightened one" is the kinsman of the sun (p. 114, n. 3).

76. Robinson and Johnson, *op. cit.*, p. 50.

77. *Ibid.*, p. 69.

78. Conze, Edward: "Buddhist Saviors," in Brandon (ed.), *The Savior God. Comparative Studies in the Concept of Salvation* (New York: Barnes & Noble, 1963), p. 78.

79. Robinson and Johnson, *op. cit.*, p. 50.

80. See Bond, George D.: "The Development and Elaboration of the Arahant Ideal in the Theravada Buddhist Tradition" in *Journal of the American Academy of Religion*, vol. LII, no. 2 (June 1984).

81. Robinson and Johnson, *op. cit.*, p. 39. Southern Buddhists may also regularly pray to the Hindu gods for mundane favors. In practice, there is a "*samsâric*" aspect to salvation which ignores the ultimate goal of *moksha*, although the official religion does not take much notice of it.

82. Quoted in Conze, "Buddhist Saviors," p. 72.

83. Quoted by Conze in "Buddhist Saviors," p. 77. It is this aspect of self-salvation by withdrawal from the world which leads Toynbee to consider the Hînayâna as (originally, at least) an idolization of the self-sufficient philosopher rather than a real higher religion.

84. Robinson and Johnson, *op. cit.*, pp. 44, 57.

85. Smart, Ninian: "The Work of the Buddha and the Work of Christ" in Brandon, *The Savior God*, p. 161. This of course is to be taken in the sense of trans-polytheism; the gods, as noted earlier, are not ultimate realities for Buddhism, and every *arahant* is above them.

86. Conze, "Buddhist Saviors," p. 73; Parrinder, *Mysticism*, p. 60.

87. Robinson and Johnson, *op. cit.*, p. 77.

88. It could not be said, however, that Buddhism preached the equality of women; see, for example, the *Vinaya-pitaka*, II, 253ff. (in Conze, *Buddhist Texts*, pp. 23ff.).

89. Robinson and Johnson, *op. cit.*, p. 36.

90. "The word 'Mahâyâna' is unfortunately used in two different senses. (1) In a wider sense it was used by European scholars of the nineteenth century to denote the 'northern' Buddhism of Tibet, Mongolia, China, and Japan. The opposite here is 'Theravâda,' the doctrine prevalent in the 'southern' Buddhism of Ceylon, Burma, and so on. (2) In a more narrow sense it is used in Indian works on Buddhism written between about 100 B.C. and A.D. 650. The opposite there are the teachings of 'the Disciples and Pratyekabuddhas.' This two-fold usage has led to a great deal of confusion. In the first case Zen and Tantra form part of the 'Mahâyâna,' whereas with the second they follow upon it and grow out of it." Edward Conze: "Introduction" to Suzuki, D. T.: *On Indian Mahayana Buddhism* (New York: Harper & Row, 1968), p. 20f. In our treatment we shall use the word "Mahâyâna" in the first, wider sense, including Zen and Tantric Buddhism—even though these were to some extent a reaction against the orthodox Mahâyâna systems.

91. Van der Leeuw, *op. cit.*, p. 633.

92. On the question of whether *bhakti* was originally a Hindu movement which influenced Buddhism, or vice versa, see Dayal, *op. cit.*, pp. 31ff. Dayal himself favors the thesis of Buddhist origin.

93. Robinson and Johnson, *op. cit.*, p. 68.

94. It is possible that the *Prajñâpâramitâ Sûtras* (*prajña* = wisdom, *pâramita* = perfection), as the principal texts of the Mahâyâna are called, contain some material which was originally written in Pâli or other dialects.

95. Literally, the Buddha denies that he practices the "teacher's fist" (*âcârya-mushti*, Pâli *âcarya-mutti*), i.e., holding back, not revealing (*Dîgha-Nikâya* II, 100.3; *Samyutta-Nikâya* V, 153.18). Dayal, *op. cit.*, p. 31. Of course, these statements may have been added by later Hînayâna scribes precisely as a polemic against the Mahâyâna claims. In any case, the Mahâyâna pretention that its *sûtras* stem from the historical Buddha is generally regarded to have no foundation. On the other hand, it demonstrates an important buddhalogical principle: the *dharma*, no matter who teaches it, is the word of the Buddha himself. See Herman, *op. cit.*, pp. 96–97, 209. See also D. T. Suzuki: *Outlines of Mahayana Buddhism* (New York: Schocken Books, 1963), p. 14.

96. In general, the Hînayâna may be called anthropocentric in its doctrines, while the Mahâyâna is Buddhacentric (in Western terms, theocentric). Herman, *op. cit.*, p. 216.

97. Sâriputra, an *arhat*, is addressed precisely to show that the wisdom proclaimed here goes beyond that goal.

98. *Saddharma-Puṇḍarîka*, trans. H. Kern (New York: Dover Publications, 1963), II. 36, 68, 120.

99. *Ibid.*, II. 36.

100. For the *nirvâṇa* of the *arhats* is in reality only a temporary repose, not the final *nirvâna*. *Ibid.*, V, 74.

101. The six perfections (*pâramitâs*) are giving (*dâna*), morality (*sîla*), patience (*kshânti*), vigor (*vîrya*), meditation (*dhyâna*), and wisdom (*prajñâ*). See *Pañcaviṁśatisâhasrikâ*, 194–195.

102. Translation from Conze, Edward: *Buddhist Texts*, p. 119.

103. On the problem of merit, see Herman, *op. cit.*, pp. 261ff.

104. Conze, "Buddhist Saviors," *op. cit.*, pp. 74–75.

105. *Ibid.*, p. 76.

106. Herman, *op. cit.*, p. 255; Conze, *Buddhism*, p. 159.

107. As Herman notes (*op. cit.*, p. 253), the idea of the Pure Lands seems to conflict with the notion of *nirvâṇa*, to which they are supposed to lead; for the heavens of the *bodhisattvas* are portrayed as paradises, where all desires are fulfilled; how can this lead to the extinction of desire? A parallel problem arises with the compassion of the *bodhisattva*, for, noble as it is, it is a species of attachment to the world, and thus conflicts with the idea of *nirvâna* as non-attachment. There is, as Herman remarks, a difficulty in reconciling the Mahâyâna's highest virtue (compassion) with its highest goal (*nirvâna* as extinction of the "I" and all attachments connected to it). As we shall see, the conflict is resolved by a profound (although not "officially" acknowledged) change in the very conception of *nirvâna*.

108. The dispute is reminiscent of the conflict between the "cat school" and the "monkey school" in Hindu soteriology, or the Lutheran and Catholic doctrines in Christianity. Amidism (devotion to the celestial Buddha Amitâbha) tends to minimize the need for works—and therefore also the place of the monastic life. While a monk may spend a lifetime in meditation, a lay person can achieve salvation by a single act of devotion—for example, by reciting the *mantra*, "Om—honor to the Buddha Amidá" (in Sanskrit, *Om namo Amitâbhâya Buddhâya*; in Chinese, *Om O-mi-to-fo*; in Japanese, *Namo Amida Butsu*). The most extreme form of Amidism in Japan, called the Shin-shu, so exalts faith in Amida's vows that it rejects all salvific works of any kind: rituals, philosophy, monasticism. All, without moral distinction, will be admitted to Amida's paradise. See Conze, *Buddhism*, pp. 206, 158–159; Robinson and Johnson, *op. cit.*, p. 114.

109. Robinson and Johnson, *op. cit.*, p. 109.

110. *Ibid.*, p. 105.

111. For a discussion of the various *bodhisattvas* and their cult, see *ibid.*, pp. 101–110.

112. It is of course dangerous to draw parallels between theologies developed in two such different contexts as Christianity and Buddhism; yet here the comparison, if not taken too far, seems apposite. The man Gautama of the Hînayâna, like the man Jesus in "ascending" Christology, is "exalted," and has re-

ceived "the name which is above every other name." Likewise, the Buddha of the *Lotus Sûtra* is the eternal Wisdom (*prajñâ*), the equivalent of the "Logos" of the Greek philosophers, which "became flesh and dwelt among us." Naturally, the differences are also striking: Jesus is exalted in being "raised up" by God, while Gautama becomes "extinguished" by his own efforts; and (as we shall see in more detail below) the "becoming flesh" of the incarnation is quite different from the creation of an "appearance body" by the Buddha.

113. So a modern Japanese Buddhist abbot writes:

> Buddhism is not atheistic as the term is ordinarily understood. It has certainly a God, the highest reality and truth, through which and in which this universe exists (Shaku, Soyen: *Sermons of a Buddhist Abbot* [trans. Daisetz Teitaro Suzuki] [New York: Samuel Weiser, 1971], p. 25).

And D. T. Suzuki explains:

> Buddhism does not use the word God. The word is rather offensive to most of its followers, especially when it is associated in vulgar minds with the idea of a creator who produced the world out of nothing, caused the downfall of mankind, and, touched by the pang of remorse, sent down his only Son to save the depraved. But, on account of this, Buddhism must not be judged as an atheism which endorses an agnostic, materialistic interpretation of the universe. Far from it. Buddhism outspokenly acknowledges the presence in the world of a reality which transcends the limitations of phenomenality, but which is nevertheless immanent everywhere and manifests itself in full glory, and in which we live and move and have our being (Suzuki, *Outlines*, p. 219).

It is interesting to note that in Muslim-dominated Indonesia, where atheism is a crime, Buddhists defend themselves with the assertion that their religion is theistic, but differs only in the matter of the name by which God is called (Dumoulin, Heinrich, S.J. (ed.): *Buddhism in the Modern World* [London: Collier Macmillan, 1976], p. 152).

114. Text in Conze, Edward (ed.): *Buddhist Wisdom Books* (New York: Harper & Row, 1972).

115. See for example the *Avalokateśvara Sûtra*, now appended to the *Lotus Sûtra*, in which Avalokateśvara is treated as the divine being, who becomes manifest in many different forms for the salvation of the world.

116. The theory of different "bodies" of the Buddha was first introduced by the early Sarvâstivâda school of philosophy, elaborated by the Yogâcâra school (see below), and later adopted by the Mahâyâna in general. See Herman, *op. cit.*, pp. 223–225.

117. Quoted in Parrinder, *Avatar and Incarnation*, p. 178.

118. It is of course impossible in a work of this nature to do justice even to

the essential concepts of these philosophical systems. For a brief treatment, see Dasgupta, Surendranath: *A History of Indian Philosophy,* vol. 1 (Delhi: Motilal Banarsidass, 1975); Radhakrishnan, Sarvepalli: *Indian Philosophy* (London: George Allen & Unwin Ltd., 1929).

119. Nâgârjuna's dialectics, as well as his conclusions, are reminiscent of the paradoxes of Zeno of Elea which support the monist view of Parmenides.

120. The *Sûnyavâda* (= "emptiness view") is also known as the *Mâyâvâda.* See Suzuki, *On Indian Mâhâyana Buddhism,* pp. 50ff.

121. Buddhist logic is based upon the *catushkoti,* the exhaustive set of four possibilities for any reality: (1) A; (2) not-A; (3) both A and not-A; (4) neither A nor not-A. Nâgârjuna is saying that none of these fits the case.

122. Text given in Radhakrishnan, Sarvepalli, and Moore, Charles A. (eds.): *A Sourcebook in Indian Philosophy* (Princeton: Princeton University Press, 1957), p. 244f.

123. Puligandla, *op. cit.,* p. 96.; Herman, *op. cit.,* p. 315.

124. Copleston, Frederick: *Religion and the One* (New York: Crossroad, 1982), p. 53f. Suzuki explicitly identifies *śûnya* with the God of Western mystics. Suzuki, *On Indian Mahâyâna Buddhism,* p. 109.

125. Text in Thomas, E. J., (ed.): *The Perfection of Wisdom. A Selection of Mahâyâna Scriptures.* (Westport, Conn.: Greenwood Press, 1952), p. 40.

126. Conze, *Buddhism,* p. 163.

127. As opposed to the Hînayâna *Abhidarma* view of *dhamma-matta,* the doctrine that *dharmas* or elements alone exist. See *ibid.,* p. 162.

128. *Ibid.,* p. 171.

129. *Ibid.,* p. 166f.

130. Robinson and Johnson, *op. cit.,* p. 93; Herman, *op. cit.,* p. 346; Conze, *Buddhism,* p. 149.

131. Suzuki, *Outlines,* p. 165. Suzuki notes that Buddhists are reluctant to talk about the relation between the individual self and the absolute, for fear of reawakening the egotism which it is Buddhism's prime concern to eliminate.

132. It will be apparent even from this brief treatment that the Mahâyâna is in many ways parallel to developments in Hindu thought. The presence of *bhakti*-type devotion; the supplanting of the *anitya* doctrine with eternal realities, like the Buddha and the *dharma;* the reintroduction of a "soul"; the philosophies of transcendental idealism and non-duality; the doctrine of Absolute Mind or *śûnya*—all bring later Buddhism much closer to the Hindu tradition than was its original form. Some conjecture that this is due to an increasing influence of Hinduism; others think it more probable that Buddhism was of its own dynamism headed toward absolutist metaphysics and pantheist religion (see Herman, *op. cit.,* pp. 207, 279; cf. p. 405, n. 277). Conze believes that the major part of the Yogâcâra system was an "invasion" of Buddhism by the Hindu Samkhya philosophy, which had been used by Patañjali to systematize yoga (ca. 450 A.D.) (Conze, *Buddhism,* p. 170f.). There certainly was Hindu influence in the *Tathâtâ* ("suchness") philosophy of Aś-vaghosa (ca. 80 A.D.), a predecessor of the Mâdhyamika school; he was himself a converted Brahmin (see Dasgupta, *op. cit.,* pp. 129ff.). On the other hand, the

classical philosophy of Śaṅkara was no doubt influenced by the Buddhist doctrines (especially that of *śûnyatâ*) which he set out to oppose. In any case, the similarities were noted by the Hindus themselves. Madhva (thirteenth century), himself a dualist, compares the Advaitins (non-dualists) to the Sûnyavâdins: "both speak of two kinds of truth, and the brahman nirgûna is not different from the śûnya" (quotation in Herman, *op. cit.*, p. 411, n. 304); and both *bhaktas* and other Vedantins have long held that Śaṅkara was a crypto-Buddhist.

133. In Yogâcâra, the self is given a theoretical basis; but even outside this school, it is covertly admitted (even though it may not be "ultimately" real; but it is as real as anything else in the world). For this reason Herman speaks of "transmigration (of souls)" in the Mahâyâna, whereas the Hînayâna doctrine is more one of "reincarnation." See Herman, *op. cit.*, p. 266. See also Conze, *Buddhism*, p. 170, for some of the other concepts under which a self has been secretly reintroduced even in Hînayâna systems.

134. Conze, *Buddhist Wisdom Books*, p. 47.

135. Conze, "Introduction," p. 10.

136. Smith, D. Howard: "Salvation in Fifth Century China" in Sharpe, Eric J. and Hinnells, John R. (eds.): *Man and His Salvation* (Manchester: Manchester University Press, 1973), p. 294.

137. *Ibid.*, p. 303.

138. *Ibid.*, pp. 295, 299.

139. Conze, "Introduction," p. 2, n. 1. Suzuki refers to Zen as Mahâyâna shorn of its Indian garb.

140. *Ibid.*, p. 8.

141. Conze, *Buddhism*, pp. 201–204. Conze notes that all these characteristics are perfectly orthodox. It was only when the inference was drawn that the disciplinary regulations could be dropped, and moral indifference was introduced as a concession to Japanese militarism, that Zen went beyond Mahâyâna teaching. Tantric Buddhism also put a new—and different—interpretation on the idea that if everything is "empty," then all is essentially pure. See Robinson and Johnson, *op. cit.*, p. 117; Conze, *Buddhism*, ch. VIII.

142. *Ibid.*, p. 204.

143. Suzuki interprets the no-âtma doctrine as a moral imperative to put off what Christians call "the flesh" or "the old man." Suzuki, *Outlines*, p. 165.

Chapter V: God's Word in Human Words—The Western Religions

1. Gómez Caffarena, José and Velasco, Juan Martin: *Filosofía de la Religión* (Madrid: Ediciones de la Revista de Occidente, 1973), p. 256.

2. There have been some instances in the West of the Platonic or Gnostic doctrine of metempsychosis, or the transmigration of souls after death to a new bodily existence (for example some of the followers of the Kabbalist Isaac Luria, today forming a part of Hasidic Judaism); but these have been exceptional.

3. This is the view adopted by the Rabbi Armand Abécassis in his essay on "Christianity as seen by Judaism" ("Le christianisme vu par le judaisme" in Lauret,

Bernard and Refoulé, Francois: *Initiation à la pratique de la théologie* [Paris: Editions du Cerf, 1982], pp. 401–421). He writes:

> Judaism is linked, in the Torah, to a people, a land, and a language. . . . Christianity, on the other hand, is neither a language, nor a land, nor a people; nevertheless, it is the bearer of the divine promise. . . . Belonging to the Church is not hereditary: the pagan becomes Christian, while the Jew is born Jewish. Certainly, one can become a Jew by conversion; but this is not the general rule, while on the other hand the entire purpose of the Church is the conversion of the pagans to the promise given to Abraham; that is, in a sense, their Judaisation. . . .
> A personal relationship with Jesus becomes the condition for belonging to the Church. Faith in him allows every pagan to obtain salvation and to gain access to the Father, that is, the God of Israel. . . . In effect, what Jesus represented for the pagans, the necessary intermediary, the inevitable mediation between them and God, the Torah is for the Jewish people. One can only reach God and the Kingdom of Heaven by two ways: Jesus or the Torah. The gentiles, according to the rabbis, have always refused to submit to the Torah. It is fortunate, then, that they have accepted faith in Jesus . . . (pp. 409–411).

4. In 1976 there were only 129,000 Zoroastrians in the world, the great majority in India. The figure is given by James W. Boyd in the "Introduction" to Kotwal, Firoze M. and Boyd, James W.: *A Guide to the Zoroastrian Religion* (Chico, Cal.: Scholars Press, 1982) p. xl. This work is the translation of a Zoroastrian catechism written in 1869 A.D. by Dastur (the Persian title for a Zoroastrian priest) Erachji Sohrabji Meherjirana, with a commentary by the contemporary Zoroastrian high priest Dastur Firoze M. Kotwal. The work shows that during the long period of its diaspora significant changes have occurred in Zoroastrianism from the classical religion which will be our principal concern. It is still a strong ethical monotheism; but there is, for example, no hint in this catechism of cosmic dualism or a primal principle of evil. Rituals and traditions form the bulk of the teachings. Several factors are no doubt responsible for the comparatively weak state of the religion: the loss of large portions of the sacred books, and the poor state of those that are extant; the influence of Hinduism and of British missionaries in the nineteenth century; the changes in the community's language; etc.

5. See Esdras 1:1–4. In the text, Cyrus ascribes his kingship to "Yahweh, the God of heaven." It is quite possible that the biblical text is fundamentally historically accurate in referring to "the God of Heaven," for this title was normal in Persian usage for Ahura Mazdâ, and a term easy to assimilate to Jewish religion. See Barr, James: "The Question of Zoroastrian Influence; The Case of Zoroastrianism, Judaism, and Christianity" in *Journal of the American Academy of Religion*, Vol. LIII, No. 2 (June, 1985), p. 210.

6. Zoroastrianism, combined with Greek ideas, is thought to have had a significant influence on the rise of the Mahâyâna in northwest India. Among its gen-

eral contributions are theism, the emphasis on "wisdom" and the importance of action rather than contemplation for salvation; more specifically, the idea of the self-sacrificing *bodhisattva* is thought by some to have been directly inspired by the Zoroastrian idea of the Fravashi (see below), spiritual beings who choose to become incarnate for the world's salvation and/or by the various saviors who follow Zarathushtra. It is also clear that Persian religion had a major influence on the Buddhist art of Gandhâra. See du Breuil, Paul: *Zarathoustra* (Paris: Payot, 1978), pp. 367ff.; Smart, Ninian: *The Religious Experience of Mankind* (New York: Charles Scribner's Sons, 1984), p. 267. The extent of Zoroastrian influence on the development of Judaism is much more difficult to gauge. Some would ascribe to such influence not only the specific concepts mentioned in the text, but also such ideas as creation and the whole current of Jewish eschatological messianism (inspired by the doctrine of the Saoshyant—see below). Others are more cautious in their estimate. See Barr, *op. cit.*, for a survey and estimate of opinions.

7. See Eliade, *History*, vol. 1, p. 302.

8. For a general treatment of the phenomenon of dualism in religion, see Gomez and Martin, *op. cit.*, pp. 207–208.

9. Kotwal and Boyd, *op. cit.*, p. 193.

10. Malandra, William W. (ed.): *An Introduction to Ancient Iranian Religion. Readings from the Avesta and the Achaemenid Inscriptions* (Minneapolis: University of Minnesota Press, 1983), p. 16.

11. Smart, *op. cit.*, p. 260.

12. du Breuil, *op. cit.*, p. 24.

13. Smart, *loc. cit.*

14. Presumably, 258 years before Alexander's conquest of Persia. Malandra, *loc. cit.*

15. Brandon, *Man and His Destiny*, pp. 261–265.

16. Smart, *op. cit.*, pp. 261–262. The six "Holy Immortals" are Good Mind (Vohu Manah), Good Order (Arta or Aśa), Kingdom or Dominion (Xshathra), Devotion (Ârmaiti), Welfare (Haurvatât), and Immortality (Ameretât). The first three are male, the second three female. For a modern Zoroastrian view of the meaning of these spiritual entities, see the introduction to Taraporewala, Irach J. S. (trans.): *The Gathas of Zarathushtra* (Avestan text with a free translation) (New York: AMS Press, 1977), pp. 33ff. It is interesting that while Zarathushtra eliminates all the *ahuras* ("lords") except one—Ahura Mazda—and makes the *daêvas* into demons, the opposite occurs with the cognate Sanskrit terms in India: the *asuras* become demons, and the *devas* are the gods. Thus in modern Western languages we end up with the word for God—Deus and its derivatives, like "divine"—and the word for the Evil One—diabolos and its derivatives, like "devil"—both stemming from the same Indo-European root (Old Iranian *daêva* = Sanskrit *deva*).

17. Malandra, *op. cit.*, p. 40, and Taraporewala, *op. cit.*, pp. 75ff. The translation I give is a compromise between these two, made with consultation of the Avestan text given by Taraporewala.

18. Although there are also other passages in which the unity of Ahura Mazdâ and the Spenta Mainyu is implied. Eliade, *History*, vol. 1, p. 310.

19. Malandra, *op. cit.*, p. 39.

20. *Ibid.*, p. 47.

21. Eliade, *History*, vol. 1, p. 305.

22. Similarly, in the *Yashts* (a later collection of hymns to various deities) when Zarathushtra asks God his name, he is told: "I am He who answers questions" (*Yasht* 1: 7). (Malandra translates: "I am He Who is to be Implored.")

23. Malandra, *op. cit.*, p. 18.

24. *Ibid.*, pp. 25, 47.

25. Zaehner, *The Teachings of the Magi* (New York: Oxford University Press, 1976), p. 15.

26. *Ibid.*, p. 11.

27. Although the language proves that much material of the Avesta is very ancient, it was probably transmitted orally and not written down until very late. Old Iranian in fact had no script, and Old Persian used its special cuneiforms only for monumental inscriptions; Aramaic was the written business language of the Persian Empire. There may have been a redaction of the sacred books prior to the sixth century, but it is unknown to us. See Malandra, *op. cit.*, pp. 29–30.

28. Text given in Zaehner, *Teachings*, p. 93.

29. "Ohrmazd" is the Parsi name for God, an adulteration of the Pahlavî "Auharmazd," from the earlier Avestan contraction "Auramazda," from the Gathic "Ahura Mazdâ" (= "Wise Lord"). Similarly, "Ahriman" is from the Pahlavî "Ahraman," from the Gathic "Angra Mainyu" (= "Destructive Spirit"). Brandon, *Man and His Destiny*, p. 281, n. 5.

30. The "Bundahishn" is the "(Book of) the primal Creation." Text in *ibid.*, pp. 35ff.

31. Eliade speculates that Zarathushtra himself probably expected an imminent transfiguration of the world; this was later projected into the eschatological future, creating salvation history. It is significant that for Zoroastrianism salvation does not lie in periodic regeneration, as in nature religions, but in a once-for-all transfiguration of the world by God. Eliade, *History*, vol. 1, pp. 312–313.

32. The *Fravahrs* or *Fravashis* are a curious and unique Zoroastrian invention. Originally they appear to have been deities, co-eternal with Ahura Mazdâ; they are then associated with the spirits of departed ancestors; and, third they appear as one of the several "souls" of humans, and/or as the "guardian angels" of each individual. On the earlier conceptions, see Malandra, *op. cit.*, p. 103f. By the Sassanian period, the *Fravahrs* are definitely creatures of Ohrmazd, and are identified with the pre-existent soul.

33. Zaehner, *Concordant Discord*, pp. 390–391.

34. Eliade, *A History of Religious Ideas*, vol. 2 (Chicago: Chicago University Press, 1982), pp. 319–320.

35. Text quoted in Zaehner, *Teachings*, p. 41.

36. On the apparent anti-feminism of the Zoroastrian theology, see Zaehner, *Teachings*, pp. 42–44; Zaehner sees the "Whore" and Spandarmat, Mother Earth,

as the two primal female principles, evil and good, just as Ohrmazd and Ahriman are the primal males. See p. 69f.

37. Eliade, *History*, vol. 2, p. 317.

38. Gayômart himself, although the primal human, does not have human form; he is semi-divine, having been born of Ohrmazd and Earth, and is round and shining like the sun. See Zaehner, *Teachings*, p. 68f.

39. *Ibid.*, pp. 70–74.

40. For a parallel of this idea with the Logos doctrine of Christianity, see *ibid.*, pp. 80–81.

41. See Smart, *Religious Experience*, p. 265; Brandon, *Man and His Destiny*, p. 288; Zaehner, *Teachings*, pp. 145ff.

42. See Brandon, *Man and His Destiny*, p. 284, for the enumeration of the constituents.

43. Different portions of this text are given in *ibid.*, p. 284, and in Eliade, *History*, vol. 1, p. 329.

44. Text given by Brandon, *Man and His Destiny*, p. 284.

45. *Ibid.*, p. 270.

46. Text in Zaehner, *Teachings*, p. 145f.

47. *Bundahishn;* text in *ibid.*, p. 149.

48. The sources are divided on the end of Ahriman; according to some, he is annihilated; according to others, simply reduced to impotence. Eliade, *History*, vol. 2, p. 321.

49. Widengren, Geo: "Salvation in Iranian Religion," in Sharpe, *op. cit.*, p. 315.

50. Text in Malandra, *op. cit.* As has been noted, in the period when the *Yashts* were written the *Fravashis* were interpreted as "gods," existing independently of Ahura Mazdâ. By the time of the classical religion, however, they are his creatures. The statement of this verse, however, still stands: Ohrmazd needs his creatures in order to "save" his creation.

Brandon notes that like Israel, Zoroastrianism sees history as the stage where the divine purpose of overcoming evil is carried out; but unlike the religion of Israel, Zoroastrianism was essentially concerned with individual human beings. *Man and His Destiny*, p. 287.

51. Zaehner, *Teachings*, p. 83.

52. *Ibid.*, p. 19.

53. *Ibid.*, p. 54.

54. Text in *ibid.*, p. 39.

55. Quoted in *ibid.*, p. 100.

56. Eliade, *History*, vol. 1, p. 309.

57. Text in *ibid.*, pp. 21, 22.

58. Ritual, always important, has taken on an especially central role in the modern religion of the Parsees. In the catechism of Meherjirana (Kotwal and Boyd, *op. cit.*), twenty-two of the thirty-two chapters—in length, by far the major part of the book—are taken up with ritual matters of various kinds.

59. Eliade, *History*, p. 320.

60. A Zoroastrian form of general confession is given in Zaehner, *Teachings*, pp. 120ff.

61. Boyd, *op. cit.*, pp. xv–xvi.

62. See Brandon, *Man and His Destiny*, pp. 295ff.

63. On Manichaeanism, see *ibid.*, pp. 299–300; Bowker, *op. cit.*, pp. 276–277. Zoroastrianism also produced several variant forms which differ from the classical dualism we have been concerned with. The heresy of Zurvanism, about which little is known, apparently restored the ancient idea that Ohrmazd and Ahriman were brothers, begotten of a primal deity identified with Infinite Time (Zurvan). They apparently treated Ahriman as a real god, to whom cult was given.

Another unorthodox strand advanced the modern-sounding idea that God, becoming self-conscious, became aware of the potential for evil within himself, recognized it for what it was, and expelled it from himself. See Zaehner, *Concordant Discord*, p. 389.

64. We shall here confine the use of the word "Judaism" to the religion which was formulated after the return from the exile and which survives today. Its antecedents will be referred to as "Yahwism" or the Hebrew religion.

65. But see Brandon, *Man and His Destiny*, pp. 106–152. Brandon shows that the official religion was in fact never simply in possession, but was always in tension with currents drawn from other religious sources which were more concerned with the individual and especially with survival after death.

66. See Kittel, G. (ed.): *Theologisches Wörterbuch zum Neuen Testament* (Stuttgart: 1933ff.), σῶζω κ.τ.λ

67. Van der Leeuw, *op. cit.*, pp. 636–637.

68. See Neusner, Jacob: "Messianic themes in formative Judaism" in the *Journal of the American Academy of Religion,* vol. LII, no. 2 (June 1984), p. 357.

69. The philosopher Philo attempted a more radical and thoroughgoing synthesis of Jewish and Greek thought, but he was for the most part ignored by Judaism, and influenced only the Christian Fathers. Eliade, *A History of Religious Ideas*, vol. 3, (Chicago: University of Chicago Press, 1985), p. 157.

70. Smart, *Religious Experience*, pp. 307–309.

71. Eliade, *History*, vol. 3, p. 154.

72. Neusner, *op. cit.*, pp. 358, 373.

73. Eliade, *History*, vol. 3, p. 154.

74. *Ibid.*, pp. 155–156; Neusner, *op. cit.*, p. 358.

75. Neusner, *op. cit.*, p. 373.

76. Smart, *Religious Experience*, p. 320.

77. Eliade, *History*, vol. 3, p. 173.

78. Smart, *Religious Experience*, p. 327.

79. Eliade, *History*, vol. 3, p. 174.

80. The *Qur'an* is divided into *sûrahs*, or chapters, and verses. In the following, sûrahs will be indicated with Roman numerals, verses by Arabic numerals.

81. "Allah" is simply the Arabic word for "God," used by Arabic-speaking Jews and Christians as well as Muslims; it is not a proper name, like Krishna or Yahweh. It appears that Allah was already worshiped in Arabia before the time of

Muhammad; he was, in fact, the God of the Ka'ba, the Creator. Along with him, however, were venerated other gods, especially his three daughters. It was from the association of others with Allah that Muhammad wished to purify religion. See Eliade, *History*, vol. 3, p. 68. In the following, we shall observe the normal usage of referring to God as Allah in the context of Islam.

82. Translation by Mohammed Marmaduke Pickthall: *The Meaning of the Glorious Koran* (New York: New American Library, 1953).

83. Compare the attitude of Krishna in the *Bhagavad-Gîtâ:*

"Whatever form a devotee with faith desires to honor, that very faith do I confirm in him . . ." (7:21).

" . . . even those who lovingly devote themselves to other gods and sacrifice to them, full filled with faith, do really worship Me though the rite may differ from the norm. For it is I who of all sacrifices am recipient and Lord . . ." (9:23–24).

84. Note that all the faithful are God's "slaves" in Islam, including Muhammad. "Abd'Allah"—"slave of God"—is an honorable title, and a frequent name.

85. The *Qur'an* emphasizes the continuity between Christianity and Islam in other ways; for example, when Jesus' disciples answer his call, they reply: "We will be Allah's helpers. We believe in Allah, and bear thou witness that we have surrendered" (III. 52; cf. V. 111). The last phrase, "have surrendered," may also be translated "are Muslims," since "*muslim*" is the participle of the Arabic verb "to surrender."

The *Qur'an* also holds Mary, the mother of Jesus, in high esteem, affirms the virgin birth, and condemns the Jews for their "calumny" against Mary (IV. 156).

It is interesting to note that the *Qur'an* adopts a Docetist position on the crucifixion: it asserts that the Jews claim that they slew the Messiah, but that: "They slew him not nor crucified, but it appeared so unto them. . . . But Allah took him up unto Himself" (IV. 157–158). The apparent motive of the assertion is the theological principle that God's prophet could not fail.

86. Brandon, *Man and His Destiny*, p. 245.

87. Zaehner points out that while Zoroastrianism insists on the goodness of God, at the expense of the unity of the absolute principle, Islam so insists on God's uniqueness that his goodness is compromised. "Since the Moslem God is as capable of leading astray as he is of guidance, it is no accident that among his ninety-nine names that of 'good' is absent" (Zaehner, *Teachings*, p. 59).

88. Compare the meeting of Ohrmazd with Ahriman in the Zoroastrian *Bundahishn;* when Ahriman promises to lead astray creation, Ohrmazd replies that he cannot finally do so; his creatures will ultimately return to him. When Islam's devil promises to lead others astray, Allah replies that he will fill hell with them all.

89. Brandon, *Man and His Destiny*, p. 241.

90. The *jihâd* receives great emphasis in the *Qur'an*, presumably because of the need of Muhammad to consolidate his position. It is not considered to be one

of the "pillars of the Faith," however, except by the Khârijite school. See Rahman, Fazlur: *Islam* (Chicago: University of Chicago Press, second edition 1979), p. 37.

91. Muhammad does not seem to have a notion of any real life of the disembodied soul after death and before the resurrection—which is actually a re-creation. His concept of "soul" seems to be close to the ancient Semitic idea of a vital principle which animates the body, rather than any kind of spiritual "substance." See Brandon, *Man and His Destiny*, pp. 248–249.

92. Brandon succinctly epitomizes the character of Islam in the title of his chapter devoted to it in *Man and His Destiny*: "Man the creature of an inscrutable God."

93. Askari, Hasan: "Unity and Alienation in Islam," in Samartha, *op. cit.*, pp. 46, 51.

94. Rahman, *op. cit.*, pp. 1, 68.

95. Smart, *Religious Experience*, p. 439.

96. Rahman, *op. cit.*, p. 2.

97. *Ibid.*, pp. 16–17.

98. *Ibid.*, pp. 21, 22.

99. Eliade, *History*, vol. 3, pp. 113–114.

100. *Ibid.*, pp. 80–82.

101. See Watt, W. Montgomery: "The Muslim Yearning for a Savior: Aspects of early 'Abbâsid Shî'ism" in Brandon, *The Savior God*.

102. Rahman, *op. cit.*, p. 172.

103. Eliade, *History*, vol. 3, p. 116, n. 11.

104. Rahman, *op. cit.*, p. 173.

105. *Ibid.*, p. 133.

106. *Ibid.*, pp. 172–173. Note the similarity to Mahâyâna Buddhism and Gnostic Christianity, both of which claim a revelation hidden by the Revealer.

107. *Ibid.*, p. 174.

108. Eliade, *History*, vol. 3, p. 119.

109. Rahman, *op. cit.*, p. 177. For a discussion of the major Shî'ite sects, see *ibid.*, pp. 175ff.; more briefly, Eliade, *History*, vol. 3, pp. 117–118.

110. Rahman, *op. cit.*, p. 173.

111. Smart, *Religious Experience*, p. 416.

112. Rahman, *op. cit.*, p. 174.

113. *Ibid.*, *loc. cit.*

114. Rahman, *op. cit.*, p. 179.

115. *Ibid.*, p. 128.

116. Smart, *Religious Experience*, p. 419.

117. Eliade, *History*, vol. 3, pp. 123–124.

118. Rahman, *op. cit.*, p. 6.

119. Eliade, *History*, vol. 3, p. 127.

120. Rahman, *op. cit.*, p. 151.

121. *Ibid.*, p. 96.

122. *Ibid.*, p. 135.

123. *Ibid.*, p. 117.

124. *Ibid.*, pp. 120ff. Rahman contends that in fact Islamic philosophy did not die; it simply changed its context and went "underground," surfacing as theosophical or Gnostic Ṣûfism (p. 126).

125. *Ibid.*, p. 140.

126. *Ibid.*, pp. 135, 138.

127. *Ibid.*, p. 156.

128. Smart, *Religious Experience*, p. 130; Brandon, *Man and His Destiny*, p. 257.

Chapter VI: A Final Word of God? The Dialectic and Convergence of Religions

1. Nietzsche writes:

> Every religion has for its highest images an analogon in the spiritual condition of those who profess it. The God of Mohammed: the solitariness of the desert, the distant roar of the lion, the vision of a formidable warrior. The God of Christians: everything that men and women think of when they hear the word "love." The God of the Greeks: a beautiful apparition in a dream (*The Case Against Wagner*. Quoted in van der Leeuw, *op. cit.*, vol. 2, p. 642).

Cf. Arnold Toynbee's attempt to link each of the major world religions with a corresponding Jungian psychological type: *A Study of History*, (New York: Oxford University Press, 1956), vol. VII B, pp. 780–781.

2. An event like the Buddha's awakening is not thought of by Buddhists as "revelation"—i.e., from another person; but it clearly fits the notion of revelation we have espoused above (the transcendental presence of the transcendent/immanent Absolute [God] coming to categorical formulation in the human mind).

3. Radhakrishnan, for example, points to the mystical dimensions present in all the higher religions to make a case that all converge toward a sort of monist or pantheist vision. See his *Eastern Religions and Western Thought*.

4. In fact, as we have pointed out above, anyone who makes a judgment or decision at all (even the decision not to form a judgment) concerning the validity of a world-view, religion, philosophy, etc., is doing so on the basis of some criteria, either explicit or implicit. There is no simply "objective" way of proceeding. A critical examination of our presuppositions and criteria is what we have attempted here.

5. It must be noted, however, that an *independent* metaphysics is a rarity outside of Western philosophy; as Lonergan points out, the normal differentiation of consciousness for most cultures is not common sense-theory, but common sense-transcendence; metaphysics is more related to mysticism than to science.

6. Furthermore, we shall find that a kind of synthesis of the two modalities is found in the concept of "incarnation," the idea that God becomes identical with his created manifestation: either a particular individual—as in the Christian notion

of incarnation—or the whole of creation, as in some Hindu and Buddhist conceptions. The former stresses incarnation as a mediation of God, the latter sees it as immediacy. In both cases, however, the unstressed pole is also represented: a "generalized" incarnation in the Christian doctrine of grace and "filiation"; a "special" incarnation in the Hindu doctrine of the *avatâra* and the Buddhist devotion to individual Buddhas and *bodhisattvas*.

    7. See Schillebeeckx, *Christ*, pp. 31–36.

    8. The recognition of "a prioris" of receptivity does not necessarily imply a Kantian position on knowledge; for such *a priori* elements may be revealing, rather than "hiding." See Lotz, J.-B.: *Die Identität von Geist und Sein* (Roma: Università Gregoriana Editrice, 1972), p. 158f.

    9. We should note a certain ambiguity in the use of the word, "experience." It sometimes refers (abstractly) to the primal *datum* of knowledge, whether external or internal (consciousness), and sometimes to that datum as known, reacted to, appropriated—i.e., made *my* experience. It is in the latter sense that we are using the word here.

    10. For a brief treatment of modern theories on mysticism, see Egan, Harvey D., S.J.: *What Are They Saying About Mysticism?* (New York: Paulist Press, 1982).

    11. Zaehner, R. C.: *Mysticism, Sacred and Profane* (New York: Oxford University Press, 1980), p. 193.

    12. For a brief discussion of the Sâmkha school, see *RH*, p. 50f.

    13. Zaehner, *Mysticism*, p. 99.

    14. Egan, *op. cit.*, p. 36.

    15. Śaṅkara, quoted in Radhakrishnan (ed.), *The Brahma Sutra*. It should be noted that even in the most famous Upanishadic text (quoted at the beginning of this section) in which it is stated "That art Thou," the context is one of personal relation; the performance of teaching itself implicitly belies a purely monist interpretation.

    16. Quoted in Parrinder, Geoffrey: *Mysticism*, p. 109.

    17. *Ibid.*, p. 110.

    18. Quoted in *ibid.*, p. 135.

    19. Zaehner contends that al-Ghazâli himself was by the end of his life a pure monist, although he generally disguised his true beliefs under an orthodox guise for fear of the authorities. See Zaehner: *Hindu and Muslim Mysticism* (New York: Schocken Books, 1969), pp. 170ff.

    20. Smart, *Religious Experience*, p. 428.

    21. There is some question whether the Vaisnavite theology of the *Gîtâ* is its original doctrine; some scholars speculate that the "incarnate" god may originally have been Śiva or simply Brahman.

    22. Parrinder, *Avatar and Incarnation*, pp. 120–127.

    23. For a description of contemporary belief in Krishna, see Klostermaier, *op. cit.*, p. 30f. and *passim*.

    24. "It is sometimes thought that only the Semitic religions believe that they have revelations. . . . But Hindus have been as insistent as Christians and Mus-

lims that they have a divine relationship which is the only way to salvation" (Parrinder, *Avatar and Incarnation*, p. 124f.).

25. Quoted in Schimmel, Annemarie: "The Veneration of the Prophet Muhammad, as Reflected in Sindhi Poetry" in Brandon, *The Savior God*, p. 129.

26. *Ibid.*, pp. 131, 133.

27. It should be recalled that the notion of "mediated immediacy," as we have used the expression, does not simply imply that revelation must have two foci, mediated *and* immediate, but rather that *every* immediacy to God is (of its very nature) mediated, and *every* mediation is founded in immediacy. This follows from the nature of the human person as spirit-in-the-world. Every immediate experience of God is mediated (at least) by the dynamism toward him which constitutes us as finite beings, that is, by our own selfhood, and must be further mediated by categorical expression (formulation) in order to be appropriated by us. Likewise, every mediation of God on the categorical level is founded in the immediate and transcendental experience of God (in the *Vorgriff* of Being) as the condition of possibility of all human knowledge and love, and the transcendental experience of God's self-revelation as the condition of possibility of "converted" existence.

Hence every religious or other formulation of revelation has the structure of "mediated immediacy." At another level, however, there is a question of the degree and kind of mediation. Because humanity is by nature communal, linguistic, interpersonal, and historical, and because the problem of salvation occurs in these very dimensions, we have concluded to the expectation of a mediation of God which is not merely interior and unthematic (as, v.g., the notion of Being), but in some way external, inter-personal, and historically active. It is on this level of mediation (i.e., the level we have called "performance" and "formulation") that the divergence between religions occurs.

28. As has been noted already, the intellectual structure of this anticipation is abstracted from our lived experience of faith; it is not (in the case of the fundamental theologian seeking the foundations of faith) chronologically, but logically prior to faith; it is that in our humanity which is answered, or fulfilled, by faith.

29. See Schillebeeckx, *Christ*, pp. 734–743.

30. It should be recalled once again that our transcendental analysis is not a function of "pure reason" or of abstract "human nature," but is existential, and hence includes rational reflection on the same conversion experience which is thematized in the language of faith.

31. See Eliade, *History*, vol. I, p. 356.

32. See Eliade, Mircea: *Cosmos and History*, trans. Willard R. Trask (New York: Harper & Row, 1959), p. 103.

33. *Ibid.*, pp. 104–105.

34. Eliade, *History*, vol. 1, *loc. cit.*

35. Eliade, *Cosmos and History*, pp. 105–106. Eliade points out that eschatological religion also includes an *anti*-historical attitude: history is tolerated because it has an eschatological function; but it is only tolerable because it will

someday cease (*ibid.*, p. 111). It is notable that some of the most world-denying episodes in Western religious history are tied up with eschatological expectations.

36. See Toynbee, Arnold: *An Historian's Approach to Religion*, pp. 10–13. Toynbee sees the idea of the "Chosen People" as inimical to the basic character of higher religion, and one which had to be transcended in Israel's history, through reflection on the experience of suffering:

> A god who had thus identified himself with a human tribe, and had led his "Chosen People" in an aggressive war of appropriation and extermination against the inhabitants of a country that had been neither Israel's to take nor Yahweh's to give, might not seem to have been a promising medium for an approach to Reality. Yet the sufferings inflicted on Israel and Judah by Assyrian and Babylonian hands during a time of troubles that dragged on from the eighth into the sixth century BC, inspired the Prophets to see, through the wrath of Yahweh the parochial war-god, another Yahweh who had more in common with the god in the Sun who was worshiped by Ikhnaton, Aristonicus, and Aurelian (*ibid.*, p. 88).

37. For the moment, we use these two terms widely and interchangeably; we shall see below that the Christian notion of incarnation differs considerably from the idea of the avatar.

38. Toynbee, *An Historian's Approach to Religion*, pp. 89–90.

39. Troeltsch, Ernst: *The Absoluteness of Christianity and the History of Religions*, (trans. David Reid) (Richmond, Va.: John Knox Press, 1971).

40. We are aware of and have already pointed out the "circular" nature of our procedure; our metaphysical anthropology itself formulates certain basic presuppositions which are a part of our fundamental existential "faith," in which the fact of Christian belief is included. Nevertheless, we have justified our procedure on the dual basis that (1) it is impossible to avoid a "hermeneutical circle" in judgments concerning foundational values, and (2) we are aware of our presuppositions and are open to revising them should it prove warranted. Furthermore, we have specifically distanced our formulations of anthropology from the formulations of Christian faith in order to subject the latter to critique on the basis of a reasoned examination of existential performance.

41. Troeltsch, *op. cit.*, p. 6.

42. *Ibid.*, p. 112.

43. *Ibid., loc. cit.*

44. *Ibid.*, p. 113.

45. *Ibid.*, p. 114.

46. *Ibid.*, p. 140f.

47. *Ibid.*, p. 142.

48. *Ibid.*, p. 114.

49. *Ibid.*, p. 143.

50. *Ibid.*, p. 144.

51. *Ibid.*, p. 146.

52. *Ibid.*, p. 114.

53. Kasper, Walter: art. "Christianity, II: Absoluteness of Christianity" in *CSM*, p. 202.

54. Troeltsch, *op. cit.*, p. 121.

55. *Ibid.*, pp. 114–115.

56. *Ibid.*, p. 122.

57. *Ibid.*, p. 123.

58. *Ibid.*, p. 121.

59. On Troeltsch's reversal of his position, see Knitter, Paul F.: *No Other Name?* (Maryknoll, N.Y.: Orbis Books, 1985), pp. 29ff.; also (much more briefly) Cobb, John B., Jr.: *Beyond Dialogue*, p. 13.

60. Troeltsch: "The Place of Christianity Among the World Religions" (lecture prepared for delivery at Oxford University, 1923, and published posthumously), in Hick, John and Hebblethwaite, Brian (eds.): *Christianity and Other Religions* (Philadelphia: Fortress Press, 1973), p. 30.

61. See for example the article by Arvind Sharma of the University of Sydney, "Playing Hardball in Religious Studies" in the *Bulletin of the Council on the Study of Religion*, vol. 15, no. 1 (Feb. 1984), pp. 1–4.

62. Troeltsch, "The Place of Christianity," p. 29.

Chapter VII: Jesus the Christ as God's Word

1. In classical apologetics, there have been two major directions in the effort to establish the validity of the Christian claim, epitomized in the doctrine of the divinity of Christ. The first direction may be called an "extrinsic" apologetic, in that it was directly based upon the establishment of the authority of the Church, rather than upon Jesus or his self-understanding. The second, or "intrinsic" approach, on the other hand, attempted to demonstrate the credibility of faith in Jesus from an examination of his own life and teaching. In a general way, Troeltsch's approach is parallel to the "extrinsic" apologetic, while Rahner's, which we shall follow in this chapter, is a reformulation of the "intrinsic" argument.

2. Rahner, *Foundations*, p. 203. Cf. p. 177:

When we say that at least today an a priori doctrine of the God-Man must be developed in a transcendental theology, this does not mean of course that such an a priori doctrine could be developed temporally and historically prior to the actual encounter with the God-Man. We always reflect upon the conditions of possibility for a reality which we have already encountered.

3. *Ibid.*, p. 209.

4. *Ibid.*, pp. 209–210.

5. *Ibid.*, p. 210.

6. *Ibid.*, p. 211.

7. *Ibid. loc. cit.*

8. We shall return later to the question of whether the absolute saving event might be plural in manifestation, or whether it must be a single person.

9. In particular we shall make use of Walter Kasper: *Jesus the Christ* (New York: Paulist Press, 1977); Edward Schillebeeckx: *Jesus. An Experiment in Christology* (New York: Seabury Press, 1979); James D. G. Dunn: *Christology in the Making* (Philadelphia: Westminster Press, 1980).

Rahner has been criticized for "neglecting" the categorical aspect of Christology (for a summary of criticisms, see Wong, Joseph H. P.: *Logos-Symbol in the Christology of Karl Rahner* [Roma: LAS, 1984], pp. 234ff.). Rahner himself was aware of the limitations of his treatment and adverts to it; this should not be seen as neglect, however, but rather as care not to go beyond the spheres of his own competence. In this, as in other areas (v.g. history of religions) Rahner recognizes his limitations and refers the student to the experts in those fields.

10. Cf. Kasper, *op. cit.*, p. 75.

11. On the distinctiveness of Jesus' use of "abba" in addressing God, see Dunn, *op. cit.*, pp. 253ff. In summary, Dunn holds that the use of "abba" was a characteristic and distinguishing feature of Jesus' prayer. To the contention that this use of "Father" (Aramaic "Abba") may have been a distinguishing feature of domestic Hasidic piety which no longer survives, Dunn replies that even if this hypothesis is admitted, Jesus' use remains to some degree unique: (1) Such usage is not found in those Jewish prayers—either from within or outside the synagogue—which have survived; the "Lord's Prayer," for example, is an adaptation of the Kaddish; what distinguishes it is precisely the introductory "Abba." (2) Nothing else approaches the regularity of Jesus' use. (3) From Rom 8:15f. and Gal 4:6f. we know that Paul considered the "abba" spirituality typical of those who possess the eschatological spirit; this could hardly be so if it was a feature of ordinary prayer. Furthermore, Jesus' use of the term indicates a unique sense of sonship; in teaching his disciples to say "abba," he probably sees their sonship as dependent upon his own. Dunn points to Mk 12:6 and Lk 22:29 (both of which he considers authentic) as indications of Jesus' sense of the eschatological uniqueness of his relation to "his" Father.

12. *Ibid.*, p. 137.

13. See *ibid.*, p. 87. Dunn believes that the earliest use of the term "Son of Man" as referring to an individual probably stems from Jesus himself, and that the term probably never was understood as meaning anyone other than Jesus. If, however, Lk 12:8 is taken as referring to a "Son of Man" who is other than Jesus (the text is ambiguous), then the argument for authenticity becomes even stronger, for the early Church would not invent such a text; in that case, the text gives a clear indication of Jesus' *functional* identity with this quasi-divine eschatological figure.

14. Rahner, *Foundations*, pp. 253–254.

15. See Kasper, *op. cit.*, pp. 91ff.; Schillebeeckx, *Jesus*, p. 189. The Gospel tradition is in fact inexplicable unless it is based upon some recollection of Jesus as a wonder-worker. Furthermore, Jesus' "miraculous" works are not denied even

by his opponents; rather, their provenance is disputed (Mk 3:22 and parallels). Even the Talmudic tradition refers to Jesus as having been a "magician."

16. See above, chapter II; Schillebeeckx, *Jesus*, pp. 180ff.

17. Kasper, *op. cit.*, p. 102; *cf.* Schillebeeckx, *Jesus*, pp. 172ff., 229ff.

18. Kasper, *op. cit.*, p. 101; Schillebeeckx, *Jesus*, pp. 200ff.

19. Kasper, *op. cit.*, p. 103; Schillebeeckx, *Jesus*, pp. 218ff.

20. Kasper, *op. cit.*, pp. 102–103.

21. Rahner, *Foundations*, p. 253. Rahner notes that the connection between Jesus and the definitive coming of the kingdom (including the eschatological judgment) cannot have been the result of Jesus' resurrection; for the primary understanding of the resurrection was as a divine vindication of Jesus' claim, apparently falsified by his death. The claim merely to be a divine messenger, a prophet, however, would not have been negated by the cross; only if the message of the coming of the kingdom was radically connected with Jesus' own person would his death have appeared as a contradiction to that message, and the resurrection as its validation (*ibid.*, p. 252).

22. *Ibid.*, p. 254f.

23. Kasper, *op. cit.*, p. 103.

24. Pannenberg, Wolfhart: *Jesus—God and Man* (trans. Lewis L. Wilkins and Duane A. Priebe) (Philadelphia: Westminster Press, 1968), pp. 81–83.

25. C. S. Lewis speaks of the horror of unending time as one of the things which repelled him from Christianity in his early life; and J. R. R. Tolkien gives the idea mythic expression in his *Silmarillion*, in which the earthly immortals envy humanity, which alone has the God-given gift of departing from the world.

26. Rahner's position includes the possibility that human "nature" (which is a "remainder" concept, arrived at by abstraction from our actual engraced situation) theoretically need not be oriented to actual attainment of that which is its only absolute end; thus grace is of another "order" of gratuity than creation. The existential hope of humanity is for a "supernatural" end, and the anticipation of that end, "being in love in an absolute way," is God's gift, or "grace"; both are the working out of the "supernatural existential." A complete eschatology would have to consider the question of the "natural immortality of the soul" and the possible natural end of humanity as the presuppositions of the supernatural existential, i.e., as an aspect of the "obediential potency" of human nature.

27. It will be recalled that Rahner also insists that immediacy to God cannot simply mean the absence of any mediation whatever (*Foundations*, p. 83f.). Even the final "vision" of God must include some mediation, at least by the subjectivity of the finite person.

28. For a dramatic literary instance, see Miguel de Unamuno's classic "San Manuel Bueno, Mártir" (*San Manuel Bueno, Mártir y Tres Historias Más* [Madrid: Espasa-Calpe, sexta edición, 1966]).

29. Modern cosmology seems to tend to the opinion that the world is not physically "eternal" (i.e., everlasting in both directions, past and future) but that space-time had a beginning. The contrary hypothesis, however, is from a philosophical or theological point of view equally admissible. See *RH*, p. 92.

30. Rahner admits that the *formulation* of the hope for "resurrection" is more successfully accomplished because of the experience of Jesus' resurrection (*Foundations*, p. 269).

31. We can however perhaps say that the notion of "resurrection"—and the anthropology it implies—*excludes* certain ideas about eternity; e.g.:

(1) Annihilation: the notion that "eternal life" is to be interpreted "existentially" as being *only* the value of human existence in *this* life, which is followed by nothing, is excluded precisely because this life, removed from its openness to a definitive mode of being, does not have *eternal* validity. (Philosophically, the thesis of the identity of "eternity" and present life fails to take seriously the nature of temporality; theologically, it raises the question of what such an "eternity" can mean for that vast mass of humanity whose present lives are spent in misery and suffering.)

(2) Immortality in the "Platonic" or Sâṁkhya sense, in which true human being is considered purely spiritual, and the body merely a sort of "prison" or exile, is excluded because it fails to take into account the intrinsically material and dialogical nature of human being. ("Immortality" in this sense logically includes the idea of the pre-existence of the soul as well as its survival of physical death.)

(3) Reincarnation is excluded because it neglects the definitive import of freedom (and with it the existential urgency of the call to conversion) and ultimately devalues the body and the world, making them respectively a series of costumes and scenes in which the "soul" appears, rather than the intrinsic determinants of finite freedom.

(4) A pantheistic "melting" into God is excluded because it ignores the essentially dialogical nature of human being, substitutes undifferentiated unity for love as the ultimate value, and empties of any sense the existence precisely of *finite* being. (It must be recalled, however, that a great deal of the mystical language which speaks in an apparently pantheistic way about our ultimate destiny—even in Hinduism—is actually a sort of poetic hyperbole which does not necessarily mean literally to deny the perdurance of the finite self, even in its union with the Absolute Self.)

32. For a more skeptical view of the factuality of the empty tomb, however, see Hans Küng, *On Being a Christian* (Garden City: Doubleday and Co., 1976): "It is scarcely possible therefore to refute the assumption that the stories of the [empty] tomb are *legendary elaborations of the message of the resurrection*" (p. 364; Küng's italics). Küng also admits, however, that "influential exegetes" hold that the empty tomb is historically probable, and cites the arguments that women's testimony, invalid in law and thus useless apologetically, would hardly be invented, and the fact that the Jewish polemic did not deny the empty tomb (p. 365). In his later *Eternal Life?* Küng dismisses the controversy about the empty tomb as "an unreal controversy," stating that "even critical exegetes allow for the possibility that the tomb might have been empty," but noting that the emptiness of the tomb does not per se prove anything, and emphasizing that "neither Jesus' resurrection nor ours is dependent on an empty tomb"—that is, the resurrection is not to be thought of as the reanimation of a corpse (p. 104).

33. *Initiation à la Pratique de la Théologie*, vol. II, pp. 384–385.

34. Rahner, *Foundations*, p. 267; cf. Kasper, pp. 132ff, 158.

35. For Rahner's explanation of the relation of his conclusion to the traditional Christological formulas, see *Foundations*, pp. 285ff. Concerning the need for re-thinking and expansion of the classical Christology, Rahner notes:

(1) The classical formulations do not and cannot exhaust the mystery of Christ; other statements can and must be added to them which are not simply "developments" of them;

(2) Within the New Testament itself there are many Christologies, not all of which are variations of the same model;

(3) Within the classical Christology itself, there is a dialectic which moves it to further development.

Presupposed by all Christologies, however, is the uniqueness of the risen Christ as the sign and embodiment of the final relationship between God and history (*ibid.*, p. 281).

36. For Rahner's reflections on the existential necessity of faith for the uncovering of the grounds of faith, see *Foundations*, pp. 238ff.

37. *Ibid.*, p. 294.

38. Even if the historical object of faith is only given as salvific in the act of faith, this does not eliminate the possibility of articulating the bases of faith to the unbeliever; such articulation is done by the believer, whose faith enters into the process and appeals to the faith experience already present unreflexively in his dialogue-partner (*ibid.*, p. 243).

39. This principle states that whatever is truly and contingently affirmed of God is constituted by the divine essence, but in such a way that a suitable *ad extra* term is demanded. See Lonergan: *Insight*, pp. 661f.

40. Rahner presents his argument for the experience of the absolute in history in several forms. Perhaps the most succinct version is in his article "Jesus Christ" in *CSM*, p. 753f. See *RH*, pp. 198ff. Our treatment here synthesizes several different versions.

41. In *Foundations* Rahner develops hope for and commitment to the world as a separate "appeal" (p. 295), along with readiness for death and absolute love of neighbor.

42. Rahner notes that to justify and explain the experience of absolute love of neighbor, it is not sufficient that God be the always-transcendent "guarantee" and limit of the absoluteness of love; such love looks for a human being in whom humanity can be loved with the absoluteness of the love for God. (This restates Rahner's basic argument that God's self-communication *at all* has as its condition of possibility a final and absolute moment—the "final cause"—of such communication.)

One might ask how the love of such a person would found or justify the love of others, who are *not* the personal identity of God and humanity. Rahner's answer presupposes the unity of all human beings and the intrinsic universality of love (*ibid.*, p. 296).

Chapter VIII: Salvation in Christ

1. Rahner, *Foundations*, pp. 217–218.

2. See Rahner, "Current Problems in Christology" in *Theological Investigations*), Vol. 1, trans. C. Ernst (London: Darton, 1961), p. 164, n. 1. Rahner here calls Christology "self-transcendent anthropology," and anthropology "deficient Christology."

3. Rahner, *Foundations*, p. 225. The statement that "the question is borne only by the possibility of the answer" is another example of Rahner's use of the idea of "final causality." The question exists because of and for the sake of the answer; in parallel fashion, the whole economy of God's self-gift depends upon the absolute savior as its final cause and condition of possibility.

4. Rahner, "Grundsätzliche Überlegungen auf Anthropologie und Protologie im Rahmen der Theologie" in Feiner, J. and Löhrer, M. (eds.): *Mysterium Salutis* (Einsiedeln: Benziger, 1965ff.), vol. II, p. 416.

5. Rahner, *Foundations*, p. 223.

6. *Ibid.*, p. 224.

7. See Rahner, "One Mediator and Many Mediations," *TI* IX, p. 174. Here Rahner speaks of the relation of the incarnation to the whole economy of salvation in terms of "mediation": precisely because Christ is the unique mediator between humanity and God, there must actually exist a saving "mediation" of salvation by the whole of spiritual history; the latter is both the effect and the necessary precondition of Christ's mediatorship.

8. While Pauline theology speaks of "grace" in terms of the juridical model of "adoption" and the image of new creation, the Johannine writings speak of "birth from God"; every Christian is, like Jesus, "virgin born" by the power of God's Spirit (see Jn 1:12f.; 3:3-8; 1 Jn 2:29, 3:1; 3:9-10; 5:1-2; etc.). On the Pauline and Johannine concepts of grace, see Schillebeeckx, Edward: *Christ*, pp. 468ff.

9. Rahner, "Methodology in Theology," *TI* vol. 11, p. 97; cf. his statement that " . . .[es] *kann von einem wahren Gottmenschentum der Gesamtmenschheit die Rede sein*": *Ich Glaube an Jesus Christus* (Einsiedeln: Benziger, 1968), p. 37; quoted in Wong, *op. cit.*, p. 140 n. 180.

10. Rahner, *Foundations*, p. 201.

11. *Ibid.*, p. 199. As we have seen above, the reason why grace for Rahner "cannot even be conceived" without the hypostatic union is that the latter is the condition of possibility of the former in the sense of being its "final cause" (p. 195). We shall return shortly to the question of why and whether this final cause must necessarily be "unique" in the sense of subsisting in only a single person, Jesus.

12. *Ibid.*, p. 287.

13. Jesus Christ for Rahner is "the unique occasion which saw the radical achievement of the *ultimate* possibility of man's existence":

> If a man receives this human essence from God in such absolute purity and integrity and so actualizes this relationship with God that he becomes God's self-expression and his once-for-all pledge of himself to the

world he calls into existence, we have what we call "Incarnation" in a dogmatically orthodox sense. ("I Believe in Jesus Christ," *TI* IX, p. 167).

14. *Ibid.*, p. 200. It should be noted that while Rahner holds that Jesus had an unthematic transcendental experience of the "vision" (i.e., intimate immediate knowledge) of God during his earthly life—this was the source of his "Abba" experience—he denies that such an experience could be the "beatific" vision which is attained after death. The transcendental consciousness of God in Jesus—like all transcendental revelation—came to categorical and explicit expression in Jesus' life; that categorical expression therefore had a history, parallel in essential structure to the history of revelation in general (cf. p. 249).

15. See Wong, *op. cit.*, chapter 3. Rahner acknowledges in his "Foreword" to Wong's dissertation that the latter's use of the theology of symbol to clarify Rahner's Christology makes explicit connections which Rahner himself had left unexpressed. Wong shows that although the word "symbol" is frequently not used in Rahner's works, it can serve as a key concept to synthesize the entirety of his thought. Wong is able to restate the argument of *Hörer des Wortes* and *Geist in Welt* in terms of Rahner's later terminology and show that these philosophical works provide the epistemological-anthropological basis for the ontology of symbol (pp. 82–98); he then shows that the concept of real symbol is the equivalent of such terms as "self-manifestation," "self-expression," etc., which form the key to Rahner's Christology and Trinitarian theology.

Rahner cautions that in speaking of this reality, we must beware the ambiguities of our language, particularly in designating God as "three persons." "Person" in modern language is generally taken to mean an independent, self-standing center of intellectual-free being; a plurality of "persons" in *this* sense is precisely what is *excluded* in the doctrine of the Trinity.

16. It should be noted that in Rahner's celebrated article "The Theology of the Symbol" (*TI* vol. IV) he begins with the thesis that *finite* being is necessarily plural and symbolic. The German text reads: "*das Seiende ist von sich selbst her notwendig symbolisch . . .*" ("Zur Theologie des Symbols" in *Schriften zur Theologie* [Einsiedeln: Benziger, 1967], vol. IV, p. 278). "*Das Seiende*" is to be understood in the light of the Heideggerian distinction between the "being of beings" (*Seiendes*) and Being itself (*das Sein*). The fact that God's being is also symbolic is not derived from a general principle of ontology, but is taken as a datum of revelation (*ibid.*, p. 280).

17. Rahner, *Foundations*, p. 304.

18. *Ibid.*, p. 223.

19. *Ibid.*, p. 293.

20. *Ibid.*, p. 211.

21. Rahner, "One Mediator and Many Mediations," *TI* IX, p. 179.

22. Rahner, *Foundations*, p. 284.

23. Rahner, "One Mediator," p. 180. This reasoning justifies Rahner's contention in this article that the one mediatorship of Christ does not exclude but

rather necessitates a mediation of salvation on the part of *each* person who is saved.

24. Rahner, *Foundations*, p. 142.

25. Cf. Wong, *op. cit.*, p. 163.

26. This catalogue of New Testament conceptions of salvation is taken from Schillebeeckx, *Christ, op. cit.*, pp. 477–511, qq.v. for a more complete treatment.

27. For a succinct treatment of Anselm's "satisfaction" theory and its sequel, see Kasper, *op. cit.*, pp. 219ff.

28. Rahner, *Foundations*, p. 284.

29. *Ibid., loc. cit.*

30. Rahner, *Foundations*, p. 221.

31. Rahner, "Observations on the Doctrine of God," *TI*, vol. IX, p. 143.

32. Rahner, *Foundations*, p. 221f; cf. "On the Theology of the Incarnation," *TI*, vol. IV, pp. 113–114:

> . . . this possibility [*scl.* of God's becoming] is not a sign of deficiency, but the height of his perfection, which would be less if in addition to being infinite, he could not become less than he (always) is.

Rahner explains that God does not alter "in himself" when he creates the world because "he does not in himself become other to himself when he himself becomes other to the world as what is other than he and derived from him" ("Current Problems in Christology," *TI*, vol. 1, p. 176 n. 1). The meaning of this rather awkward formulation seems to be the differentiation of Rahner's thought from that of Hegel. For Rahner, God is not self-alienated; his creation of the world as his "other" and his giving himself in grace do not imply a need of the world in order to be or to realize himself; rather, they express the overflowing of his being as free love.

33. *Ibid.*, p. 220.

34. See Wong, *op. cit.*, pp. 129, 192f. In *efficient* causality the agent establishes the other *as other* and becomes present in/to it to some extent; in *formal* causality the agent constitutes the other as *its own* reality, and is fully present and manifest in it (*ibid.*, p. 192). (Rahner uses the term "*quasi-*formal" causality to refer to God's relation to the engraced creature in order to signify that the self-expression on God's part is free and that there is a "real and major" distinction between God and the creature; in other instances of formal causality, on the contrary, the "formal cause" exists *only* by virtue of its "real symbol" or self-expression. Rahner explains this notion at length in his notes for the course "Theologische Anthropologie II: Die Lehre von der Gnade," given at the University of Münster in the summer session of 1968.)

With regard to God, however, the distinction between these two forms of causality cannot be absolute, because—as we have seen above—even the "otherness" of creation is "within" God, and its distinction from him is constituted by himself. The distinction between "efficient" and "(quasi-)formal" causality is in fact a distinction between *degrees* of divine "presence."

35. See Rahner, "The Theology of Symbol," *TI*, vol. 4, pp. 245–247.

36. Wong notes that although Rahner calls all creatures "sacraments" of God, he reserves the term *"Realsymbol"* (with the correlative and distinguishing *"Ur-sakrament"*) to Christ (Wong, *op. cit.*, p. 194).

37. Rahner, "Observations," p. 143.

38. *Ibid.*, p. 152.

39. This again clarifies why there *must be* an eschatological or absolute moment to God's self-revelation: in order that God-in-his-other become fully identical with God-in-himself.

It also makes clear the continuity (as well as the theoretical distinction) between the orders of creation and "grace." All creation is by its nature a "self-symbolizing" of God, through his positing of the "other" which is distinct from but dependent upon himself. The order of revelation-incarnation-grace is the definitive mode of God's self-expression in his other; through this sharing of himself, God makes his other identical with himself, not by absorption into undifferentiated selfhood, but by making us his beloved, united in communion of life and distinction of personal being. The deficient mode of self-symbolizing which is creation (abstractly considered—i.e., apart from the existential order of grace) is possible precisely as the condition of possibility for the definitive mode; but the latter remains always gratuitous. (This gratuity is existentially felt as the tension which accompanies our achievement of transcendence; it is the reason why we must "die" to self in order genuinely to "live.")

40. Rahner, *Foundations*, p. 65; cf. "Observations," p. 136. See also *RH*, p. 168f.

41. Schillebeeckx, *Christ*, p. 655. The effect of such "positivism of revelation" has frequently been the evacuation of faith of a truly historical consciousness, and the substitution of a Monophysite understanding—or imagining—of the incarnation. Such "Christocentric" faith is actually an alternate "theocentrism," simply substituting "Christ" for "God."

42. Rahner, "Theologische Anthropologie II," p. 65. Rahner admits that our coming to an anthropological-philosophical horizon which serves as the hermeneutic of faith itself takes place from the starting point of our actual experience, including religious and Christian conversion and their expression in our tradition; indeed, Rahner's transcendental theology is a reflection on the conditions of possibility of faith. Nevertheless, it cannot simply be reduced to the content of that faith, but requires an independent reasoning.

43. Rahner, *Foundations*, p. 218f.

44. Küng, Hans: *On Being a Christian* (Garden City: Doubleday, 1976), p. 125.

45. Pannenberg, *op. cit.*, p. 106.

46. Rahner has no difficulty in calling the imminent eschatological expectation of Jesus—if we leave aside the question of the exact meaning of "imminent" for Jesus—an "error" of his human mind, at least in the sense that Jesus apparently did not explicitly reconcile the inconsistency of expecting the end "soon" with the necessarily *unknown* character of "the day and hour" of God's coming. At the same

time, Rahner points out, this "error" was in a deeper sense the bearer of truth: for it was the only concrete means for Jesus' mind, given its cultural setting, to thematize the reality of his own "absolute" closeness to God. See *Foundations*, p. 250.

47. Pannenberg, *op. cit.*, p. 107.

48. *Ibid.*, p. 108.

49. Kasper, *op. cit.*, p. 132.

50. *Ibid.*, *loc. cit.*

51. Schillebeeckx, *Christ*, p. 465.

52. These texts are cited in Knitter, Paul: *No Other Name? A Critical Survey of Christian Attitudes Toward the World Religions* (Maryknoll, N.Y.: Orbis Books, 1985), p. 182. See also the texts quoted in Schillebeeckx, *loc. cit.*

53. Schillebeeckx, *Christ*, p. 465.

54. *Ibid.*, p. 466.

55. Rahner, *Foundations*, p. 218 and *passim*.

56. See Wong, *op. cit.*, p. 159.

57. Rahner, *Foundations*, p. 224.

58. For this criticism which has been leveled against Rahner by Wiederkehr, see Wong, *op. cit.*, p. 234.

59. See for example *Foundations*, pp. 305ff.

60. *Ibid.*, p. 251.

61. Rahner, "One Mediator," p. 183.

62. Cf. Rahner, *Foundations*, p. 218:

Any idea that this union of God and man has to take place in the case of every man because this union of God and man is the most radical culmination of man's essence is forgetting that historicity and personhood must not be reduced to the level of nature, to the level of what is given always and everywhere.

63. *Ibid.*, p. 294f.

64. Knitter, *op. cit.*, p. 183.

65. *Ibid.*, pp. 182ff.

66. Pannenberg, *op. cit.*, p. 129.

67. It is interesting that popular Christian piety—although not official doctrine—has (because of its frequently Monophysite understanding of the incarnation) at times sought in the figure of the Virgin Mother the *human* embodiment of absolute love, exalting her (so far as human qualities go—that is, excluding the ontically conceived reality of the hypostatic union) to a position of virtual equality with Jesus.

68. Rahner notes that a presupposition of soteriology is the essential unity of history and the solidarity of all humanity (*Foundations*, p. 284). Could such a unity and solidarity be given in the case of other worlds—especially if the immense distances in both space and time between stellar systems should preclude any contact between intelligent beings that may inhabit them, so that each world of intelligent beings would be, in effect, a "closed system" with regard to all others?

69. Tillich, Paul: *Systematic Theology*, vol. 2 (Chicago: University of Chicago Press, 1957), pp. 95–96.

70. Knitter, *op. cit.*, pp. 198–200.

71. On the intrinsic interrelationship of event and interpretation, see Schillebeeckx, *Christ*, pp. 31ff.

72. Knitter cites Sobrino's principle that the uniqueness of Jesus can be manifest only in concrete embodiment, i.e., in praxis. He suggests that we "may encounter religious figures whose vision offers a liberating praxis and promise of the kingdom equal to that of Jesus" (*op. cit.*, pp. 195, 197).

73. Tillich, *Christianity and the Encounter of World Religions*, (New York: Columbia University Press, 1963), pp. 68–69.

74. *Ibid.*, pp. 70–71.

75. Whitehead, *Religion in the Making*, p. 55.

76. Knitter, *op. cit.*, p. 110.

77. *Ibid.*, p. 118.

78. Rahner, *Foundations*, p. 280.

79. See Dunn, James D. G.: *Christology in the Making* (Philadelphia: Westminster Press, 1980), chapter IV.

80. Not every religion therefore need share the historical memory of Jesus as the center of its God-relation; but each will share and express the "memory" (in the Augustinian sense) of the *future* and final Christ who is manifested proleptically in the resurrection.

In this sense the image of the "new Adam" must be complemented by that of the *final* human being, Christ with his entire "body," the "Omega" point. The historical Jesus is the "beginning" of a new humanity in history—its "threshold"—on the thematic level, insofar as his experience of intimacy with God allows him to live and teach the indispensable personal dimension of relation to the Father. The resurrected Jesus is the "final cause" which, on an unthematic level, draws all humanity—even apart from the knowledge of the history of Jesus—to that same relation.

81. Rahner repeatedly insists upon the difference in "natures" which is defined by the Chalcedonian formula. He points out that the *modern* concept of "person" does not correspond to Chalcedon's "hypostasis"; because in modern terminology "person" means a single center of intellective-volitive activity, it carries with it, when applied to the hypostatic union, a danger of Monophysitism. It can lead to overlooking "the fact that the man Jesus *in* his human reality exists with a created, active and 'existential' center of activity vis-à-vis God and in absolute difference from Him" (*Foundations*, p. 292). If this is kept in mind, there seems to be no reason why another such intellective-volitive reality (whether "human," i.e., earthly, or not) could not be united to the Logos in the same way.

82. Knitter points out that such confessional language (v.g. the "you alone are the Holy One, you alone are the Lord" of the prayer "Glory to God") is testimonial, not dogmatic; it belongs to the same "language game" as declarations of love ("there is no one like you in the world . . ."). See Knitter, *op. cit.*, pp. 184–185.

83. Quoted in *ibid.* p. 138. As we have seen, Rahner seems to reach a similar conclusion, and to consider it sufficient for the act of Christian faith. Reflection need not be able to exclude all other possibilities of salvation, but only to affirm that it can find no better. If we conceive the existential human desire for salvation as a "searching Christology," then "we would simply have to ask where else this searching Christology could find what it is searching for, and what it affirms at least as a hope for the future, and ask whether Jesus and the faith of his community does not justify an act of faith that what is in any case being sought is found in *him*" (*Foundations*, p. 295).

84. Cf. *ibid.*, p. 186.

85. *Ibid.*, pp. 192, 200–202, 205.

86. For a review of past and current Christian attitudes toward other religions, see Knitter, *op. cit.;* also, more briefly, Cobb, *op. cit.*, chapters 1 and 2.

87. Rahner, *Foundations*, p. 313.

88. *Ibid.*, p. 320.

89. For a consideration of negative judgments about religion, especially from a Barthian standpoint, see Knitter, *op. cit.*,pp. 80ff., 101ff.

90. Rahner, *Foundations*, p. 318.

91. *Ibid.*, p. 316.

92. At the risk of oversimplifying, we might say that the truth of monism is in the affirmation of the essential unity of all being, while its difficulty is in accounting for multiplicity, freedom, and evil. The truth of dualism lies in the insight that evil is the "surd," and that the only proper existential attitude toward it is opposition; but dualist systems have difficulty in explaining the unity of being. The truth of theism is the reality of finite being as the "other" posited by God, and the essential relation of personality, freedom and creativity to being in the world; the difficulty of theism is its proclivity to anthropomorphism. The truth of non-representational religion is the utter transcendence of the Real to any conceptualization and its revelation in the existential attitude of self-emptying; its difficulty is in the lack of a positive analogy of being which permits the affirmation of the primacy of person as the supreme revelation of God.

93. See Griffiths, Dom Bede: *The Cosmic Revelation* (Springfield, Ill.: Templegate, 1983); *Vedanta and Christian Faith* (Los Angeles: Dawn Horse Press, 1973).

94. See Klostermaier, *op. cit.*, p. 34.

95. *Ibid.*, p. 115.

96. Rahner, *Foundations*, pp. 44ff.

97. Conze, Edward: *Buddhism: Its Essence and Development* (New York: Harper & Brothers, 1979), p. 64.

98. *Ibid.*, p. 166.

99. See Radhakrishnan, *Eastern Religions and Western Thought*, p. 21.

100. Tillich, *Christianity and the Encounter of World Religions*, p. 23.

101. O'Flaherty, Wendy Doniger: *Dreams, Illusions and Other Realities* (Chicago: University of Chicago Press, 1984), p. 158.

102. Zaehner points out this danger in particular with regard to certain tend-

encies in Hinduism. See *Concordant Discord* (Oxford: Clarendon Press, 1970), p. 128.

103. Küng, Hans: *On Being a Christian* (Garden City: Doubleday, 1976), p. 110. Cobb, *op. cit.*, gives a profound reflection on the kind of *mutual* transformation which can come from a dialogue between Christianity and Buddhism.

104. The Christian doctrines of creation and grace—and especially of the incarnation—permit the conception of a unity or continuity between the present and the eternal which is to some extent lacking in the Oriental religions, particularly in Buddhism. As we have seen, it is common Buddhist teaching—inspired by the Mâdhyamika school—that all desire or attachment, including the desire for Nirvâna, is to be extirpated. At the same time, the highest virtue is proclaimed to be compassionate love. There thus appears to be an inconsistency between the goal and the means to attaining it. The development of the Christian tradition, on the other hand, led to the distinction between *eros* and *agape*, the latter being ultimately identical with God, and the former having various levels, including the deepest transcendental "desire." The Christian philosophical tradition can therefore affirm an analogy of being and of love, in which present human being and the world are not simply negative factors, although they are to be transcended. There is a continuity between the transcendental goal and our present existence.

105. Knitter, *op. cit.*, p. 219.

APPENDIX

Diagrammatic schema for theological anthropology showing the correlation of method and content. (Part I represents the contents of *The Reason for Our Hope*; Part II the present work).

METHOD ←——————————————————→ CONTENT

Part I

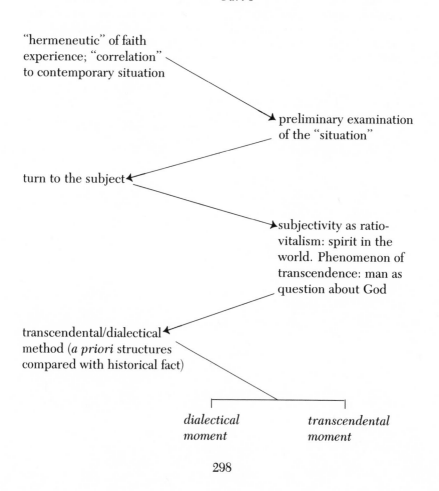

"hermeneutic" of faith
experience; "correlation"
to contemporary situation

preliminary examination
of the "situation"

turn to the subject

subjectivity as ratio-
vitalism: spirit in the
world. Phenomenon of
transcendence: man as
question about God

transcendental/dialectical
method (*a priori* structures
compared with historical fact)

dialectical   transcendental
moment   moment

298

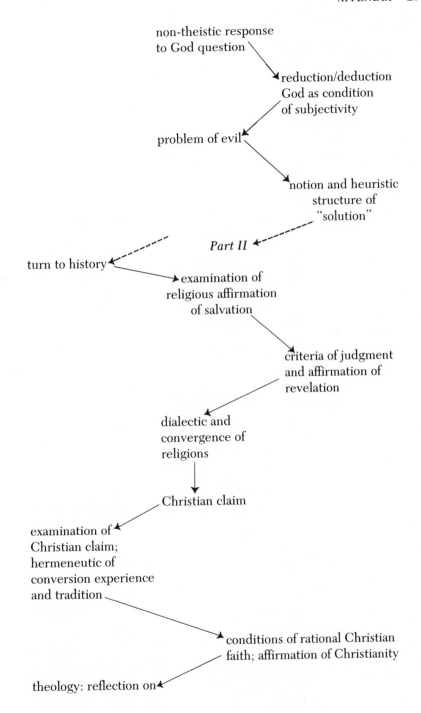

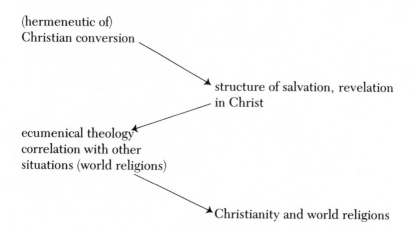

(hermeneutic of)
Christian conversion

structure of salvation, revelation
in Christ

ecumenical theology
correlation with other
situations (world religions)

Christianity and world religions

INDEX

Epicureanism, 97
epistemology, 14
epochal occasions, 55, 84
eschatology, 132
essence, 62, 63, 68
eternity, 206, 207, 208, 287
Eutychianism, 232
evil, 31, 33, 142, 163, 165, 186, 187, 200, 209
  moral, 25, 29–32, 35
  mystery of, 252
  origin of, 133
  physical, 25, 28–33, 35, 36
  problem of, 11, 15–17, 19, 22–24, 30–37, 45, 95–98, 102, 137, 163, 182, 229, 252
evolution, 29, 30, 32, 34, 63, 65, 68, 70, 76, 77, 83, 86, 91, 92, 98
Exile, 130, 143
existential, 65
  supernatural, 63, 169
existential interpretation, 54, 55
existentialism, 17

faith, 5, 6, 8, 11, 13, 14, 35, 38, 52, 54, 55, 66, 67, 82, 85, 86, 88, 89, 121, 129, 140, 144, 159, 164, 237, 240
  in Hinduism, 108, 109
  salvation through, 164
fall
  of angels, 27, 29
  of humanity, 27, 30
fanah, 173
fatalism, 16, 19
Fātima, 155
Faust, 15, 20
Fichte, 43
foundations (functional specialty), 11
Four Holy (Noble) Truths, 111f.
fravahrs, 137, 138, 140, 275, 276

fravashi—see *fravahrs*
frawashis—see *fravahrs*
Frazer, 262
freedom, 15, 19, 30, 34, 35, 36, 43, 55, 56, 61, 64, 70, 84, 131, 157, 165, 201, 207, 226, 241
fundamentalism, 7, 52, 53, 54, 55, 67

Galileo, 91
Gandhi, 250
Gathas, 133, 134, 135, 139
Gautama, 98, 110, 111, 122, 123, 124
Gayōmart, 137, 138
Genesis, 27, 50
Gilkey, 51, 52
Gnosticism, 23, 145, 157, 159, 160, 227
God, 16, 18, 22, 81–83, 92, 95, 98, 103, 104, 107, 108, 109, 114, 115, 117, 124, 131, 133, 134, 135, 137, 140, 142, 143, 144, 145, 146, 147, 148, 152, 154, 155, 156, 158, 159, 160, 163, 164, 165, 167, 170, 172, 173, 176, 180, 181, 190
  absoluteness of, 44, 45, 254
  act of, 46–70, 80f.
  antecedent and consequent nature, 257
  and becoming, 229, 230
  attributes of, 38–44, 66, 133
  biblical, 53
  collaboration with, 88, 103
  dipolar, 55
  distinction from world, 131
  and evil, 16, 17, 19, 21–25, 29–36, 53
  existence of, 6, 11, 14, 15, 17, 24, 39, 41, 44, 53, 60, 61
  experience of, 15, 64, 84, 85